# THE GREAT BOOK
# OF THE
# PACIFIC

ROSELENE DOUSSET
ETIENNE TAILLEMITE

# THE GREAT BOOK OF THE PACIFIC

CHARTWELL BOOKS INC.   CHARTWELL BOOKS INC.

CREATED AND PRODUCED

BY

EDITA LAUSANNE

Translated by

ANDREW MOURAVIEFF-APOSTOL

Published by Chartwell Books Inc.,
a Division of Book Sales Inc.,
110 Enterprise Avenue, Secaucus,
N.J. 07094.

ISBN 0-89009-242-7
Library of Congress Catalog Number 79-84758

EDITA S.A., 3 rue de la Vigie, LAUSANNE

Printed in Italy and bound in Switzerland

# CONTENTS

Publisher's Introduction . . . . . . . . . . . . . . . . . . . . . . . 9

THE DISCOVERIES
by Etienne Taillemite
The First Voyages . . . . . . . . . . . . . . . . . . . . . . . . . . . . 11
The Earth is Round . . . . . . . . . . . . . . . . . . . . . . . . . . . 12
Empire planning . . . . . . . . . . . . . . . . . . . . . . . . . . . . . 17
The Pacific in the Seventeenth Century . . . . . . . . . . . . 25
Scientific Exploration . . . . . . . . . . . . . . . . . . . . . . . . . 35
General Conditions . . . . . . . . . . . . . . . . . . . . . . . . . . . 36
The Growth of Knowledge . . . . . . . . . . . . . . . . . . . . . 54

MEN OF THE PACIFIC
by Roselène Dousset-Leenhardt
The Civilization . . . . . . . . . . . . . . . . . . . . . . . . . . . . . 68
Anthropology . . . . . . . . . . . . . . . . . . . . . . . . . . . . . . . 69
The Habitat . . . . . . . . . . . . . . . . . . . . . . . . . . . . . . . . 79
Techniques and Economics . . . . . . . . . . . . . . . . . . . . . 91
Customs . . . . . . . . . . . . . . . . . . . . . . . . . . . . . . . . . . . 106

COLONIZATION
by Roselène Dousset-Leenhardt . . . . . . . . . . . . . . . . . 151
Awakening Interest in the South Seas . . . . . . . . . . . . . 152
Missionaries and Mariners . . . . . . . . . . . . . . . . . . . . . 154
Economic and Political Factors . . . . . . . . . . . . . . . . . . 166
The Colonized Territories . . . . . . . . . . . . . . . . . . . . . . 173
Australia . . . . . . . . . . . . . . . . . . . . . . . . . . . . . . . . . . . 174
New Zealand . . . . . . . . . . . . . . . . . . . . . . . . . . . . . . . . 200
The Other Pacific Islands . . . . . . . . . . . . . . . . . . . . . . 207
The Myth of Paradise Lost . . . . . . . . . . . . . . . . . . . . . 221

THE PACIFIC IN THE TWENTIETH CENTURY
by Roselène Dousset-Leenhardt
Conflict of the Great Powers . . . . . . . . . . . . . . . . . . . . 229
Development from 1900 to 1940 . . . . . . . . . . . . . . . . . 230
The Pacific War . . . . . . . . . . . . . . . . . . . . . . . . . . . . . 244
The Pacific Today . . . . . . . . . . . . . . . . . . . . . . . . . . . . 253
Changes in the Pacific . . . . . . . . . . . . . . . . . . . . . . . . . 276

Index of Geographical Names . . . . . . . . . . . . . . . . . . . 281

# PUBLISHER'S INTRODUCTION

The new and improved navigational techniques, together with the progress made in ship-building, enabled Western man to launch himself into the discovery of the earth he inhabited. The last, but perhaps the most interesting, secrets lay in the Great Southern Sea – the Pacific. Here the great exploratory movement, launched in the fifteenth and sixteenth centuries, continued to make fresh discoveries until the end of the nineteenth century.

Throughout this long period, the South Seas saw the best and worst of Western penetration. Myth and romance clung to it – the dream of balmy islands, where nature provided man with all his needs, turned the Pacific Islands gradually into the Earthly Paradise, peopled by 'noble savages'. Nor was this idea so far from the truth – as will be made clear. Inevitably, however, the Western impact eroded the special way of life, man in harmony with nature, producing a steady decline that is only now being halted.

What follows will, we feel, reveal the truth behind the legends and the myths. The first section, THE DISCOVERIES, sets out the story of the early voyages to the South Seas, and tells of the hopes, fears, and sheer determination of the men who took their lives in hand to venture into the unknown. Gradually, science came to their aid, and by the beginning of the nineteenth century, a vast body of scientific and cartographic knowledge had been built up. But still much remained to be done. The second section, MEN OF THE PACIFIC, shows the reader the peoples the explorers found, who had already a well-developed social system that suited their environment perfectly. They knew what was useful to them to know, and their social, religious, and technical knowledge was quite sufficient for their needs. Western intrusion upset an age-old balance. The third section, COLONIZATION, describes the impact the colonizing powers had; their aims, and the ways in which these were achieved. For cupidity, religious intolerance, slavery, and crass ignorance, this story is hard to beat. Finally, the section THE PACIFIC IN THE TWENTIETH CENTURY takes the history of the South Seas down to the present, describing the effect of two World Wars and their aftermaths, and the gradual decolonization and growing independence of the area, and the West's slow realisation of the native values, and its attempts to encourage and preserve traditional ways of life before they finally disappear.

T.R.C.

MER OCEANE

Capode bonne efreance

TERRE AVSTRAL

# THE DISCOVERIES

## THE FIRST VOYAGES

Man's spread beyond Europe, or, to use Pierre Chaunu's well chosen term, 'the great development of the dialogue between man and space', slowly altered conditions of life on earth.

For thousands of years man knew but a tiny section of the world. Even in the thirteenth century civilisation was sparse and scattered, existing mostly without any contact between one settled area and another, and these areas of settlement scarcely covered one third of the planet. Earth still consisted of 'but a collection of individual island-universes without any communication between them'. Land was still sparsely occupied, here and there. A few relatively densely settled centres (the Mediterranean basin, China, India, Mexico, Peru) maintained individual existence, completely separated from one another by empty land spaces, deserts, steppes, forests, not to mention the ocean wastes which could not be traversed for lack of adequate craft. When these craft finally made their appearance, it was the sea which first provided the means to break the bonds of isolation, and formed the first link between far-flung human settlements.

For obvious geographical reasons the Pacific was the last area to be embraced by this great movement, which started in the fourteenth century but only reached the Southern Ocean two centuries later, and even then sporadically and at irregular intervals. Most parts of the Pacific indeed remained unknown and unexplored even superficially until the second half of the eighteenth century, and in many cases well into the nineteenth century.

We know very little of the Pacific before Magellan's time, save that the occasional European or Asian navigator must have reached it, but we cannot say exactly when.

Recent archaeological and ethnological research suggests that the Vikings first reached South America, and then moved on as far as Polynesia where we find groups of fair-haired humans who might be described as nordic types. In the sixteenth, seventeenth, and eighteenth centuries, explorers like Quiros, Schoutten, Wallis, Bougainville and Cook were surprised to find white-skinned men with blue eyes and fair hair on various archipelagos such as Tahiti, the Marquesas and Hawaii.

Jean Poirier, the ethnologist, noted that 'their existence can only be attributed to some recent contact with humans of the same type, i.e. Nordic people. And we do know today that Scandinavian navigators did travel deep into North America. It is therefore only logical to suppose that some of them must have reached Polynesia.'

Did Chinese navigators get as far as the coast of Mexico prior to the twelfth century? Experts are still debating this. According to J. Needham, China's early fifteenth century commercial expansion 'covered every area from Zanzibar to Kamchatka and every island of the western Pacific with the doubtful exception of Austrialia'. By then China possessed all the techniques needed for world-wide discovery, but instead suddenly withdrew within her own borders to open up her interior. So technical ability is not everything: psychological motives also play their part.

The Don Cossacks' advance across Siberia suffered a like fate when it reached the Pacific coast in 1645.

Pre-Colombian America's 80 million inhabitants at the end of the fifteenth century, as reckoned by most recent studies, seem to have been equally untempted by the Pacific which stretches for so many thousands of miles along its shores.

This map from *Cosmographie Universelle* by Guillaume Le Testu (1546) shows the legendary 'Terra australis', believed by contemporaries of Christopher Columbus to be situated south of the Cape of Good Hope. The search for the imaginary continent with its extraordinary animals encouraged men to explore the oceans, and especially the Pacific.

# THE EARTH IS ROUND

It was from Western Europe that the explorers eventually came who, with periodically increasing and decreasing tempo, were gradually to bring the Great Ocean into international economic life. But many intermediary steps had first to be taken before reaching those distant horizons. Among the foremost were the designing of suitable ships and elaboration of navigational systems without which such distant voyages far out of sight of the home coasts could not be attempted.

The first improvements to sailing ships slowly appeared at the end of the twelfth and beginning of the thirteenth centuries, when England and Flanders introduced the swivelling rudder and variations in the design and usage of sails. Soon the heavy round hull became more elongated, and the ever closer contacts between the Mediterranean and Northern Europe led to new inventions. New types of vessels emerged from the interchange of techniques which had produced the Mediterranean and North European galleys, giving birth to the Hanseatic *kogge*. Presumably at this period there appeared in the Bay of Biscay the first long caravelles with their impressive sets of sails, made more manoeuvrable by an able combination of square driving sails and lateen manoeuvring sails. Were they inspired by the design of Chinese junks, as has been claimed? This will doubtless long remain a subject of study and debate. At first the caravelle was but a tiny 40-50 ton craft, made suitable by the sixteenth century for voyages of discovery by her speed, which by then already approached that of the fastest eighteenth century frigates.

But having the ships was not enough. Man had to be able to use them on the high seas, which meant knowing how to reckon their position by the stars. When was this knowledge first acquired? Experts do not know precisely. Maybe around the middle of the fourteenth century, by the Portuguese, under Henry the Navigator's inspiration, although the invention is credited to Italy. The first compasses appeared in the Mediterranean at the end of the eleventh century and in China in the twelfth century. Italy produced the first marine charts, mostly in Genoa, consisting of lines showing the routes between ports, since navigation at the time was by estimate only. This technique spread from Italy to Catalonia, to reach Spain's Atlantic coast in the fifteenth and England only in the sixteenth centuries. Empiricism remained essential. It enabled the Polynesians to travel from Tahiti to Hawaii, and the Vikings to reach Greenland and later Vinland and presumably even more distant shores. Navigators in those days derived their knowledge from certain signs like the colour of the water, the flight of birds. They knew too how to steer by the stars.

Real navigation by astronomy was first used only in about 1484-1485 AD when the latitudes of the west coast of Africa were charted and the earliest navigational instructions drawn up. King John II of Portugal is credited with the 'great merit of making technical use before any other state of the

Vasco Nuñez de Balboa reached the Pacific on 29 September 1513 with a small group of Spaniards. His men saw him halt, start to quiver, raise his arms and fall to his knees. In full armour the General then entered the water up to his chest, brandishing his sword and proclaiming official possession of the South Seas in the name of the King of Spain.

theoretical knowledge available in his reign (1445-1495)'.*
As usual at that time, progress was slow and there was long
delay in putting scientific discoveries into practice. As Pierre
Chaunu wrote, 'By and large nautical knowledge sufficient
for discoveries was available by the end of the thirteenth
century. University scientists by the second half of the century knew all that was required for navigation by astronomy, such as was practised from the fifteenth century until
the discovery of the chronometer at the end of the eighteenth century. But from that great moment (at the end of
the twelfth and the start of the thirteenth centuries) when
men of knowledge possessed all the intellectual means
necessary for maritime discoveries, two long centuries of
adapting, groping, teaching were to go by before this vital
potential was more or less completely in pratical use in the
closing decades of the fifteenth century.'**

It was only in the sixteenth century, then, that the development of navigational astronomy became advanced
enough to give a new impulse to discoveries which would
at last join the old and new worlds. By the beginning of that
century men were indeed beginning to measure latitudes
regularly by the sun with the aid of astrolabes and the
Jacob's staff. Nevertheless they did not progress beyond
what has been called the 'empiric-scientific age' for a long
time. By then latitudes were indeed able to be fairly accurately measured, but not so longitudes. These remained
deplorably vague until 1770-1780 with the introduction of
the chronometer and of reckoning by lunar distances. Thus
navigation by astronomy in the strict sense of the term can
only be said to have been practised since the end of the
eighteenth century. The problem was only resolved for
good with the coming of wireless.

How did man become aware that the Earth is round, as
already divined by Aristotle?

It all started in the mid-fourteenth century with the first
sorties into the Atlantic by Italian navigators. The Canary
Isles and Madeira were discovered between 1320 and 1350.
Jaume Ferrer, the Catalan navigator, is belived to have
reached Senegal from Majorca in 1346. But, for lack of vessels suited to the Atlantic waters, these first efforts were not
actively pursued. No-one did much about exploring the west
coast of Africa for another 100 years: Gil Eanes first
rounded Cape Bojador, of evil reputation, in 1434.

Intrepid spirits gradually pushed further and further
south, slowly acquiring knowledge of the winds and currents which alone dictated outward and homebound routes
until mechanical propulsion was invented. This dependence
on winds made the Iberian penninsula the inevitable start-
ing-point for all voyages of discovery.

Portugal's Diego Cão discovered the mouth of the Congo
around 1482-1486 and pushed on towards the Cape of Good
Hope, which was rounded the following year by another
Portuguese mariner, Bartholomeo Diaz, Portugal again playing a vital rôle in that adventure. A small country with less

*  See Bibliography, Beaujouan.
** See Bibliography.

than a million inhabitants at the time, she was fortunate in
her rulers being willing to finance such undertakings of discovery from the State's treasury, which was well supplied at
that time.

That the world appeared to be expanding beyond belief
was due mainly to two men, Colombus and Vasco de Gama,
whose voyages led to the discovery of the Pacific, and to the
epic circumnavigation attempt of Magellan.

It is likely that it was about 1480 that Christopher Colombus first heard from his parents-in-law, the Perestrello family, Italians living in Lisbon, of the charts and notes
assembled by Portuguese navigators. The great dream of
the time was to find a new way to India to bring back the
spices which Europe was consuming in increasing quantities. The Portuguese were looking eastwards; why not try
westwards? The possibility had been discussed for some
time and had the support of Paolo Toscanelli, the Florentine
doctor and astronomer, who died in 1482. But real courage
was needed to sail out into the unknown Atlantic Ocean.
The experiences of the Vikings had long been lost in the
mists of time, as witnessed by the 1492 map of the world
drawn by Germany's Martin Behaim.

The only areas marked on it that demonstrate a reasonable accuracy are those coasts which had been followed for
decades by Portuguese navigators, namely south-west
Europe and West Africa. Further north, inaccuracy and
sheer imagination start at the level of Scotland and Scandin-
avia. Somewhere in the middle of the Atlantic lies an island
called Antilia. The Pacific Ocean is simply wiped out,
because Behaim, basing himself on Marco Polo and Toscanelli's reports, stretched the Asian continent eastward and
southward out of all proportion and with not the slightest
resemblance to reality.

Strangely, Columbus' achievement was helped by his
chain of errors of distances and location. The Greek geographer Eratosthenes had estimated the world's circumference fairly accurately at 24,902 miles (252,000 stadia), but
greatly under-estimated the distance from Western Europe
to East Asia. Marco Polo and Toscanelli made the same mistakes, so that Columbus thought the earth was much
smaller than we now know. According to their reckoning
Japan was only 2,400 miles from the Canaries, whereas the
real distance is over 10,000 miles. Appalling mistakes
ensued. They placed China near the Bahamas and the southern tip of Japan near Guyana. Fortunate mistakes these
proved! If they had not existed neither Colombus nor anyone else for generations would have had the temerity to
undertake their perilous voyages. On his first journey, Colombus had to keep altering his estimated positions to pacify
his crew, only too ready to mutiny. Comparing Behaim and
Toscanelli's ideas of the continents' contours with modern
maps easily explains why Columbus kept trying to find
Japan and India in the West Indies.

After failing with John II of Portugal, Columbus had a
hard time persuading Queen Isabella of Spain to back his
venture. It took him six years (1486-1492) to complete negotiations and overcome intrigue. But luck came to his aid.

Granada fell on 2 January 1492 and the Spanish sovereigns could once more turn their attention to new discoveries, now that they had broken the Moorish kingdom and virtually completed the *Reconquista*. After many serio-comic episodes, including not a little shadow boxing, Ferdinand and Isabella on 17 April 1492 awarded Columbus and his descendants, at the surrender of Santa Fé, the rank of Admiral of Castile, Life Governor of the discovered lands, fiscal rights, commercial monopolies and other enviable privileges.

With the active help of Martin Alonzo Pinzon three celebrated ships were fitted out: the PINTA, the NIÑA and the SANTA MARIA. The King of Spain put up half the funds required, the Pinzon family the remainder.

The tiny squadron set out from Palos on 3 August 1492, the remarkable thing being that Columbus had from the outset set a course which was to remain the best to and from the West Indies until the coming of steam. On 9 August they reached the Canaries and stayed till 6 September, when they sailed on to the west. After erroneously mistaking a cloud formation for land on 26 September, land was actually sighted on 11 October by look-out man Juan Rodriguez Bermejo de Triana, who thereby earned a life-income of 10,000 maravedis a year. At day-break Colombus, the Pinzons, and Escovedo the notary went ashore and planted the standard of Castile, the event being duly recorded. But it was not Japan, just Guanahani, a tiny isle of the Lucaya group, which Columbus re-christened San Salvador, now known as Watling Island.

The Indians proved friendly and barter was started, to last for almost 400 years, until the whole world had been discovered. Moving from island to island Columbus landed in Cuba on 20 October, and stayed until 12 November. He was struck by the apparent wealth of the country, its commercial opportunities, the density of the population and their gentle and friendly nature which gave rise to the long lasting myth of the 'friendly savages'.

After Cuba came Haiti on 6 December. He was sure he had at last reached Cipango! He named it Hispaniola and noted that the natives were quite happy to barter their gold. Everything was going fine when at midnight on Christmas Eve disaster struck: thanks to the crew's negligence the SANTA MARIA broke up on a reef and had to be abandoned. Her timbers were used to build a fortress, called Navidad (Christmas).

Columbus had to rejoin Pinzon, who was cruising round, exploring the Haitian coast in the PINTA. On 16 January he set sail for home meeting two bad storms, and stopping in Lisbon on the way to pay a triumphant visit to King John II. On 15 March he sailed into Palos, and on 31 March was received by his sovereigns who promptly granted him all they had promised.

But he had not achieved his aim and would have to go back and explore further to find, if possible, the desired passage to China. So he set sail once more on 25 September 1493, this time with a much bigger squadron: fourteen caravelles, three transport ships and 1,500 men. Taking a course much more to the south, he landed on 3 November at Desirade in the heart of the Lesser West Indies, and set out to reconnoitre the neighbouring islands: Dominica, Guadeloupe, Montserrat, Saint Thomas and Porto Rico.

But this time he no longer faced the peaceful welcome of the Sarawaks but the formidable cannibal Caribs. Continuing further north and west they came to Haïti to find that the garrison they had left behind at Navidad had been massacred by the Indians. So he built a town nearby, which he called Isabella City in honour of his Queen and continued exploring the island.

On 11 April 1496 he returned to Cadiz, where he found his welcome less warm. On 30 May 1498 he managed to sail out again, with six caravelles, taking a route still further south and landing at the southern point of the West Indian arc, in Trinidad. After briefly reconnoitring the south west portion of the mouth of the Orinoco, he returned to Haïti to find serious complications had developed in his absence.

From now on he no longer had the field to himself. Rival explorers were becoming active. Hojeda, Juan de La Cosa and Amerigo Vespucci, who had set out in February 1499, found the coasts of modern Venezuela. In January 1500, Vicente Yanez Pinzon reached the north shores of Brazil and the mouths of the Amazon and the Oyapoc.

But Columbus managed to put together a fourth and last expedition, which sailed in May 1502 and enabled him to cruise along the east coast of Central America from Honduras to Venezuela. Here he just missed discovering the Pacific as he passed the narrowest part of the Panama isthmus. He came back to San Lucar exhausted on 7 November 1504 and died at Valladolid on 21 May 1506.

His successes proved a 'disaster for Spain and a turning point for Europe', wrote Jean Amsler.[*] For Spain it was catastrophic because the Iberian peninsula was now launched on an unbridled race for colonies with no solid economic or demographic base, in which she would unavoidably exhaust herself.

Columbus had found a new route, but he had not discovered the Pacific, whose existence he ignored. This achievement fell to Vasco Nuñez de Balboa who set out to colonise the Darien Isthmus. Informed by the Indians, he crossed the peculiarly hostile forests with 190 men, 9 dugouts and a pack of hounds... and beheld the ocean on 25 September 1513, and reached it on 29 September at the mouth of the Sabana. 'At low tide, say some, or high tide according to others, he strode into the water up to his chest, fully armed from head to toe, brandishing a naked sword and waving the banners of Castile and Aragon, to take possession officially of the South Sea, her islands, and her coasts to north, south, east and west.'[**] This theatrical gesture was fraught with consequences. For more than two centuries Spain followed a doctrine which was still valid in Grotius' time, claiming that this 'capture' was valid in law and signified that the Pacific was held as Spain's private property; which was to cause many a diplomatic and military battle.

[*] See Bibliography.
[**] J. Amser, *Op. cit.*

Stopping in the Philippines, Magellan forgot about the spices for which he came and become embroiled in the skirmishes of the local chieftains. An alliance with the King of Cebu drew him into war with the inhabitants of the neighbouring Mactan Island where, on 27 April 1521, he was ambushed and killed by poisoned arrows.

The Portuguese and their King Manoel, successor to King John II, had been profoundly struck by Columbus' discoveries, and decided to push ahead with his ideas for a route towards oriental India. They equipped a new expedition commanded by Vasco de Gama and entrusted to Bartholomeo Diaz. On 8 July 1497 the SÃO GABRIEL, the SÃO RAPHAEL and the BERRIO SÃO MIGUEL with one transport set out from Lisbon. Near Cape Verde Gama turned south until he reached the Tropic of Capricorn, then east. They rounded the Cape on 22 November and sailed up the west coast of Africa to Mombasa, where they anchored 7 April 1498. Avoiding all traps placed in his way, the Admiral reached Capocate, north of Calicut, on 20 May.

With tremendous effort Portugal managed within a few years to secure the monopoly of the Indian Ocean. From 1509 to 1513 Abreu and Serrão explored Indonesia from Malacca to Ceram.

Columbus to the west and Vasco de Gama to the east had opened up new routes. Now for the Pacific, already sighted by Balboa! This would fall to a little Portuguese settler in the service of Spain.

Fernão de Magalhaes, whose name was pronounced by the French Magellan, had started his career in the Indian Ocean, various missions taking him to the Celebes Islands. There he saved the life of one Francisco Serrão, one of the first Europeans to settle in the Moluccas, or Spice Islands.

Magellan returned to Portugal and conceived the idea of joining his friend by the western route. Like Leonardo da Vinci and Vespucci, he felt it must exist in the extreme south of the Americas, that passage so vainly sought by Columbus in the West Indies which Juan Diaz de Solis thought he had found in the River Plate in 1516.

Brought home to Portugal, he crossed into Spain and managed to convince a few people at the Casa de Contractation in Seville. With the authority that the future Emperor Charles V granted him on 22 March 1518, he found backing from a wealthy Spanish ship owner, Christobal de Haro, of Antwerp, who hoped to rival Portugal.

On 20 September 1519 his squadron of five ships, the VICTORIA, the SAN ANTONIO, the CONCEPCION, the SANTIAGO and the TRINIDAD, sailed out of San Lucar with 265 men including a number of convicts earmarked for specially dangerous missions. On 13 December they reached Rio de Janeiro. In January they explored the River Plate and in April Saint Julian's Bay. Mutiny broke out but was ruthlessly put down. The VICTORIA'S captain, Mendoza, was beheaded on 7 April. Meanwhile, the first contact had been made with the Patagonians.

On 18 October the squadron headed further south and on 2 October reached the Virgins Cape behind which appeared a passage which the SAN ANTONIO and the CONCEPCION set about exploring. Casting prudence to the winds, Magellan sailed into the straits amid Dante-like scenery of desolate, barren, snow-covered mountains. The sloops moved ahead of the ships, sounding the depths. After twenty-seven painful days, they finally passed the last cape, and found themselves in the Pacific.

Aided by winds and currents they sailed north and then west. Magellan had but one thought: to reach the Moluccas, whose latitude he roughly knew, but not their longitude. After sighting a few deserted islands, hunger began to set in. 'Our biscuits were no longer bread, but a mixture of dust, worms, and mouse urine, smelling revoltingly', wrote Pigafetta. On 6 March, after 110 days at sea, they sighted three islands. Natives came out to meet them in dug-outs which they handled with great skill. Food, no matter how scarce, was essential. Those islands were part of the Marianas group; Magellan named them the Ladrones after the thieving inhabitants.

More land appeared on 26 March. Magellan put his sick ashore on an uninhabited island. On 28 March some natives came to visit them and contact was easily established. A chieftain called on them with a large escort. Some days later Enrique, the Malayan slave whom Magellan had brought back from a previous voyage, found he was able to talk to some men in a canoe. The circle had been completed. For the first time man had sailed around the world. Enrique managed to persuade the chief to come aboard, and a solemn reception with high mass was held and guns fired.

On 4 April the squadron set out for Cebu with King Calambu aboard.

Magellan had succeeded in persuading the leaders of his peaceful intentions, and a treaty was made by which the king agreed to be converted to Christianity, and the Spaniards received exclusive trading rights and agreed to help the king extend his powers further afield. This was asking for trouble, and trouble was not long coming. Magellan sailed to attack a rebellious vassal on 26 April on Mactan Island. Reefs prevented his ships from approaching the land, and the tiny landing force of fifty-nine men had to move in without artillery cover. They were attacked by thousands of natives and quickly routed by their poison arrows. Despite his faithful Enrique's help, Magellan was fatally wounded and died there.

Deprived of their leader, tragic days lay ahead. The Malayans waylaid them on 1 May and a bloody fight followed. One officer, Carvalho, took command, but proved incapable. Without pilot or interpreter, and only 108 survivors, many of them weak from disease, the expedition seemed doomed. But they managed to escape total disaster thanks to the energy of a few led by Juan Sebastian Elcano, a Basque from Getaria, who had earlier been condemned for selling his ship but was now to emerge as leader.

From May to November 1521 the survivors wandered painfully around. The CONCEPCION, in a parlous state, was broken up and abandoned after everything of any use had been taken out of her. The TRINIDAD was blown ashore, fortunately without damage. Carvalho, more interested in the lovely Javanese girls than in the welfare of his men, lost all authority and Elcano took over. They had to find the Moluccas, fill up with spices and return to Europe. With indomitable tenacity Elcano achieved this madly ambitious aim despite the limited means left at his disposal.

By 6 November they made Gilolo and on 9 November were at Tidore where Sultan Almanzor had his palace. More tactful than his commander, Elcano carefully avoided religious subjects with this good Moslem, and stuck to business. Agreement was easily reached, and on 21 December they weighed anchor with 750 bushels of cloves on board. Christopher Columbus' great dream had come true. The western route had joined the eastern, and they could now prove that the earth was really round.

All they had to do now was to get back to Spain. The original squadron's last survivor, the VICTORIA, had only forty-seven men left as crew. A further thirteen Malayans were signed on at Tidore, and Elcano managed to make Timor and take on supplies. On 13 February 1522 they set sail for Europe.

The tragic homeward journey was fraught with unimaginable difficulties. They could not return by the same risky route and had to continue westward through seas jealously guarded by the Portuguese. At that season the sea-lanes were free, presenting little danger of hostile encounters, but anchoring in occupied ports was impossible. Despite this alarming prospect, Elcano stuck to his guns, crossed the entire Indian Ocean and anchored to the East of the Cape of Good Hope, firmly resisting the efforts of some of his crew who wanted to give up and surrender to the Portuguese at Mozambique. After weeks of headwinds, he was round the Cape by 18 May and ready to sail north with the

16

---

Magellan discovers his strait and crosses the Pacific

As soon as we entered on this water, imagined to be only a bay, the Captain sent forward two vessels, the SAN ANTONIO, and LA CONCEPCIÓN to examine where it terminated, or whither it led, while we in the TRINIDAD and the VITTORIA awaited them in the mouth of it...

Two days passed without the two vessels returning, sent to examine the bottom of the bay, so that we reckoned they had been swallowed up during the tempest; and seeing smoke on shore, we conjectured that those who had had the good fortune to escape had kindled those fires to inform us of their existence and distress. But while in this painful incertitude as to their fate, we saw them advancing toward us under full sail, and their flags flying; and when sufficiently near, heard the report of their bombards and their loud exclamations of joy. We repeated the salutation, and when we learnt from them that they had seen the prolongation of the bay, or, better speaking, the strait, we made toward them, to continue our voyage in this course, if possible.

When we had entered into the third bay, which I have before noticed, we saw two openings, or channels, the one running to the southeast, the other to the southwest. The Captain General sent the two vessels, the SANT' ANTONIO and LA CONCEPCIÓN to the southeast, to examine whether or not this channel terminated in an open sea...

On Wednesday, the twenty-eighth of November, we left the strait and entered the ocean to which we afterward gave the denomination of Pacific, and in which we sailed the space of three months and twenty days, without tasting any fresh provisions. The biscuit we were eating no longer deserved the name of bread; it was nothing but dust, and worms which had consumed the substance; and what is more, it smelled intolerably, being impregnated with the urine of mice. The water we were obliged to drink was equally putrid and offensive.

We were even so far reduced, that we might not die of hunger, to eat pieces of the leather with which the mainyard was covered to prevent it from wearing the rope. These pieces of leather, constantly exposed to the water, sun, and wind, were so hard that they required being soaked four or five days in the sea in order to render them supple; after this we broiled them to eat. Frequently indeed we were obliged to subsist on sawdust, and even mice, a food so disgusting, were sought after with such avidity that they sold for half a ducat apiece.

Nor was this all. Our greatest misfortune was being attacked by a malady in which the gums swelled so as to hide the teeth, as well in the upper as the lower jaw, whence those affected were thus incapable of chewing their food. Nineteen of our number died of this complaint (scurvy), among whom was the Patagonian giant, and a Brazilian whom we had brought with us from his own country. Besides those who died, we had from 25 to 30 sailors ill, who suffered dreadful pains in their arms, legs, and other parts of the body; but these all of them recovered. As for myself, I cannot be too grateful to God for the continued health I enjoyed; though surrounded with sick, I experienced not the slightest illness.

In the course of these three months and twenty days we traversed nearly 4,000 leagues in the ocean denominated by us Pacific, on account of our not having experienced throughout the whole of this period any the least tempestuous weather. We did not either in this whole length of time discover any land, except two desert islands; on these we saw nothing but birds and trees, for which reason we named them Las Islas Desdichadas (The Unfortunate Islands). We found no bottom along their shores, and saw no fish but sharks. The two islands are 200 leagues apart. The first lies in latitude 15 degrees south, the second in latitude 9 degrees.

From the run of our ship, as estimated by the log, we traversed a space of from 60 to 70 leagues a day; and if God and His Holy Mother had not granted us a fortunate voyage, we should all have perished of hunger in so vast a sea. I do not think that anyone for the future will venture upon a similar voyage.

ANTONIO PIGAFETTA, *Premier Voyage autour du monde par Magellan* (vers. Léonce Peillard)

winds behind him and the Benguela current helping him.

The VICTORIA reached Cape Verde on 9 July in such a sorry state that the Portuguese at first readily believed their story of having been savagely attacked and the victims of terrible storms. The local authorities soon became suspicious, however, and the VICTORIA had hurriedly to cast off in distress when a boat-load of armed men was seen approaching.

But this halt had brought an extraordinary mystery to Elcano's notice which he sought in vain to elucidate: by his records he had tied up there on a Wednesday, yet the Portuguese insisted it was Thursday. This enigma remained a mystery. The conception of the Date Line was still unknown.

There were now only eighteen men left of the original crew. They had to work day and night pumping as the ship was leaking so extensively that some of the precious cargo had to be cast overboard. But fortune favoured the brave. The lookout man sighted Cape St Vincent on 4 September, and by 6 September they were lowering the anchor at San Lucar, just over three years after they had set out. Elcano, the first European to sail right round the world, was knighted by Charles V, and awarded the device: *Tu primus cirumdeisti me* (You were the first to go round me).

The task of reporting this extraordinary exploit fell to Antonio Pigafetta. He paid special and well deserved tribute to Magellan. To the Grand Master of the Order of Rhodes he wrote: 'I trust that Your illustrious Order will see to it that the memory of this valiant and noble captain will be kept for ever bright and never allowed to pass into oblivion in our times. Among his many virtues was greater constancy in the face of the worst adversity and the most important events ever witnessed. In maritime skill he was the most expert and knowledgeable man the world has seen. No man before has ever displayed such skill, such bravery, or such knowledge as he displayed in laying down the orders which led to this success.'

This first crossing of the Pacific marked a vital date in the history of exploring the world. But much remained to be done, especially tracing out the routes to be followed and finding the way back. It was not much good being able to go and then not be able to come back. In the Atlantic Columbus had managed this double feat from the start by charting what the Spaniards called 'la volta', the circle. Magellan had no such luck. Charting the two-way Asia-America route would still need trial and error over many a year. Intent as ever on their spice market, the Spaniards tried a number of times to reach the Philippines by sailing from the Americas. In 1521 Gil Gonsalez tried this in vain, as did Saavedra and Pedro de Alvaredo. In 1542 Villalobos succeeded in reaching the Philippines from Mexico for the first time, but could not get back. Finally two Spaniards, Legazpi and Urdaneta set out from Navidad, 450 miles north-east of Acapulco in 1564 and managed to find their way back in 1565 by the North Pacific, thereby making the occupation of the Philippines possible.

1565... a prime date in the history of the world. After the 'volta' of the Atlantic, the Pacific 'volta' now completed the link between the old world and the new, which could now begin to be integrated into the economic life of Europe. The circumnavigation of our world was now truly completed and the first exploration achieved. But in the field of knowledge, and even more so of economics, this was but the merest first step. The rest would have to be taken in the centuries ahead.

# EMPIRE PLANNING

After discovery comes development. The tremendous spread of the human habitat in the sixteenth century could not fail to arouse greed and desires which must inevitably end in conflict. As P. Chaunu wrote 'During the first half of the sixteenth century the new expansion of Europe stirred up the world, but during the second half the rest of the world began to shake up Europe. Strangely, it was Central Europe which gained most from the new-found wealth rather than Mediterranean Europe which discovered it.'*

From the end of fifteenth century the Spanish monarchs began to establish their rights over the new lands. With that in mind King Ferdinand obtained the famous Papal Bull *'Inter coetera'* from Pope Alexander VI, his fellow Aragonian. This drew a meridian 100 leagues west of the Azores dividing the world in two halves: the discovered and the to-be-discovered. Everything east of this line was proclaimed Portugal's; Spain had everything west of it. This unilateral arrangement naturally provoked the most vehement objections from Portugal. The two royal houses agreed to negotiate, and on 3 June 1494 the Treaty of Tordesillas was signed, setting the dividing line 370 leagues west of Cape Verde. But such vague boundaries were never to be very strictly observed in those days of limited and uncertain geographical knowledge. Spain aimed at securing a free hand in the Americas. This she largely achieved thanks to the arrival of Alvarez Cabral on the Brazilian scene in the year 1500.

But others not included in these 'arrangements' were starting to take an interest in this overseas expansion: England, Holland, France. They contested the Bull's validity or simply ignored it. Thus by the end of the sixteenth century the Bull had become a dead letter.

Foremost among the great imperialist plans of the time, some of which in fact later became reality, were those of Spain. Rapidly following the road opened up by Columbus, the Spaniards took firm hold of San Domingo. Conquered in 1495, the island was thoroughly explored and came to be the base for the expeditions which set out from there between 1509 and 1515 to conquer the other larger islands of the West Indies. In 1509 Juan Ponce de Leon occupied Porto Rico and Esquivel occupied Jamaica. In 1511 Diego Velasquez was appointed Governor of Cuba, and Havana was founded in 1515. The mainland was already being vis-

* See Bibliography.

ited by the first colonisers, Alonso de Hojeda exploring Darien, where Vasco Nuñez de Balboa soon became Captain-General. By 1515 San Domingo thus became the centre of a first 20,000 square mile empire which would soon expand beyond expectation. From its larger islands, attacks on the mainland were launched.

In 1517-1518 the coasts of Yucatan were reconnoitred by Velasquez; and those of Mexico by Hernandez de Cordoba and Juan de Grivalja, while the invasion of Mexico itself was being prepared under the command of Hernando Cortès, Velasquez' Secretary who already had considerable experience of the Americas. Why such haste? They were undoubtedly driven partly by their thirst for gold, but an important factor was the need for manpower, as the Indians kept falling victims of the Europeans' microbes and diseases.

The invasion was carried out with astonishing speed despite the apparent lack of means at their disposal. Leaving Cuba on 18 February 1519 with only 3-400 men and 6 guns, Cortès landed in March. He immediately secured the support of a remarkably beautiful and intelligent woman who became not only his mistress but his political mentor. She was heart and soul for the Spaniards, bore an implacable hatred for the Aztec state which she was determined to see destroyed. The latter, it is true, was based on absolute male supremacy.

Left in the lurch by Velasquez, Cortès pushed ahead and founded the city of Vera Cruz, had himself prematurely proclaimed chief by his men, and sent an envoy to Madrid to justify himself. Taking every advantage of the rivalries splitting Cuba and San Domingo, he courageously pursued his personal aims and entered Tenochtitlan on 8 November. Mexico was his. On 14 November he captured the Aztec emperor and gradually took over all his powers. He had to fight off a small force sent against him by Velasquez in May 1520. But this meant leaving Mexico in the care of one of his lieutenants. The latter lost his head completely during some fiesta and massacred the Aztec nobility, which led to a general uprising against the Spaniards who, after the 'noche triste', the sad night of 30 June, had to withdraw from Mexico City. Cortès rushed back and righted the situation thanks to his friends and allies. He retook Tenochtitlan on 13 August 1521 and the Aztec empire gave up. On October 1522 the conqueror received his letters patent from Charles V sanctioning his action and approving the constitution for New Spain. In 1525 Mexico was under Spanish domination right through to the Pacific. Within a few years Cortès had achieved what the Aztec emperors had vainly attempted for two centuries. Next came the turn of the Mayas to be subjugated by Pedro de Alvarado.

How could such a seemingly powerful empire crumble so quickly before a mere handful of men? The contributing factors were military, diplomatic and religious. Spain's military superiority cannot be denied. Cortès commanded a well-trained, well-armed and perfectly disciplined force. They knew how to fight, how to make use of terrain, how to lay siege, whereas the Aztecs only knew how to charge wildly ahead. As previously mentioned, the Spanish leader

After long sailing the South Seas in the company of John Hawkins, the pirate, England's Sir Francis Drake (circa 1540-1596) completed his voyage round the world 1577-1580 in the *Golden Hind.*

Drake's favourite cup was the gift of Queen Elizabeth I recalling his achievement, a globe cut at the equator and surmounted by an armillary sphere.

18

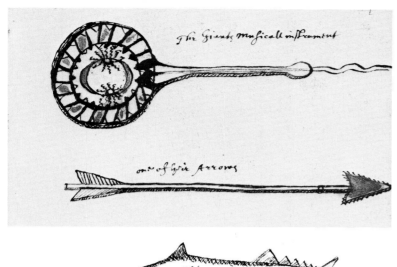

A member of Drake's crew, Francis Fletcher, included in the journal he kept drawings of fish, arrows and utensils (left), and a Pacific volcanic island (above). Below, a map of the *Golden Hind*'s course, engraved by Nicolas Van Sype and 'checked and corrected by the said noble Drake'.

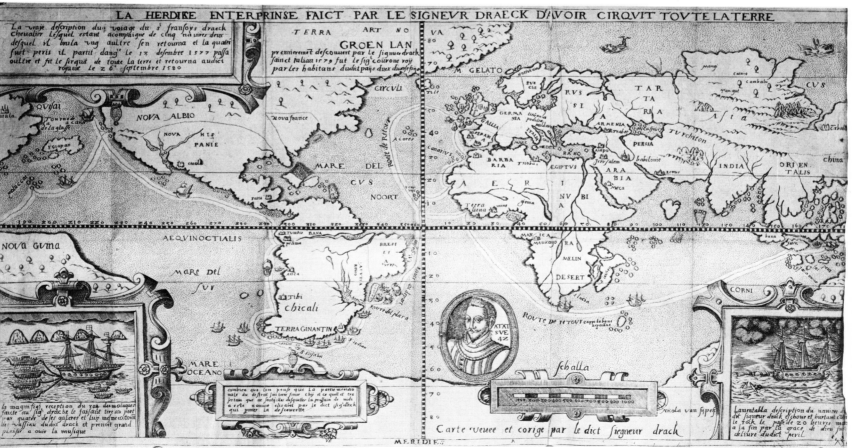

was an adept at profiting from his enemies' internal differences, but his successes owed much to mystical and religious factors, the Aztecs equating him to Quetzalcoatl the god of vengeance, whom they could never hope to defeat.

As can be imagined, such lightning conquests did not give rise to permanent or continuous occupation. Occupation was irregular and piecemeal, limited to certain areas of strategic or economic importance, without regard to huge untouched territories which might remain unvisited and unconquered. Thus vast areas remained almost totally unknown until quite recently while the conquerors stuck to the most profitable areas.

After Mexico it was Peru's turn to be taken over in very similar manner. Founded in 1519, Panama became the base for conquering the Pacific coast just as Cuba had done for the conquest of the West Indies. The southward advance down the Pacific was accomplished in stages. A first attempt was made in 1523 by Pascual de Andagoya who got no further than today's Colombia. But the resultant rumours of colossal riches were enough to encourage Francisco Pizarro, Almagro and Luque to form a company to explore the area. The means at their disposal were even less impressive than those enjoyed by Cortès. After a first fruitless efforts Pizarro returned to Spain to seek royal patronage and reinforcements. On 26 May 1529 he was successful and on 19 January 1530 he was off the northern borders of the Inca empire, then in the midst of a civil war, which was once again greatly to facilitate his task. On 15 November 1532 Pizarro met the Inca emperor Atahualpa at Cajamarca. Atahualpa dropped the Bible offered to him: despite their tremendous numerical inferiority the Spaniards took him prisoner and his whole empire collapsed. Just one year to the day after his capture, Pizarro entered Cuzco and set up a kind of protectorate under Manco Capac.

Chile was the invader's next goal. Almagro set out from Cuzco on 3 July 1535. This time his forces were very different and plentiful: 1500 men and a hoard of Indian bearers. He tried to achieve what the Incas had always failed to do, to overcome the war-like tribes of the Picanches, the Puelches and the Huiliches. But the great distances and the fierce resistance put up by the Araucanians combined with the Peruvians' attacks were too much for him. Pedro de Valdivia tried again in 1540. Marching along the coast, he founded Santiago in February 1541 and Conception in 1551, and sent scouts down towards the south. But he had crossed the Bio-Bio River which the Araucanians regarded as their natural boundary. On Christmas Day 1553 they killed and devoured the Spanish leader whose army was wiped out at Tucapel by Lautaro, a kind of Indian Black Prince who was later glorified as the hero of a novel. The Spaniards avenged their shameful defeat in 1558 and crossed the Andes (1560-1562) towards Mendoza. But the Araucanians kept up the fight for another 300 years.

South America's South Atlantic coasts were far from forgotten. As we have seen, Juan Diaz de Solis tried to find a way through to the Pacific but was killed and eaten in 1516 while exploring the River Plate. Later, Sebastian Cabot's 1526-1531 expedition fared no better, but the Spaniards remained undaunted. With a fairly well equipped expedition Pedro de Mendoza managed to found Buenos Aires in 1536 and his followers Juan de Ayolas and Martinez de Irala sailed up the River Parãna and the Paraguay to settle Asuncion. From January 1541 to August 1542 Francisco de Orellana coasted down the east-bound rivers to discover the Amazon in the course of a phenomenal 2,500 mile journey.

Towards the middle of the sixteenth century Spain's American empire could be largely outlined with its extension towards the Philippines, that final outpost towards which all sea lanes converged, which were linked by the umbilical cord of the galleons regularly crossing the Pacific between Manilla and Acapulco. This age-old link was only broken centuries later by Napoleon's conquests and the wars of independence.

Navigators of the day were terrified by the immense wastes of the Pacific. But one man was prepared to attempt it from the American coast: Alvaro Mendaña who set out in November 1567 from Callao, in Peru, towards the Philippines. Heading southward, he discovered an island in February 1568 which he named Santa Isabel, where he came across cannibals of Papua. Searching around, he found other islands: Guadalcanal, San Cristobal. But skirmishing with the natives cost him too many men and he had to leave. In June 1569 Mendaña returned to Acapulco. He had discovered the Solomon Islands which became a sort of myth, an Eldorado which many an explorer vainly tried to locate again up until the eighteenth century.

A long period of inactivity followed this unsuccessful attempt. On 16 June 1595 Mendaña tried again from Peru with 4 ships and 400 men, a Portuguese pilot, women and children to found a colony. The head of this expedition enjoyed a number of privileges, including royalties from any conquered islands. On 21 July he reached the Marquesa Islands. Heading further west he found an island which he called Santa Cruz, where he landed to settle, not without considerable native resistance. On 17 October Mendaña died. His wife Isabel took over command. On 18 November she gave orders to depart. After stopping at Guam, what was left of the expedition reached Manilla on 11 February 1596. From there Isabel, already remarried, returned to Acapulco.

Thus ended Spain's great exploration attempts started by Columbus, which gave birth to a fabulous empire, so widespread and so varied. It lasted for 200 years, held together more or less firmly by loyalty to the crown and to Christ, but also and mainly by its rivals' preferring to enjoy its weakness rather than to seek its destruction.

The Spanish empire based itself on the Atlantic, the American continent, and to a certain extent on the Pacific, and left the Indian Ocean to the Portuguese. Despite her impoverished state, or maybe because of it, Portugal soon started gearing her expeditions towards commercial gain. Except for Brazil, which was to become a real colony, the Lusitanians at that time set up fortified markets aimed at controlling commercial exchanges. For lack of sufficiently extensive private capital, it fell to the state to carry this out by founding first the Guinea House, then the India House, which provided capital and retained almost complete monopoly for itself.

The twin empires of Spain and Portugal rubbed shoulders in the key area of the Celebes, sole source of spices. Malacca and the Moluccas, where the first settlements appeared in the early sixteenth century, were the anchor of the whole chain of Portuguese markets: Cape Verde, Luanda, Mombassa, Goa. Stabs towards China and Japan (1545-1549) had been less successful but 'within a century and a half poor underpopulated little Portugal led the way for European expansion and continued to play its part in Africa, Asia and much of America. Lisbon is at the height of its glory; all northern Europe flocked to Portugal to buy overseas commodities'*. But in many areas it was a fragile commercial empire, ill able to stand up to its commercial rivals.

In the second half of the sixteenth century those countries not included in the Tordesillas Treaty took on increasing importance in Europe and gradually overcame their internal problems which earlier prevented them from looking overseas. The British and the Dutch soon became powerful partners who had to be reckoned with. The French only came into the picture in the seventeenth century.

In Northern Europe the first to take to the high seas were the British. On 2 May 1497 Giovanni Caboto, long settled in Bristol under the name of John Cabot, set out towards the north of America to find a passage to China, armed with letters patent from Henry VII. By June he was off Labrador, but found nothing encouraging. A second trip fared no better. It was not until the middle of the following century that such voyages were to be resumed, possibly more inclined towards piracy than discovery. Such was the case of John Hawkins and his second in command Francis Drake. By 1562 they were seriously harassing the Spaniards in the West Indies. In 1577 Drake set off for the Pacific with 5 ships and 160 men, ostensibly to find the southern continent but in reality to pillage the ports and ships of Spain along the Peruvian coast. Having accomplished this satisfactorily, he sailed up to California, crossed the Pacific, visited the Moluccas and the Philippines, and so accomplished England's first round the world voyage. He was back in Portsmouth on 26 September 1580.

He was followed by Thomas Cavendish in July 1586 with 3 ships and 120 men. Passing the Straits of Magellan, they raided a series of Spanish trading posts in Chile and Peru, captured a large 700-ton galleon, and took off across the Pacific, making the crossing in the record time of 45 days, and getting home to Plymouth on 9 September 1588. A few years earlier Martin Frobisher had led three unsuccessful expeditions (1576-1580) to Labrador looking for the North-West Passage towards the Pacific, the target of so many navigators right up to the nineteenth century.

Spain was for the first time having what she considered her private preserves raided by rivals. Soon this would

extend to the American continent: in 1584 Sir Walter Raleigh sent a small group of settlers into a previously ignored area, which was later to become Virginia. A stroke of luck? Brilliant intuition? This area was particularly well chosen since it offered the best point from which to sail back to Europe. But it was not until the mid-seventeenth century that England's real drive for colonies began, after William Baffin (1612-1615) and Henry Hudson's expeditions had concentrated their attentions too far north. At least the latter did discover the river and its huge bay which now bear his name, before vanishing, abandoned by his mutinous crew (1609-1610).

England's vast emigration movement of the early seventeenth century was due to many factors: her capitalist form of economy, religious and political conflicts leading to persecution and banishment, the problems brought on by the Thirty Years' War. 'The take-off of Anglo-Saxon America started around 1620', wrote P. Chaunu.* 'It was stimulated by two main causes. Foremost was tobacco, the economic justification. Europe discovered the use of tobacco between 1615 and 1625. Regarded as a medicine for almost a century, it suddenly became a highly popular stimulant.' The other factor was the lack of native population. Devoid of Indians, Virginia began to attract a wave of whites who at first led a life of virtual slavery, somewhat along the lines of the first French colonies which were being formed at about the same period. The new country developed comparatively quickly under an aegis of strict religious observance.

After Virginia and Maryland (1620-1640) came the turn of New England, also stimulated by religious troubles at home, though for different reasons. Virginia's economy had been mainly farming. New England soon turned its back on the land and concentrated on trade with the West Indies.

It became the north-eastern corner-stone of a four point trading system between Europe, Africa and the Caribbean.

But the Dutch were lying in wait. Between 1624 and 1633 the Dutch West Indies Company was busy setting up a chain of trading posts based on New Amsterdam and strung out along the Hudson and the Delaware. Their apparent power soon faded away just as it did in Brazil. By 1664 all the coast was occupied, but rather loosely and with no foreign enclave. Expansion continued all through the 1660's in various directions, inwards to open up Pennsylvania and southwards towards North and South Carolina.

England was still far from the dominant power she would be in the mid-eighteenth century. The Spanish-Portuguese mononpoly's main rival long remained the United Provinces. It can be fairly said that from 1550 to 1650 the Dutch dominated the century, on the high seas and beyond, as they set about taking over large portions of Portugal's overseas possessions and her vital commerce in the Indian Ocean. But the decline of Portugal was only relative. The loss of her Indonesian positions was well compensated to that country by the growth of Brazil and the new African colonies.

Holland's appearance in the Indian Ocean appears to

* See Bibliography.

* See Bibliography.

have been brought on by an unfortunate decision of Philip II. In 1594, when Spain and Portugal were uniting into a single kingdom, he barred the port of Lisbon to the British and the Dutch. Scared of an economic collapse when they were so dependent on oriental produce, they promptly decided to set up bases in the centres of production. Their project was facilitated by the Portuguese having always maintained only lightly defended trading posts everywhere, all constantly on bad terms with the native rulers, who were themselves for ever waging war against each other.

Without hesitation the Dutch set up bases in the Moluccas and in India in 1598. That same year, on 2 July, Oliver van Noort took 4 ships with 248 men from Amsterdam on a voyage round the world showing the United Provinces flag. After passing Guinea, Brazil, and the Magellan Straits, he set about raiding the coasts of Peru and Chile, which action was by now becoming almost a habit among intruders, and sailed across the Pacific to the Philippines, where he sank two Spanish warships. He returned to Holland on 26 August 1601 with less than one third of his crew left.

Founded in 1602, the Dutch India Company seized Ambon and Tidore and negotiated a treaty with the local rulers: Dutch protection in exchange for sole rights to the spices. These developments prompted Hugo de Groot, the famous legal authority better known as Grotius, to publish his famous *Mare Liberum* (1609). In it he propounded eloquently the theory of the freedom of the seas and of free trade, both considered as man's natural rights. It is noteworthy that after basing themselves on these fine theories to justify throwing the Portuguese out of the Moluccas, the Dutch soon forgot them when they set up their own monopolies; for 150 years they went to great effort to keep all foreigners out of their precious archipelagoes and prevent anyone knowing what lay concealed there. They maintained that trade must be free everywhere except where contracts or treaties existed. Holland had such treaties with Ambon, Ternate and others, so the natives had to observe these strictly and no foreigner was allowed to try and persuade them to break them. This inflexible stand brought on sharp conflict between 1610 with the British India Company, which tried hard to break into the Indonesian Islands as well.

The Dutch saw that the weakness of the Portuguese empire lay in its purely commercial nature. Led by their Governor-General, Coen, they aimed at political domination and at diversification of sources of profit by developing trade with other parts of the Indian Ocean.

As part of this plan they formed a settlement at Jakarta on the Island of Java, which later became Batavia. The city prospered despite the terrible climate and soon became one of the foremost outposts of the Far East. Continuously extending their zone of influence, often by somewhat dubious means, they soon had a huge chain of well selected trading centres: after the Moluccas, permanently installed from 1628 onwards, came Ceylon (1636), Negapatam, Malacca (1642), and, to insure a well-located shipping base, the Cape of Good Hope in 1652. In addition to these fully controlled

RELACION DE VN memorial que ha prefentado a fu Mageftad el Capitan Pedro Fernandez de Quir, fobre la poblacion y defcubrimiento de la quarta parte del mundo, Auftrialia incognita, fu gran riqueza y fertilidad: defcubierta por el mifmo Capitan.

Con licencia del Confejo Real de Pamplona, Impreffa por Carlos de Labayen. Año 1610.

Above, the frontispiece of an account of an expedition by the Portuguese Pedro Fernandez de Quiros, published in 1610. He passionately believed in the existence of the fabulous Austral continent, visualising it as reaching from the South Pole to the heart of the Coral Sea below the Tropic of Capricorn. When he reached the New Hebrides on his journey with Luis Vaez Torres 1605-1607 he was convinced he had at last found the 'Australia of the Holy Ghost'.

Most Holy Father,

I hereby humbly bring to Your Holiness' feet these several million men, beseeching you with as much insistence as humility, to admit them to that Sacred Flock which Divine Providence has entrusted to Your care on this earth and outside which there is no salvation. They are the peoples of those areas shown on all maps as the unknown Austral Lands, of such immensity as to form their own portion of the Universe, yet of such import as to have earned from many the name of the Third World...

These poor, miserable creatures of the Pole have suffered for centuries beneath the yoke of Satan and now are filled with hope at the mere mention of the name of the greatest among Conquerors, who so often regretted having but one world to conquer. This convinces them that, having assumed this name, on assuming the Sovereign Pontificate, Your Holiness will deign to bring their Third World under Your sweet laws and unite it with the other twain which bow before Your Throne and Your Crown. Most Holy Father, do not disdain their hopes and command that they may be granted salvation.

Canon PAULMIER DE COURTONNE, *Notes on the establishment of a Christian mission in the third world otherwise known as the Austral, Southern, Antarctic and Unknown Land, dedicated to our Saintly Father Pope Alexander VII by a churchman from that same land,* Paris 1663, 1664

esfaxente es desta bayadesan millan sonyndios algg blancos sus armas son Arcos azzo xadicos ymacanas sus basti mentos sony ñames cañas duçes pan de maluco pueuos y muchas frutas

esfaxente es dela baia s felipe y s tiago donde senos fuela q pitana sonneqto cuer pos fros dinarios sus armas son flechas Dardos ymaeianas efterzaffnal ysana tapanlar vezeuencas con ojas Deauoles

esfaxente es del remate dela nueba guinea esjeneze bemoa sus armas son dardos es flechas lanças largas mlontan tisdoal f eeqas los contrarios ajo vsande

areas of their own, they also set up a chain of trading posts stretching from Persia to Japan.

From all this a curious social mixture with little racial prejudice sprang into being. Many of the Dutch men married Asian women. These embraced Christianity and became Dutch citizens along with their children. There was broad tolerance towards Chinese and Moslems. They lived in Batavia and were able to worship according to their respective beliefs. But this liberal attitude did not extend to economic life. There the colonial power was inflexible. On some islands they deported or killed off the inhabitants or turned them into slaves, binding others inescapably to their service with advances of cash or goods with such stringent conditions that the unfortunate debtors could never hope to become clear of debt. Working under the closest supervision, the spice growers had to stick to tight production quotas which they were strictly forbidden to exceed. Any overproduction was mercilessly seized and destroyed, and the plants ripped up. When Bougainville visited the Moluccas in 1768 he was astounded to find such malthusian practices still being followed.

Holland's colonial expansion was not limited to the Indian Ocean. It spread to the Atlantic and the American continent. By 1609 the first settlements were springing up in Guyana. In 1614 they built Fort Orange, near Albany on the Hudson, entrance to the fur territories. In 1621 the West Indies Company was created, which organised the Hudson Valley trading posts and founded New Amsterdam. An expedition under Jakob Willekens and Piet Hein led to the start of the Dutch presence in Brazil, which lasted until 1654. As though following a pattern of taking over Portugal's colonies, the Batavians seized a number of posts along the West African coast: Arguin, Elmina, Luanda. But the British and Portuguese soon put their feet down, and this exagerated advance was stopped, collapsing almost as fast as it had developed. By 1642 the Dutch were being driven out of Brazil and Angola. In 1664 New Amsterdam fell to the English and was renamed New York. A treaty was signed in 1668, leaving the New Provinces holding only Elmina, but retaining many worthwhile trading concessions. Meanwhile they had set up a base on Curaçao in the West Indies. This little island was to became a source of great wealth thanks to its clandestine trade with the Spaniards.

The Dutch West Indies Company could not but succumb to such repeated losses. But its sister company, the East India Company, prospered beyond its wildest dreams and provided a base of solid and lasting prosperity for the Dutch.

Torres landed on New Guinea in 1606, where Prado Tovar, his captain, made the first known drawings of South Sea natives. Without realising it, Torres just missed Australia and sailed through the Straits which today bear his name.

TARTARIA

IAPAN

MAR NEGRO O

Islas

Islas de las
velas, o
de los Ladrones

Filipinas

ARCHIPELAGO DE S. LAZARO

MA

Tropicus Cancri dat is Creeftes Sonnewend of Noorder Sonnestandt

Linea Æquinoctialis, dat is de Middellijn

Nueva Guinea

Illas de Salomon

Tropicus Capricorni dat is Steenboex Sonnewend of Zuyder Sonnestandt

MAR

By Heffel Gerrits z.
met Octroy
van de E. H. M. Heeren
de Staten Generael
der Vereenichde Nederlanden
cIɔ.Iɔc.xxv.

QVIBIRA

LA FLORID

DEL·SVR

ACIFICO

# THE PACIFIC IN THE SEVENTEENTH CENTURY

The seventeenth century seems a period of comparative stagnation after the power struggle of the sixteenth, during which Europe found the Pacific and timidly commenced to discover some of its possibilities. The demographic explosion which went on from 1434 to 1560-1570 was followed by a long pause of indifference and even retreat, with but little progress, and that of minor importance. Man did not yet possess adequate instruments to fix with precision the positions of the newly discovered lands.

What caused that long pause in the drive for discovery? A number of factors, psychological, economic and political, lay behind it.

A profound change of outlook had come into being. The heroic age of the conqueror gave way to the more prosaic attitude of the mathematician, the economist, and the trader; an age which shunned mad adventure and discouraged risky investments in overdaring enterprises offering but illusory chances of profit.

In the field of economics the seventeenth century gave rise to a new development, that of the trading companies based on monopoly such as were being created by first Holland, then England, both new powers with which the pioneers had to reckon. Arming their own fleets and erecting their own fortified trading posts, these companies were not interested in promoting any new discoveries which did not offer immediate profit. To do so was not their business. They concentrated instead on making money out of the new-found lands, not on conquering them. Moreover, their efforts bore fruit. Maritime commerce developed enormously in those years both in European waters and in more distant regions such as Newfoundland, the West Indies and the Indian Ocean, to all of which there were regular sailings.

Politics in Europe at the time were also not conducive to such expeditions. The power of Spain was seriously weakened in the first half of the century by the Thirty Years' War. The power of Portugal crumbled in its wake. As a result the dual monopoly of these two empires began to disappear after having earlier been responsible for 75 per cent to 90 per cent of commercial interchange between Europe and overseas. It was now Northern Europe's turn: Holland, England, France began their own expansion which was to lead to continuous conflict until the Treaties of Utrecht (1713), which laid the foundations for England's tremendous power growth.

Nevertheless the seventeenth century had by no means turned its back on new discovery. How could that happen in a period of such extraordinary scientific progress? The 1620-1630 decade witnessed the start of perhaps one of the

This map, attributed to Hessel Gerritsz (1581-1652) gives a rough idea of what was known of the Pacific around 1630. Neither Australia nor New Zealand are shown. Yet early in the century Dutch sailors had explored the coasts of Australia without realising it.

greatest revolutions in scientific thought: the world's adoption of mathematics. In 1623 Galileo came out with his famous pronouncement: 'nature is written in mathematical terms'. This was the period when the first scientific societies were born, first in Italy until the decline of the maritime power of Genoa and Venice put a stop to all practical development, but most particularly in England and in France. At practically the same time, the 1660s witnessed the foundation in England of the Royal Society, which published its *Philosophical Transactions,* and in France of the Royal Academy of Science with the *Scientists' Journal.* The very trading companies began to set themselves up as promoters of geographic and cosmographic study. This was, in fact, first done by the East India Company in England, and this was followed later by that of France. Governments followed their example. In London, the India Office became a vital information centre. In Paris Colbert became Secretary of State for the Navy in 1669 and at once set about forming a collection of maps and charts which, half a century later, was to form the basis of the *Dépôt des Cartes et Plans de la Marine,* which gathered in one collection all the scientific and geographic data brought home by naval officers from their campaigns.

Thus, gradually, discovery ceased to seek purely mercenary gain and instead began to be geared towards scientific aims. But ship owners for the first time were perceiving that scientific research could pay tangible dividends. Progress in navigational instruments, ship design, charting, food conservation all made a direct contribution to profits. Crew maintenance was no longer left to chance. The years 1600-1740 may have produced little new exploration, but essential knowledge was all the time being accumulated which would make possible the great leap forward of the late eighteenth century, and the hundred years to follow.

What was known of the Pacific under Henri IV and James I? Very little. Its secrets were still quite unknown a hundred years after Magellan, and Europeans had only seen some of its coastal fringes, such as Peru, Northern Chile or the Philippines. The latter's compact formation made it easy for the Spaniards to start developing it fairly extensively from 1570 onwards. Right up till the mid-seventeenth century stagnation, the new colony progressed rapidly from 1630-1640 on, when it too became affected by the same factors as slowed down Europe's economy.

Except for those two distant target areas, the rest of the world can fairly be said to have remained unknown. Map makers vaguely dotted the seas with odd islands, inaccurately prolonged the North American continent towards Siberia, and put in an Austral land mass, of which nothing much was then known, somewhere in the South Pacific. Much would be written and vaguely theorised about this almost hypothetical land mass for 200 years.

Any purely scientific observation was impossible for lack of adequate measuring equipment. South of the fortieth parallel visiblity is generally bad due to mist and cloud, so it was not surprising that the early navigators claimed to have 'seen' lands which did not exist and mistook an island for a continent. As late as 1739 Bouvet de Lozier thought he had discovered Australia when he first sighted the tiny island which today bears his name. All kinds of myths were created in this way, based, as in this case, on the belief that Austral continent must infallibly exist to keep the balance of the planet.

Like Columbus' illusions, such theories did in fact serve a useful purpose in that they sparked many a voyage of exploration which all added to the elementary knowledge of those far-off parts of the world.

The first man to tackle the problem seriously was Pedro Fernandez de Queiroz or Quiroz, Mendaña's pilot on the 1594 expedition. Convinced of its existence, he visualised the Australian continent as stretching up to the Tropic of Capricorn, reaching towards the Coral Sea and the Solomon Islands. He tried to persuade the King of Spain to back further exploration, halted by the death of his leader. He did not succeed, and in 1600 went to Rome to seek the support of the Pope and at the same time to study the Vatican's rich store of geographic material. Tipped off by the Pope, Philip III finally decided to back the project and on 21 December 1605 Quiroz, Prado and Torres set out from Callao with three ships. Their idea was to sail west-south-west along the thirtieth parallel and then to turn up northwestward towards the tenth parallel in an attempt to reach the Island of Santa Cruz de Medaña. But the prevailing winds kept the three men all the time north of their intended course. Passing through the Tuamotu, they recognised Tahiti, which they called Sagittaria. On 1 May 1606 they landed on a large island which they named Terra Australis de Spiritu Santo, Quiroz being convinced that it was part of the Austral continent. He took possession of the island and drew up a superficial but enthusiastic list of its resources and loudly proclaimed the marvels of his discovery, even though several of his crew were poisoned by eating some of its fish. 'I can justifiably state that there can exist to no more delightful, healthy and fertile land than this', he reported. So Espiritu Santo entered world history, though in reality it was but one of the New Hebrides. However, Quiroz' companions did not share his enthusiasm and urged him to return to America. At first little importance was given to his discovery and his many reports to the King of Spain on the subject remained without reply. He finally received permission to try again, but died in Panama in 1615.

When he left the New Hebrides Quiroz had become separated from his companions who continued on towards Malaysia or the Philippines. Crossing the Coral Sea, they reached the eastern point of New Guinea, followed its southern coast and found the straits which today still bear the name of one of them, Luis Vaez de Torres, but without realising its significance since they were unaware of the existence of the Australian continent. This discovery remained buried, however, for 200 years because Torres' report was filed away in the archives in Manilla and did not see the light of day until 1762 when the British conquered the city. Even they did not make it known until 1806. Not realising the importance of marking such spots on the charts covering the area between America and the China Seas, the Spani-

Verraders Eylandt
Isle des traistres

Above, Schouten and Le Maire anchor off Tonga, where inquisitive Niu-atoputapu natives climb aboard and make off with everything they can lay hands on.

Below: New Guinea Papuans honour the 'white gods' with a lavish banquet. A Dutch brass band played, while Schouten and Le Maire bartered trinkets for spices.

ards themselves paid no attention to these results. The Dutch thought otherwise. Settled, as we know, on the Indonesian islands since the late sixteenth century, they set about reconnoitring the surrounding areas in a series of expeditions devoted to trade and discovery.

In 1605 Willem Janszoon left Bantam in the DUIFKEN (the Little Dove) for New Guinea, where he examined the southern coasts. Without realising what he was doing, he reconnoitred part of the coast of Australia but returned to Java the following year, discouraged by the hostile reception of the natives and the desolate appearance of the country.

The founding of Batavia in 1619 by Jan Pieterzoon Coen set off a new series of discoveries in those parts. In 1619 Houtman made studies of large portions of the west coast of Australia, followed in 1627-1628 by Peter Nuyts and de Witt. Back in Holland, ever bigger expeditions were being organised. Isaac Lemaire, a wealthy Amsterdam merchant, decided to follow Magellan and Drake's indications of the previous century. On 25 June 1615 Texel set sail with Isaac Lemaire's son Jacob, and William Schouten. After passing within sight of the mouth of the Magellan Straits they continued south and discovered the States Territory, still called Lemaire today. On 24 January 1616 they sailed round a cape which they named after one of their ships, the HOORN, and entered the Pacific, thus being the first to do so by the route which has now become so well known. On the way north they stopped at Juan Fernandez before crossing the Pacific between the Tropic of Capricorn and the Equator, passing the Tuamotu, Samoa, and the Tonga and Solomon Islands before hitting the northern coast of New Guinea.

In Batavia they faced a hostile reception from Coen, who accused them of trespassing on the East India Company's rights by taking on spices at New Guinea. Both Lemaire and Schouten died shortly afterwards. But at least their journey had proved that the southern tip of America was not connected to the hypothetical Austral continent.

All these expeditions helped trace the vague outline of the coast, stretch by stretch. These still had to be put together and accurately drawn, a task entrusted in 1642 to Captain Abel Janszoon Tasman by Governor-General Van Diemen. Starting from the Island of Mauritius, then in the hands of the Dutch, he crossed the Indian Ocean south-eastwards close to Australia but without seeing it, and landed at an island which he named Van Diemen and which is now called Tasmania. Continuing eastwards, more or less along the fortieth parallel, he found a new shoreline, which he naturally assumed to be that of the continent he was in search of. It was New Zealand. In the face of the violent hostility of the native Maoris he was unable to land. Sailing, without realising it, through the narrows which separate the two islands, Tasman turned north to Tonga, rounded the Fijis and set out west. He charted the north coast of New Ireland, which he thought was New Guinea, and returned to Batavia via the Moluccas. He had little to show for his efforts, having sailed all round Australia without seeing it. Many years were to pass before any precise knowledge of the latter continent was available.

The middle of the seventeenth century thus marked the end of a chapter in the history of discovery. All the expeditions described above had shown disappointing results for several reasons: the quality of the ships then in use, superficial charting due to inadequate instruments, and above all bad planning and organisation.

So far discovery had been purely empirical, left to individual initiative, only secondary importance being attributed to scientific requirements. The findings of each journey were carefully shrouded in secrecy. Each country, each navigator, was careful to keep the latest discoveries from public knowledge. Under such conditions, what progress could be expected when no-one knew what the others were doing and no attempt was made to co-ordinate the information available? Further, the findings of the great geographers of the past like Ptolemy were still regarded as sacrosanct.

By the middle of the century things began to change with the formation of the new scientific societies. These began to publish the findings they had assembled. P. Fournier's *Hydrography* (1643) was a real encyclopedia of navigational science. It was followed by P. François' *Science of Geography* (1652) and P. Athanase Kircher's monumental work*, in which he attempted for the first time to explain the physical make-up of our globe. At about the same time the first observatories were being built — at Greenwich with the blessing of Charles II and in Paris with the support of Louis XIV and Colbert. 'By the Great Century exploring had ceased to be an adventure, but was conducted to provide precise facts and figures needed to complete man's knowledge of his physical world, of geography, ethnography and natural history.' (P.J. Charliat**).

The rewards of all this effort were slow in coming, and little progress in exploring the Pacific was noticeable until the end of the seventeenth century. An uninterrupted series of wars from 1668 to 1713 did little to help scientific research. But it was not completely halted. Some interesting facts were being gathered by a few scientists, while others emerged from such unexpected sources as piracy and commerce. The first scientists to make the Pacific trip were, one after the other, Father Louis Feuillée (1660-1732), a mathematician and botanist, and Amédée Frézier (1682-1773), the King's Engineer.

After surveying the Levant and the West Indies, Father Feuillée set sail in 1707 from Marseilles in the ST JEAN BAPTISTE as correspondent of the Paris Science Academy. He stopped at Teneriffe and Buenos Aires, sailed round Cape Horn, visited Chile and Peru and only returned to France in

* See Bibliography.
** See Bibliography.

Reefs and the local inhabitants permitting, halts were made at every possible opportunity after long and often dramatic crossings in order to take on fresh water and victuals, by then often spoiled or exhausted. The rich nature of the Pacific provided plentiful fruits and coconuts. After stocking the holds, the men can recuperate on shore. Opposite, an enchanting view of Moorea, the Society Islands.

August 1711, bringing with him a rich harvest of new scientific knowledge. These filled a number of volumes published between 1714 and 1725, including the *Journal of Physical, Mathematical and Botanical Notes Made on the East Coast of South America* and a *History of Medical Plants in Peru and Chile.*

Frézier owed his voyage to the then state of war. A military engineer, he was sent to Chile and Peru to restore the forts there, which took him from January 1712 till August 1714. He had an enquiring mind and took advantage of his stay to do some purely scientific research, including a careful survey of Tierra del Fuego, the Lemaire Straits and especially the completion of the first good map of South America. His 1716 report on his travels brought him into lively conflict with Father Feuillée.

Much has been written about the exploits of adventurers of the time, but they did more than indulge in adventure for adventure's sake. They were not all rough and tough; many of them proved capable of useful observations. A prime example was Wiliam Dampier (1652-1715), an Englishman who could truly be called a Pliny among adventurers. Intelligent, cultured, with a good scholastic record, he was the son of a Welsh farmer. A keen observer, a good writer, an outstanding sailor, he started by sailing to the West Indies and Newfoundland, where he teamed up with the pirates of Turtle Island. In 1683 he sailed round Cape Horn in the REVENGE, raided a few Spanish bases, went on to California and then across the Pacific to attack the Philippines. After good pickings in the China Seas he returned to England where he only escaped the punishment he doubtless deserved thanks to his friends in high places. Without ever giving up his pirate's activities, this extraordinary man kept a diary of his observations, drew up charts and coastal maps, and made a study of herbs, which brought him the friendship of Hans Sloane the botanist, with whom he corresponded while preparing the publication of the notes on his journey. Dampier's hydrographic studies attracted the attention of the Royal Society, thereby earning him an officer's commission from the Admiralty which engaged him to carry out an official mission of discovery.

Early in 1699 he left England for Brazil in the ROEBUCK. Avoiding Cape Horn, he re-crossed the South Atlantic and sailed through the Indian Ocean to land on the west coast of Australia. He carefully surveyed some thousand miles of its shores but was then forced to sail off towards Timor by the attitude of his men, who were put off by the arid barren aspect of what they could see of Australia. He sailed along past New Guinea and New Britain, making notes as he went of their geography and natural history. On the way home they were shipwrecked at Ascension Island but managed to make two sallies between 1706 and 1708. He took the opportunity to note carefully the position of the Falklands and to push as far south as the sixtieth latitude south without ever realising that he had in fact already discovered the famous Austral continent. Returning by the Pacific, they put in at Juan Fernandez, where they found the original Robinson Crusoe, Alexander Selkirk, who had been living there in solitude for some years.

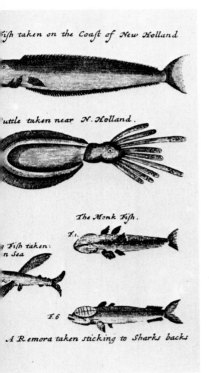

William Dampier (1652-1715), nicknamed the Pliny of Piracy, filled his notebooks with reports and drawings, indulging in botany and map-making between expeditions. Above: fish caught off Australia, and birds seen in New Guinea.

Left: Coral reefs are a sailor's worst enemies. Many a crew has been shipwrecked for failing to spot them. Out on the high seas coral forms wonderful barriers, as seen here off New Caledonia.

At the turn of the century a number of French merchant ships were for the first time to be seen in the Pacific Ocean. In 1697 Pontchartrain, France's Secretary of State for the Navy, had created a Pacific Sea Company, directly after the Augsburg League war was over, to promote French trade with Spanish America. The war of the Spanish Succession was to bring this project to nothing but it was revived by private enterprise. Ships out of St Malo began to pay frequent visits to Chilean and Peruvian ports. At least eleven of them went round the world, mostly in the accepted direction of the Atlantic, Cape Horn, the Pacific and the Indian Ocean. Only one of them, in 1714, went the opposite way round.

These purely commercial ventures were not without geographic interest. In 1699-1700 Jacques Gouin de Beauchesne carefully explored the surroundings of the Magellan Straits and completed a new chart, while in 1713 another St Malo man, Marcand, discovered the Sainte Barbe Canal, a previously unknown passage between the Straits and the Pacific. In 1708 Lamarre, from Caen, sailed straight across the South Atlantic from Cape Horn to the Cape of Good Hope. The following year Frondad took the St Antoine over the previously unattempted northern crossing of the Pacific, where no-one else followed until Cook.

'The honour of dispelling the traditional fear of the Cape Horn passage fell to the ships of France,' wrote E.W. Dahlgren*. 'They soon realised that the dangers of the Magellan Straits, until then regarded as the only gateway to the Pacific, were far worse than those presented by the currents and storms prevailing around the southernmost point of America.' Bougainville was to find this out to his cost at the end of 1767.

These trade voyages stopped after 1715. The Spaniards, worried by such competition which they were unable to face, managed to have them forbidden. Nevertheless a number of expeditions were carried out between 1715 and 1750, several of which were of great scientific value and added greatly to contemporary knowledge.

Relative newcomers to the Pacific were the Russians, who began to show up there when Vitus Bering entered the Tsar's service and was instructed to survey the borders of Asia and America in the far north, and if possible to make contact with the Spaniards in California. He sailed from Kamchatka in July 1728 and passed through the straits which carry his name without really noticing it. Several years later an international team of scientists and artists put together a far more imposing expedition. They left Petropavlosk in 1741 in two ships under Bering's command, sailed through the Aleutians and reached Alaska. But storms and scurvy stopped them from getting any further. Bering himself died in December 1741, and what was left of the expedition returned home in August 1742.

Two important journeys were made at the time into the South Pacific by Jacob Roggeven of Holland and George Anson of England. The first was a truly scientific effort; the other was the result of war operations.

Roggeven (1669-1729) wanted to check the reports made by seventeenth century explorers, particularly Lemaire and Schouten. He left the Texel on 21 August 1721 with three ships and entered the Pacific via the Lemaire Straits. On 14 April 1722, Easter Day, he sighted an island which he called Easter Island. He and his companions took the time to visit it and were naturally struck by its extraordinary statuary. They next made Makatea and later New Britain and New Guinea, where the natives proved extremely hostile. In Batavia Roggeven was arrested by the Company's managers and had his ships confiscated. The Hague government intervened and he was set free. But he died before being able to publish his report which only saw the light of day in 1911. Once again there was little to show for such heavy expenditure.

Anson's campaign, undertaken thanks to the Anglo-Spanish war of 1739, was more fruitful. The British Admiralty decided to send a squadron to the Pacific to hit the Spaniards below their money-belt. Anson sailed out of Spithead on 18 September 1740, flying his broad pendant in the 60-gun Centurion. He passed Cape Horn in a terrible storm and put in at Juan Fernandez. In Peru he sacked and set fire to Paita in the best traditions of piracy. He tried the same trick at Acapulco, but the Spaniards were ready for him, and he had to make off in sorry shape across the Atlantic to reach safety at Tinian Island on 27 August 1741. On 19 December he reached Macao where he signed on new men. On 19 April 1742 he sailed out to intercept the Manilla galleon, in which he was successful after a brief encounter. Crossing the Indian Ocean, the squadron was back at Spithead by 15 June 1744. On the way Anson accumulated copious information, together with notes on the importance of currents which upset all estimates, and, of particular interest, secret Spanish documents captured aboard the galleon showing an outline of the north Pacific route.

An accomplished writer, Anson immediately published the records of his voyage. It was a tremendous success throughout Europe and aroused the enthusiasm of Voltaire who devoted a whole chapter to it in his *Précis of the Century of Louis XV*. The book deserved its success. Besides its undoubted literary qualities, *Anson's Voyage* opened a new era in the field of discovery and marked the transition from expeditions which must be termed empirical to those which were to become more and more scientifically based.

But it must be honestly admitted that in the middle of the eighteenth century the Pacific was still the Great Unknown. Two hundred years of strenuous effort had produced but meagre results, always for lack of technical equipment, a barrier that nobody had been able to overcome. Langlet du Fresnoy provided the clearest proof of this in his *Method for the Study of Geography* published in 1742. Referring to the celebrated Austral continent he wrote: 'That continent embraces not only the lands below the South Pole but all the other lands in the area which cannot be joined to that southern continent due to their distance from other land masses. The Antarctic is bound by the Mer Delzur or South Sea, the Ethiopian Ocean or Sea, and the Indian Ocean or Sea. Its

* See Bibliography.

principal countries or islands are New Guinea, Papua, the Carpentaria, the Solomon Islands to the south, the Austral land of the Holy Spirit, New Zealand, Horn Island, the Coco Islands, Traitors' Islands and other minor ones round about, Tierra del Fuego Island, the States Island, particularly Austral Land, Van Diemens Land and New Holland.'

This strange mixture shows how great was the ignorance of the times and how much still remained to be done by future explorers. But the first requirement would be to find new methods, and reduce technical obstacles.

This engraving of Admiralty Strait, Tierra del Fuego, gives an excellent impression of the desolation and savage scenery to be found near Cape Horn and the Magellan Straits.

The Dutch and Australia

Though an infinity of evils attends the wars with which states and kingdoms are afflicted by the Divine permission, yet they oftentimes procure unexpected benefits. The same Providence that humbles the sinner furnishes means to raise him upon a due repentance. The scourge of war that punishes men may contribute, when the Divine Providence thinks fit, to whet their spirits, and render them capable of any enterprise.

This was the scourge that galled the United Provinces for so long a time; and constrained 'em to range o'er the remotest countries, in quest of the means of subsistence, of which the King of Spain had robbed 'em, not only by laying their country desolate with fire and sword and exercising the cruellest acts of tyranny upon their persons.

If the Spaniards had not seized their ships, and exposed their persons to the rigor of the Inquisition, probably they had never extended their navigation beyond the Baltic Sea, the northern countries, England, France, Spain, and its dependencies, the Mediterranean, and the Levant.

One would have thought that the tyrannical usage of the Spaniards would have ruined their country, and extirpated the people. But on the contrary, it occasioned the welfare and prosperity both of the one and the other. The people, being conducted by such sovereigns as were naturally wise and (if it be possible) become wiser by the sense of danger; being supported by the prudence and animated by the valour of their renowned General and Stadtholder, Prince Maurice of Nassau—the people, I say, under these encouragements, happily set out in order to find under another firmament, and among barbarous savages, the succors that were refused 'em by their neighbours.

Of all the countries that were visited in the way of this forced trade, none have contributed more toward the riches and present happiness of the United Provinces than the East and West Indies. Now in order to reach these countries, they were obliged to avoid the meeting with the Spaniards or the Portuguese; and that difficulty seemed to be in a manner unsurmountable.

They conceived that by steering northeast they might afterward run along the coast of Tartary, and so reach Cathai, China, Japan, India, and the Philippine and Molucca Islands. The execution of this project was committed to two excellent mariners—namely, William Barents and James Heemskirk—and divers others.

While they were in quest of this northern passage, one Cornelis Houtman, a Hollander, happened to be in Portugal, and there satisfied his curiosity by a diligent inquiry into the state of the East Indies, and the course that one must steer in order to come at it. He had frequent conferences upon this subject with the Portuguese, who gave notice of it to the Court. At that time all foreigners were strictly prohibited to make such inquiries, and upon that score Houtman was put in prison, and ordered to lie there till he paid a severe fine.

In order to raise such a considerable sum of money, he addressed himself to the merchants of Amsterdam, and gave 'em to know that if they would pay his fine, he would discover to them all that related to the East Indies and the passage thither. Accordingly, they granted his request, and he performed his promise.

*A Collection of Voyages Undertaken by the Dutch East-Indies Company, for the Improvement of Trade and Navigation,* London, 1703.

# SCIENTIFIC EXPLORATION

Discovery of the world, and especially of the Pacific, belongs to two great periods: the sixteenth and seventeenth centuries which led the way, and the eighteenth and nineteenth centuries which completed the task. They might broadly be described as the era of the adventurer and the era of the scientist; the time when chance played a large part and the time when man succeeded in dominating nature, thereby winning the game.

In this field, as in so many others, the great changes came in the mid-eighteenth century. Around 1740-1750 some 80 million square miles of ocean were known and in regular daily use by some 180-200 ships. By the time of the French Revolution the area had grown by 50 per cent and the number of ships had grown ten times. Two phenomena had contributed to this: Europe's unprecedented economic expansion, and its technological progress. These two would gradually revolutionise methods of navigation and hence of exploration. Europe's grip on the world would strengthen beyond belief. At the start of the eighteenth century Europe's overseas empires were still very loosely knit together, except for a few very small areas under firm control. These seemingly imposing legal edifices ill concealed the truly modest reality.

Why this sudden explosion of Europe? Because Europe had long ago started its great economic and technical takeoff, albeit that progress was uneven, and other continents were all way behind it. The technological distance between the rest of the world and first the Mediterranean countries and later Western Europe was growing unceasingly, and this was so ever since the thirteenth century. This phenomenon of increasing separation, as observed today between the industrialised countries and under-developed or developing countries, has in reality been in existence for 700 years, and has its roots in a number of different causes.

Two are particularly important: better nourishment and a massive use of animal traction. Europeans, especially in the north, are great meat eaters and 'luxuriously fed' compared to other populations, this despite all crises and periods of shortage which would only disappear in the nineteenth century. As early as the thirteenth century the European had adopted the yoke and put his livestock to work, thus securing a source of energy unknown to, or scarcely used by, peoples elsewhere, 'It is a surprising fact that by the middle of the eighteenth century, and probably before the end of the seventeenth, every European native already possessed an average of 25 times as much energy as his own muscle-power could provide.'[1].

Stemming from this, Europe had greater means at its disposal than all the rest of the world put together. The Enlightened Century would bring into full view that disparity which would not cease to grow despite fluctuating dynamic progression. By 1800 Europe, and especially England, controlled every ocean. Its demographic leap forward would provide further fuel for expansion, further need of space, and thus send out ever more men on land and sea. The empires described in earlier pages grew rapidly. For instance Anglo-Saxon America jumped from 890,000 inhabitants in 1740 to 4,000,000 within fifty years. This new conquest, infinitely greater than the first, was based on more favourable economic circumstances, and would no longer proceed by leaps and bounds but would make continuous progress, the conquerors slowly pushing their frontier outward without leaving empty, unoccupied spaces behind. Europe reached a position of supremacy throughout the world.

[1] P. Chaunu, *op. cit.*

# GENERAL CONDITIONS

From the middle of the eighteenth century governments themselves began backing nearly all major voyages of discovery. This new attitude helped greatly to improve the conditions under which such expeditions took place thereafter.

Previously officialdom's attitude to overseas adventure had been one of indifference. Although the Spanish and Portuguese monarchs had protected and even partially financed some of their discoverers' expeditions, this was more with a view to financial gain than scientific progress. The main burden was taken up by private enterprise which explains the long pause in such research after the seventeenth century. The great post-1650 surge of academies and scientific associations served to focus the attention of heads of state on the problems of science. Around 1750 a number of scientists, including many leading figures, began to demand that exploration be resumed more actively. In Volume I of his *Histoire Naturelle* Buffon in 1749 complained: 'There is still much to be found out and vast areas to be discovered despite all we have learned from mathematics and from our great explorers. We know almost nothing of the areas around the South Pole. All we know is that they exist and are separated from the rest of the world by the ocean. We still have much to uncover in the arctic and must regretfully admit that our appetite for new lands has waned severely. We seem, possibly rightly, to prefer the profits to be made from the lands we know to the glory to be derived from discovering the unknown.'

In 1752 Moreau de Maupertuis, member of the *Académie des Sciences* and President of the Berlin Academy published a *Letter on Scientific Progress* addressed to Frederick II of Prussia, and through him to monarchs everywhere, appealing for their active collaboration in the great field of discoveries 'which require far greater resources than can be provided from private sources'. The finding of the Austral lands was the most important, according to him. 'We all know that there is a huge unknown space in the southern hemisphere where there may well exist a continent larger than any of the other four. Yet no prince has been moved to find out whether it conceals a land mass or new seas at a time when navigation has been brought to such a high degree of perfection.' Emphasising the crass ignorance of the period, he went on: 'This is a world on its own. We cannot tell what we will find in those isolated Austral lands. We may open up great treasures both for commerce and for physical geography. The Austral lands surely are not limited to the great continent of the southern hemisphere. There must be numerous islands of possibly great importance between Japan and the Americas. Surely those precious spices now so eagerly sought by Europe do not grow in one area only, an area now in the hands of a single power? Does that very power possess that knowledge, and keep it dark for selfish reasons? Discoverers have already reported seeing savages on those islands, hirsute, possessing tails and constituting a kind of link between monkey and man. Give me an hour's conversation with one of them rather than with the finest wits of Europe!'

His concluding words to the Prussian King were: 'I have aimed at merely pointing out to you what are, in my opinion, the most important discoveries to be made. According to what you may yourself select, we can always discuss the best means of carrying them out. But it would surely be no severe burden for a great prince to send out two or three ships every other year on such undertakings. No matter the outcome, this would serve to prepare commanders and pilots for all phases of navigation and would in all probability lead to some great discoveries since our globe still contains so much that is unknown.'

De Brosses made a similar appeal in his *Histoire des Navigations aux Terres Australes* in 1756: 'The noblest, grandest, most useful task open to a sovereign today is the finding of the Austral lands, which would perpetuate his name for ever. To achieve glory is a king's dominating passion. But kings err in seeking it by force of arms, hence through the sufferings of their subjects and their neighbours. In the case of discovery, the gains from the outcome are added to the greatness of the objective. Here the outcome would mean adding a new world to the one we have now. In recent centuries has any king achieved the fame of Christopher Columbus? It can be stated without fear of contradiction that the greatest glory a monarch can attain is by discovering new lands, and that the most valuable service a contemporary sovereign could perform would be to be able to give his name to the Austral world. Only a king, or the combined resources of a trade-minded republic, can attempt this. No private undertaking, not even a Trading Company, I believe, would have the means of so doing.'

The best placed person to make the attempt, President de Brosses felt, was the King of France himself. He had much helpful advice to give the latter to assure his success.

'Much perseverance will be required. The findings of previous explorers must be carefully studied. Nor must profits be a concern until the final successful outcome; these will follow of themselves afterwards. We must first keep geography in mind and the pure search for knowledge, for new lands and new peoples.'

Intending explorers had to be persuaded to take along a team of scientists. 'A ship's complement must include people capable of drawing maps, observing eclipses, taking measurements of the heights of mountains above sea level, classifying plants, drawing natural history, and even stuffing birds and animals or preserving flowers and leaves.' The disappointing results of earlier expeditions were partly due to the absence of qualified observers on board. Rousseau may have gone too far in asking whether sailors were really humans, but undoubtedly many of them did not possess the qualifications required by leaders of such expeditions. Now ships officers were for the first time being inculcated with a taste for research under the influence of such institutions as the French Marine Academy, which soon after its foun-

In 1785, Louis XVI handed La Pérouse detailed instructions regarding the scientific and hydrographic observations he wanted made, the specimens to be brought home and the attitude to be adopted towards the natives. The authorities were more interested in overseas discoveries.

The most important objective for safety in navigation is to fix the latitudes and longitudes of one's destinations and of those one may meet on the way. To this end, the astrologist employed on every frigate must be told to follow with utmost precision the movement of marine clocks and chronometers and to check with the shore on every possible occasion whether their time-keeping has remained accurate during the journeys and what changes may have occurred in their daily movement, so that he may take such changes into consideration when reckoning the longitudes of any islands, capes, or other points of note that may be sighted between two such checks. Whenever conditions permit, he should measure the distances between the moon and the sun or the stars to determine the ship's longitude and compare it to that shown at the same time and place by the marine chronometers and clocks. To obtain optimum precision this will have to be done several times to find the mean result between the various reckonings. On sighting an island or landfall where no stop is planned, he must try, when the time comes to measure the meridian of the sun or some star, to steer a course parallel to it to help reckon the ship's latitude; he must use the same point's meridian when later observing the longitude. This will obviate any error in fixing position and distance which can adversely affect his calculations.

LA PÉROUSE, *Memorandum from the King to be used as special instructions,* 26 June 1785

dation in 1752 became a branch of the Science Academy. Its officials met in Brest and helped solve many a problem.

The many calls for active resumption of exploration finally produced results after the close of the Seven Years' War, when France and England took up the challenge. They were soon followed by Spain, the United States, Russia. The initiative now came from another source. It was governments that became responsible for organising and financing new expeditions. Officers charged with such missions began to receive precise instructions before sailing, being told just where to explore and what kind of information was wanted. As this meant considerable preparatory work, teams of scientists were gradually constituted to guide the expedition leader like a scientific general staff. After 1770 no important expedition was set up without its group of specialists in various fields such as astronomy, or natural history. These groups were constantly being broadened in the fields of science covered.

Thanks to such increasingly rational organisation, voyages were being ever better prepared and assisted by more comprehensive documentation. This close collaboration between scientists and governments led to great improvements in the field of discovery which at last entered the age of science. The academies and associations mentioned not only helped this collaboration but played an important part in preparing and even initiating these scientific voyages, as in the case of the arrangements made to observe the sun's 1768-1769 eclipse by Venus. The new importance attributed to science sometimes provided internationally recognised protection for crews. Thus at the start of the American War of Independence France ordered her officers to help Captain Cook, and when Baudin set out in 1800 to do so he was given a British passport.

Exploration was further assisted by a new willingness to share fresh knowledge and discovery with others and to publish the facts and conclusions quickly, instead of keeping them secret as before.

The centuries old tradition of secrecy began to break down after the mid-eighteenth century. On 3 June 1766 the French Ambassador in London, Count de Guerchy, reported Byron's return to his Secretary of State for the Navy in these terms: 'I have reason to believe that the Britsh government did not wish his destination to be known. I was even assured that the crew on one of the ships under his command arrived some time before him and were promptly transferred to another ship headed for Jamaica. The aim was to prevent the crew from spreading news in England about the cruise. But the secret soon came out.'

By then Anson had published the report of his trip. This now became standard practice. Bougainville, Cook, and their successors all published full and precise reports with every kind of new information very soon after they came back. Henceforth chance would play an ever diminishing part in voyages of discovery as the reports of each successive expedition added to the store of available knowledge. As Bougainville wrote in 1774: 'No longer is every new discovery shrouded in secrecy.'

But more still remained to be done. Ships and their instruments badly needed improvement as did navigational methods, maps, and the food and hygiene for the crews.

The sailing ship of the mid-eighteenth century had altered substantially in appearance, bearing but little resemblance to those in use a couple of centuries earlier. The frigate and the corvette gradually took over from the caravelle. Shipbuilding was rationalised, especially after those fateful years of the 1750s when so much was changing. Empiricism gave way to science and art, the carpenter to the technical engineer. So far, shipbuilding had always been a job for craftsmen. Every ship's carpenter had his secrets and kept them carefully to himself, only reluctantly sharing them with his children or some close friend. Every unit had its particularities and there were no series or classes of ships as we now know them. These were not to appear until, around 1780, types of ships began to be standardised.

Treatises and theoretical studies began to be published by mathematicians and engineers as they started examining the problems of ship building scientifically. There appeared in quick succession Bouguer's *Traité du Navire* in 1746, Eurler's *Scientia Navalis* in 1749, Duhamel du Monceau's *Les Eléments de l'Architecture navale ou Traité pratique de la Construction des Vaisseaux* (1752), *Treatise on Shipbuilding* (Murray, 1754); and *Architectura Navalis Mercatoria* (Chapman, 1768). The latter brought in the mathematical formula for calculating a ship's centre of gravity and hence means to improve stability. The first school to turn out shipbuilding engineers was founded in Paris in 1765.

After the 1760s stronger ships became available as the binding of hulls was being strengthened with metal joints, and more manoeuvrable craft thanks to improved sail designs. England introduced a major improvement in 1765, followed later by France, by providing copper sheathing to protect the hull against parasites and corrosion. This was shown to be more efficient and practical than wooden or lead bottoms or the use of large nail heads as previously adopted. Stowing arrangements and internal fittings were also improved. Lightning conductors were introduced, and greater attention was paid to galleys and holds. Thanks to these improvements, and to the talents deployed by great designers of the time, the sailing ship attained a new kind of perfection in England and France by the 1780s. The new features were obviously to play a decisive rôle in the successes of future voyages.

The improvement in navigational methods was just as noteworthy. We have already seen how shortcomings in this field handicapped earlier expeditions. In those days navigation was limited to estimates made from solar observation of the latitude each day at noon, with compasses having to be re-set likewise every day. With these rough aides the navigator had to estimate his speed and his course. But such estimates could be but approximate as compass and log were far from perfected. Men knew little of the systems of prevailing currents and their influence, so that drift could not be calculated. Of course every ship's officer did his best to check his estimates whenever he could see a coast line, but the absence of adequate maps and charts made even this of little use. Since the coast lines had themselves been traced in on an estimated basis, often with tremendous error, sighting land was of but scant use.

The deplorable quality of map-making instruments constituted a serious handicap for navigators. At the start of his career, Beautemps-Beaupré, one of the fathers of modern hydrography wrote in 1785: 'The maps of the area around Brest which are made available to navigators are frighteningly inexact.' The quality of maps of areas further afield can be left to the reader's imagination.

Some important publications appeared in the middle of the century, including d'Après de Mannevillette's *Neptune Oriental* (1745), covering the Indian Ocean and Bellin's *Hydrographie Française*. Even in this last, Bougainville found when he started out that British maps showed the Salvage Islands off Gibraltar as lying 30 miles west of the position on Bellin's map, which in fact was all wrong. Nevertheless it remained in use until the start of the nineteenth century, its errors being undoubtedly a contributing cause of the wreck of the MÉDUSE, which made a considerable stir in France.

Maps everywhere could only be drawn from the information provided by mariners. We know what this was worth.

Cook's *Endeavour* bark was a 370-ton sailing vessel built to carry coal. Stronger and more spacious than other ships of like tonnage, she required a smaller crew, carrying only 94 men. The hull was of exceptional size, enabling enough supplies for 15 months at sea to be carried. Her great beam made it easier to approach the shore and provided stability if she grounded on a bank. She could also be easily careened.

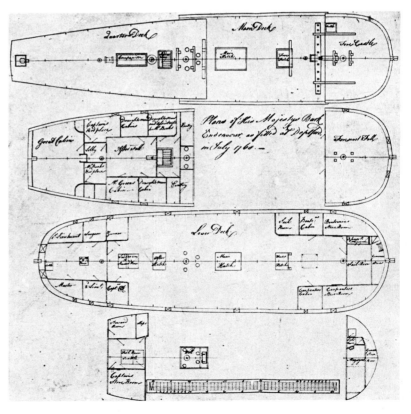

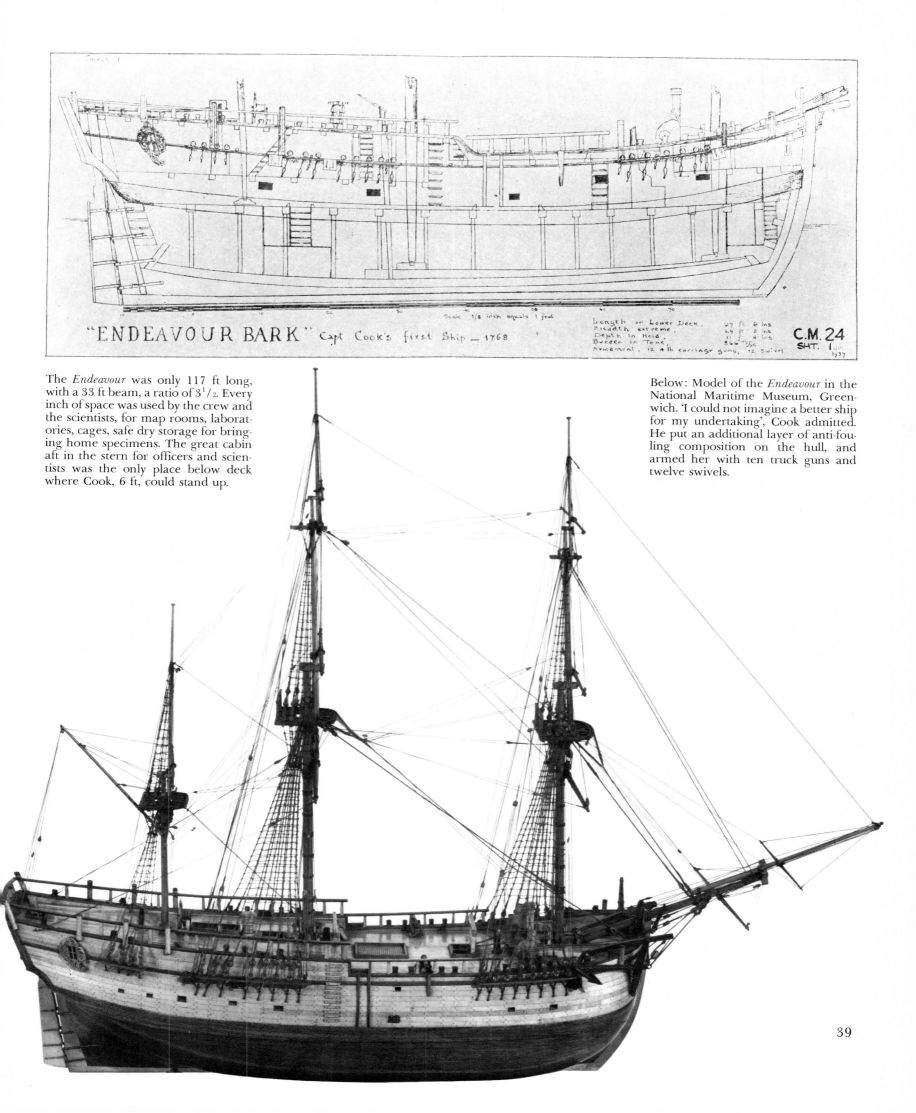

"ENDEAVOUR BARK" Capt. Cook's first Ship — 1768

Scale 1/8 inch equals 1 foot

Length on Lower Deck,        97 ft 6 ins.
Breadth extreme,            29 ft 2 ins.
Depth in Hold,              11 ft 4 ins.
Burden in Tons,             366 71/94
Armament, 12 4 lb carriage guns, 12 swivel

C.M. 24
SHT. 1 Jun
1937

The *Endeavour* was only 117 ft long, with a 33 ft beam, a ratio of $3^1/_2$. Every inch of space was used by the crew and the scientists, for map rooms, laboratories, cages, safe dry storage for bringing home specimens. The great cabin aft in the stern for officers and scientists was the only place below deck where Cook, 6 ft, could stand up.

Below: Model of the *Endeavour* in the National Maritime Museum, Greenwich. 'I could not imagine a better ship for my undertaking', Cook admitted. He put an additional layer of anti-fouling composition on the hull, and armed her with ten truck guns and twelve swivels.

The great problem was to find how to work out longitudes. To fix a position, two coordinates are required: latitude and longitude. With only one of these known, a position could be anywhere along that line. It was of little use discovering new places if these could not be correctly marked and thus revisited. Typical were the positions given the Solomon Islands, discovered by Mendaña in 1567 and thereafter wandering strangely all over the place in seventeenth and eighteenth century maps. England's highly respected hydrographer Alexander Dalrymple thought they were New Britain. On other maps they appeared as being variously situated between the 170° and 190° longitudes, whereas the centre of the archipelago is at 150°. With such errors of 300-700 leagues, it is easy to understand how such navigators as Surville and Bougainville sailed right through them without realising it. Maps were actually geographical gibberish.

Two methods to work out longitudes were developed almost simultaneously: reckoning lunar distances and using chronometers.

To find the longitude of any place, it is necessary to select the meridian as starting point and work out the difference between the time at that place and the time at the meridian selected. It was easy to establish the local time from the angle of the sun at that hour. The difficulty lay in maintaining the time of meridian zero throughout a prolonged trip. To keep track of GMT or Paris time with precision meant having as perfect a chronometer as possible. We shall be seeing that attempts in this direction started being made in the first half of the eighteenth century, but success came slowly. So mariners and astronomers began looking for another way out: lunar distances.

They had already become aware that the distance from the moon, which moves rapidly, to the sun and the planets and stars, varied according to a regular pattern corresponding to specific physical times and could thus be used as a celestial clock. But this method required two things:

1. An adequate instrument to take measurements of much greater precision than a Jacob's staff since any mistake in working out a distance meant a mistake thirty times greater every hour. Thus one minute wrong in calculating an angle meant an average error of two minutes in time or 15 miles (28 kilometers) at the equator, or four minutes at latitude 60°. Such instruments of greater precision were first perfected in England thanks to the development of the first machine tools — which made it possible to engrave graduations with reasonable precision — and of the science of optics as well. England's great opticians, the Dollonds, began around 1750 to turn out the first achromatic lenses which proved an instant success. Hadley turned out an octant, later succeeded by the sextant, and later still by Borda's reflexion circle. Cook and Bougainville both adopted Hadley's octant, father of the telemeter.

2. A set of astronomic moon tables drawn up by an observatory, from which to calculate a distance close to the one required. With this established, the basic angle can readily be found. Abbé de la Caille, (1713-1762), the renowned author of the catalogue of southern hemisphere

For reckoning the angles of sun and stars to chart their courses, sailors first used the astrolabe, a tenth century Arab invention, later the fourteenth century Jacob's staff (above, left), and then the Davis quadrant (above, right) which eliminated the necessity of looking straight at the sun. Cook's more elaborate version was made in 1768 by John Bird (below). Two foot high with adjustable weights and stand, this forerunner of the sextant provided quite accurate reckonings.

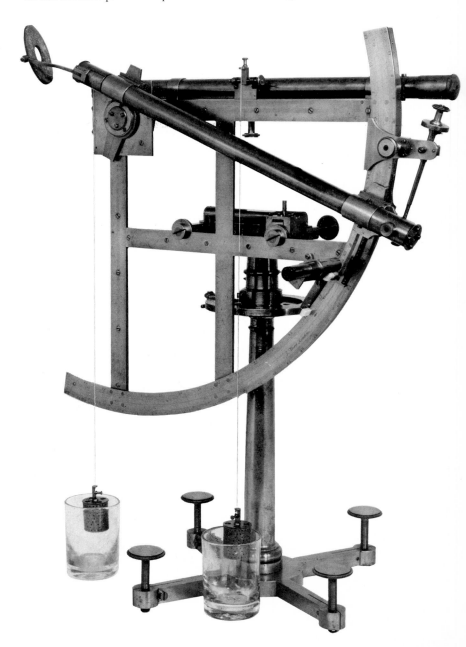

The compass was first used by the Chinese some 1,000 years before Christ and made long distance navigation possible by showing the relationship of a ship's course to magnetic north. Above is shown the elementary compass used by Drake to sail round the world in the sixteenth century.

An inclination, or dipping, compass has a magnetised needle on a horizontal axis. It showed the angle of the earth's magnetic field relative the horizon. The principle was worked out by Robert Norman at the end of the sixteenth century. Cook's was probably one made in London in 1772 by Edward Nairne to the order of the Board of Longitude.

stars, had urged that a nautical almanac be composed, listing the distances from the moon to the sun and the principal stars. His 1761 *Connaissance des Temps* (Knowledge of Times) served as a model. The project was only completed in 1766 when the British astronomer Maskelyne published his *Nautical Almanac* giving lunar distance tables for 1767.

The first to propose adoption of this method were Abbé de La Caille and d'Après Mannevillette (1707-1780), captain and hydrographer in the employ of the Compagnie des Indes who had tested it in 1736 on a trip to China. But it was Bougainville, aided by his astronomer Véron and Chevalier du Bouchage, who perfected the system and first used it continuously.

For over a century longitudes were calculated by the simultaneous use of lunar distances and chronometers, checking each against the other. This method only ceased to be used at the beginning of the twentieth century, *Connaissance des Temps* only dropping the tables in 1904. It was a complicated system requiring lengthy calculations too complex for the average navigator. Something easier had to be found, in other words a time-keeper proof against roll, changing temperatures and all other natural hazards. Leibnitz and Newton's earlier trials in this direction had proved ineffective. In 1714 the British Parliament offered a prize of £20,000 to the inventor of such a time-keeper which could be used to work out longitudes. France's Académie des Sciences and Ministry of the Navy followed suit. In England Harrison wrestled with the problem for thirty-five years, finally coming up with a large clock which was tested on a trip to Jamaica with reasonably good results. Parliament awarded him half the promised prize.

Meanwhile on the continent a French high precision mechanic named Julien Le Roy, and a Swiss watchmaker, Ferdinand Berthoud, were competing for the stakes. After ten years of effort, Berthoud proffered his first contribution in 1764, which was tried out in Brest and found to be half a degree out. He pronounced this excessive and produced another in 1768 which was carried in the frigate ISIS. With Fleurieu in command and Pingré of the Academy in charge of the tests, his longitude was only a few minutes out, and he was given a £3000 pension and the titles of Watchmaker-Mechanic to the King and to the Navy.

Le Roy's clocks were first tried by the French Navy in 1767 on the corvette AURORE, but success was only conceded in April 1769, after a ten-month test trip in the frigate ENJOUÉE to the West Indies and back, when the Science Academy awarded him their prize.

On a third trial voyage, both types of clock were checked against each other in the frigate FLORE which sailed out of Brest in October 1771 with a scientist officer in command, Verdun de La Carenne, and Pingré and a number of younger scientist officers on board. FLORE and her clocks visited Spain, the Canaries, the West Indies, St. Pierre-et-Miquelon, Iceland and the Faroes and found that neither heat nor cold nor even the firing of the ship's guns affected their precision. This scientific triumph at last insured the accurate calculation of the longitude and astronomic navi-

41

gation becoming a precise science, causing P. Chaunu* to exclaim: 'The overcoming of time is among the greatest achievements of the seventeenth and eighteenth centuries. The coming of the clock spells the end of our ancient civilisation of the more-or-less.'

Truly scientific exploration of the earth and the oceans could now be attempted. Comparing the results of La Pérouse's journey in 1786 with that made by Bougainville but a generation earlier clearly shows the momentous importance of the new discovery. Pérouse wrote: 'Using both lunar distances and the new chronometer kept us never more than half a degree off course.' Bougainville was seldom less than several degrees off.

Each forward step in the development of ever finer ships and their navigating equipment was always loudly proclaimed by historians. Yet they seemed to ignore a far more vital requirement: the welfare of the men sailing in them, their health, their food and hygiene.

Some of the terrible human losses among the crews suffered by the great explorers of earlier centuries have been mentioned in previous chapters. The navy literally devoured its men. In the sixteenth century, expeditions to the West Indies and the Indian Ocean saw some of the worst such losses, killing off 15 to 25 per cent of the crews. On the run to the Philippines the toll might reach 35 per cent. The odds in favour of a safe homecoming from the Far East were low enough, but lower still on round the world trips, as Magellan's and Anson's men were to find out to their cost. Crew losses of one in five were not uncommon in Compagnie Française des Indes ships on their 24-month return trips to China.

Only after 1750 was any real attention paid to the men's welfare, with real improvement coming at the end of the nineteenth century when refrigerated storage was first introduced. Until then a man had to be healthy indeed to embark on a career at sea, where life was always tough and physically demanding, with appalling lack of comfort or even decent food.

In spite of advanced studies and strict regulations, technical problems remained unsolved and ship's crews continued to be appallingly fed until the end of the nineteenth century.

The French navy's great Ordonnance of April 1689 included a chapter entitled 'Concerning Victuals', which remained in force for 100 years and has been frequently admired for its attention to detail.

It listed daily rations for sailors including biscuits, salted meat or fish, dry vegetables, cheese and spices, totalling some 4,000 calories, plus beverages. A working man on land certainly fared far less well.

The quantity stipulated was generous enough. But not so the quality. Strict supervision made it impossible to cheat on provisions delivered to the ships; suppliers made up for this by sending the worst cuts of meat in poor condition. Waterproof wrapping was unknown. Salt was the only known preservative, and provisions became uneatable all too soon

* P. Chaunu, *op. cit.*

---

Inaccuracies in hydrographic surveys

If every calculation made at sea were perfectly accurate, the map maker's task would be easy; unfortunately it is all too often not the case. Bad weather can shake a compass; sometimes the compass card face moves too slowly. The needle is often affected by outside influences, such as atmospherics or magnetic waves from some coast. At other times it may be impossible to take bearings on the stars, especially when too close to land. And even this method cannot be always followed as the calculations it requires make it too cumbersome.

The general principle must therefore be admitted that a certain proportion of fixings are not absolutely accurate and some are downright faulty, for reasons outlined above, not to mention the many other sources of error that can arise.

F. PÉRON, L.-CL. DE FREYCINET, *Voyages de Nicolas Baudin aux terres australes*, Paris 1807-1816

---

Marine Chronometers

M. Dagelet is writing to you separately about his observations, so I will not touch on these. It will suffice if I tell you that the combined use of our two methods, observing distances and using marine chronometers, has completely solved the problem: our margin of error in working out longitudes has consistently proved less than in the results obtained in latitude reckoning ten years ago when wooden octants were in use, and maybe four times less than when the astrolabe and the quadrant were in use.

LA PÉROUSE, *Lettre à Monsieur Fleurieu*, Botany Bay, 7 February 1788

A ship's position can be determined by means of a sextant, but longitudes can only be reckoned with the aid of a truly reliable clock, impervious to roll and temperature changes. In 1712 Britain's Parliament offered a £20,000 reward to anyone who could produce such a chronometer. John Harrison worked at it from 1726 to 1761 and came up with a 70 lbs monster fulfilling the requirements (below). Harrison's clock No. 4 (above), a perfected marine chronometer, was taken by Cook for his second and third voyages. He was delighted with it.

John Harrison (1693-1776) was a brillant, self-taught doctor. In this portrait, by T. King, he is shown holding one of his inventions in his hand. The possession of a truly reliable marine chronometer meant safer navigation and more accurate maps, no longer only on the meridians but now also along the parallels. The Pacific could now be explored scientifically.

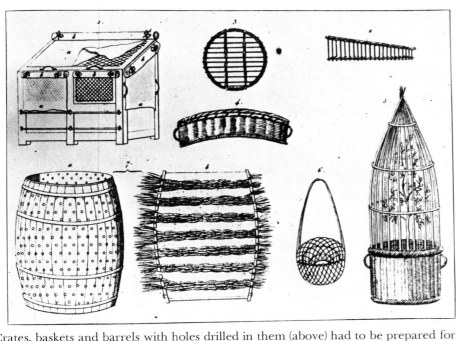

Crates, baskets and barrels with holes drilled in them (above) had to be prepared for the scientists to be able to bring their plants and exotic animals safely home. What could not be carried home had to be sketched and described in detail (right: plant of *umbelliferae* family drawn by Philibert Commerson, Bougainville's botanist). On shore special tents (below) were set up to protect the scientific instruments.

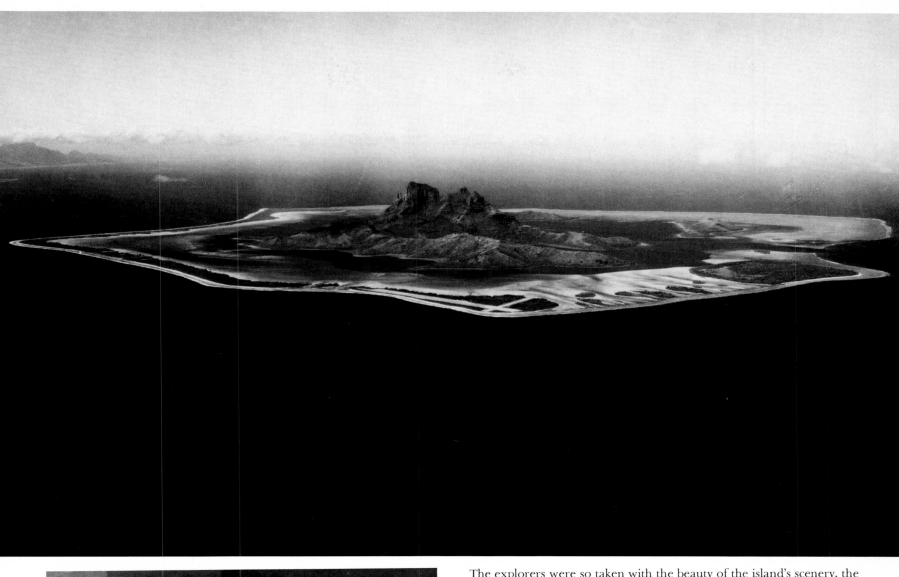

The explorers were so taken with the beauty of the island's scenery, the charms of its inhabitants and their freedom of life that the Societies became synonymous with Heaven on Earth. Above: an aerial view of Bora Bora gives point to their opinion.

Captain James Cook (1728-1779), son of a Yorkshire farmer, was a hard taskmaster with a keenly observant eye. He brought more progress to knowledge of the Pacific than all who had preceded him put together. His scientific harvest was so rich that La Pérouse could but exclaim: 'M. Cook has achieved so much that all that is left for me is to admire his work'. Cook's portrait is by Nathaniel Dance.

Following double page: Cook anchored in 1777, during his third voyage in the *Resolution* and the *Discovery,* at Tongatabu of in the Polynesian Tonga archipelago, which he named the Friendly Islands for the warmth of his welcome. He was showered with gifts, and gave a firework display.

This map of Oceania shows the principal voyages of discovery from the sixteenth century until the beginning of the nineteenth. There are some omissions, but the routes of Magellan, Byron, Bougainville, Furneaux, Cook, Clerke, La Pérouse, Vancouver, Flinders and Krusenstern are shown. Although the map dates from 1837, the outlines of the South Sea Islands are faithfully portrayed, exception being made for New Guinea.

48

after sailing, especially on long voyages. The poor quality of French salted meat was notorious. To contend with the problem experiments were made with live animals. Thus the COMTE D'ARTOIS, belonging to the Compagnie des Indes, sailed out of Lorient in 1766 with 89 sheep and 514 chickens on board. But all too many perished before they could be eaten. Except in port, the only improvement to shipboard diet came when fresh fish were caught or live turtles hauled on deck in the tropics. When stocks were really low the men had to eat rats, of which there were always plenty in wooden vessels.

Drinking, especially water, was no better. The problem of fresh water, bulky to store and difficult to keep, was always a headache until the end of the days of the sail. It was always stored in wooden barrels, where it soon became undrinkable despite every kind of empirical remedy, such as putting old rusty nails or stones inside. Metal tanks were not introduced until around 1825. So in the seventeenth century many inventors began to set about trying to find a method to turn sea-water into fresh, especially in England, France and Holland. William Walcot patented a distilling apparatus in 1675 which seems to have worked, since a company to manufacture it was formed in 1701, and records exist of at least one having been observed working in 1705.

Another type, invented in Nantes by Dr Jean Gautier (1679-1743) seems to have been less successful, despite its claim to produce 'water as from a spring with no trace of salt' after being tested on several of the French king's ships in 1717. Some years later another doctor, Pierre Poissonnier, designed a kind of still which he called a 'cucurbite' and which was installed in a number of ships' galleys at Lorient in 1763, using the crews' galley stove for heat. Bougainville and La Pérouse had one on board when they crossed the Pacific, as did Cook. Its use was limited by the amount of fuel available and by its having to be shut down during rough weather. Nevertheless these predecessors of the modern boiler proved invaluable and saved many a crew from otherwise unavoidable shortages.

The bad quality of food undoubtedly was responsible for many shipboard diseases, against which doctors of the times had but the scantiest resources. Foremost among these were scurvy and tropical diseases.

Recognised for centuries, scurvy made a brief but lethal appearance at the time of the crusades and to a greater degree throughout the period of the great discoveries. Vasco de Gama suffered from its effects. Hawkins called it 'Sea Pest'. Although navigators of the time did notice that it soon disappeared, if it had not already taken too strong a hold, as soon as fresh fruits and vegetables were added to the diet, they seem never to have drawn any conclusion before our day as to the real cause of the disease. Of course vitamins were still unknown, but some sea-faring men did find their own practical solutions. As early as 1593 Hawkins was using lemon juice to prevent it, and wrote: 'God in his secret wisdom and power has provided this fruit with a specific and unknown remedy against scurvy'. But his discovery, which might have saved thousands of lives, failed to attract

---

Magellan's navigation

The Antarctic has not the same stars as the Arctic Pole; but here are seen two clusters of small nebulous stars which look like small clouds, and are but little distant the one from the other. In midst of these clusters of small stars two are distinguished very large and very brilliant, but of which the motions is scarcely apparent. These indicate the Antarctic Pole. Though the needle declined somewhat from the North Pole, it yet oscillated toward it, but not with equal force as in the Northern Hemisphere. When out at sea, the Captain General directed the course the pilots should steer, and inquired how they pointed. They unanimously replied they bore in that direction he ordered them. He then informed them that their course was wrong, and directed them correct the needle, because, being in the Southern, it had not an equal power to designate the true north as in the Northern Hemisphere.
When in midst of the ocean, we discovered in the west five stars of great brilliancy, in the form of a cross.
We steered northwest by west till we reached the equinoctial line in 122 degrees of longitude, west of the line of demarcation [laid down by Pope Alexander VI]. This line is 30 degrees west of the meridian, and 3 degrees west of Cape Verde... After we had crossed the line we steered west by north. We then ran 200 leagues toward the west; when, changing our course again, we ran west by south until in the latitude of 13 degrees north. We trusted by this course to reach Cape Gatticara, which cosmographers have placed in this latitude; but they are mistaken, this cape lying 12 degrees more toward the north. They must, however, be excused the error in their plan, as they have not like us had the advantage of visiting these parts.
When we had 70 leagues in this direction and were in latitude 12 degrees north, longitude 146 degrees, on Wednesday, the sixth of March, we discovered in the northwest a small island, and afterward two others in the southwest. The first was more lofty and larger than the other two.
The Captain General meant to stop at the largest to victual and refresh, but this was rendered impossible, as the islanders came on board our ships and stole first one thing and then another, without our being able to prevent them. They invited us to take in our sails and come on shore, and even had the address to steal the skiff which hung astern of our vessel. Exasperated at length, our Captain landed with forty men, burnt forty or fifty of their houses and several of their boats, and killed seven of the people. By acting thus he recovered his skiffs, but he did not deem it prudent to stop any longer after such acts of hostility. We therefore continued our course in the same direction as before...
The sixteenth of March, at sunrise we found ourselves near an elevated land 300 leagues from the islands De los Ladrones. We soon discovered it to be an island. It is called Zamal [Samar]. Behind this island is another not inhabited, and we afterward learnt that its name is Humunu. Here the Captain General resolved on landing the next day to take in water in greater security, and take some rest after so long and tedious a voyage. Here likewise he caused two tents to be erected for the sick, and ordered a sow to be killed...
Perceiving around us a number of islands on the fifth Sunday of Lent, which also is the feast of Saint Lazarus, we called the archipelago by the name of that saint.
*Voyage Round the World,* by the Cavellero Antonio Pigafetta, London 1812 ed.

The names of the Society Islands – Tahiti, Moorea, Bora Bora, Raiatea, Hauhine – conjure up idyllic visions of palm trees swaying in the breeze to the sound of the langorous Polynesian music. The Utopian way of life of the islands has always fascinated the traveller. Right: Motu Tapu, near Bora Bora.

Between 1772-1775, Cook visited almost every archipelago of the southern hemisphere. He discovered New Caledonia, and sojourned in the New Hebrides. Here William Hodges shows the peaceful welcome given him in July 1774 by the people of Malekula. Cook often had to use much diplomatic skill as other Melanesians were not always as friendly.

Below: Cook was killed on 14 February 1779 by the people of Hawaii in Kealakekua Bay, Sandwich Islands: on top of a diplomatic error – he had ignored a local taboo – one of his men ignited this already explosive situation by firing off a shot in fear. He and his party were massacred and devoured in full sight of his crew.

Above are portraits of Jules-Sebastian-César Dumont d'Urville(centre), who headed the most remarkable expeditions made under the French flag; Robert Fitzroy (right), commander of the *Beagle* when young Charles Darwin sailed in her; and Charles Wilkes (left), of America, who added to Pacific knowledge by tracing the southern Antarctic.

Below: In December 1818 the *Uranie,* with Louis-Claude de Freycinet in command, dropped anchor in Rawak Bay in the west of Papua (New Guinea). Freycinet and his team of scientists were following Baudin's route, mainly with a view to correcting and completing the latter's reports in the light of science.

attention until scurvy caused so much trouble to Anson and his men that something had to be done about it, since over two thirds of his men fell victims to it. In 1747 James Lind of Scotland tried out oranges and lemons, with such excellent results that he published his *Treatise of the Scurvy* in 1753. This was not an immediate success, because doctors of the day continued to insist that scurvy was caused by humidity. It was only later, during the wars of the French Revolution, that another Briton, Gilbert Blane, managed to convince Admiral Rodney to make an issue of lemon juice compulsory for all crews. Results were immediate and it can truly be said that by enabling England's squadrons to stay at sea lemon juice was largely responsible for the fall of Napoleon.

Rats constituted another antidote against scurvy. According to A. Carré, when a rat eats putrid foods, its secretions make them digestible to the rat. In the process it emits a little surplus Vitamin C. It was this which, unknown to them, kept sailors free from scurvy when they ate rats.

Besides scurvy, tropical diseases took a severe toll. Amoebic dysentery, pernicious malaria and what was then called Batavian fever were the main ones. The latter laid out almost half of Cook's men on his first trip. On his return to St Malo after an absence of two years and four months, Bougainville was overjoyed to find he had lost only 10 men out of 220. Of these only 6 had died from disease. Along with progress in other fields, there was thus visible improvement in the effects of such voyages on the health of the men.

## *The Growth of Knowledge:*

# HYDROGRAPHY

Nearly sixty-four million square miles, twice the area of the Atlantic and fifteen times that of Europe – such figures give an idea of the difficulties awaiting navigators taking to the Great Ocean, but also of the resources it had to offer scientists. Despite its size the Pacific was never an unsurmountable obstacle to contacts between men and civilizations, owing to the large number of archipelagos spread over much of its surface, providing a series of stepping stones.

Even before the fourteenth century the Polynesians had reconnoitred the centre from Hawaii to New Zealand, while the Melanesians were familiar with all the area between New Guinea, the Fijis, the Carolines and the Marshall Islands. Both used astronomy to navigate, greatly to the wonder of Bougainville, but did the Europeans learn much from their nautical knowledge? It would seem not.

Europe's naval forces were the only ones capable of organising research expeditions. They played an important part, mainly between 1750 and 1850, in furthering scientific knowledge in the fields of both navigation and natural science. In the words of F. Braudel* 'Glorious Europe meant

* See Bibliography.

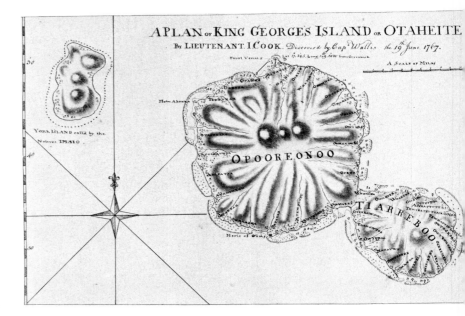

The map of Tahiti above, was drawn up in 1769 under Cook. The island had been named King George's Island. This map is rather crude, compared with the one below, made thirty years later, in 1797, by Captain James Wilson while on a missionary voyage. The sketch of the island's west coast, right, was made from the *Endeavour*, anchored in Royal bay in 1769.

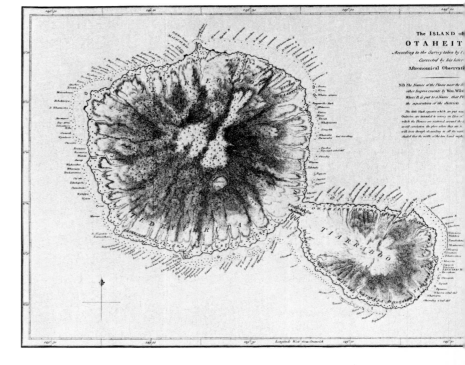

fleets, ships and more ships, voyages across the high seas; truly a people of mariners, ports and shipyards.'

In this highly important area knowledge only progressed slowly at first, as was typical of all technical advances in the middle of the eighteenth century. Around 1650 the Pacific had still been but superficially explored and everything still remained to be done. Mendaña, Quiros and Tasman had identified a few spots on the map, which still contained huge blanks. Very little was known about such lands as had been discovered, and myths and reality were alarmingly confused.

Knowledge only really began to improve in the eighteenth century. The first useful voyage was Bougainville's, although the results he obtained were somewhat disappointing, as in the final analysis he adhered to the South Pacific routes which Magellan had made commonplace. By contrast, Cook was the first to perfect and follow a systematic method for exploring the areas assigned to him. In 1769 he spent a month in Tahiti discovering the many islands of the archipelago, later sailing all round New Zealand and making detailed studies which revealed that it was composed of two large islands separated by a strait. He then explored part of the east coast of Australia, the New Hebrides and New Caledonia, and set out due south to abolish for ever the legend of the austral continent. The true discoverer of Polynesia, he was the first to recognise the unity of the Polynesian nation. He was also the first person to present a picture of the Pacific as a whole, reveal its borders, and position the main archipelagos.

But there remained much to be discovered of the coasts of North America, beyond California towards the extreme North, Alaska, Kamchatka, Japan. That was left to La Pérouse, Vancouver and Belcher. Information on the New Guinea and Solomon Islands region was still insufficient and needed completing. Krusenstern's *Atlas général du Pacifique* published in 1827 was still very inadequate.

In that second half of the eighteenth century the new factors added to marine knowledge were mostly the establishment of links between separate sketchy entities: the American Pacific, the southern part of which had been widely travelled for a good hundred years; the Chinese Pacific, also well travelled at least up to the latitude of Canton; the central Pacific, the vast central area which had long remained unknown except for a few narrow passages opened up in the north by the Manilla galleon, and some of the south by an occasional navigator. Contact between those separated worlds was no longer so rare. By about 1800 only the Japanese archipelago remained completely closed, despite Krusenstern's brief visit to Nagasaki in 1804. All the other major islands had been found.

The essential was known, and map-making had progressed substantially since Bellin and Dalrymple, yet much detailed work still had to be done. Around 1820 Freycinet* wrote: 'Today we can no longer flatter ourselves that the unexpected discovery of a large piece of land is going to

* See Bibliography.

excite the public... We need only to complete details to improve geographic knowledge rather than increase it.' This would clearly be less spectacular. The days of great discoveries were over. From then on what was wanted was research in depth, made feasible by the technical progress achieved over the previous fifty years. 'After 1800, navigators possessed a solid scientific background, with instruments and proven methods; increasing numbers of maps which were improving with each expedition. A veritable travel library accompanied every trip and numerous documents would be checked and corrected on the spot.'*

The great missions carried out in the nineteenth century were very different from those of the preceding hundred years. Too little is known even today about the great scientific progress they achieved. They were truly scientific undertakings which led to the old system of vague reconnoitring being abandoned in favour of precise and detailed hydrographic surveys around certain archipelagos or along set coastal sections. This required much more careful preparatory work and called for the active participation of the *Académie des Sciences* and the *Dépôt des cartes et plans de la Marine*, which had the task of drafting instructions for the navigators, as was the case for Baudin, Freycinet, Dumont d'Urville and many others.

Reverting to previous custom, a number of scientists were sent on Baudin's expedition at the start of the century. But they had some difficulty in adapting to conditions aboard ship, as had happened with Cook and Bougainville. So preference was given to finding scientists within the Marine corps. Among such were Quoy and Gaimard, doctors, and Gaudichaud and Lesson, chemists, as well as a number of ship's officers who became distinguished in various scientific fields, such as Dumont d'Urville, Jacquinot, Bérard, Jules de Blosseville, Admiral Paris. Dumont d'Urville was a remarkable forerunner of the travellers of today. He turned out to be the 'type of methodical and conscientious explorer who was never interested in pursuing any other trade or ideal. It was without doubt he who did the most to perfect the map of the Great Ocean. For a whole century the *Service Hydrographique* work depended on what he had observed'.**

This tremendous international effort produced impressive results. Thanks to the progress in navigational science due to the widespread use of precise chronometers, it gradually became possible to locate the exact positions of regions visited. The work carried out by Baudin and his officers, foremost among whom was Beautemps de Beaupré, one of the founders of modern geography, enabled a first complete map of Australia to be published in 1807, incorporating data discovered on Entrecasteaux's voyage. In 1814 an admirable report on the same region was published in England by Mathew Flinders and George Bass, greatly improving available knowledge about the coasts of Australia. In May-June 1824 Duperrey carried out the first sur-

\* See Bibliography.
\** See Bibliography J. P. Faivre, *op. cit.*

*CARTE GÉNÉRALE*
de la Partie Sud-Est de la
**TERRE DE DIÉMEN**
*d'après les travaux*
de MM. Beautemps-Beaupré, en 1792 et 1793.
L. et H. Freycinet, Boullanger et Faure en 1802.

Above: It was necessary to wait until 1802 before the first detailed chart of Van Dieman's Land (Tasmania) appeared, although the island was discovered by Tasman in 1642. Below: Various Australian peaks and mountain ranges as seen by Baudin in 1804. From top to bottom: Mewstone (1A), Witt isles (1B), Tasman isle (not to be confused with Tasmania), the Pyramid (3D), the Kent archipelago (3e), Wilson's Promontory (4f), and part of the west coast of Decres island (5). Right: This map, dated 1769, shows the relief of New Zealand superimposed on Cook's outline. There are errors; the island has been extended to the east, confusion existing between islands and promontories.

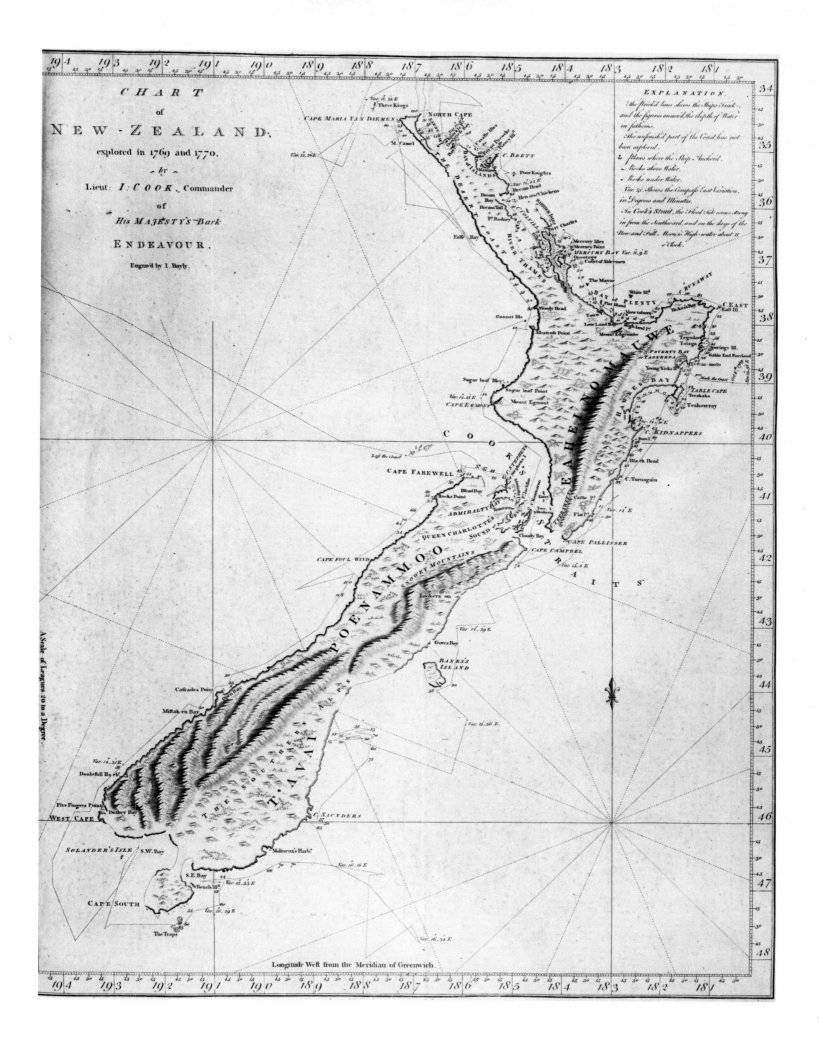

CHART
of
NEW-ZEALAND,
explored in 1769 and 1770,
- by -
Lieut: I. COOK, Commander
of
His MAJESTY's Bark
ENDEAVOUR.

Engrav'd by I. Bayly.

EXPLANATION.

The prick'd lines shews the Ships Track,
and the figures annex'd the depth of Water
in fathoms.
The unfinish'd part of the Coast has not
been explored.
⚓ shews where the Ship Anchor'd.
Rocks above Water.
Rocks under Water.
Var. 30. shews the Compass East Variation
in Degrees and Minutes.
In Cook's Strait, the Flood Tide comes strong
in from the Southward, and on the days of the
New and Full Moon, is High-water about 11
o'Clock.

A Scale of Leagues 20 to a Degree.

Longitude West from the Meridian of Greenwich.

Left: An aerial view of Bora Bora. Below: The same island, drawn in 1824 by Lejeune, when a member of the Duperrey expedition. The water colour, made from a ship at anchor, shows proof of a strong imagination.

By comparaison, John Webber's water colour, made in 1777 (above right) during Cook's visit, and the photograph taken in 1970, nearly 200 years later (below), show how exact the artist was in setting down the characteristic scenery of Moorea.

vey of the Gilbert Islands and the Caroline Archipelago, in the COQUILLE. On his first journey Dumont d'Urville made a hydrographic survey of the Bass Straits between Australia and Tasmania, established the positions of some 120 islands of Samoa, noted the Loyalty Archipelago and explored more than 750 miles of almost unknown coasts of New Guinea. He brought home fifty-five maps or plans executed with greatest care.

Fitzroy's hydrographic surveys of the Patagonian channels made in 1831 were of such perfection that they are still used on maps today.

On Dumont d'Urville's second voyage between 1837 and 1840, Vincendon-Dumoulin, hydrographer, helped further to improve the hydrographic data on a number of archipelagos, mainly the Fiji, the Solomon and Loyalty Islands and, of course, part of the Antarctic. That journey produced fifty-seven new maps, of such outstanding quality that many of them were never revised until after the Second World War.

Subsequent publications reveal the scientific importance of those voyages. Between 1815 and 1850, eighty-five volumes of notes and observations were published in France, highlighting the various fields of physical and natural sciences studied. Of these Dumont d'Urville alone accounted for forty-two, apart from his atlas, and the Russians for seventeen, the British thirteen, the Americans nine. French navigators alone brought back such a huge mass of documentation that some of it has never been published to this day. But, apart from log books and ships' journals, many scientific works have been preserved: astronomical observations, longitude and latitude tables, tables of soundings, notes on tides, surveys and views of coasts, many very artistically drawn, meteorological observations, and so on, as well as numerous natural history studies. On those journeys studies were not only made of nautical science but of botany and zoology as well; many specialised books being published on those subjects as a result.

# BOTANY

Advances in botany were due to a large measure to the great voyages of the second half of the seventeenth century. It was then that knowledge of exotic flowers was extended by travelling clergy like Plumier, Feuillée, du Tertre as well as some navigators like Dampier, that prototype of botanist mariner whose work was so important. The latter pioneered botany in the Pacific and his account of his journey round the world provided the first known data on the flora of the islands which he visited.

The eighteenth century was the golden age for botany. As before, mariners and clergy were greatly encouraged in their work by King Louis XV's doctors, particularly Lemonnier, who in that respect inherited the mantle of Fagon, who lived Louis XIV's reign. Europe's finest minds were pursuing the herb cult at the time, especially after Rousseau made it

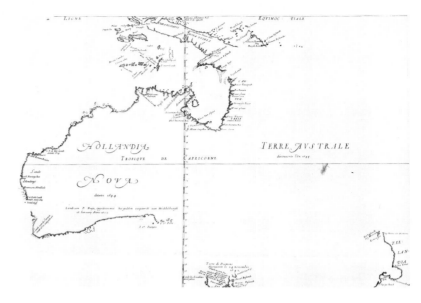

Above: Before Cook's discoveries, New Holland (Australia) was not thought to be an island, hence the inaccuracies of the eastern portion of Melchisedec Thévenot's chart, dating from 1663. However, Luis Vaez de Torres had coasted the south of New Guinea in 1606, which should have enabled navigators and cartographers to be more accurate. This map does contain, though, the details given by Abel Tasman, who had traversed the western coast of the continent in 1642-1643, and discovered the island that bears his name.

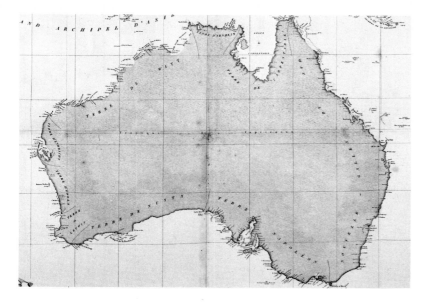

Baudin's map of Australia, made in 1802, is very close to reality, with the exception of a few points on the north coast. At this time, the interior was practically unknown. It was not until 1839-1841 that Eyre explored the centre, and it was 1862 before Stuart made the first traverse.

Gaudichaud-Beaupré was the botanist of the Freycinet expedition of 1817-1820. He is shown with two companions collecting specimens among the ruins of an ancient *marae* on Rota, in the Marianas. During his voyage on the *Uranie,* he collected some 4175 plants, which were presented to the Paris Museum.

a fashionable science. But beyond the fashionable craze, there were true scientists who set about organising systematic research overseas, either by going there themselves like Tournefort and Adanson, or by sending specialists and making use of their findings, like Linnaeus and Buffon. Linnaeus sent his 'missionaries' to China and the East Indies. One of them, Peter Thunberg, even managed to travel as far as Japan and returned to Sweden in 1779 with a rich haul. Others followed both tactics; Sir John Banks (1743-1820) went on Cook's first voyage with Solander of Sweden, and brought back a large botanical and zoological collection which he shared with anyone interested. Although he did not publish anything himself, Banks played an important part as guiding spirit, being both President of the Royal Society in London and director of Kew Botanical Gardens. Like Linnaeus he had a number of explorers working for him and was largely responsible for introducing almost 7,000 exotic plants to England in the reign of King George III. It was Banks who provided scientific backing for Flinders's and Bass's voyage to Australia on which Robert Brown collected some 4,000 vegetable species which enabled him to publish his *Prodromus Florae Novae Hollandiae et Insule Van Diemen.*

Johann Forster (1729-1794) was one of the botanists who did not blink at the risks attaching to such voyages. With his son Johann-George he took part in Cook's second voyage and described about 100 new types of plants, publishing several works on Oceanian plant life.

Philibert Commerson (1727-1773) deserves special mention. He accompanied Bougainville on part of his journey. Before leaving France, this indefatigable naturalist had drawn up a '*sommaire d'observations d'histoire naturelle*' as a programme for studies to be made in the realms of anthropology, zoology, botany, meteorology and mineralogy. It was much too extensive for him to carry out, but it provides an idea of the widespread interests of the encyclopaedic century. Botany occupied an important place in the list. 'Vegetables', he wrote, 'constitute natural history's richest store of species and individual specimens on earth. But we shall be seeing each one of them being put to use for teaching, for economic, mechanical or medicinal purposes, so that they will all become consumer or commercial objects. We cannot yet devine the limits of that fine science, which can take up all the time of the most indefatigable observer. Those limits only help us perceive the wealth awaiting us.' Commerson died on the Ile-de-France (Mauritius) before being able to return to Europe. His botanical and zoological collections were sent back to the *Musée d'histoire naturelle* in Paris but were not given very good care. Like Banks, Commerson did not publish anything, but Jussieu and Lamarck made good use of his observations. Cuvier paid him a fine tribute: 'His herbarium and his manuscripts were shockingly neglected... He was a man of inexhaustible energy and deepest scientific knowledge. If he had himself written about what he found, he would be one of the greatest naturalists.'

The Vanikoro disaster robbed science of the fruit of the work done by Lapérouse's men, but fortunately the same did not occur with d'Entrecasteaux. On that journey Jacques-Julien de la Billardière (1755-1834) collected over 4,000 plants of which threequarters were not known, and which were saved from total destruction by Sir John Banks's intervention when the expedition was broken up. Besides his *Relation du voyage à la recherche de Lapérouse,* la Billardière published two volumes of descriptions of Australian plants. Flourens wrote of him: 'He must be regarded as one of the first naturalists to bring to our knowledge the singular vegetable life of the austral lands, which have added so much to the science of botany, either by reason of their anatomy or their contribution to classification.'

Each voyage between 1800 and 1850 provided its share of new elements for botany. Foremost was Baudin's, thanks to the presence on board of two naturalists, François Péron (1775-1810) and Jean-Baptiste Leschenault de La Tour (1773-1826). The GEOGRAPHE's chief botanist, Leschenault travelled along the Australian coasts and landed at Timor in 1803, from where he went on to Batavia. He only returned to France in 1807, bringing with him a rich collection for the Museum. According to Cuvier: 'Leschenault's involuntary stay in Java greatly added to the value of the last expedition'. Péron devoted most of his attention to zoology. We will return to him later.

Under the French Restoration, the marine chemist Charles Gaudichaud-Beaupré (1780-1854) joined Freycinet on his journey on the URANIE and collected 4,175 vegetable species, mainly from Australia, Samoa and the Marianas. Unfortunately part of his precious collection was lost when the corvette was shipwrecked off the Falkland Islands, but Gaudichaud did not lose heart, and set off again a few years later in the BONITE (1836-1837), publishing the results of his botanical research when he returned.

Duperrey's voyage in the COQUILLE was also fruitful. Dumont d'Urville was on board, and brought back some 3,000 plant specimens, 400 of which were previously unknown. They were accompanied by detailed descriptions and studies on their uses and possible acclimatization in Europe. His flora from Tahiti unfortunately disappeared on the way.

René-Primevère Lesson (1794-1849), then attached to the Rochefort botannical gardens, was in charge of plant research on the ASTROLABE mission (1826-1829). The scientific world was highly satisfied with his work, and Cuvier pronounced his benediction in 1829: 'The best proof of the fine work performed by our naturalists is the problem faced by the *Jardin du Roi* to store all it has received from recent expeditions.'

Sailors and professional scientists were not alone in helping the progress of scientific knowledge. In the nineteenth century, the Pacific archipelagos had many visits from Protestant missionaries from the London Missionary Society, and Catholics of the Picpus Order and the Society of Mary. As Father O'Reilly observed, they made very important contributions to discovery, especially in the field of natural science. To mention but one example, William Ellis, the English missionary, lived in Polynesia from 1816 to 1824

A drawing of breadfruit (*artocarpus incisa*) from Micronesia, made by L. Choris, who sailed with Kotzebue (1815-1818). There are many different species of breadfruit, recognised mainly by variations in leaf-form. One breadfruit tree may produce two or three crops per year throughout a life-span of fifty years. Originally, breadfruit was the principal crop throughout a large part of Oceania, but was later replaced or complemented by bananas, sweet potatoes, and coconuts.

A trigger-fish, or file-fish, from the Rawak islands and Waigeo (north-west New Guinea). The fish gets its name from the serrated spines on the dorsal fins, which can be raised and lowered by muscular action. This example was painted by Bévalet, after an original by Taunay, who was a member of the 1818 Freycinet expedition. Freycinet brought back 25 species of mammals, 313 birds, 45 reptiles, and 164 fish. His work was published in 17 volumes.

and left his *Polynesian Researches,* a work of fundamental importance to our knowledge of the ancient Pacific, particularly its flora and its fauna. For instance, the book contains thorough descriptive notes on certain plants like the breadfruit tree, arrowroot, the sweet potato, the yam, the coconut palm, their uses, and the myths that surround them. There are also details on the introduction of new plants like the grapefruit tree.

Naturally the French were not the only contributors to scientific progress. The English botanist and doctor, Sir Joseph Hooker, who went on the Ross mission to the Antarctic (1839-1843), published two volumes in of his *Flora antarctica,* describing many new plants. By comparing species found on that voyage, he helped greatly to advance available knowledge of the laws governing the distribution of plant life across the face of the earth. On his second voyage in the SAMARANG, Sir Thomas Belcher took along a surgeon, Adams, who described elements of the flora of the Dutch East Indies (Moluccas, Philippines, Malaysia) and of the history of animals found there. Thus zoology was at once a motivation and an end in the widening of knowledge of the Pacific.

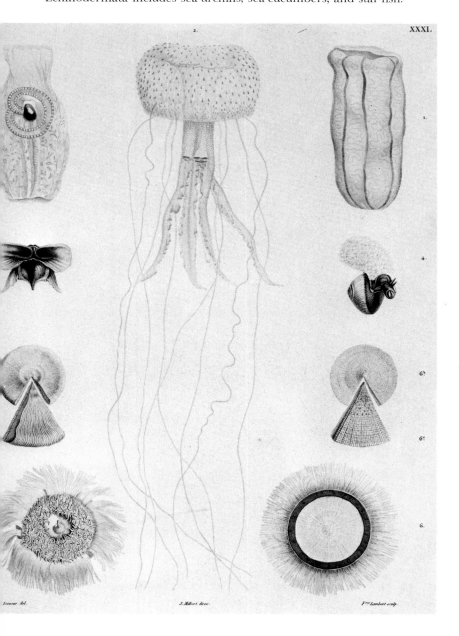

Molluscs and zoophytes drawn by F. Péron during a South Sea voyage with Baudin (1800-1804). The term zoophyte, or animal plant, was given by Cuvier to one of his four divisions of the animal kingdom. This branch is now divided into coelenterata and echinodermata. The coelenterata phylum, all invertebrates, embraces coral, jelly-fish, and sea anemones. Echinodermata includes sea-urchins, sea-cucumbers, and star-fish.

# ZOOLOGY

Botany and zoology were in fact linked in the thinking of most navigators and naturalists. Diversification which scientific progress later made necessary only came in very gradually. 'The fundamental object of zoology is to list animal forms and classify them methodically, analysing their structure, their growth, their relation to each other and to their surroundings. Such strict notions only emerged slowly, and people were content to limit zoology to mere descriptions up till the time of Darwin, whose *The Origin of Species* was published in 1859. Only later did specialists take up 'interpreting and discussing phenomena within the perspective of the distribution of animals'.

Although some early seventeenth century reports by travellers contained occasional very detailed descriptions of birds, most observations by contemporary navigators were sketchy. Bougainville carefully described a few insects, but in reporting on the birds of the Pacific his terminology was so vague that his journal was of little interest to zoologists, while unfortunately nothing was left of the work carried out by Commerson during his crossing of the Great Ocean. We shall never know how far he advanced in his ambitious programme for studying quadrupeds, birds, fish, insects, reptiles and shells. But his *Sommaire* does provide an excellent glimpse of the ideas on zoology prevailing around 1760. About insects he wrote: 'Insects are unjustly scorned; today they are only vile in the eyes of the vulgar. They are much

With the exception of the dingo, which appeared comparatively recently on the continent, all the native Australian mammals are either marsupials or monotremata, the egg-laying mammals, such as the duck-billed platypus. The kangaroo is a marsupial: 1: first kangaroo ever seen by Europeans, sketched by Sidney Parkinson in 1770; 2: striped kangaroo, now extinct, discovered on Baudin's voyage (1800-1804). The newly-born young find their way instinctively into the maternal pouch. Unfortunately, many species of kangaroo have disappeared, the animals having been exterminated for their hides, or finishing in tins of cat-food. 3: The wombat, a nocturnal marsupial, the teeth of which grow continuously like other gnawing animals. The sketch was made on Baudin's expedition.

4: A dasyure, or native cat, discovered by Freycinet at Port Jackson in 1818. This marsupial is carnivorous, nocturnal, and extremely ferocious. It feeds mostly on birds, and is found in New Guinea and Australia. 5: Cuscus, or phalanger. This specimen was found on Waigeo by the Freycinet expedition. It possesses a prehensile tail, and is arboreal. 6: Chameleons are also found in the Pacific.

more diversified in appearance than other animals. Their different metamorphoses, their importance in the general economy of nature which uses them quietly to keep down the excessive luxuriance of the vegetable kingdom, to free the earth's surface of the foul bodies which would soon poison it, and to prevent polution of stagnant waters by rapidly consuming matter which would otherwise putrify there, their organization and mechanism, their ingenious methods, all the ways in which they often trouble us – all this is admirable and proves they are nature's best servants because they are the smallest of them, the most numerous and the most active.'

Linnaeus's work had provided zoology with a clear frame and a nomenclature which might serve as a basis for research. But it was not until the nineteenth century that it really developed as a science, with the great journeys around the world naturally playing a decisive part by encouraging discoveries and the study of vast numbers of species previously unknown. In that respect Baudin's expedition is of particular interest. With instructions from Cuvier and Lacépède, and assisted by several naturalists like Mauger and Levillain, François Péron brought back an enormous collection of mammals, birds and tortoises, in fact more new animals than had been mentioned by all earlier scientists. Jussieu announced that 'never had the Museum been so richly reinforced, especially in the realm of animals'. This extraordinary contribution enabled Lacépède to describe some previously unknown animals, including various Australian reptiles. Publications being prepared by Péron and Freycinet after Baudin's death were enriched by fine natural history plates.

After Baudin's expedition, the most valuable for zoology was Freycinet's in URANIE, bringing home 25 species of mammals, 313 birds, 45 reptiles and 164 fish, all unknown new varieties.

The presence of Dumont d'Urville and Lesson on board contributed to the utility of the COQUILLE voyage. The future commander of the ASTROLABE did not study botany only but devoted his attentions to insects. He returned with 1,100 species, of which some 450 were lacking in the Museum collections, plus 300 never previously described. Lesson's contributions included descriptions of numerous fish and moluscs, which were almost unclassified until then, and the discovery of forty-six species of birds, twenty of reptiles and eighty species of totally unknown fish. Lesson had the task of writing up the medical and zoological part of the COQUILLE expedition.

Even though science may not have been the main purpose of these epic expeditions, it was always kept in mind, and they did not fail to produce indirect and important scientific results. It was while sailing in the BEAGLE from 1831 to 1836 that Darwin first felt his vocation as a naturalist, when he noticed the problems presented by the distribution of animals across continents and islands. Without the patient labour of all those naturalists, great works like L. Schmarda's *Die geographische Verbreitung der Tiere*, which came out in 1853 with a summary of the existing state of

zoology during the eighteenth century and the first half of the nineteenth, might never have been written. These works were published one after the other from 1650, and gradually assembled the necessary basic information. Marine fauna also began to be studied, and the theory that no life was possible below the surface was completely destroyed after 1819 when Sir John Ross described living creatures 6,000 ft down. But it was not until 1850 that large-scale exploration of the sea bed began to be organized.

The tremendous growth of scientific knowledge in all sectors, hydrography, botany, zoology, which characterized the second half of the nineteenth century and the twentieth century, was only made possible by the world-shaking but patient groundwork so truly laid by the great savants. As Adam Smith wrote in 1776: 'Discoverers performed a useful deed in uniting the far-spread parts of the world and making them able to supply each other's needs, thereby mutually increasing each other's well-being.'

The Pacific islands – particularly eastern Indonesia and New Guinea – are noted for their butterflies, which include some of the most colourful in the world. These studies were made during Dumont d'Urville's expedition (1826-1829), and show only two of the 1100 insect specimens brought back by him.

# MEN OF THE PACIFIC

## THE CIVILIZATION

The hallmark of Pacific civilization is totemism. Somewhat forgotten in Micronesia, it remains a vital force in Australia and Melanesia, even though its existence is hidden and kept secret from the uninitiated.

In Polynesia, at the beginning of the Christian era, a time known as *Manahuné,* the *Aïtou* — or totems — were affectionately respected as animals, plants, natural phenomena, and were local and familiar; *mana* and *ora,* the vital elements, affected, and belonged, equally to plants, animals, minerals, or cosmic forces just as they affected man himself. The great objective was the omnipresence of life. Civilizing heroes, such as Tiki, the first man, and Maoui, who fished up the islands from the sea, were also venerated.

Then the noble *Ariki* arrived from the far west, coming from a fabulous homeland, Hawaiiki. Despised because they were 'godless', the *Manahuné* were dominated by the *Ariki,* who saw themselves as the equals of their gods, Tané, Tu and Rongo. These gods, to be properly appeased, demanded human sacrifices. From this moment on, humanity was divided into two classes, superiors and inferiors. Places of worship became more and more elaborate, and *marae* began to be built. The most important, Taputapu-Atéa, near Opoa on Raïatéa, made the island the cultural centre of Polynesia, but the biggest *marae* was on Tahiti at Mahaïtéa. Other *marae* were set up on the Cook Islands, the Marquesas, Tubuaï, Hawaii. A new god, Tangaroa, divinity of the sea, was accepted after bloody wars, during which those tribes that remained faithful to Tané were destroyed. On Raïatéa and Tahiti, the god Oro founded the *Arioi* society, while on the Marquesas the *Kaïoï* society arose, and on Hawaii the *hula* dancers honoured the goddess Pélé. Oro was not widely accepted, and his cult encountered a stiff resistance throughout Polynesia, so much so that a great palaver, a kind of Oecumenical council, was called at Opoa for all the chiefs from all the islands of Polynesia. They were unable to reach agreement, and a murder took place in the Taputapu-Atéa *marae.* From then on, the *Arioi* were confined to Tahiti. This was a check to the autocratic regime dominated by the *Ariki,* and when the 'discovery' of the Pacific began, explorers found Polynesia to be a society in crisis.

By contrast, in Melanesia, Australia and Micronesia, 'typical' society still existed. Thus, in order to explain the essentials of Pacific civilization, in relation to our own, I have chosen to concentrate on these regions. The section on 'Customs' will deal mainly with totemism, parenthood, and initiation. The case for Polynesia is different, and the reader is referred to the illustrations and the extracts quoted outside the main text.

The rhythm for this dance, performed in Cook's honour at night by the women of Hapai in the Tonga archipelago on 17 May 1777, was provided by long hollow poles. What most struck the Europeans in those ballets of a by-gone age was the precision of the movement and the unison of the dancers. Polynesian dances and songs were mostly about love, but everyday labours, victories, journeys to neighbouring islands and tribute to the land of birth also came into them. Some dances had to be performed by men only.

# ANTHROPOLOGY

Stretching from the Arctic to the Antarctic, and from the West Coast of America to Indonesia, the Pacific Ocean covers one third of the globe, dotted with countless islands and atolls.

Of all its vast space, people tend only to think of Oceania and to dream of the 'Southern Seas'. Yet the Pacific, at the opposite end of the world for Western man, possesses its own characteristics and constitutes a cultural whole. Despite obvious differences to be found in its various latitudes, this huge stretch of water has given rise to its own peculiar manner of living and thinking. This book intends to focus on these special features of the Pacific, which embraces the vast lands of Oceania and connects Asia to America by means of the 56-mile icy bridge of the Bering Straits between Alaska and the Chukotskiy Peninsula.

Oceania lies in the Southern Pacific in an area bound in the east by the South American coast at the level of Peru and Chile and in the west by Indonesia and Malaysia, which geographers have named the Wallace frontier, a line drawn at the level of Timor. Besides Australia, whose area is roughly equal to that of the United States and even of all Europe, the Pacific embraces three great land units: Micronesia, Melanesia and Polynesia.

Micronesia is a mass of small islands including the Carolines, the Marshall, Gilbert and Ellice Islands, the Palau and the Marianas.

Melanesia forms an arc around the Coral Sea, justly referred to as the Pacific's Mediterranean. Below the Equator lies the great bird-shaped island of New Guinea, with its western coast near to Arnhem and the York Peninsula, the north points of Australia, which some anthropologists include in Melanesia. Further east, going from north to south, lie the Archipelagos of the Admiralty, Mathias and New Hanover, Bismarck, New Ireland, New Britain, Louisiade, Solomon, Santa-Cruz, and New Hebrides groups. Then comes New Caledonia with the four Loyalty Islands, and lastly Wallis and Futuna linking Melanesia to Polynesia, some authorities including them in the former, others in the latter. It is among the dark-skinned peoples of these areas between New Guinea and Fiji, sometimes known as the Negroes of Oceania, that Oceania's civilisation and rich traditions are still best preserved and least spoiled.

The islands of Polynesia are in a triangle centred on the Society Islands with its points at Easter Island, New Zealand, and Hawaii, formerly the Sandwich Islands, where Cook met his end on 14 February 1778.

Together these land masses cover some 6,500,000 square miles of the Pacific, Australia alone having 2,974,581 square miles and New Guinea another 90,540 square miles. The Melanesian islands are often long and narrow, while Micronesia, as its name suggests, contains only small islands. Polynesia likewise contains thousands of minor islands and atolls with the exception, in the extreme south, of New Zealand's 103,569 square miles. In the centre of the triangle the archipelagos are relatively close to one another, becoming further apart towards the sides. Thus Cook Island is 1,400 nautical miles from New Zealand. The Polynesians used to do the trip in their canoes without once sighting land except possibly tiny Kermadec Island.

The North Pacific gets narrower towards the Bering Sea and the Arctic Ocean, its waters bearing flotsam from the South Seas, coconuts and fragments of palm tree, right into the Bering Straits, to which Cook gave its name although he did not himself discover it. When he entered the Straits he met a man who handed him a sheet of paper which neither he nor any of his men could understand. It was written in Russian. They were left wondering who were the explorers or merchants who had been there before them. Today we know that Russian Yermak Cossaks settled Western Siberia in the sixteenth century, soon reaching the Straits and the Pacific. A century later one of their descendants, Simon Dejnev, managed to take three ships through the Straits after first being blocked by the ice. He left us the first known description of American Eskimos.

Across from the Straits, the southern edge of the Bering Sea is marked by the Aleutian Islands. The underground homes of their mongoloid Eskimo inhabitants are described in Cook's records. To the South, beyond the Kamchatka Peninsula, the Kurile Island chain almost reaches Japan. Everywhere else the North Pacific is just one vast stretch of uninterrupted water over which it is possible to sail for days without sighting any land.

The Pacific people tell of a land miraculuously saved from a flood or deluge similar to our own tale of Noah and his Ark. According to Stephen Gilson, a scientific Christian tradition holds that: 'The true philosophers descending from Seth and Noah clearly preceded any of the pagan philosophers, ancient poets or the Sibyls. God gave them six hundred years to live to give them time to complete their philosophy, and especially their difficult laws of astronomy. God revealed all knowledge to them and gave them long life to enable them to complete and try out their philosophy. Not unlike our story is the Oceanian belief that the waters covered all the world except the little coral island of Taomarama, which is flat, whereas Tahiti has mountains where it would be logical for survivors to seek refuge. When the missionary Ellis put this to the natives, they always replied that Taomarama, the Ark, was never covered by the waters which covered everything else including mountains, as the *farere* (corals, shells, and other marine deposits) left behind by the retreating waters prove. The Tahitians' mythical origins seem thus more scientifically based than our own account of the Ark and Mount Ararat.'

Less flimsy explanations of the origins of the peoples of the Pacific have been sought. It was first thought that their islands were remains of some vast continent long vanished. Another suggestion was that they may have been Negritos descended from the negroid races of Africa, and chased out of Asia thousands of years ago, who wandered around the world for centuries. They would have been joined by Ainoids and Vedoids, who were stone polishers and may have come from South East Asia. This would account for the Indonesians being a mixed race of mongoloids, whites and proto-malaysians. A double migration has been suggested,

Above: the drawings of the two Hawaiians are from Cook's third journey (January-February 1778). The man is wearing a *mahiolé,* the well-known plumed helmet worn by important Hawaiian chiefs. It was made of wicker covered with a net, in which are stuck feathers of red and yellow, the sacred colours.

Sailors reacted differently to the Polynesians. Some were seduced by the charms of the young island girls (below left, a Tahitian girl in her 'mission clothes', about 1900), while others objected to the girls' excessive obesity. This is in fact frequent throughout the islands, as can be seen from the picture (below, left) of the fisherman in his diving goggles. Pearl divers take considerable risks and seldom reach old age. Opposite: Tahitians crowned with flowers photographed around 1920.

The first arrivals in New Ireland (Bismarck Archipelago) and nearby islands were astonished by these Papuans (drawn in 1823) with their rare beards and thick hair. The latter is covered with grease, which discolours the hair but makes it hard, therely acting as a protection against sunstroke. The hair is plaited in one or two almost perfect circles and surmounted with a wooden comb.

Inhabitants in New Guinea and near-by islands are noted for the wealth of their ornamentation. Men generally wear a loincloth of vegetable fibre, a belt and a penile hood. These human types all belong to the Papuan race, distinguished by their hooked noses from the negroes of Africa or the Melanesians. Right: A man of the Orokaiva tribe in ceremonial dress at a sing-sing at Kokoda (Papua-New Guinea); he wears a cassowary feather headdress and a necklace of animal teeth and shells.

with melanesians landing on the west coast of America from the sea, others coming by land via the Aleutians, who later would have given birth to the Eskimo peoples.

Various other migrations from Asia or America have been suggested, and the ethnic origins of every island have been the subject of all kinds of other knowledgeable explanations, including a suggestion that two successive waves landed on Easter Island at the easternmost point of Polynesia, one from America and one from Polynesia. But well founded objections to this were raised on the grounds of the numerous traces of characteristic Melanesian Art. Modern research by Soviet, Chinese, American, French and Scandinavian geomorphologists and anthropologists is opening up new vistas. Monocentrism is giving way to polycentrism. Contemporary thinkers, such as Okladnikov, Giddings and Malaurie are inclining towards a belief that humanity had its start in Eastern Siberia.

The human groups all over the vast Pacific are very varied. In Micronesia, Melanesia, and Australia, the Oceanian natives have skins ranging from golden copper to chocolate brown, and black, the latter having thick curly hair. The Polynesians, though swarthy, are lighter and have smooth hair. All Oceanians belong linguistically to the Austronesian family group, noted for the richness of its spoken literature. The natives of the North Pacific islands are almost white and belong to the hyperborean or paleo-asiatic linguistic family group.

Many of the varied theories advanced concerning the origins of these islands peoples have been subject to modification. Anthropologists of the polycentric school have shown a more open spirit and have helped throw a little light on the general ignorance. There is still much unknown. This lack of knowledge is well illustrated in the case of the Aïnus. This little-known race came from the North and bear certain similarities to the inhabitants of New Guinea and Australia. Their skin colouring is duller than that of Europeans, yet they are much lighter than the Japanese and are peculiarly hairy. Living on the Sakhalin and Kurile islands in the North Pacific and spit up into small totemic groups, the Aïnus went after fish wherever the chase took them, and left traces all along the coasts of Siberia and Mongolia. Batchelor's Aïnu-English-Japaneses dictionary tells us that ancient Japanese came across Aïnus installed in areas which now form part of Japan. They fought them fiercely for several centuries. The Japanese managed to advance slowly and drive a wedge between the intruders, who were obliged to escape, some to the north, the others to the south. Fighting only ceased for good in 1884 when the Russo-Japanese Treaty awarded the volcanic Kurile islands to the Japanese. The Aïnus on the Kuriles were moved to Hokhaido Island. By 1920 there were scarcely 20,000 of them left. By now, after being bound for years to the Japanese by ties of culture and servitude, they are almost extinct as a race. But their language is still spoken by 20,000 inhabitants of Hokhaido. They have left many unmistakable traces and their blood still runs in the veins of natives as far away as Melanesia with their 'canac-ainoids. The fashion still found on many islands

These two Maori women, photographed about 1920, show Polynesian characteristics, in contrast to some of their compatriots, who are more negroid. Maori traditions speak of a great migration in about 1350 from Hawaiiki (Raiatea?) to 'Aotearoa' (New Zealand).

A Maori chief, Te Reapa Pualaata, of Otuku, can be recognised by his robe and staff of office. Chiefs were also priests, – the word *tahunga* means specialist – although priestly functions might be confided to close relations.

The curved forms of these 1846 tattoo markings show them to be of Maori as opposed to Marquesa Island origin, the latter being more angular. Most Polynesians adorn their bodies, or used to, with tattooings, the word *tatu* being of Polynesian origin. The marks are inserted under the skin with the aid of a comb made of bone, with sharp points, covered with a pigment made from smoke black. The complicated tattoo on these two men shows that they are chiefs. On women the tattoo is limited to the lower lip and chin (above).

74

of plaiting their prolific long hair in halo-like shape round the head may well have been a tradition of the ancient Aïnus, who were notoriously proud of their fine appearance, which they held to be a sign of vitality. It is a peculiar characteristic of the peoples of the Pacific.

The demographic collapse of the Aïnus noted by Batchelor after the Russo-Japanese Treaty is no exception. It is only necessary to observe what modern times have done to the population of the Pacific everywhere. The first explorers found the islands heavily populated. Their reports, and more recent archeological research, show beyond dispute that the islands were thickly populated with sufficient resources to provide for their own needs. Cook's estimates were at first thought to have been greatly exaggerated because, when he saw the numbers that gathered on the shores where he landed, he 'wrongly' thought the rest of the island was equally full of people. Far from it. Although still hotly debated, known history suggests the populations of the area have fallen by 80 per cent between the coming of the European and the end of the nineteenth century. Thus there were 5,000 people in Tasmania when the whites began hunting them down, and actually drove them into the sea in 1830. The few survivors were driven into exile where the last Tasmanian native died in 1877... a true example of genocide coupled with ethnocide. In 1788 Australia had a million aborigines. A hundred years later there were only 250,000 left, and a few decades later they were down to 40,000, or 175 times less, whereas in 1843 some South Australian tribes had as many as 12,000 members. In Melanesia and Micronesia overpopulation of the limited land space, as for instance in the Ellice Islands, was achieved by limiting biological, or nuclear, families to two children and resorting to abortion and slaughter of new-born children. The demographic drop was just as spectacular: the population of Micronesia alone fell from 300,000 to 90,000 and of Polynesia from 1,000,000 to 20,000. Cook visited Tahiti a number of times and once counted 720 boats manned by 40 warriors each; his botanist Forster noted enough bread-fruit trees to feed 204,000 persons. Within little over a century Tahiti was left with but 9,000 native inhabitants!

Recent studies have shown that Cook's estimates were right. José Garanger's excavations in Tahiti prove that the island's entire liveable space was occupied. In the furthermost areas traces have been found of *marae* (ancient temples), basements of houses, terraces for crops, and remains of irrigation canals leading out of the rivers. The remains are so numerous and wide-spread that there is no doubt that the whole interior of the peninsula was completely inhabited right up to the highest point of every valley.

From the warm springs of Rano Mafana in Madagascar to Easter Island's Lake Rano Raraka 'Oceania is a single ethnographic unit, from the coast of Madagascar to the tip of Easter Island', wrote Maurice Leenhardt*. He based his opinion on ethnolinguistics, which confirm his findings, for all languages throughout Oceania belong to the same linguistic group, austronesian. This group embraces also the languages and dialects spoken in Madagascar, Indonesia, the Philippines, Malaysia, the Malay States, South-East Burma and South-West Siam (Thailand), as well as the languages used by the Chams on the coast of Vietnam and Cambodia, by the Jorai on the Central Vietnamese plateau and in Eastern Cambodia, and to the south by the Formosa hill people.

Exceptions to this are Australia, Tasmania, and Papua, including the interior of New Guinea and a few minor islands north-east of Papua-New Guinea. These formed a single land mass at the time of the last glacial period, the Würm, and were populated at least 25,000 years before the rest of Oceania. Archaeological excavations carried out in Australia by Australian universities revealed three series of cultures. Carbon 14 tests indicate the oldest as dating from the sixteenth to the third millenium BC. Around 1750 BC the earliest known large stone blades with polished edges appeared. Such discoveries might well confirm a widely held theory that civilisation came to the area from Asia, where similar stone blades have been found to have existed in the South East since the year 2000 BC: this would be contradicted by the latest discoveries in Arnhem where similar blades dating from the year 22,700 have been found, which would reverse the position. Further, skeletons 26,000 and 32,000 years old have been found in the dunes around Lake Mongo. Again in South Australia, forty tombs were dug up in which human remains were found, very different from the ancient Australians, bearing a pre-sapian appearance and recalling the pithecanthropian man, although they were dated as being only 14,000 years old.

The ornamental objects in the tombs are similar to those still in use today. This proof of age-long continuity is significant. It shows that the peoples of the time had reached a degree of civilisation sufficent to permit them to attain a certain level of existence.

We can only deplore the stupidity of the nineteenth century when cannons were turned upon the stone monuments of oceanian classical design, thus depriving succeeding generations of their irreplaceable beauty. In his *Journal*, James Cook indignantly decried the harm done by the mere presence of the white man in those areas. But it would seem that the detailed and often perfect descriptions of those Stone Age peoples and their lives only served to encourage visitors to destroy them.

* See Bibliography.

## Cook meets the Australians

Tuesday, [July] 10. ... In the A.M., four of the natives came down to the sandy point on the north side of the harbour, having along with them a small wooden canoe with outriggers, in which they seemed to be employed striking fish, etc. Some were for going over in a boat to them; but this I would not suffer, but let them alone, without seeming to take any notice of them. At length two of them came in the canoe so near the ship as to take some things we throwed them. After this they went away, and brought over the other two, and came again alongside, nearer than they had done before, and took such triffes as we gave them. After this they landed close to the ship, and all four went ashore, carrying their arms with them. But Tupia soon prevailed upon them to lay down their arms and come and set down by him, after which most of us went to them, made them again some presents, and stayed by them until dinnertime, when we made them understand that we were going to eat, and asked them by signals to go with us; but this they declined, and as soon as we left them they went away in their canoe.

One of the men was something above the middle age, the other three were young. None of them were above 5½ feet high, and all their limbs were proportionally small. They were wholly naked, their skins the colour of wood soot, and this seemed to be their natural colour. Their hair was black, lank, and cropped short, and neither woolly nor frizzled; nor did they want any of their fore-teeth, as Dampier has mentioned those did he saw on the western side of this country. Some parts of their bodies had been painted with red, and one of them had his upper lip and breast painted with streaks of white, which he called *carbanda*. Their features were far from being disagreeable; their voices were soft and tunable, and they could easily repeat any word after us, but neither us nor Tupia could understand one word they said...

In the morning four of the natives made us another short visit; three of them had been with us the preceding day, the other was a stranger. One of these men had a hole through the bridge of his nose, in which he stuck a piece of bone as thick as my finger. Seeing this, we examined all their noses, and found that they had all holes for the same purpose; they had likewise holes in their ears, but no ornaments hanging to them; they had bracelets on their arms made of hair, and like hoops of small cord. They sometimes may wear a kind of fillet about their heads, for one of them had applied some part of an old shirt which I had given them to this use.

Thursday, [July] 12... About this time five of the natives came over and stayed with us all the forenoon. There were seven in all—five men, one woman, and a boy; these two last stayed on the point of land on the other side of the river about 200 yards from us. We could very clearly see with our glasses that the woman was as naked as ever she was born; even those parts which I always before now thought nature would have taught a woman to conceal were uncovered...

Saturday, [July] 14. ...Mr. Gore, being in the country, shot one of the animals before spoke of [Kangaroo]; it was a small one of the sort, weighing only 28 pound clear of the entrails. ...

*Captain Cook's Journal during the First Voyage round the World Made in H.M. Bark 'Edeavour' 1768-71, a literal transcription of the original MSS by Captain W.J.L. Wharton, London, 1893.*

There is much divergent argument about the origin of the Australian race. It is probably the result of successive waves of settlers, as proved by the difference between the physical features of the old man at left (recalling the Veddas of Ceylon) and the others, who are more negroid. Above right: an Australian hunter brandishing a boomerang, in the company of his son. The boomerang used to exist in other parts of the world. It is used for hunting birds and small animals, and is a small curved board designed to return to its point of departure. Below: the picture on the left dates from 1957; somewhat posed, the picture is less idyllic than the one on the right showing inhabitants of Port Jackson (Sydney) seen by Freycinet in September 1818.

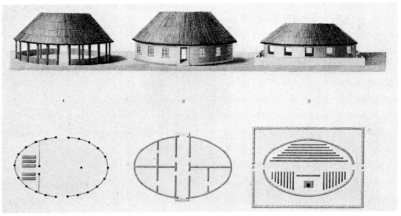

Above: Outline and plan of three types of dwellings in the Society Islands as seen by Duperrey in 1823. From left to right: a native home, a missionary's house and a joint school, inspired by native architecture.

Above left: Rangi haeta's house on Mana island, New Zealand, drawn in 1826, represents the best of Maori architecture. The red ochre façade and the decorations bore witness to the greatness of the chief. The houses below, drawn in 1819, belonged to Kraimoku, counsellor to the King of Hawaii. In the foreground, a woman weaves, while a warrier looks on.

# THE HABITAT

It is climate that determines man's habitat and his needs.
But in the Pacific Islands, with their notoriously soft balmy
air, what needs does he have? Cook wrote about the life of
Australia's aborigines and how they slept under the sky
wherever they happened to be; he described the type of
light shelter of interwoven fibres which Tahitian native
chiefs took around with them on their travels on land and
sea, a fragile covering which lets the cooling breezes
through yet keeps the sun's hottests rays out. In New
Guinea's central mountains the inhabitants use little round
huts erected wherever they work, and throughout the
Pacific those little huts of straw can be found, woven
branches and leaves which the natives put up wherever they
settle, on the ground, in trees, on stilts over the water, and
which they abandon when they move on. These are not
really houses, still less homes, but simple temporary shelters, like those put up on a beach at holiday time. In such
countries, free of dangerous wild animals, where the climate is soft and nature kind and peaceful, man has no need
of protection. It is necessary to have lived on those islands,
whose conditions are so often all too wrongly likened to the
harder climate of Africa, to realise how true were the
reports of early travellers extolling the softness of the ocean
breezes before western man came to deforest and colonise
the area, upsetting the environmental balance and ruining
the soil so as to destroy the climate and nature's action.

In former times, except for a few places and those islands
near the tropics where the south wind brings in cold air currents, the oceanic climate was so balmy that for shelter the
simplest lean-to or leafy roof was all a man needed. With
nature everywhere friendly and no contrast between
indoors and out, no-one needed a house in the same way
that western man does to keep warm and cosy *inside* to
guard against the cold, wind and rain *outside*.

In those days man was part of nature. Oceania's civilisation did not divide the world into human, animal, vegetable
and mineral kingdoms; everyone and everything was alive,
possessing one or more souls. Man, the master of the earth,
was concerned with preserving that life and organising its
movement and keeping its balance. In such a society man
had his place, but not a dominant one for life was one and
the same for all. It was the totems which held life and passed
it on.

The earliest discoverers have left us descriptions of the
beauty of the villages they saw, with their dwellings hidden
in the greenery amidst the singing of birds. Made of leaves
and boughs and of remarkable design, the home, according
to Oceania's legend, was created by the female. In all civilisations it is the woman who gives rise to culture and devel-
ops it. In Oceania her place was particularly important since
it was through her and her blood that the life of the totem
was transmitted and the spirit of the ancestors reincarnated.
The legend goes:

'One day a woman woke up to find the hut she shared with her man too cramped, and longed for a better home. "I shall close my eyes," she said, "and wish that when I open them we may see two big and beautiful houses." Before their astonished eyes there appeared, at the end of a long avenue, a tall house with round and pointed roof. On either side of the entrance stood two carved, wooden figures, effigies of their ancestors come to bring their blessing to her young man, their latest descendant, while in a side avenue stood a round house with a roof of golden straw: the woman's home.

'From that day on everyone began to make houses for their wives, helped by everyone else, as shown in the story of the Chief of Koné; who decreed "Bring us a master post and a joist. Make up bales of lianas, grasses, straw, bark and binding fibres. You others stay and dig a mound as base, so that we can finish the job today and you can get back to your tasks tomorrow with this young woman's house finished."

'The men were so moved by this speech that they at once began digging and working.

'They set about doing everything they had been told, cutting, carrying, loading, unloading, stacking. They measured the space for the house, set up a central wooden post, fixed on cross-bars, planted stakes all round, put the joists in place, tied the frames with many bindings... The roof was tightened down and surmounted with a spire of shells, white as a sparkling cascade.

'And it was all completed in a single day, as their chief had asked them. When the house was ready the man brought his wife and showed her the big building with its spire of shells, the *moaro,* the village centre-point, and nearby on a side-avenue, her own small dwelling: "Here is your house" he said, "You will live here." And from then on they lived there together.'

The living were not alone: the spirits of the dead stayed in their surroundings. The Abelans, of Central Sepik in the Maprik region of New Guinea, bury their dead under the house, while in many areas including Madagascar and Indonesia, the dead are mummified and kept in the house until a great funeral day, or until they are cremated, as in Indonesia. Elsewhere they may be placed in caves or dark spots in the forests, guarded by mourners. But the important point to remember is that, one way or another, the dead stay present always in the village. Sometimes they return to pay visits to the living, sometimes their heads are mounted and painted to look alive and beautiful with their hair in place, their ears made of clay and their eyes glazed. These skulls are lined up in *korwars* in various forms, acting as homes for the departed. In some parts of New Guinea a small body is carved out of wood to support the skull.

Everywhere the village way of life maintains this duality for the living and the dead, for the male and the female.

Villages are laid out in circular form in Melanesia, New Guinea and the Hebrides, with the cemetery in the middle with a clear space for dancing, as a centre for the ancestors and the dead, and for the ceremonies which dominate village life. All round, in a circle cut by an avenue, are situated

The Hawaiian chiefs

The young chiefs, unless they otherwise desired, were always borne on the shoulders of attendants; their only exercises were games, sufficient to excite and amuse, without greatly fatiguing; no care or toil was theirs; the abundance of the land and sea were at their disposal; and, from the quantity they daily consumed, particularly of that most nutricious diet, poi, it is not surprising they gave such material evidence of their training. Did they overeat themselves, (a common case,) menials were always ready to do that for the system, which otherwise, active exercise only could have effected. People were especially trained to *lomi-lomi;* a kind of luxurious kneading or shampooing, and stretching and cracking the joints, which served completely to renovate the system, when suffering either from a surfeit or fatigue. The fatter the chiefs, the more they required this operation. Their most common position was reclining upon divans of fine mats, surrounded by a retinue, devoted solely to their physical gratification. Some fanned, brushed away insects, and held spittoons; others fed them, *lomi-lomied,* or dressed their hair or persons.

JAMES JARVES, *History of the Hawaiian or Sandwich Islands,* Boston 1843, pp. 87-88

Throughout the Pacific the communal house plays an important rôle. Opposite, above: The wall of one at Apia (Samoa: 1838 drawing) is outlined by a circle of pillars. The woodwork is itself upheld by a row of central pillars and the roof is covered with fibres and pandanus (screw-pine) leaves. The whole recalls an open umbrella. Below: Of somewhat similar appearance, this Hawaiian chief's house (1846) differs in the absence of columns and beams, which make it possible to open and close the walls.

Maori Houses in New Zealand

Their houses are the most inartificially made of any thing among them, being scarcely equal, except in size, to an English dog-kennel: they are seldom more than eighteen or twenty feet long, eight or ten broad, and five or six high, from the pole that runs from one end to the other, and forms the ridge, to the ground: the framing is of wood, generally slender sticks, and both walls and roof consist of dry grass and hay, which, it must be confessed, is very tightly put together; and some are also lined with the bark of trees, so that in cold weather they must afford a very comfortable retreat. The roof is sloping, like those of our barns, and the door is at one end, just high enough to admit a man, creeping upon his hands and knees: near the door is a square hole, which serves the double office of window and chimney, for the fire-place is at that end, nearly in the middle between the two sides: in some conspicuous part, and generally near the door, a plank is fixed, covered with carving after their manner: this they value as we do a picture, and in their estimation it is not an inferior ornament: the sidewalls and roof project about two feet beyond the walls at each end, so as to form a kind of porch, in which there are benches for the accommodation of the family. That part of the floor which is allotted for the fireplace, is enclosed in a hollow square, by partitions either of wood or stone, and in the middle of it the fire is kindled. The floor, along the inside of the walls, is thickly covered with straw, and upon this the family sleep.

J. HAWKESWORTH, *Lieutenant Cook's Voyage Round the World,* London 1773, pp. 157-158.

the chief's house and those of his wives and children, others for guests and parents and for storehouses.

Christianity later brought changes to the central space, putting a church in the middle. But these churches, with their saints and images, remain surely the homes of the dead?

These particular arrangements in northern Melanesia are repeated in some of the islands nearby. Dumont d'Urville noted some at Rotouma. Others have been found at Wallis and on the Fiji Isles. On the Trobriands, the central space was for the men-folk, whereas the circular lane was kept for women. In the rest of Polynesia the village planning is not so clearly defined: the houses sometimes stretch along the lagoon, sometimes line a broad avenue parallel to the sea-shore, or may be placed in a number of different ways.

But in the south of Melanesia, villages are set out quite differently. The chief's house is the collective home for the men, and is built in bee-hive shape, a particularity of New Caledonia. It is sited on a rise to give broad views. The author remembers with surprise hearing a group of old Kanakas, seated in deep contemplation at the top of the steps of the Château de Versailles exclaim 'Our ancestors used to build this way.' The Melanesian author and sculptor Boesoou Erijisi left a detailed description with drawings of the building of these houses. Maurice Leenhardt published it in his book *Gens de la Grande Terre,** describing 'those long avenues planted with fresh grass' and bordered by arocaria and coconut trees leading to the chief's house. In the middle, a central wooden post, the *rhea,* with 5–7 ft long laths forming a framework to which the joists are fixed. The roof, shaped like an elongated cone, had deeply impressed early explorers, and its tremendous height was greatly admired by Cook. It is peculiar to the south of Melanesia. On either side of the entrance is a sculpted transom holding up the roof and representing tribal ancestors. In front, stakes, *juxes,* are planted with little gardens around them: these signify the presence of the dead.'

The same in different form can be found in the extreme north of Melanesia, in New Guinea, and in men's houses among the Asmats of Indonesia. There, in the centre of the *Yen,* a tall cylinder of palm leaves is found, containing food. It represents the tree of life, the female element, while the hearth supports are sculptured to represent the village's ancestors and the dead are buried in front of the house. When the *Yen* is inaugurated, the women dance all day around the tree of life, being themselves the life-spring. When they withdraw the men go in. With a single blow the chief smashes the tree of life, and the feast starts. Adrian A.

* See Bibliography.

Interior of a *dubu* or house for men in a Papuasian village, in New Guinea. It differs from the other huts by its size and rich decorations. Shown here is a gathering of men; with ceremonial masks and decorated bark shields leaning against the beams.

In the Pacific most houses are covered with thatch (of pandanus leaves or coconut palm) but they vary in shape from island to island, and sometimes from tribe to tribe. Left: Photographed around 1885, these tree houses at Sadera Makera (Papua-New Guinea) are for unmarried women. Above: interior of a hut at Lebuka (Fiji). This 1838 picture shows woven objects, wicker and pieces of pottery. The Fijians excelled in all those arts. Below: A village street scene in 1885 at Moapa, Trobriand Islands (Papua-New Guinea).

Gerbrand describes the *Yen* in his book *Wow-Ipits—Eight Asmat Woodcarvers of New Guinea,** clearly revealing that this house, with a communal centre available to everyone, represents indeed the centre for the community of the living and the dead.

A little further south, still in New Guinea, in certain parts of Central Sepik are circular houses surmounted by very high roofs similar to those of New Caledonia, rare in the Pacific.

In Polynesia, houses may be oblong, square or rectangular, with or without stilts, often set on a hillock. Cook clearly described the big, two-sided open barns of Tahiti with symmetrically placed support posts, used for both working and sleeping. Such communal houses are built to hold two or three thousand people.

The Pacific's biggest country, Australia, is the only one not to have possessed a real architecture. The natives were nomads, living off the land and hunting, mostly sleeping under the stars or in temporary shelters without any communal buildings for their big meetings, the *corroborree*. Nevertheless, houses made of bark have been found in Arnhem with paintings inside of Australia's night sky, birth, the voyage of the dead, the rainbow, and constellations.

All necessary building material can be found on the islands and archipelagos of Oceania, such as stone, wood, vegetable matter. But the weatherproof house, made necessary by the Western climate, was not only unnecessary there, but appears incongruous and unaesthetic. Totems, like lizards, had to be able to settle without hindrance in the thatch. Man must not, nor did he need to, be caged in by four walls, separated from the cosmos. Houses were not even waterproof among the ancient Aïnu of the north Pacific, now Japanese inhabitants of the Hokkaido and Sakhalin islands. This people built differently to others in the Pacific: they started from the roof. Four wooden posts were laid on the ground in a rectangle, and rafters bound to them and to a long pole held horizontally above which would form the ridge of the roof. From the roof's ridge to its base other rafters were tied. Posts were stuck in the ground, interwoven with thin poles at regular intervals. Then the roof frame was put into place and thatched over. Next, the *inao* was made where the ancestors could be worshipped. The *inao* was a rod of willow or similar wood surmounted with hair and stuck in a base of reeds before being set up by the cradle of a new-born child whose titular guardian angel it would become. But the house itself was a living person and had from its initiation to be given its *inao* hanging from windows and joists to protect it. Further off, the store-house, raised on stilts, and other dependencies were built. If the house was for newly-weds, a smaller version would be built. When it became too small, far from pulling it down, it would have a bigger one built on to it, and become a sort of veranda or porch for the larger house. The houses were so much alive that they had their own soul and life like their owners.

* See Bibliography.

These buildings used no stone. If the Oceanian peoples used stones it was to fashion those huge statues which are a marvel of Easter Island, or smaller ones like the jade *tiki* of New Zealand or the basalt *tiki* of Hawaii; or for the ritual or magic stones, *churingas,* of central Australia, tablets depicting totems where the souls of the dead hunters gathered; the *Féi* of the Pelew islands, those big wheels of pink and mauve stone serving both as objects of worship and as religious moneys, placed before each house; or to make tools, pestles and axes, some of real beauty such as the *o'kono,* the round axe of New Caledonia which served equally as a weapon, a chief's sceptre, and a magic device when the sun's reflexion on its green jade side was used to call down rain.

All these objects show that the peoples of Oceania were superb masters of stone-craft. But for the home stone was almost never used since they built on mounds, called a *marae* in Tahiti and a *paepae* in the Marquesa Islands, which acted as supports for their houses and as altars for their gods and ancestors. The beautiful constructions on the Society Islands, often of gigantic proportions, did indeed stand in large stone enclosures within which square or rectangular terrasses, bordered on either side by high stone and basalt walls, formed the *marae*. The *marae* was the place where the chiefs and priests had their seats, a hallowed public place for meetings, worship and sacrifices, a refuge and at the same time church and town hall. The individual family *marae* was of smaller size. The bones of the dead were buried there after the family had removed the head, which was hung inside the house, which was made of wood and vegetable matter. On the Marquesa Islands, the *paepae* consisted of a high terrace made of carefully positioned black stones and was reached by a ladder. On this stone elevation stood a rectangular wooden house with thatched roof, one side of which came down to the ground and the other curved up like a porch, the whole constituting an architectural entity of great beauty, powerful yet light. The family houses were built on small mounds of slate. But communal houses, built to hold large numbers of people, were given terraces of immense proportion; a strong sense of admiration is evoked by the confrontation with the beauty of the work carried out by those tremendous movers of stones.

After the Romans colonised Europe, their stone buildings were preserved. But when those same westerners came to discover Oceania in Dupetit-Thouars' time, they used their guns to destroy the islanders' majestic buildings and vast public squares with their sloping terraces, and pillaged the priests' seats and the sacred statues. These constructions were often too enormous to disintegrate under cannon fire. But the missionaries with their pious campaigns against idols finished the job. Many statues were too colossal to move, so to preserve decency, they mutilated their sexual organs. They were followed by settlers, officials, ethnologists, all of whom for different purposes stole the treasures which now fill homes, museums, and the galleries of commercial collectors. Piece by piece all remains of those religious, artistic and architectural achievements were to disap-

Only specialists are capable of building these Niutao (Ellis Islands) houses called 'sleeping houses', where food is cooked outside. They are made of mats and boards from the pandanus tree and covered with leaves from the same tree, and shown here in various stages of construction.

pear from the places where they belonged and where they had been created.

Thus vanished a plastic and architectural art of great cultural significance. All across the Pacific its beauty had been a living, modulated demonstration of a rich, affective life which combined its small, intimate homes and its huge houses where 3,000 people could find shelter.

Today we understand the eminently social and religious rôle played by the habitat in Oceania: a complementary duality between man and woman, a constant interchange between the dead and the living, an intimate participation in the cosmos. All this was expressed in architectural works of remarkable finesse, constructed out of the most perfectly appropriate materials. Stone, mounds and sacred ornaments, timber and vegetable matter for the house itself... each played its specific part; soul and object were intimately mingled. The aim naturally may be to create a fine work of art, but the prime aim is not art itself but to act 'in a suitable manner' so that the world, the cosmos, can maintain its harmony and its movement. Being a part of the cosmos, man must at no time be cut off from it; so his habitat must not be a closed, isolated world with the inside separated from the outside. It must be a single, living unit: this striving for permanence and continuity is well illustrated by the Aïnus' refusal to be shut up in a coffin, so that their spirit could depart freely from the body at the time of death: life is indivisible, and the habitat is an integral part of life.

Dwellings on Easter Island

These houses are shared by at least a whole village or district. I measured one of them near our base: it was 310 ft long, 10 ft wide, and 10 ft high in the centre; its shape resembled a canoe resting on its gunwhales; entry was by two doors 2 ft high, thus access was on hands and knees. This house could shelter more than 200 people: it was not a chief's house, for there was no furniture, and in any case, so vast a space would be useless to him. This house alone formed the whole village, with two or three small houses some distance away.

LOUIS ANTOINE MILLET-MUREAU, *Voyage de La Pérouse autour du monde,* Paris 1792, vol. II, p. 10 (April 1786)

Dwellings on the Sandwich Islands (Mowee)

On our walk we encountered four little villages of ten to twelve houses each; they are made of straw with straw roofs and are shaped like those of our poorest peasants. The roof slopes on two sides; the door is in the gable-end and is only 3 1/2 ft high, so it can only be entered by bending down. It is closed by a simple latch that anyone can open. For furniture these islanders only have mats which form a very clean floor like our carpets, and on which they sleep. Their only cooking utensils are very large gourds which can be shaped at will when green. They varnish them and trace out in black all manner of designs on them. I also saw some which were stuck together to form very big containers. It appears that the glue used withstands humidity; I would very much like to know what it is made of.

LOUIS-ANTOINE MILLET-MUREAU, *Voyage de La Pérouse autour du monde,* Paris 1792, vol. 2, pp. 143-144

An engraving of Chief Matutaera, standing in front of an ornamented house near Aukland, New Zealand, in about 1865.

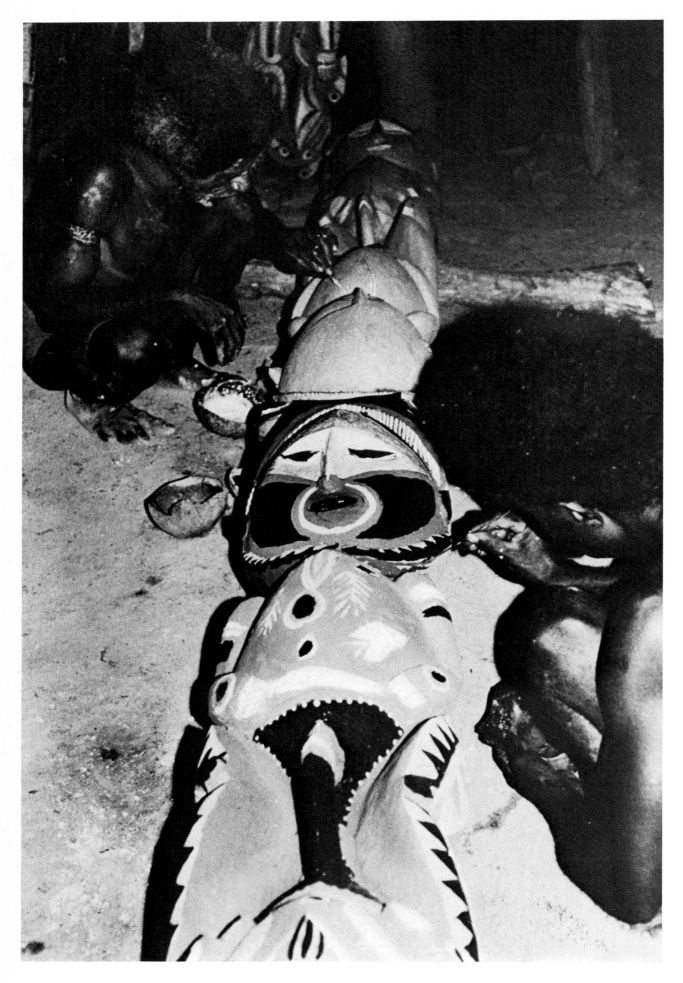

# TECHNIQUES AND ECONOMICS

Economic life in Oceania is based on barter and those skilful techniques in which individual brain and muscle-power play a vital rôle. Like Michel Angelo, who would go and choose himself the precise slab of marble at the quarry for the sculpture he had in mind, so do the men in the Pacific invariably select themselves the stone or the tree from which they will later carve out the corner stone or the central pillar of their home, or the well-balanced dug-out fit to face the rigours of the ocean. Before making anything, the men personally go out to choose with care the correct stone, tree, branch or bark for their purpose; the same applies if fibres, leaves, feathers, bones, sands or shells are needed.

The Pacific inhabitant has a very precise notion of the powers and limitations of his body, which he looks after. All its components are a well-studied and exercised unit where optimum use is continuously made of the bare foot, the leg, the arm, the hand, with all their muscles, the mouth with its saliva so useful for transforming fibres or clay. These are his tools, as efficient for him as any man-made device.

To achieve their triumphs of architecture or navigation, of polishing or carving, they depend on six senses: touch, sight, hearing, smell, taste and, most important, judgement.

On festive occasions they show off their brilliant tattooing, their jewels, feathers, and mother-of-pearl, their fine cloth made of vegetable fibres and broad belts of bark. But for everday work they stay as lightly-clad as possible to keep freedom of action, using but light belts, bracelets or thongs round arms and legs into which they slip the tools they may need. Only when fishing or hunting do they suddenly reveal all the taut perfection of their muscle power.

Their simple tools include a small pointed stick which is turned at speed against a piece of wood to produce a spark to ignite a few dry twigs which are then blown on gently until the flame takes hold. The Australian native perfects the operation by scooping a hole in the piece of wood and filling it with a mixture of kangaroo droppings reduced to powder with pulverised dry twigs. This produces first smoke and then its own flame. Thicker sticks, either pointed or forked at the tip, are used to dig up roots. They use wood also for bows and arrows, boomerangs, heavy clubs, axe handles, shields. Bone or stone may be employed as well for other axes or head-crushers, for knives, needles or ceremonial spoons, mortars and pestles, dishes and water carriers.

Wood is used for all manner of flutes, horns, or drums, including the water drum designed to project sound against smooth surfaces, and in combination with skin for other types of drum or with feathers to close the mouthpiece of ceremonial flutes such as are used by the Mundugumors of the Sepik. The *rhumbus*, a sound-producing disc said to emit the voices of the gods in Melanesia, Malaysia and Australia, and the ancient Australian *churinga* carved tablets could be of wood or stone. Wood too, or bamboo, is used for the

Left: Papuan artists on Kalabu Island (north of New Guinea in the Maprik region) painting a ceremonial post. Some 14 ft long, it is made from wood which has been previously soaked in m... d then painted with colours composed of earth and soot. Above: This diadem of feathers, or *ta'avaha,* was brought back from the Marquesa Islands by Cook on his second journey (1772-1775). It is made of vegetable fibres decorated with strips of mother-of-pearl on which leaves of chiselled tortoiseshell are applied. Stylised *tiki* designs appear on the tortoise-shell discs.

89

Below: An actual village in the Trobriand Islands. In other areas of Papua-New Guinea there are no villages, houses being disseminated all over a tribe's territory. Only the house for ceremonies is made of wood, the others being of woven fibres. They are built on stilts to keep out of reach of animals.

Right: These New Hebrides huts were photographed in 1972; they are covered with coconut palm leaves. They are dwellings for women or couples. Houses for men are more luxurious. The sites selected are shaded and blend perfectly into the natural surroundings conforming to the Pacific ideal in which men, animals and vegetation all form a whole.

chiefs' truncheon on which the history of the clan is carefully carved, for the Australian *yarkilla* or message stick, for the Easter Island memo-pad board, and for the painted bark pieces of Australia.

Wood was required, with tapa, shells and feathers for the masks of New Ireland, particularly for the *Malangan*, the purpose of which was to proclaim the presence of the gods at certain ceremonies, at the conclusion of which they would be left in the bush to rot. The masks of the areas around the Torres Straits between New Guinea and North Australia were fashioned in human or animal shape from large shells joined together with fibre. Wood too for the New Guinea *korwar*, representing the dead in the form of a seated man. At Geelwink Bay the *korwar*'s head was the dead man's, his body being concealed by an elegant shield. Supports, and hooks carved like faces to hang up human skulls were also of wood, as were the *oha*, small boards bearing the painted effigies of ancestors and hung on the walls of the men's dormitory beside the skulls of their victims. In parts of Australia whole trunks of trees carved with geometric lines were used to mark a notable's grave or the places used for the initiation ceremony.

Hardwood posts and beams hold up the roof of the tall cathedral-like Houses of the Spirits in New Guinea. The roof is of palm leaves bound to a bamboo frame – the palm there is known as the tree of life. The roof overhangs considerably, to protect the painted side walls from the rain. At the base is a wall of interwoven bamboo 20 ft high. In the centre of the front wall, under the overhang, hangs a 133 ft long wicker chain. More wood was used for their temples on stilts, shaped like canoes turned upside down, as at Dorei, west New Guinea and Geelwinck Bay, and the whole building held up by columns carved to represent the tribal ancestors. More wood was used for the pillars and lintels, and rot-proof wood painted red made the splendid carved sarcophagi of New Zealand's Maori chiefs. And wood for their canoes, which, credited with a life of its own, carries a prow in the shape of an ancestral totem.

The small fishing canoe is hewn out of a single trunk with two transversals joined to the hull, forward of hardwood, aft of pliable wood. The war canoe is twin-hulled like a catamaran, joined by a platform holding carved columns. Long distance canoes have twin hulls bearing twin masts with sails, and bamboo shelters on the connecting platform. The whole craft is dug out of tree trunks. Ironwood is used for the masts, coconut fibre for rope, gum and matting for the sails. The only tools used are axes and awls made of bone, a gimlet of bone or shell, and a plane of coral.

There is a multitude of other uses for wood, beyond those briefly listed. Native skill enables them to use it with surprising precision, as in the case of the boomerang, which may be engraved and then painted as in Australia, or may be engraved or carved, as in other places.

Extensive use is made of bark, to make covers, clothes, or shrouds, and decorated accordingly, and of leaves, for roofs and mats. This is one of the last skills existing, which has survived the onslaught of civilisation, in use in Oceania.

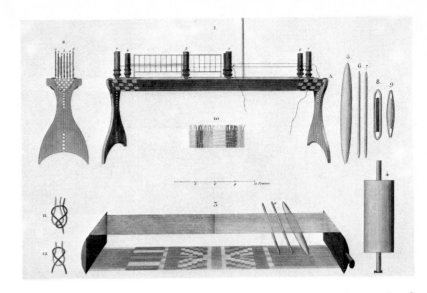

Above: A loom on Oualan Island, Carolines, in 1824. Textiles, made of fibres from banana or hibiscus leaves, used to be rare in Micronesia. In New Zealand the climate was colder and the Maoris needed thick warm clothes, and especially capes which they made from strong fibres from a local type of flax, *phormium tenax*. It was woven by hand by winding the thread round two stakes in the ground. Below: weaving in a hut at Rangihireta Pah.

The finest combs made in Melanesia are found in the Admiralty Islands (in the north of the Bismarck Archipelago). The teeth are made of wood or bamboo, the handle being painted in bright colours. They are always finely worked.

Since trees are so vital to their economy, the peoples of
the islands devote special care to planting and cultivating
them. They themselves plant the thousands of palm trees
which are such a feature of the Pacific islands. With its multiple uses for their everyday life, the tree is a sign of wealth.

Before the wood came the stone age. The rich stone civilisation of the area can still be divined from the remains,
mostly enormous, to be found in the jungles. Among these
are the huge flagstones on the terraces of the Polynesian
*marae*, the stone basements of temples and houses, stone-
faced irrigation canals and supporting walls, stone monuments often of colossal size as on Easter Island. The *tiki* of
the Marquesas Islands, huge round-eyed heads with thick
lips on massive bodies and limbs, were copied a thousand
times by Polynesians everywhere in wood and bone as well
as stone. Some, like the *Ji-Po* on the Marquesas, were made
from the bone of an ancestor and used to decorate boats,
drums or the headgear of chiefs and warriors. The *tiki* is still
an ornamental theme for native jade in New Zealand today.

The meanings of many of the petroglyphics of the time
are still unknown. But many of these earlier stone carvings
appear to be identifiable with later human tattoo marks and
with designs found on engraved bamboos and on ancestral
pillars by the doors of the houses, like the New Caledonian
*talé* and the Australian carved tree-trunks at sites of initiation ceremonies.

Earth was mainly used for pottery. The Fiji water pots are
famous for their varnish and original forms. Of simple
manufacture, they were covered with *kaori* gum while still
hot from the oven, which imparted a particularly fine glaz-
ing. But they are not fire-proof. Their decorations of dotted
lines are reminiscent of the Spiritus Sancto potteries of the
New Hebrides.

At the beginning of the twentieth century it was still possible to find in New Caledonian villages earthenware cooking pots. Though rather coarsely made, they were decorated
in relief with sacred animals or human faces showing the
fine melanesian nose and broad nostrils. These were always
made by the women. Only before going to war did the men
make a special coarse little model pot.

In parts of New Guinea the ridges of houses are made of
pottery. In some of the stilt houses the hearth was of pottery. Often the heads of the dead were covered with clay
and painted over.

Inhabitants of north New Caledonia would exchange
their pottery for the *asu* bracelets made by the tribes in the
centre. In New Guinea, the Port Moresby Motus would load
their *lakatoi* canoes with pottery and sea-shell ornaments,
and sail down to the Papuans at the Gulf to barter them for
the Papuan dug-outs.

Pottery was always an object of barter. Yet for a long time
it was believed that no pottery existed in Polynesia, mainly
because it had all vanished before the age of discovery
began. Only later was some found in the Marquesas, Samoa
and Tonga. It is now possible to identify three separate
schools of ceramics of prehistoric Oceania, the oldest being
Lapita pottery, named after a New Caledonian village. The

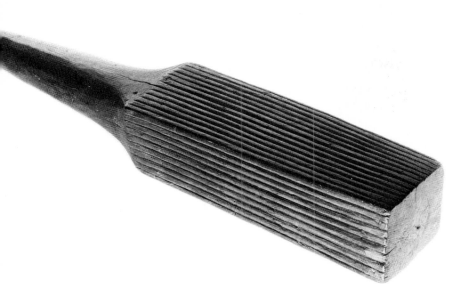

Left: The coat of feathers above belonged to King Kamehameha I of Hawaii (end of eighteenth century). The feathers are stuck into a netting of touchardia. Below left: Polynesian ceremonial axe; the stone blade here is perpendicular to the handle. Below right: This bowl, or *oumekela'au* is 5¹/₂ ins across and was used to drink *kava,* a drink made with pepper. Bottom: A head-rest or *kali,* pleasant to sleep on in hot countries like the Tongas, with air circulating round the head and with no danger of deranging the hair-style, which is often complicated. The wooden mallet (above) from the Hawaii islands is used to hammer bark cloth (*tapa*), previously wetted to increase its surface. The mould below (Samoa islands) is for printing designs on the material.

Lapita pieces, believed to have been pre-Polynesian, were made from rectangular slabs beaten into shape on a kind of anvil. Some are very fine, others more ordinary. Some were quite plain, but most have dotted geometric designs. Of the other two schools, remains have been found of post or spheroid shape with designs chiselled in and reliefs stuck on, and others of ovoid shape with designs stamped on by an engraved block.

Another specialty of the region worth mentioning is the use of polyps in house building. This does not mean coral proper, the uses of which little is known, but what the island people call live coral, the mass of shells from which reefs are formed and which can be dug from the bottom of the sea and brought up in large lumps. These are put on a pile of logs over a pit, and the logs burnt. When the fire is out the pit is filled with a fine, strong, very white lime which is covered with palm leaves and collected when required for building. Other heaps of live coral would be piled up into a V-shaped fish trap, with a narrow opening leading into a tank. There the fish could be kept alive until eating.

Thus widest use was made of every kind of raw material. Tools were made from shells. So were musical instruments, particularly from conch shells which are found everywhere except in Australia. Smaller shells were used to decorate canoes and other objects. They were often considered sacred when worn by men, as in Melanesia's white shell bracelets and in New Caledonia's necklaces made of starfish discs with pendants. 'Pearl money' consisted of bits of shell strung together on fibres, often several yards long, and was particularly highly prized.

Feathers were widely used. In Australia officials guarding the sacred tablets at totem ceremonies were covered with down stuck on with blood, while feathers carpeted some of the ground and formed a light covering for the tablets. Patiently collected yellow, black and red feathers with little tufts of red down were said to guarantee the presence of a god. In Polynesia feathers were kept in long, carved boxes for ceremonial occasions. The Hawaiian coat was of yellow down with red triangles, being worn with a light wicker helmet surmounted with red feathers and yellow plumes.

The wealth of the island people is amply demonstrated by the brilliant variety of their dress and the beauty of the things they made, engraved, painted or carved. But for all of them their greatest treasure was their canoe or dug-out.

In the North Pacific the Aïnu sew planks together to make their boats, which have rounded prows. But the canoe is in general use throughout Oceania, West Madagascar and South-East Asia, light and perfectly balanced. It is a thrill to watch their pilots patiently waiting outside the reef for the right wave, and then paddling frantically to get across. Some of their war canoes, all larger and better decorated, were almost of the size of the ENDEAVOUR.

Now passed into history, they were greatly admired by Cook and his contemporaries. In his *Ancient Canoes of Tahiti\**, Jourdain wrote: 'A canoe in a squadron is a

\* See Bibliography.

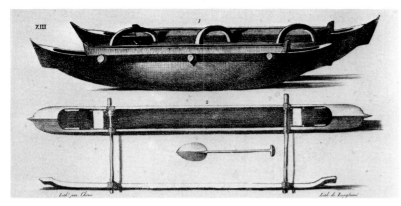

In the Hawaiian islands canoes were carved out of a trunk of a single *koa,* a kind of acacia, or an Oregon pine which occasionally floated up on to the shore of one of the islands. They were generally 26 ft long, and 1 ft wide, seldom weighing more than 60 lbs. The outrigger canoes (lower drawing) were steered by a simple paddle, in contrast to the double war canoe which was longer and had three or four straight or curved cross-bars, and which required two kinds of paddles, one for steering and one for paddling.

Canoes in the Society islands are akin to those of the Marquesas but differ from Hawaiian designs. Opposite: ancient sailing canoes with outriggers held two to six men. They were made for crossings taking two to three weeks. The bottom was in one piece for smaller craft or two or three pieces for larger canoes. The mast could be as much as 25 ft high. War canoes (below) had no outrigger. The largest sizes could hold up to 100 men. The prow was often provided with a decorative figure.

powerful instrument of war. Their beauty, like that of the big sailing canoes built for long distance exploration, and their technical qualities can justly be compared with those of the great sailing ships of Europe and America of the nineteenth century'.

A star was selected as a guide for the eventual return home at departure. In some parts, steering was done with the additional aid of a coconut with holes in it acting as a kind of wind compass. Prevailing winds were taken into consideration, as were strong currents which come from certain directions at specific times of the year. The island mariners knew how to tell that land was ahead from changes in the clouds and waves, from the flight of birds and the reflection of the surfaces of lagoons in the clouds.

In 1831 a missionary, Ellis, noted that in Huahine the native word for the white man's compass was *aveia,* their name for the star-pilot by which they steered home.

Their sea-faring knowledge, passed on from one generation to the next, is not lost, and Europeans and Polynesians are trying to revive it today. Australia's National University gave David Lewis a grant in 1968 to make a study of Micronesian and Melanesian systems of navigation. Lewis set out for Puluwat in the Carolines in a 39 ft ketch with an auxiliary engine and enlisted the support of an Oceanian sailor, Hipour. Another native navigator joined them at Pilini in the Santa Cruz group. The three men proceeded to cover 13,000 miles, including 1,680 miles out on the high seas, without any modern instruments or aides. At the end of his book *We, the Navigators,* * Lewis writes: 'When Europeans first reached the Pacific, Oceania already possessed a real and elaborate science of navigation. It was not the same everywhere but was always based on lists of stars whose movements had been correctly noted, and valuable information on terrestrial and maritime signs and phenomena affecting sailors. Apprentices received strict training, both on land and at sea, lasting several years.'

Further important light on the subject is provided, thanks to the work of Stockholm's Ethnographic Museum, by Kjell's *Astronomy and Navigation in Polynesia and Micronesia.* **

The great explorers and settlers were the Polynesians, who travelled from Hawaii to the Celebes, Tahiti to New Zealand and as far as New Caledonia's Loyalty Island.

The Maoris were the astronomers. They stayed up all night, those *tchunga kokorangi,* observing the *raririki* stars. They forecast weather changes far further ahead than modern meteorological men can. They not only observed, but loved and worshipped their stars, regarding their movements as the travels of their ancestors. Their astronomers recalled the past and repeated the teachings of their forebears. They worked not as scientists but as members of their tribe and its religion, and their women hailed the stars with songs and dances.

Even their canoes had to be built according to ritual. The chosen tree was dragged solemnly to the village square or

* See Bibliography.
** See Bibliography.

97

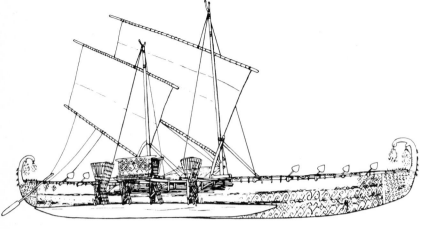

The big twin-masted sailers from Luf (Agomes, Hermit islands, Melanesia) were easily recognized by the float fixed to the boat. The hull was of one piece with the bulkheads reinforced and well padded. Such craft could carry up to 50 men out on the high seas. They sat so as to act as counter-weights against head winds. The last of them, also utilisable as war canoes, date from the beginning of the twentieth century.

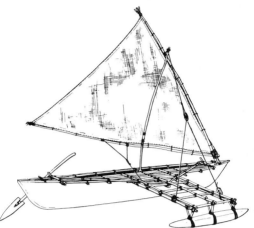

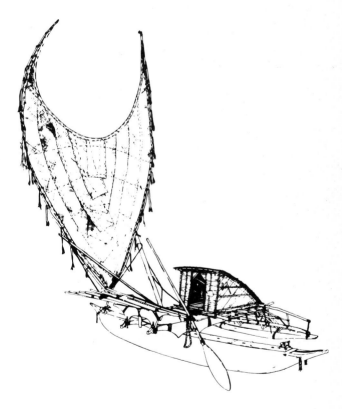

This ocean-going craft of Santa Cruz (Melanesia) is one of the great triumphs of Oceanian naval construction. Waves can submerge the hull without sinking it. Covered with boards, the two ends are identical, making it easy to reverse direction. The beams in the centre follow exactly the shape of the boat. All the parts are tied down with lianas. A side cabin, covered with sago palm fibre, is set on two cross-bars. The sail is of a type known as 'micronesian lateen'.

Below: In the Marshalls (Micronesia) they used 'maps' made with small sticks right up to the beginning of the twentieth century. They proved invaluable to navigators. Their existence demonstrates how well they knew the oceans and islands. The peoples of the Marshalls were as a matter of fact the only ones to have invented the system. The map at left is 5 ft 2 in long and 28 in wide and depicts the Ralik Archipelago. It does not give the exact position of each island but it does show marine currents and the direction of the waves. Where the sticks cross, winds are shown to be contrary. Islands are marked by shells. There is thus no similarity with European maps.

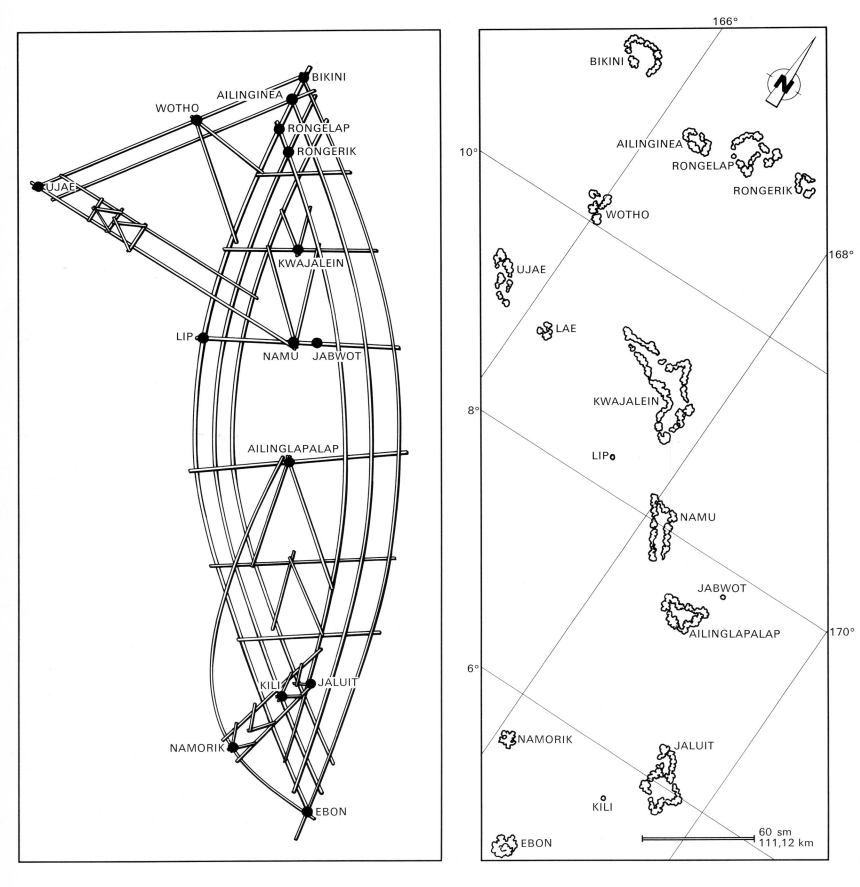

There were various ways of fishing. In New Caledonia they used harpoons (above, left), while in Polynesia the inhabitants used curved baits, or nets, as in this Tahiti river fishing scene (below, left). Below: fishing at Bora-Bora on 14 July 1972. French Polynesia celebrates 14 July with canoe races, the canoes having 3, 6 or 16 men paddling. The celebrations go on for nearly a month.

to the beach. Coconut fibres bound the various pieces together and the sides were carved. A broad platform was laid over the cross-bars and all cracks well stuffed. The boat had to be painted black, yellow and red, with a triangular sail assembled from strips of leaves sewn together.

The whole village in full regalia came down to the launching, their bodies covered with coconut oil and their faces white-washed and painted with perfumed red and black resin. The canoes then visited every village collecting contributions for their bartering, which was a special characteristic of the *kula* cult in the Massim area, the south of Papua and New Guinea.

Bronislaw Malinowski describes the *kula* barter system in his *Argonauts of the Pacific.** The basic items are *mwali* (bracelets of big white shells with little balls and shreds of fibre) and *soulawa* (necklaces several yards long of red starfish discs with a pendant). In the Papua and New Guinea area and the neighbouring islands these are taken around on trips lasting up to three years, the *mwalis* going east, the *soulawas* west.

As the *mwali* and *soulawa* acquire new mystic virtues at each barter operation, from their temporary owner, they must never be owned by any individual but pass from hand to hand at special ceremonies which lead to the barter of more utilitarian objects like fire-sticks, nuts, pottery, precious woods or whatever may be each island's products. In New Caledonia it is jade, the centre of the island producing green axes and the south serpentine necklaces. From there these items will continue the round of the islands and return to their starting point several generations later.

Several friendly tribes will gather at a great feast, the jade on show in the fine avenue facing the Great House. They are exchanged for some strings of 'pearl money', signifying an alliance or a new life. One chief, who had given a French official his clan's green axe, was utterly dismayed when he called later in Paris to collect his counter-gift and was told that the Frenchman would not even receive him. The official had in the meanwhile become President of the Republic, but the chief never forgave this breach of honour, and remained an implacable enemy of France.

For centuries alliances, formed by the tribe's forefathers, have given rise to such circular trips which must follow a prescribed route, which may however be extended since, as has been seen, new alliances may always be in the making.

In this manner the canoe broadens the living space of the islanders. The goods offered are not basic necessities, being things like jade axes, mother-of-pearl, or the *mwali* and *soulawa* of the Massim *kula* followers. The aim is not barter or economic survival. These journeys provide occasion for a series of social gatherings and merry-making where past alliances are renewed and new ones sealed by the giving and accepting of gifts of aesthetic and not monetary value, and the sharing of knowledge and news.

Each year these journeys of friendship are resumed with a resulting valuable interchange of information. And each year their canoes bring with them the tribe's mythology

*See Bibliography.

104

The Australian's traditional economy, hunting and gathering, can be compared to that of the Bushmen of South Africa. Hunters shown here are trying to improve their ordinary fare of grain, roots, and fish eggs, by climbing an eucalyptus to try and kill lizards, squirrels or bats. This watercolour dates from about 1820.

In this recent photograph, an Arunta hunter in central Australia has been snapped brandishing a javelin. Some javelins have forked points, others are carved and are used for ceremonial occasions.

These women on the Trobriand islands off New Guinea, photographed about 1970, are digging sweet potato (*taitu*), basic fare throughout the archipelago. Botanists have never yet identified the origins of the sweet potato, they may have come from America.

carved on their powerful prows. This makes the artist a highly respected man, for among these races the beautiful, the good, beauty itself, constitute an element of unity. Every line, every dot of colour traced on the boat is significant, denoting life itself and the continuing presence of the totem and the ancestors.

Such is the system which in Oceania embraces all the facets of social life and, as has been observed, gives rise to an inclination to take another look at western man's concepts of rights and interest-based economics, savings and utilitarianism. The economy of Oceania is not one of survival but an economy of sumptuous generosity.

Food in Tahiti

Scarcely can it be said that they earn their bread with the sweat of their brow, benevolent nature hath not only supply'd them with necessarys but with abundance of superfluities. The sea coast supplies them with vast variety of most excellent fish but these they get not without some trouble and perseverance, fish seems to be one of their greatest luxuries and they eat it either raw or dress'd and seem to relish it one way as well as the other, not only fish but almost every thing that comes out of the sea is eat and esteem'd by these people. Shell fish Lobsters Crabs and even Sea Insects and what is commonly call'd Blubbers of many kinds conduce to their support. For tame Animals they have Hogs Fowls and Dogs the latter of which we learnd to eat from them. (...)

Cookery seems to have been but little studied, here they have only two methods of applying fire, broiling and Baking as we call'd it, the method this is done I have before described and I am of opinion that Victuals dress'd this way are more juicy and more equally done than by any of our methods, large fish in particular, Bread fruit, Bananoes and Plantains Cook'd this way eats like boild Potatoes and was used by us by way of bread when ever we could get them. Of bread fruit they make two or three dishes by beating it with a stone pestil till it makes a paste, mixing water or cocoa nut liquor or both with it and adding ripe plantains bananoes Sour paste &c[a] this last is made from bread fruit in the following manner. This fruit from what I can find remains in season only 8 or 9 months in the year and as it is the chief support of the inhabitants a reserve of food must be made for those months when they are without it; to do this the fruit is gather'd when upon the point of ripening, after the rinde is scraped off it is laid in heaps and cover'd close with leaves where it undergoes a fermentation and becomes soft and disagreably sweet, the core is then taken out and the rest of the fruit thrown into a hole dug for that purpose the sides and bottom of which are neatly laid with grass, the whole is cover'd with leaves and heavy stones laid upon them; here it under goes a second fermentaition and becomes sourish in which condition they say it will keep good 10 or 12 Months, as they want to use it they make it into balls which they wrap up in leaves and bake in the same manner as they do the fruit of the tree, it is then ready for eating either hot or cold and hath a sour and disagreable taste. In this last state it will keep good a Month or six Weeks, it is calld by them Mahail and they seldom make a meal without some of it one way or another. To this plain diat salt water is the Universal sauce, hardly any one sits down to a meal without a cocoa nut shell full of it standing by them in which they dip most of what they eat especialy fish, drinking at intervals large supps of it out of their hands, so that a man may use half a pint at a Meal.

*The Journals of Capt. James Cook or his voyages of discovery* (First Voyage), ed. by J. C. Beaglehole, Cambridge 1955, pp. 121-123 (1769)

# CUSTOMS

## Totemism

Just as the sumptuary economy of the *kula* does not observe our western distinction between law and economics, between liberty and obligation, liberality, generosity, luxury and savings, in the same way Oceanian customs, though they may explode exuberantly in the dance, are solemn and of sterling value in everyday life. There may be no distinction between the sacred and the profane, but that is precisely because the life of each man is continually coupled to an abstract conception: the totem, which guides his actions. The master of a canoe standing in the prow by the totem, a real work of art, is regarded by his crew as holding a position which is simultaneously sacred and profane.

Can the same be said of the religion which dominates these countries? No: totemism is not strictly speaking a religion. It has precise rituals and forbidden places, but no sacred area as opposed to a profane area. What is held sacred is life. Life can be seen every day in its simplest and most basic form, in the lizard, at once both animal and totem, sleeping in the thatch of the roof over the hut; in a bird, in a drop of water, in thunder or in the wind's roar.

Far from being shut up in a church, these totems – lizard, blade of grass, bird, drop of water, and all the others – are the most normal parts of everyday life.

Let it be said from the outset, the term totemism as used in Oceania is but a makeshift. Totem is in fact an Algonquin Indian term.

The word first made its appearance at the end of the eighteenth century in J. Long's *Voyages and Travels of an Indian Interpreter* (London 1791). Its use was limited to North American Indians until the time Grey first noted similar customs in Australia in his *Journals of two Expeditions in North-West and Western Australia* (1841). But we really owe the first coherent description of totemism, also in Australia, to Baldwin Spencer and F. J. Gillen in *The Native Tribes in Central Australia* (1899) and *The Northern Tribes of Central Australia* (1904). Later the term became vulgarized and misused by Baden Powell's boy scouts.

What is known as oceanian totemism can best be understood by examining its manifestations around the Coral Sea. The Coral Sea has been chosen because the civilization there seems to have stayed closer to its origins than elsewhere: the Papuans in the interior of Papua-New Guinea have preserved their race and their culture; both of which were once far more widely spread, judging by the traces left on the Indonesian islands of South America. A number of links and similarities can be traced between them and certain North Australian aborigines and some of the New Hebridean and New Caledonian Kanakas.

In Oceania, totemism is not polytheism, for it is the author's opinion that the problem should not be simplified to the extent of considering as polytheistic a world where there is no distinction between 'gods' and 'men'.

Easter Island's 'talking' tablets, numbering about a score, conceal the island's most fascinating enigma. All that is known for certain is that priests held one in their hands when reciting their canticles or sacred texts. Discovered a century ago, many a paleograph and cryptograph has tried to decipher them, but with conflicting conclusions. One of the latest theories is that the signs do not represent real writing, but a kind of pictographic code where ideograms mix with puzzles and letters as such.

For years people thought that Easter Island's monumental statues were the work of a race of giants now extinct, and that the island was the last remains of a sunken continent, which might explain the existence of such immense stones. These tufa-stone busts vary from 11 ft to 18 ft in height. The elongated heads have almost geometric features. The use of stone is due to the lack of wood on the island, the stone from Rano-raraku, one of the island's mountains, being easy to work. Transporting them must have been a problem.

Above: The sacrificial altar at the Kayakakowa (Hawaii) royal *marae*, which is surrounded by a palisade of statues. Beside it stand French officers from Freycinet's crew, 1819, to give an idea of the scale. In the background, the skeleton of a large quadruped seems to be an anachronism. Left: An execution witnessed in Hawaii in about 1819 by Marini, a Spaniard. Below: Cook felt obliged to watch a human sacrifice on Tahiti on 15 September 1777.

The totem carried in woman and transmitted to her children through her blood can certainly not be called a god. It is life, it is sex, it is the deepest 'essence of self'. It is never worshipped, but deeply loved and respected for carrying and transmitting the life of the tribal ancestors. It is the keeper of life. All morals and ethics will therefore tend to harmonize life into one 'cosmomorphism' responsible for seeing that the various fragments making up the universe are maintained in their places: sky and stars, sun and moon, waves, the drop of water, storm and wind and all the other totems springing from animal, vegetable and mineral life. Man, that thinking reed of Pascal, is only capable of observing fragments of the universe. What is called the totemic system tries to relate man, and those scanty fragments that are gently but always in motion, in such a way that they may not harm each other, and that life may keep its eternal nature. So there appears to be no strife, but a vibration of life giving birth to a social organization based on complementarity.

In order to understand that organization better and to prevent the charge of complication being levelled at it – whereas in fact the organization is merely 'different' from Western ideas – in short, to grasp what totemism means, the effort should made to relate it to Western experience. To do so, a rough examination should be made of the principal distinctions between Christianity and totemism, and their consequences: Christianity recognizes one God Almighty, Maker of heaven and earth, according to a set dogma which does not necessarily conform to the material nature of the world. Totemism is not bound by a limited number of totems. It is wide open, for life can be found everywhere in nature. Its church, or rather its tribe or home, is the universe.

Christianity offers a new world, 'new heavens' and a 'new earth'. Thus there is a separation between the Church and the world. The Christian Church no more reflects the world than the world reflects the Church: 'My kingdom is not of this world'. Totemism is of this world. It seeks to perpetuate and relate to life. Society is so organized, founded on the family and the clan, as to reflect the cosmic order.

Christianity is personalized. It believes in the salvation of the individual through faith. Totemism sees man as a fragment of nature: human, animal, vegetable and mineral matter are part of one and the same life. Men and things are not separated, or, perhaps, may be regarded as equally possessing a soul.

For Christianity, the life of humanity moves forward along a line starting with the original sin and ending with the Second Coming. Beyond that time limit there is no salvation. So man must work for his salvation during the whole of his earthly existence. For him it is all decided during his brief stay on earth; afterwards it will be too late. This line of time has a complete and irreversible break between past, present and future, between life and death. With totemism life is all one: the daily flow between the various facets of life is continuous: past, present, future, the world of the living and the world of the dead all merge.

It is hard to conceive what syncretism could fuse such

Australians resort to music and dancing to act out events or precepts passed on by word of mouth from myths. Above: a dance by painted men imitating the love parade of the crane. Below: Inhabitants of the McDonnell Ranges solemnly reciting the sacred chants which precede the totemic ceremony of the serpent.

Taken in about 1935, this photograph shows people of North Australia in ceremonial dress behind their totem pole. The designs on this are repeated at the top of the participant's head-dress.

opposing systems into a homogenous whole. Currently it is possible to detect a double life among many tribes, the official and the clandestine. Official life takes place generally in western languages. Marriage ceremonies, funerals, are first held in church, then in secret, or rather in private, far from the eyes of the whites, in traditional form. In the most 'culture-affected' and even bi-cultural places, where the chiefs have gone to perfect their knowledge to schools and universities, a double layer of contradictory beliefs is noticeable, which frequently upsets and puzzles people.

Admittedly reducing Christianity to a monotheistic, personalized, speculative religion with a conception of linear time does not offer a complete picture; furthermore the West is not just Christian. But the aim is to outline a general framework, no matter how summary. It has been said that 'Mystery is the religion of others'. Before attempting to understand the magic of Oceania it will be useful to recall the main features of western mysticism. This holds that God triumphs over nature and man has only the few decades of his life on earth to earn his salvation. In Oceanian beliefs, the world is a place where gods and men, visible and invisible creatures, live in harmony. The West is concerned with overcoming 'self' and triumphing over nature, Oceania with respecting life.

And such respect shall be paid as much to evil 'gods' as to good 'gods'. The difference between good and evil has but little meaning. Thus a converted tribe referred to the God of Christianity by a word which in the vernacular means a devil. Yet this god was deeply respected: the idea was to see that he was satisfied and left the people in peace. There is no notion of sin, just a notion of error, of an inadequate attitude. There lies a fundamental difference between Western and Oceanian thinking; it is possible to talk of Western ideas as a civilization of guilt and Oceanian as a civilization of shame.

In the civilization of guilt, when a sin has been committed, the sinner feels overcome by his own remorse and feels guilty towards himself; in the civilization of shame, when an error has been committed, an inadequate action performed, or a wrongful gesture made, the trangressor will not show himself, he is ashamed before the other members of the clan whose harmony has thereby been disturbed, however slightly.

For the Oceanian, the world holds its own harmony within itself and its ultimate meaning, whereas Western man is for ever trying to move ahead, either mystically, through religion, or physically, in a world which he only sees as a means of assuring his own survival, that is to say of satisfying his own ego, of possessing more, and not of being.

Totemic civilization has virtually disappeared in Polynesia, but there are still slight traces of a certain original ethic. Governor Deschamps recently said of the Tahitian: 'Social rules hardly bind him any longer because his traditional society has vanished and has only been replaced by Christianity to a limited extent. Of his heritage and unity he still retains a certain sense of what is permissible and what causes shame (*mea hoama*). It is a rather strange cocktail: he

Tahitian dances

The young girls when ever they can collect 8 or 10 together dance a very indecent dance which they call *Timorodee* singing most indecent songs and useing most indecent actions in the pratice of which they are brought up from their earlyest Childhood, in doing this they keep time to a great nicety; this exercise is however generaly left of as soon as they arrive at years of maturity for as soon as they have form'd a connection with man they are expected to leave of dancing *Timorodee*.

*The Journals of Capt. James Cook or his voyages of discovery,* ed. by J. C. Beaglehole, Cambridge, 1955

These young Polynesian girls (1777) look more like Mayfair ladies than Tahitian dancers. It is due to the early explorers' ethnocentrism and excessive prudishness. It is enough to compare this scene with the photographs on the following page. The dress is surmounted by a farthingale while the breasts are decorated with shells and tufts of feather. The headdress is made of *tamau* tresses or human hair.

Music in Tahiti

Their only musical instruments are flutes and drums; the flutes are made of a hollow bamboo about a foot long, and, as has been observed before, have only two stops, and consequently but four notes, out of which they seem hitherto to have formed but one tune; to these stops they apply the fore finger of the left hand and the middle finger of the right.

The drum is made of a hollow block of wood, of a cylindrical form, solid at one end, and covered at the other with shark's skin: these they beat not with sticks, but their hands; and they know how to tune two drums of different notes into concord. They have also an expedient to bring the flutes that play together into unison, which is to roll up a leaf so as to slip over the end of the shortest, like our sliding tubes for telescopes, which they move up or down till the purpose is answered, of which they seem to judge by their ear with great nicety.

To these instruments they sing; and, as I have observed before, their songs are often extempore: they call every two verses or couplet a song, *Pehay*; they are generally, though not always, in rhime; and when pronounced by the natives, we could discover that they were metre.

J. HAWKESWORTH, *Lieutenant Cook's Voyage Round the World,* London 1773, pp. 204-205.

Festivities were frequent. Among dancers on the high plateaux of Papua-New Guinea masquerading played an important part. They might adopt mud masks like the dancers on the left, or paint their faces like these performers at a sing-sing in the 1970s, wearing wigs and birds of paradise feathers. These plays were of educational nature: the object was to commemorate through miming scenes in which the heroes created the world, being sometimes men and sometimes animals, or both at the same time. The actors reproduce the actions and gestures of the ancestral hero who presided over the creation.

Left: This performer of the Small Nambas (*nambas* means the penis covering) on Mallicolo Island (New Hebrides) has daubed his body with soot or earth. He wears a bright twin-faced mask and is adorned with flowers, leaves and feathers.

The shape of this mask, with its nose shaped like a snout, is typical of middle Sepik (northern Papua-New Guinea). The hand drum from the area of Lake Sentani (northern Indonesian New Guinea) provides the rhythm for ceremonial dances and for sending out messages. Below: Maoris brandishing paddles in front of their pah during a war dance (New Zealand 1846).

Young Maoris used to enjoy playing *volador*, as seen in the 1846 drawing by George Angas (left). It is a kind of huge supple mast with a number of ropes set up beside the sea so that participants can swing round it and jump into the water. Right: a picture of a similar game carved on bamboo by a New Caledonian artist.

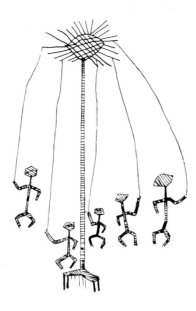

In this Hawaiian game, seen by Freycinet in August 1819, adversaries stand forehead to forehead with their feet touching, and push themselves upright without using their hands. Moving their feet backwards, they keep this up until the first one to lose his balance is defeated.

noticeable in the Society Islands when they departed in their long canoes to build their *marae* everywhere, those temples or sacred places destined for their gods. The Ariki imposed those new gods, on whom their power rested, by means of bloody battles in the course of which whole tribes were decimated. Such was the case of the proud Mangaïa tribe on Cook Islands, who remained loyal to the god Tané and refused to worship Oro, the latest of the Polynesian gods.

## Ancestors and totems

In Oceania ancestor worship is pre-eminent in what is rightly or wrongly called totemism today. The connection between ancestors and totems is not very clearly discernible, but the conflict between totems and gods is fierce. In the same way it is impossible, properly speaking, to determine the separation between feelings for ancestors and feelings for totems. A totem will be addressed affectionately in such terms as 'elder brother' or 'grandfather', and ancient legend recalls many an occasion of that elder brother or grandfather, the totem, coming to the assistance of a man of his own blood. Once help has been given, the totem 'leaves and returns peacefully from whence it came, leaving the man the totem assisted to continue with his job without worry'.

A totem is just simply there with a man throughout his life; he is joined to it by a kind of affectionate family relationship without in any way looking upon it as an object of worship. The totem gives life, and remains the loyal companion while always enjoying the same respect.

In Australia totemism first came to Western attention through the works of Spencer and Gillen, and it was later studied by Elkin. He distinguished between various forms of totemism; individual, sexual, shared (meaning dividing the tribe in two groups by a formula of family relationship and descent, either paternal or maternal), sectional and sub-sectional totemism, local, clan and finally multiple totemism.

Elkin concluded that a totemised man, if the term may be permitted, is one who 'is at home with nature' and 'sees to it that nature is at home in his organization of society'. It would be interesting to define that wide-ranging word 'nature' in order to find out whether 'totemised' man, the *homo sapiens* of the stone age, can organize his life among societies living on another level of civilization. In the opinion of the author, it seems that this question can be answered in the affirmative. Elkin shows this clearly, when he says: 'One has a feeling that a kind of link exists between man and the whole range of species and objects in nature; everything on earth and in the heavens, including man, is distributed in halves, in clans, cultural groups or sections. Totemism thus becomes a system for classifying natural phenomena owing to its integrating them into man's social and cultural groups, thanks to the principle that the life of nature and the life of man are one', and, 'strange as it may seem to us... lightning and thunder, rain, clouds, hail and winter are crow, the moon and stars are black cockatoo...'.

In other words, in contrast to our Western society, the various classes of totemic civilizations do not serve to establish any hierarchy since the crow is not more highly esteemed than thunder, nor the moon than the cockatoo. Further, the silvery moon may be distinct from the cockatoo, but is not separated from it any more than lightning is from the crow. It can be understood that such classifications help to unify and not to separate.

So what really counts is the relationship between terms, and not the terms themselves. This makes it possible to build up very stable societies where men do not live apart, isolated, but where, as Elkin says, 'totemism acts as a sort of hyphen between everyday social life and the life secret and mythical', that secret life which will be revealed forcibly and in the same way to all the tribe's children at their initiation.

Each line may be descended from one ancestor, but it is the totem which guarantees their life. There are many islands where whole clans claim descent from the same totem. More often than not it may be an animal to which a woman gave herself, or simply a fruit or a tree from which they are all descended.

This explains why we find sculptures everywhere showing totem and ancestor significantly juxtaposed. We have seen how the New Caledonian habitation has the ancestor carved over the lintel of the door and again over the geometric designs of door-frames, watching those who enter. In front of the door will be a pole representing the bones of the dead, surrounded with live flowers. On the top of the house is placed the totem. It should be noted that the design of the door-frames is not unrelated to the carved trunks of Australia. The same meanings are often found widely distributed.

The carvings erected in New Zealand in memory of ancestors are more historical representations than in New Caledonia. Likewise in New Guinea and the New Hebrides the artist tries to make the carved skull look like the dead man, but what is more important is that is denotes the presence of the dead among the living, rather than having any great resemblance to any particular individual.

Totem and ancestor remain united everywhere in one and the same life. The same is not true of the 'gods': the conflict between 'gods' and 'totems' is the fight between power and life, between life and the proud striving for prestige, for 'progress' which ignores respect for life and tramples on anything standing in the way of personal achievement. Politics are more or less connected with certain gods, and men lose confidence in them if the political project is not successful... unless of course it is not the god's fault but that of some man. But the totem stays well outside the temporal problems of victory or success. To it belongs life in its deepest unity, so that sentimentally it is not really disassociated from the ancestors but remains separated from the gods.

All this takes effect at the level of the family and dwelling-place. With regard to the habitation, we have already observed the making of the big house erected on a mound, the *moaro*. Each member of the clan harks back to that *moaro* and identifies himself as belonging to this or that *moaro*. All political life revolved around the *moaro* and its big house with lofty or pointed roof, beneath which only the men

## Tahitian Wrestling

After we had sat here some time a Message was brought to the Chief who immidiatly went out of the Boat and we were disired to follow and were conducted to a large Area or Courtyard on one side of his Long House where we were entertaind with publick Wrestling. Tootaha seated himself at one end of the place and several of his principal men sat round him in a semicircle, We were desired to sit down here likewise but we rather choose to walk about. Every thing being now ready several men enter'd the Theater, 8, 10, or 12 and some times more, these walked about in a Stooping dancing posture forming a large Corve with their arms and almost every moment app[l]ying their left arm bent near their bodys and with their right hand open struck with a smack their left fore arm [and] breast, in this Manner they walk'd about untill one challenge'd a nother which was done by motion and gesture without speaking one word. The Two antagonist[s] would then meat and endeavour to seize each other by the thighs, but if that faild they would seize each other by the hair of the head or where ever they could and then wristle together untill by main Strength the one or the other was thrown on his Back, this was always (except once) follow'd by three hurras from some old men who sat in the house and at the same time a nother compney of men would dance for about a Minute, the wrestlers all the time continuing their game without takeing the least Notice of any thing else. The only dexterity the wrestlers seem'd to make use of was in first seizing each other for after they had close'd it was all decided by main Strength. It would sometimes happen that neither the one nor the other could throw his antagonist, in this case they would either part by mutal consent or were parted by others. The conqueror never exulted over the Conquer'd, neither did the Conquer'd ever repine at his ill luck, but the whole was carried on with great good humour.

*The Journals of Capt. James Cook or his voyages of discovery* (First Voyage) ed. by J. C. Beaglehole, Cambridge 1955, p. 90-91 (1769)

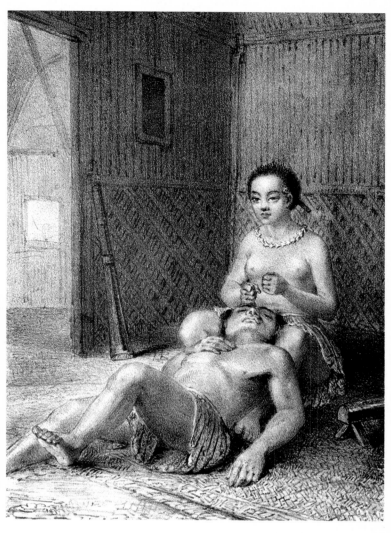

The islanders generally gave Cook a warm welcome, as shown in this picture (above, left) of the boxing match given in his honour on 17 May 1977 by the chief of Hapai Island in the Tongas, and the impressive feast (below) given 2-14 May 1977 at Nomuka in the same archipelago. That welcome earned the archipelago its name of Friendly Islands. Above, right: Dumont d'Urville was struck by the langourous love life of the Hapia royal family in the Samoans (1838) and generally by the easy ways of the Polynesians.

Left-hand page: A long avenue of ancestor images, several yards tall, stood in front of the entrance to the house for men, or *tambaran ambunti,* in the Sepik (Papua-New Guinea).

These cathedrals made of bark (Maprik, Papua-New Guinea), right, may be as much as 72 ft tall. The facing is of bark and pandanus leaf dyed with ochre. On the front are paintings of effigies of the spirits, each bearing a name and a replica inside, in the form of a statue or cast.

Cook brought back this Maori club (*kotiate*) made of whalebone. The slashes on the side were decorated with feathers to distract the adversary's attention. Below: Opulu (Samoa) inhabitants armed with assegais and clubs attacking Dumont d'Urville's men in 1838. The Samoans are using large canoes with open ends, some equipped with sails and some without.

A fight between two canoes, Louisiade Archipelago (Melanesia)

The natives in the canoes had pointed at two other canoes paddling out from two different islands towards each other. They made it very clear that they were going to attack one another and that the winners in one canoe would slaughter everyone they caught in the other canoe and eat them. They left no doubts about their intentions and showed signs of greatest joy, as though they would be partaking in a banquet. The two canoes did indeed accost each other a few minutes later: The opposing crews stood up in the bottom of their canoes, holding stones in one hand and a shield in the other. Stones flew through the air for five or ten minutes, aimed with great skill and force. Then, either because the results were not decisive or because they had resorted to reconciliation, the two canoes finally separated and made their ways home to their respective islands.

ROSSEL, *Voyage d'Entrecasteaux,* Paris 1808, pp. 421-422 (June 1793)

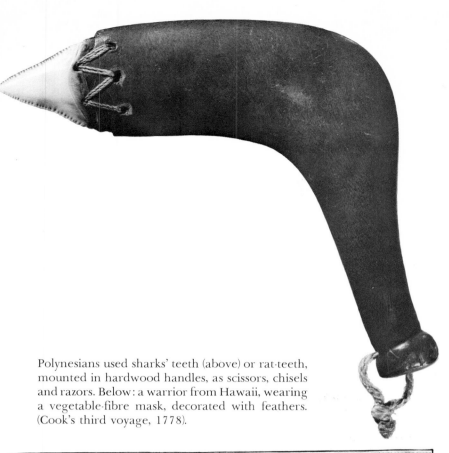

Polynesians used sharks' teeth (above) or rat-teeth, mounted in hardwood handles, as scissors, chisels and razors. Below: a warrior from Hawaii, wearing a vegetable-fibre mask, decorated with feathers. (Cook's third voyage, 1778).

could gather. The central post, the *rhea*, supported the house as a symbol of the clan's unity. When several clans gathered together, they built and inaugurated at a joint festivity, in which they proclaimed the name of each *moaro*, a house with a *rhea* or central post for each family; the huge mass of *rheas* placed next to each other held up a slender dome with a light thatched roof symbolizing the strength of sworn alliances.

As translation of the word clan, Maurice Leenhardt's French-Ajiè dictionary – Ajiè is the language spoken on the east coast of New Caledonia – offers three local alternatives: *moaro, perene, ba*.

We have just seen how the word *moaro* encompasses all the stones forming the base of the big house, and by extension, all the members of the clan, members of one and the same *moaro*.

*Perene* refers to the genealogical origin, to all the descendants of a single ancestor. It is the shell, the gourd, the hard and shiny surface of a hollow reed; it is an ancestral object, tree, rock or totemic stone.

Finally *ba* means the crowd.

Thus for that single word 'clan' we have three levels of different relationships.

Within the clan, marriage is exogamic and husband and wife thus have separate totems, and it is the wife whose totem is taken over.

The mother passes on her totem to her children, in other words gives them her name, but hers is not the ultimate authority in the family. She obeys her husband.

The child is of its mother's blood. A group of mothers forms a maternal clan which embraces not only the mothers but the brothers, descended from the mother's brothers. But their spokesman is not the mother but a male representative, the *kanya*, the mother's brother. Like the mother, the uncle refers to the new-born child as 'life of my blood'. The father represents, as it were, the brother, in the Melanesian sense of the word; he merely calls the child modestly *moru* ('life'), for the child does not belong to him but to the maternal line represented by the *kanya*. So the term *moru* must not be interpreted in its organic meaning but in the generic meaning of the life of the clan. *Go moru* 'I am alive, I am in complete safety, I feel well, I lack nothing', in other words 'I am at one with my totem, with my life'.

As to the term 'life of my blood' (*moru wara xynia*), that refers to the continuity of the maternal blood flowing back and forth from one clan to another. It denotes a dynamism in the life of the group among the descendants from both maternal and paternal sides. In case of accident or death of a child, the maternal relatives can come and claim the blood due to them; if they fail to obtain satisfaction they may sack the whole village. Some whites have witnessed acts of vandalism and brutality which were really only facets of a different form of social justice.

The child will call 'mother' not only its actual mother but its aunts, her sisters; similarly it will call 'father' its uncles who are its real father's brothers. Consequently, for the

125

child all children of its 'fathers' and 'mothers' will be its 'brothers' or 'sisters'. The same holds good today when Oceanians invariably speak a language which is not their mother tongue but that of the colonizer. But the term 'maternal uncle' used by ethnologists has not penetrated their language. However, the author has often heard Melanesians talk of their 'father-in-law' in French when referring to their maternal uncle. It is not known whether the term has become generalized, but it is worth noting that ancient China had one and the same word for the mother's brother and the father-in-law.

Melanesian totemic society is based on family relationship: a child bears the name of its mothers' totem. It is the matriarchal line of descent. Although the terms is unsuitable to a society which has no 'property' in the Western meaning of the word, a child is also said to 'inherit' from its maternal uncle. That means it inherits his totem, his *tapa* and all 'his personal belongings'. This is the equivalent of paternal authority, *patria potestas,* which thus becomes split in two. The father plays the part of the everyday source of authority, since the child lives on the same land as he, while the maternal uncle, living further away in the village from which his sister departed to her husband's village, will only have a say on important occasions. For that reason when a child is born, say among Kanakas in Grande Terre (New Caledonia), a messenger is at once despatched to inform the maternal clan, bearing gifts and a fine coin of pearls for the *kanya* and announcing the child's birth in the following terms: 'He has appeared here thanks to you. It is you who permitted him to come and who gave him, you, his maternal uncles'.

Does that mean that the biological father is of no account? Far from it. He represents the paternal clan, the line of power and is hence aware of his responsibility for the child's safe arrival. But after she has been made pregnant by the husband, the wife can be seen wandering in places where the ancestral spirits might be found, in the woods, by the sea; another force is still required to enter the child's body, an ancestor, or a totem, to help it acquire human shape during the ensuing nine months.

And that totem or ancestor represents the line of life of the maternal line. A father may love his son, but the coming of a nephew through his sister will be of great importance to him, as the nephew will contain his mother's blood and become his 'heir'. So it is easy to understand why the messenger sent by the father of a new-born child to inform the *kanya* comes loaded with gifts and words of gratitude: only the *kanya* can represent the life of the new-born.

That is why those societies have been referred to as matriarchates, whereas in fact women are far from exercising the real authority since it is the paternal clan which represents power. Surely it would be simpler to refer to them as totemic societies, for, as now becomes apparant, totemism can only exist in societies where the family is the clan. In a totemic civilization every family nucleus, father, mother, child, represents both the line of life and the line of power, i.e. the whole world. The biological father, the paternal clan,

Maori fortifications

This Village is built upon a high promontory or point on the north side and near the head of the Bay. It is in some places quite inaccessible to man and in others very difficult except on that side which face'd the narrow ridge of the hill on which it stands, here it is defended by a double ditch a bank and two rows of Picketing—the inner row upon the bank but not so near the Crown but what there was good room for men to walk and handle their arms between the Picketing and the inner ditch: the outer Picketing was between the two ditches and laid slooping with their upper ends hanging over the inner ditch, the depth of this ditch from the bottom to the Crown of the bank was [24] feet. Close within the inner picketing was erre[c]ted the strong posts, a stage [30] feet high [40] in length and 6 feet broad, the use of this stage was to stand upon to throw darts at the Assailants, and a number of darts lay upon it for that purpose. At right Angles to this and a few paces from it was a nother of the same construction and bigness, this stood likewise within the Picketing and was intended for the same use as the other, viz. to stand upon to throw stones and darts upon the Enimy as they advanced up the side of the hill where lay the main way into the place; it likewise might be intend[ed] to defend some little outwoorks and hutts that lay at the (...) and this side of the hill, these out-woorks were not intended as advanced Posts but for such of the Inhabitents to live in as had no room in the main work but had taken shelter under it. Besides the works on the land side above described the whole Village was pallisaded round with a line of pretty strong picketing run round the edge of the hill. The ground within having not been level at first but did slooping, they had divided it into little squares and leveled each of these; these squares lay in the form of an amphitheatre and were each of them pallisaded round and had a comunication one with a another by narrow lanes or little gate ways which could easily be stoped up, so that if any enimy had force'd the outer picketing he had several others to incounter before the place could be wholy reduced, supposing them to defend every one of the places one after another. The Main way leading into this fortification was up a very steep part of the hill and thro' a narrow passage about 12 feet long, and under one of the Stages; I saw no door or gate but it might very soon have ben barricaded up. Upon the whole I looked up[on] it to be a very strong and well choose post and where a small number of resolute men might defend them selves a long time against a vast superior force, Arm'd in the manner as these people are. These seem'd to be prepared against a siege having laid up in store an immence quantity of firm roots and a good many dry'd fish.

*The Journals of Capt. James Cook or his voyages of discovery* (First Voyage), ed. by J. C. Beaglehole, Cambridge 1955, p. 198-199 (1769)

Right: a scene witnessed and described by Dumont d'Urville: chief Bouni-Bouni of New Guinea offers his fiancée the heads of his rivals, as a wedding present. Before the birth of a child the father presents the future mother the skull of an enemy, whose name will be given to the baby. Below: Cook and his companions were much impressed by this fortified village on a vaulted rock at Tolaga (New Zealand) on their first voyage.

This warrior from the Gulf of Papua (eastern New Guinea) is bearing a 38 in high shield for ceremonial purposes. As may be seen, it does not protect the arm.

represents what Western people regard as the real family, the blood family.

The *kanya* hands over some money as his counter-gift and thanks the paternal clan: 'I receive your news. I receive your food, yams and taros, eels and fish...' and whispers the *Rhevana*, the totem-in-force, into his nephew's ear:

'May his spirit be blessed and his totem be tall, may he perform all the natural functions, may his ears be keen, his eyes bright and sharp, his limbs powerful, and may his breath be exalted by his fathers and grandfathers who gave it to him by virtue of the word which passes back and forth as the tide ebbs and flows, in the clan of his maternal uncles'.

This intimate celebration of birth sometimes, when there are a number of children, gives way to one of those great ceremonies around which the entire totemic life is centred and which are today known in New Caledonia as *pilous* or *pilou-pilous*. This is the whites' onomatopaeic name for it, because of the rythmic hammering noise of feet on the soil where the *karo* is erected, that carved post around which the dancing takes place. Everyone's life is studded with *pilous*, a *pilou* at birth, an initiation *pilou*, others for weddings and mourning. The aim on each such occasion is to propitiate the ancestors on the maternal side and especially to tighten and strenghten the bonds at every critical stage of life between members of the maternal and paternal clans, alive and dead.

Melanesia has other very different customs, like those of the Marind-Anims of the west coast of Papua-New Guinea, north of the Torres Straits. As can be seen from the grotesque drawings by a western artist on page 127, there the father has to go to war before his child is born, and bring the future mother back a skull from some slaughtered enemy, so that the child can bear the latter's same. The breath of life is not enough to ensure the arrival of a new man into the world of the living. It must also be provided with a personality, usually that of an ancestor. And there, as in the Massims' country, they do not possess masks to represent their ancestors.

In some parts of the same archipelago the child must touch the beaten earthen floor of the family hut the moment it is born, thereby entering in contact with the soil, as was apparently performed in ancient times throughout Australasia and in ancient China. In other parts they also observe the so-called 'manchildbed ceremony'. In the north of Grande Terre, if a mother has any difficulty with the delivery, the men begin a non-stop dance to give her the energy needed to bring the child to birth successfully. Customs seem to vary between places which may not be very far apart, but if they are examined carefully, the idea is always found to be the same: to maintain the continuity of the life of the clan, to provide each child with spiritual potential from the moment it is born, with a shadow protector. To digress for a moment, it should be noted that New Zealand Maoris have their priest pronounce a benediction over the new-born, while in the rest of Polynesia abortion and infanticide were common customs. It was preferable to get rid of girls, but children of either sex would be smothered to death at birth if social or religious requirements called for an infanticide, as was the case in Tahiti during the god Oro's period of influence.

The life of the newly born man evolved in constant interchange between three currents of influence, as he belonged, in Western terms, to three communities: his family by marriage, the paternal relation in the village where he lived; his blood family, the maternal relations living in the area the mother came from, which might be confused with his totem family if they had the same totem; and the totem family representing his own life, plant, animal, stone or element such as the wind, thunder or the rain drop.

Each of these families will give him special protection and will expect him to fulfill specific duties to them. He must never eat his totemic animal except in certain well-defined circumstances. He must in case of need provide assistance to that animal and to all his maternal relations sharing the same totem. In Grande Terre he must learn from his earliest youth to look towards his maternal relations living far away in that other village in an area which he does not yet know but which his mother teaches him to love because that is where, among his maternal folk, a woman will be waiting for him when the time comes for him to marry.

For that reason, when a young Melanesian calls a girl by the name of her totem, it is said with a due sense of its seriousness. It is the equivalent of a marriage proposal since he is thereby invoking the name of the totem which will be his children's.

The child first grows up in the women's hut, cherished as much by his brothers as by his mothers, as well as by his fathers who feel they should play with him and surround him with love and affection. Such tenderness is displayed quite naturally and unrestrainedly, as though it were quite natural for every member of the clan to share the mother's feelings for the child. But he will be in the company of others of his age. As soon as he is weaned he leaves the net in which his mother carries him around wherever she goes, and begins to play with other children, to fish for shells, pick fruit and perform various manual tasks.

His liberty is subject to no threats or reproaches, but if he does not behave properly he will be laughed at and covered with shame. Education will come to him through laughter and comic plays showing him how to behave. Sarcasm will not be used to upset him, but the others will be constantly putting him in his place. He will be challenged, teased, and helped. Mutual assistance, or feeling for neighbours, is always present, even when challenges or jokes are involved. The object is not to dominate or exercise authority by forcing him to obey, but to bring him up in the image of the clan and make a 'real man' of him so as to preserve the eternity of the clan, and therefore of the world.

As he grows up the boy will soon start to imitate his elder brothers and his fathers. Then comes the crucial moment for his initiation, when he will stop running around naked, and will be clothed, as it were, in the spirit of his ancestors.

It is always difficult to discuss matters which are only known from the outside, western observers having such little knowledge of their beauty. But the subject of the initiation must be approached, however awkwardly, as it has very deep significance. In so doing an awareness of our ignorance and lack of perception must remain. All unhealthy curiosity or exotic inquisitiveness should be stifled, and racial feelings of superiority towards those differences, which are fed on details and anecdotes which are not fully understood, should be repressed.

What do whites know about initiation? Mostly what Spencer and Gillen described about initiations in Australia. The Larakias went in for administering heavy blows at random, the Urabumas made the novice lie down and hit him fiercely before slashing his back symmetrically on both sides of his spine; young Aruntas are made to lie on a bed of leaves spread over glowing embers. The idea behind all this pain is to change the nature of the adolescent, make him virile and purify him. Is this in some way the equivalent of Western tradition and the belief held by some of the part played by military service in helping form the character of young men? It should be noted that these endurance tests may sometimes be harsh, but they are never repressive. The idea is not to teach the youth obedience but to make him worthy of the continuing ancestral tradition. Likewise, there is a basic difference with Western ways of attaining manhood in that in Melanesia everyone acquires the same knowledge when they are initiated.

There is no specific age for initiation. Its forms differ substantially from area to area, but it usually takes place at the time of adolescence. The child will then be given his secret name, meaning his place, which makes those societies very united. In Polynesia it is different. There a caste system has taken over from the old civilization. Initiation is reserved for priests and children of royal families. Initiation has lost the profound meaning there that it has in Melanesia, and which the Melanesians keep secret. This is true of initiation for young men or initiation in several steps and throughout life, as is the case in the New Hebrides, especially at Malikula, where the novice carves a statue at each new step and hands round large quantities of food. Initiation, or knowledge, can thus only be acquired through personal sacrifice. He then becomes an *ambat-meleum*, blessed with a wisdom which destroys all fear of the forces of nature.

In addition to these initiations which help a man progress, there are others, such as those of very advanced nature reserved for those who fortify men spiritually, known to white Australians as medicine men, the wise men of Australia. Spiritual healers and mediums in touch with the Rainbow Serpent, with mother-of-pearl shells and shining quartz, theirs is a particularly important rôle; they must watch over the health and psychological balance of society and of each of its members.

It is they who restore sanity to the group in times of panic caused by the death of a loved one and the troubles which arise when the deceased is no longer there to carry on with his tasks within the family or society. Socially, death cannot be regarded as a natural phenomenon. It may sometimes be regarded as a failure to devote enough care to the person who has left the group. Or someone may have been to blame, may have wanted to be rid of the person who has just died. The guilty person may have acted through a sorcerer, using the magic of the pointed bone cast in the direction of the individual whose death was desired, or some other form of magic. But it should be noted that such black magic is seldom resorted to as it might well turn against the person who employed it.

When the funeral is over the guilty party has to be found, the mistake sought, the lack of attention faced, even possibly the guilt of being responsible for the death. Everyone works hard at trying to find the answer, particularly anyone harbouring any special ill feelings. So an enquiry has to be held, conducted with tact and skill and close knowledge of any jealousies or troubles between the men of the area. If the medicine man declares anyone guilty, meaning responsible for the death, which Westerners would describe as a natural death, that man will himself be put to death. But often no ill feelings can be traced within the group, or they may exist but can be cured, for instance by the guilty party's tribe sending one of its sons to be initiated within the tribe of the dead person − in a word, if the medicine man's enquiries fail to produce a guilty party, on such occasions it is conclued that the dead man must have disobeyed some taboo and died for it. The society's ethics become strengthened thereby and more closely united than ever.

To conclude, there is a correlation between the society and the forms which the initiation takes. In Polynesia, like everywhere else, it includes circumcision, ear piercing, and other forms, but the great ceremonies there are reserved to children of royal blood, who thus become set apart from the rest of the people.

## Initiation of boys in New Caledonia, New Guinea and Australia

Initiation has twin purposes: to test the novice's strength, agility and physical and mental powers, so as to help him attain a certain degree of independence; to teach him true knowledge.

The idea was, on becoming a man, to become familiar with various skills necessary to suport life. In classical Oceanian societies before the coming of the whites, this meant the arts of fishing, hunting, navigation, sculpture and the various social duties which a man might have to undertake.

But it was also necessary to learn the myths, ancestral history, relationships, legends and genealogies; in short, to learn Oceanian man's position in relation to his totems, ancestors and the dead. Maurice Leenhardt has described initiations on Grande Terre which are generally conducted when the first mangrove shoots begin to appear.

Before the time of his initiation, the child has run around freely in a village where relations between male and female vere clearly demonstrated around each dwelling. Vegetation was divided between dry and living plants; cordyline

A member of the *dukduk* secret society is seen surrounded by Melanesian warriors of New Ireland (Bismarck Archipelago) armed with lances and clubs. He can be recognized from his conical mask which covers the breast as well as the head. *Dukduks* symbolize the male spirit. Their society has a special house of worship.

War in Tahiti

Their methods of waging war are cruel indeed. According to what Aotourou told us, men and male children captured in combat are slaughtered. They peel the skin off their chins complete with beard and carry it as a trophy. Only women and girls are spared; the victors do not disdain to take them into their beds. Aotourou is himself the son of a Tahitian chief by a captive mother from Oopoa Island, a neighbouring island frequently hostile to Tahiti. To this mixture I attribute the difference which I noticed between the types of men. As to their wounds, I do not know how they treat them but our surgeons were very impressed with their scars.

LOUIS-ANTOINE DE BOUGAINVILLE, *Voyage autour du monde de la frégate* LA BOUDEUSE *et la flûte* L'ETOILE, Paris 1958 (orig. ed. Neuchâtel 1772)

In this duel between Australians (New South Wales), watched by Jacques Arago in 1839, each of the adversaries tries in turn to dodge his opponent's club.

stood for man while the soft pulpy wood of erythrina stood for woman, indicating at the entrance to the village what Leenhardt called 'the sex of each avenue'. Now the youth must get to know his place in the village.

As his two parents belong to two different totems, he must find his place in relation to his *kanya*, his maternal uncle, brother of his mother, and to his father and their respective totems and ancestors. In that classical dualism where the totem is represented by the maternal line (the female principle), and ancestors rather more by the paternal line (male principle), the novice has two representatives: on the one hand his *kanya*, through his mother, the *kanya's* sister, and on the other his father, for his future children who will belong to his wife's clan.

For some weeks he will no longer have been playing naked as previously. His grandmothers have put a little *bagayou* on him, a cloth of bark fibre called *tapa* wound round his penis and kept in place by a thin string round his waist.

The *bagayou* is like a Roman toga, only covering the penis instead of the shoulders. The two ends of the *tapa* cloth round his waist crossed in front and hung down in olden days, the length depending on his importance. When the first whites saw this covering, they described it discreetly as '*Caledonici cum tela aut fronte mentulam celant*'. Important chiefs wore the *bagayou* artistically draped in broad folds to make a train which might be 6-7 ft long. When a meeting took place with a marriage in view, they took off their clothing and each put on the other's. It was their seal of loyalty. There are similar customs on other islands. So the first time a novice wore a *bagayou* it had a real significance.

The initiation took place in some isolated spot located between a lake or a river, where the novices could bathe, and the cemetery, where the ancestors' skulls were kept. The place is marked by a pole, the *karoti*, barring the entrance.

Then came the day for superincision, not circumcision. That minor operation consists of cutting a buttonhole in the foreskin with a sharp piece of bamboo, and passing the male member through it. When the scar forms, the foreskin rolls back to form a circular growth which, being swollen at the bottom, will better hold the binding of the *bagayou*.

While the scar is healing the old women of the village bring the young patients their food. Once cured, and up to the day of the initiation *pilou*, the boys must not look on any woman. They must find their own food, and by night, as they must not be seen. But they stay in warm contact with the people of the village by drawing pictures on the ground of every fish and bird which they manage to catch. In the morning these proofs of their skill are noted with joy and admiration, and the mothers will be comforted by the knowledge that their isolated sons are all right. Finally, when they have recovered and successfully demonstrated their skill and knowledge, they plant in full view a pole decorated with balls made of leaves and crowned with a strip of balassor. The pole, called a *ti*, shows that their strength has returned and that they are ready to enter the world of men. At that point, some ten weeks after the operation, they

Left: In the Hawaiian isles a thief is sentenced to have his hand crushed. Behind him stands a warrior ready to execute him with his sword if he flinches. Below: a group of Maoris rubbing their noses in greeting. This ceremony (*ongi*) is observed in a number of Pacific islands and even as far away as North America.

The first contacts between Europeans and Australians often led to an exchange of gifts (opposite: Freycinet and his companions landing in Australia on 12 September 1818). It was more a form of introduction than a hope for gain, the humanitarian aspect being more important than the mercenary.

Below: Nuku-hiva (Marquesas) women dancing on board the *Zélée* (1838). In olden days Polynesians used to welcome visitors by boarding their ships singing and dancing.

wear their first real *bagayou,* put on by the mourners. These will have first piously cleaned the ancestors' skulls. Then they collect leaves like those put on the child's head when it is born and start by wrapping up 'that which the *bagayou* is supposed to contain'. After putting *bagayou* on each novice, they pull up the ends, cross them around the belt, tie them at the back and let their folds hang down to form a long train.

The *bagayou* draws attention the boys' virility rather than concealing it, and shows their strength which was exalted in wars waged with phallic-shaped bludgeons. Similarly, 'virility stones' serve a very different purpose to the aphrodisiac aims of graffiti on walls in Western countries. These stones have a special shape, with a round hole in the middle through which the warriors pass their assegais before going off to do battle. The edges of the hole are marked with parallel lines. Similar lines surround the forehead of the ancestor, whose effigy is carved on the window frames of the huts. They represent the strings of their sling, symbolising the sling itself. There is a whole symbolic lore to bring solace and encouragement, since it is the same force which animates the ancestor who watches over the living, their sling (or their assegais) and over the arm of the living man who throws the assegai.

The novices are now ready. From now on, and all through the *pilou* in which they will be taking part, they do not leave the side of the mourners.

Poles are next erected on the spot earmarked for the *pilou,* some to commemorate the dead, others to honour the 'new *bagayous*'. As Leenhardt wrote in his *Gens de la Grande Terre,* 'before offering a *pilou* to the maternal relations, all the obligations of the clan are grouped to be discharged at the same time, in order that everyone can enjoy the brilliance of the ceremony: a birth celebration, when there are gifts for the uterines; an initiation, when the young novices are presented; a funeral, to mark the separation from the deceased. The *pilou* will include political undertones calculated to promote harmony: speeches for or against the whites, and all concerns of interest to the community'.

When the *pilou* 'master of ceremonies' signals the arrival of the mourners, they come on followed by a line of the novices, each of them blowing on a conch. They receive enthusiastic applause; the cries of joy demonstrate the pride of the parents at finding their son has become a 'real man'.

As the parents belong to different clans, coins are exchanged between paternal and maternal relations, after which the novices start their dancing, waving a bouquet, the *poeti.* This bouquet of leaves is put together by the young folk of the paternal group who send it to the young people of the maternal group, thereby ensuring the friendship of the new generation or 'age class'. From that moment the novice is able to assume his righful place in the universe, which is represented by the complementary maternal and paternal totem groups. He will know how to behave correctly. Thanks to the part played by the mourners and the presence of the poles representing the ancestors the child has become part of society.

It appears that the deep purpose of the initiation is integration with the dead, with the ancestors, an essential prerequisite for human fertility. We are already familiar with the New Guinea dwelling places, and the importance of the *yen,* the house for men which is the centre for the community of the living and the dead. At the time of his initiation, the young lad is seated in the *yen,* leaning forward in an attitude of humility and holding the skull of a recently slaughtered foe against his penis.

This is the difficult moment when chilhood must be left behind and life must be faced if he is to become capable of assuming his responsibilities as a man within the community. The boy's elders are there to help him, but the women are not allowed to see him. As a matter of fact they only enter the men's house on very specific occasions like the consecration of a new *yen.* At such times the women dance around the huge cylinder composed of palm leaves piled six to ten feet high, and filled with a particularly delicious food, consisting of larvae like little white worms. The cylinder is the tree of life, the sago palm, identified with woman.

The child will stay in those solemn surroundings for a long time, without moving, surrounded by the living and the dead, and by the male and the female essences which pervade the *yen.*

After meditating for several days men and novice leave the *yen* and get into their canoes, to paddle out towards the setting sun, with the child, now 'growing older', curled tightly over the skull in a soft little bundle. Then the men throw the little living bundle with his skull into the sea.

After this immersion the novice can start his life as a man, as an Asmat. According to Adrian A. Gerbrands in his book *Wow-Ipits,* As-mat means 'us, the tree people'. The tree of life is the woman, and its fruit is identified with the skull. The people known crassly as 'head hunters' are merely bird-men on the look-out for fruit-skulls so that life may be perpetuated. They kill so that their children may become men.

The Mailus in the South-East of Papua-New Guinea have the same conception, as the one symbolising the birth of a child for the Marind-Anims and the initiation for the Asmats. In *Unknown New Guinea,* written by W. S. V. Saville, a missionary, for which Malinowski wrote the preface in 1925, we find descriptions of women waving branches by the shore as they wait for the return of the war canoes. When the warriors approach near enough to distinguish the widows of men who fell on an earlier expedition, they throw them heads taken from their defeated foes. Then the brother of each widow takes a head and decorates it. Novices, nominated by the chief, queue up behind each other with their feet apart, and the chief rolls the skulls between their legs. Chanting can be heard all through the night from the *dubu,* which the novices are allowed to enter with the warriors for the first time. Then their maternal uncle hands them their manly dress, died yellow and black, and makes them chew betel.

In other parts of Papua-New Guinea, a hole is dug inside the *tambaran* at the time of the initiation, and filled with water. Water drums are sunk into the water and beaten.

Extraction of one upper incisor is associated with the water totem among Australians. This ceremony was sketched by Jacques Arago during Dumont d'Urville's second expedition (1839).

Reproductions of the carvings on the wood of the drums are tattooed on the back of the novice. The tattoo shows the clan's identity marks in the novice's flesh. The lobe of his ear, and his nostrils, are then pierced. This permits him thereafter to wear all manner of ornament, while the mother-of-pearl which is inserted as decoration makes his eyes shine with particular brilliance. But the important thing at initiations where this custom is observed is that the nostrils should bleed copiously, so that from then on he should be free of his mother's blood and become wholly man, devoting himself solely to the social duties required of him. Finally the young novices are handed flutes, which neither children nor women may hear, for their music is taken to be the voice of the ancestors.

Through the flutes' music the novices come directly into contact with the world of the ancestors. The ancestor is still present in the dancing. He also appears carved on the stoppers of the lime gourds carried by the novices to hold their betel which is known to be a stimulant constantly used in Indonesia, giving so many old men scarlet mouths and black teeth. In Melanesia, it is mostly chewed in New Guinea. A betel leaf is dusted with lime powder made from roasted shells, and then chewed, together with betel nut and aromatic seeds. That is the purpose of those carved calabash lime gourds with spatulas made of bone or wood, the handle of which acts as a stopper.

Carving these stoppers is one the tests of skill which the novices have to pass. The group can thereby discover their future artists. Elisa Maillard pointed out to the author that some of those gourds have decagonal stalks emerging from a double wheel. Now it is easy to divide a circle by six or eight, but much more difficult to divide it by ten. Those beautiful rosettes with their ten branches tipped by a light scroll represent the cosmos itself.

Not far away, on the Solomon Islands, at the festival closing the initiation ceremonies the boys blow on huge horns which are believed to give forth the voices of the ancestors. The ancestor appears on the horns in the shape of two arms and a face which ends in a phallic shape. There are also rhombuses with the images of the dead engraved in enamel. In the New Hebrides some conches are likewise decorated with two heads and a face. Also worthy of note are the long flutes of Papua, sometimes associated with the crocodile totem, and drums in the shape of crocodiles.

So all through the initiation the ancestor will be present thanks to his carved effigies, his gestures reproduced in the dances, his voice heard in the music of the various instruments described above, and finally at the closing banquet there will be his flesh.

Once initiated, the boy can meet his future wife. Young Papuan boys and girls in New Guinea receive their amorous education during the *kanaka,* which are vigils where boys and girls embrace and sing beautiful poems of love under the watchful eye of some matron who sees to their changing partners at appropriate times. Later the boy will get married and acquire more and more responsibilities within the clan until, if he is qualified, he joins the group of wise men, the

Above: two flowers growing in New Guinea, a calliandra (left), a leguminous relative of the pea, and a *strelitza reginae* above. Opposite, left: an hibiscus flower or tropical hollyhock. Right: one of the thousands of species of arborescent fern, the cyathea of the Forest of Koghi (west coast of New Guinea). Below: Australia's red-flowered resinous eucalyptus can grow up to 500 ft high.

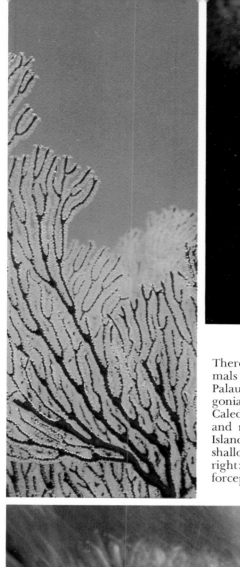

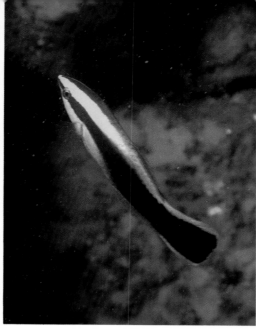

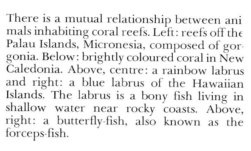

There is a mutual relationship between animals inhabiting coral reefs. Left: reefs off the Palau Islands, Micronesia, composed of gorgonia. Below: brightly coloured coral in New Caledonia. Above, centre: a rainbow labrus and right: a blue labrus of the Hawaiian Islands. The labrus is a bony fish living in shallow water near rocky coasts. Above, right: a butterfly-fish, also known as the forceps-fish.

elders. Gradually old age creeps on, that half-life, half-death where grandfather and grandson form a pair of brothers, as in New Caledonia, or bear the same name, as in Australia, until finally the old man crosses from 'this side' of life to 'the other side'. The dead man's flesh will rot away, leaving behind the world of the living, but his skull and bones will be preserved and his spirit will go to join the ancestors.

In Polynesia the Ariki believe they come from a legendary land called Hawaiiki, and men will return to that home of their ancestors when they die. In some places the bodies were put in boats to be carried away by the currents of the sea back to Hawaiiki. In Tahiti 'common people', according to Ellis, were buried sitting up, with bandages round their bodies and their knees bent, on the day after they died, but 'the chiefs' bodies were embalmed and kept for months in temporary shelters' – in former times they would be kept in the home on a kind of platform. When the body has completely decomposed the bones were buried within the *marae*, but the skull was detached and hung up from the roof of the family home. Indeed the *mana* resides in the head and the son will inherit it, so it must be kept nearby. Hence the importance attached to the hair in those countries. Elsewhere, when a body was embalmed, a hole would be carefully dug for burying the faults of the dead in it. The priest then placed a bouquet near the body, saying 'There is your family! Here is your mother! Here is your wife! Here is your father! Here is your mother! Be happy over there. Look not back at those who have stayed behind in this world'.

In Australia the spirit of the dead would go home to his *churinga,* that sanctuary of the souls, until a new mother could be found in whose belly he might enter and be reincarnated.

Initiation is possibly hardest in Australia, the trials of endurance going as far as to eliminate the weakest. In that arid land, its centre a vast desert, the long marches which the novices had to undertake must have been exhausting when no water could be found. The families could follow their progress from afar thanks to their fires. What hope of finding game, fish, caterpillars, birds when the water kept receding, water-holes drying up more and more until, as often happened, they vanished altogether?

It is vital for Australians to have access to a water-hole, and tribes on the move go from water-hole to water-hole and not from camp site to camp site. The importance of these water-holes may help to explain a custom which was described by explorers in detail yet with remarkable lack of comprehension: removing a tooth.

Across the endless dunes of the Simpson desert this custom is compulsory among the Arandas, the totem of whose territory is water. Only rain and water clans observe the custom which makes its initiates look like their totem with a gap for the missing tooth, like a cloud presaging rain. On pulling out the tooth, an upper incisor, the owner displays it to all present and then throws it with a shout in the direction of the mothers' ancestral camp. When this is done a girl, she takes up her *pitchi,* a basket of bark which she will later use for carrying her baby, fills it with sand and shakes it as though winnowing. This is a symbol of the motion she will later have to carry out daily for sorting out what she picks to feed her family. The *pitchi* is a kind of scoop-shaped dish. It is used alike for rocking babies, holding grain, carrying water and any domestic task. It is the Australian woman's main utensil.

This custom is associated with water-holes, and involves women more often than men. The rites differ from place to place: the Warramungas make their girls go into the water, fill their mouths and spit the water out all around. The broken tooth is crushed and mixed with meat which the mother has to eat.

Boys' initiations in Australia are performed in stages. Each stage has its own name by which the novice is called all through his trials. The ceremonials differ according to place across the huge continent, but they follow the same general lines. The initiation starts with a sort of kidnapping. Some men, messengers, come and seize the boy in his own camp. Although the father knows all about it and himself fixes the time for the kidnapping, he puts up a show of fierce resistance for as long as possible as though unwilling to let the child go from his family. There are cries and shows of grief at the coming separation, the women throw their assegais, and everyone demonstrates their emotion at this serious moment in the parents' lives when the child, so recently a baby in arms, is about to be accepted into society. The child himself is given no choice, being seized and carried off by the messengers who paint him all over with red ochre or blood. He can decide nothing, not yet being capable of it, and must yield to this solemn moment in his life: the beginning of a long apprenticeship in preparation for his life, his own independence and responsibility. When he returns home he will be a man, with new bonds between himself and his parents. In New Caledonia these new bonds are expressed by the dual name by which the mother calls him from then on: 'You, father and son'. This clearly highlights the purpose of the initiation which is to separate the boys from their mothers and introduce them into the society of real men.

In Australia it is customary for the messengers to carry off their novices to a *corroborree* square where each of them sets up his camp 'on the side facing his home', Elkin tells us. First a banquet is served, then over the following days various rites are held which differ from place to place. The novice may be thrown in the air, have his scalp bitten or a tooth pulled out. The important factor is not so much the customs, the secret meanings of which we do not know, as the fact that, as in Melanesia, the novice 'is treated exactly as though he were dead', writes Elkin. 'He must remain silent, and may not even call for what he needs. He may only nod his head to answer questions put to him'.

Circumcision, or the tooth extraction, are performed in an isolated spot and mark the start of the period of solitude already noted in New Caledonia and elsewhere, the duration of which varies. But the boy will not be alone to find his food. In Australia novices stay in pairs and help each other. They must go for long expeditions and learn to look after

Australian aborigine techniques: Man is at home with nature, and even manages to come to terms with reptiles. This engraving, made in 1889, shows a young aborigine beating a boa out of a tree, forcing it to fall to the ground where it will be despatched and eaten.

There are many species of birds, often of very bright colouring, found in the South Seas. Australia alone has sixty types of parrots and other *psittacidae.* Left: a small rainbow lorica takes nectar from flowers by means of its brush-tipped tongue. Below: a male cockatoo. Cockatoos live in flocks all over North and East Australia, eating beetles and seeds. Opposite, above: The Raggi bird of paradise thrives all over New Zealand. Right: As a courtship display, it spreads out its wings, which makes it easier for the female to couple with the finest males. Right, centre: Iiwi feathers and feathers from another now extinct species formed the headgear of Hawaiians. Thanks to its beak, the iiwi could delve deep into flowers. Bottom left: The Australian wood kingfisher is related to the kingfisher but eats reptiles and rodents. Bottom right: according to legend the New Guinea royal is the king among birds although it is the smallest among birds of paradise, being only 6 in long.

The cuscus is a tree-dwelling kangaroo (left). Above, centre: the feather of the kiwi, New Zealand's national bird, looks like hair. Above: the koala bear is a marsupial living exclusively on the eucalyptus leaf, which contains enough water for it to be able to live without drinking. Left: a spiny porcupine, which lives off ants and termites. Below: the male kangaroo can grow to 7 1/2 ft tall and weigh as much as 250 lbs.

themselves, following the examples of their ancestors, and are sent out to discover the water-holes, that is to say camp sites. At a certain moment they will have their nostrils pierced and a small bone inserted as sign of their maturity. In some places an operation of sub-incision is performed. This consists in making an inch-long button hole in the urethra. In the *Arunta* (1927), Spencer and Gillen tell how the child's father and mother have to practise absolute chastity at the time their boy is undergoing this and waiting for the scar to heal. This operation is peculiar to Australia and is essential if the ceremony known as *andatta* is to be properly performed: this is a totem celebration for which the men dress up in bird feathers (*andatta*). The men open up the sub-incision scar and draw out the blood to use it for sticking the *andatta* feathers to their skin. This totemic ceremony is generally associated with initiation ceremonies. A post some 16 ft high is set up, daubed with human blood and covered over with feathers. The Great Ancestral Serpent is depicted on the post, on the ground and on totemic tablets.

But the initiation has a climax more important than the circumcision or the sub-incision, which are comparatively recent in Australia: obtaining the *churinga* and the bull-roarers. When these are displayed, writes Elkin, 'the sight of them causes deepest religious awe, akin to the emotions of Christians at the moment of the Holy Sacrament in their churches. The bull-roarers are usually kept in sacred places and may not be touched without permission from the chiefs. Non-initiates must keep away from these sacred places. But if an animal fleeing from the hunt takes refuge in one of them, its life is spared. Under similar circumstances a fugitive from justice may be granted his pardon. I know of no more impressive sight than a group of aborigines seated around their sacred symbols in a secret enclosure and chanting the myths they must preserve'.

The bull-roarer dangling on the end of a string gives out the sound of the ancestors' voices, which terrifies the women and children. Only initiates who have heard it can reach the land of the ancestors while his double travels in a solar craft. Europe's museums have a number of such craft brought back from Indonesia and Melanesia by early explorers and thought to be models for canoes. Paul Rivet understood that those solar craft had the same significance as the *churinga* in Australia.

Sprinkled with the blood of the ancestors, purified by fire and fortified with blood, the novice is ready to receive the revelation of knowledge. When he sees his own *churinga* he discovers who he is. He finds the markings on his back are engraved on the *churinga*. At that solemn moment the two of them, covered with blood and feathers, are living in the Land of Dreams.

Thus set free and at last capable of living in the age of the myth, the novice is told his 'secret name', as he is now in possession of the tangible sign of his spiritual double who will reveal his dream, in other words his cultural totem. The new man is now in position to incorporate his death as well as his life. When his body comes to die, with his skull and some of his bones piously cleansed and preserved, and with others made into tools or decorations for the living, his descendants, then his soul can withdraw to his *churinga* to wait for the right moment for re-incarnation.

It reassures him to feel that he will be able to re-live his free and hard life of a 'real man' on this beloved earth. Probably the most characteristic feature of these 'real men' is their ability to combine the spiritual with the material. In the Pacific, the stone age seems to have achieved a degree of spirituality which should make for a re-evaluation of that distinction between *homo faber* and *homo sapiens*, on which is based the conception of man's evolution.

The *churinga* has been mentioned a number of times. The *churinga*, so peculiar to Australia, brings us to one of the most mysterious and significant elements involving the education of 'real men', the novices. An attempt should now be made, by descriptions and by myths, to give an explanation of the *churinga*, using an Aranda term likewise designating rites and myths, which is the most important of all ceremonial objects and the presentation of which is the focal point of the initiation. The author has decided to limit this study to an examination of totemism, family ties and the initiation culminating in the acquisition of the *churinga*, because it is felt that this is the fundamental point of the characteristic difference between those countries and ours.

The *churinga* has the shape of an oblong tablet some four inches long, on which various geometric designs are carved or painted. In eastern Australia it is decorated with spirals and semi-circles, in the west with dotted lines, squares and concentric lozenges. For ordinary wood engraving, quartz points can be employed, or sharp bones or pieces of shell, but for engraving these tablets which contain the ancestral spirits only oppossum teeth may be used.

The paintings on *churingas* and all the other ceremonial objects are handed down by a mother serpent. Pursued by hunters, she was trying to reach the safety of the holes in the Pedinga where many snakes have their abode. But she was caught and wounded before being able to reach it, and dragged herself painfully to Mulboutu, where she still lives. The red ochre is her blood, the white ochre her excrement and the yellow her urine. So it was from a woman, a mother, that the Australian palette had its origin, with its ochres offset by white from lime and black from charcoal.

The knife was also invented by a mother seeking to limit her son's suffering. Géza Röheim, the psychoanalyst, in *The Eternal Ones of the Dream* (1945), tells of a legend he picked up from the Pitjantjara people near Lake Amédée. There coarse firewood sticks were used to circumcise the boys, many of whom died as a result. The woman said to the men: 'I became a woman thanks to the *kunkaringu* (meaning incision = knife). Use that on the boys, and leave the fire for cooking meat'.

The bull-roarer was likewise formerly the property of the women. Spencer has helped us to understand its importance by telling the story of the myth of Kunapippi, a large-footed creature who went around with a bag full of the spirits of children, all boys, and of bull-roarers. Wherever he

Above: Australian Dingo, drawn in 1889.

The duck-billed platypus is certainly among the most curious of mammals. Its teeth have developed into a beak, its feet are webbed, and it is amphibious. Its manner of reproduction is bird-like, laying eggs through the cloaca. The female secretes milk through numerous ventral glands, which spreads into the water, and is drunk by the young while swimming after her. This peculiar animal is found in Central Australia, New South Wales, and Tasmania.

stopped Kunapippi performed impressive ceremonies. Kunapippi is also known as Numina or Kadjeri and is often referred to as the Old Woman.

There is also a myth about the Rainbow Serpent who swallowed the two Wawilak sisters and restored them to life, thereby creating the spirits of children. The two women, the younger one pregnant and the other already a mother, went around hunting and collecting food. As they went along they gave names to the animals and plants which they ate. The younger sister gave birth to her child near the Mirrirmina water-hole. Its name means water-hole 'of the back of the Python of the rocks', which is the abode of Yurlunggur, a python and totem of the Dua half. It happened that the two Wawilak sisters were the products of an incestuous love. They had been conceived in the land of the Wawilaks where the men and women are all Dua and may therefore not marry each other. So when the two

mothers set about circumcising their sons and some menstrual blood from the elder fell on to Yurlunggur at the bottom of his well, he rose up and flooded the whole world, swallowing everyone including the mothers and their sons. But then he spat them out again. Since that day, Yurlunggur the giver of life possesses a womb. He is both male and female. From that time on the blood used by men to decorate their bodies and their emblems on ceremonial occasions is not only their own blood but also the blood of the two Wawilak sisters. The blood of the men and of the two women are one.

It has been noted how future mothers on Grande Terre walk around meditating in isolated areas where the spirits of the ancestors are thought to reside, thus enabling one of them to enter into her and 'give life' to her child. The same happens in Australia. As the plant grows in the earth so does the child's body grow in its mother's womb, but a 'child spirit', a 'double', has to come and give it life. Those doubles live in the land of the ancestors and at the appropriate time enter the body of the pregnant woman.

That double will stay by the newborn child all its life. Sometimes it will leave the living body when it is sleeping, and only return to it at sunrise. That explains the importance attributed to dreams. They are actions performed by the 'double', for which the living creature is as responsible as for his own acts performed while he is conscious.

The Land of Dreams is where the great ancestors came from. But, as has been observed, they appear in specific places on earth, totemic wells like Mirrirmina, springs, places where there is water. If they were never conceived, they are nevertheless creatures of the earth linked to a totemic animal. The totem is the symbol of life, linked with the reproductive functions of women, the family name of the clan, and the ancestor, brother and uncle, protector of the clan. It is this overlapping which the Western mind and its corollary, Cartesian reasoning, find most difficult to grasp, although it can be seen written all over Oceanian art: the carved face of the ancestor being changed into a bird; man, alive or an ancestor, being swallowed by a totem. And the child-spirits are always there, in life or waiting for a new life. There is harmony between the imaginary and the real, between the spiritual and the physical.

That civilization of naked men is founded on the harmony between mind and spirit. It has been observed that in Australia the double is connected to the *churinga*. *Churingas* are secret signs, permanent symbols, of the Time of Dreams. As Elkin writes in *The Australian Aborigines*, 'They are themselves the Dream, from which life and strength reach men through their intervention. That is why passing a *churinga* over the body of the sick restores their health.

Although small and having scarcely 1,500 inhabitants, Bora Bora Island is one of the best known of the Society Islands for the beauty of its scenery. It was an American base during the Second World War. Following double page: an aerial view of Mooréa. Page 148: rock, hibiscus and other wild flowers on Bora Bora.

Taking one with one to go hunting is a guarantee of success, but the game killed under these conditions becomes sacred. It may only be eaten by men who are fully initiated, after observing certain minor rites. Friendship is renewed or strengthened by lending a *churinga* and thereafter possesses the sacred features pertaining to everything connected with the Time of Dreams. Finally, when a novice is rubbed with such objects or permitted to see or handle one for the first time, he is fully aware that, by so doing, he enters into contact with the eternal Time of Dreams. That explains why in some tribes, maybe in more of them than one imagines, every man has his personal *churinga*, different from the others, possibly specially made for him, and why his spiritual double is in principle almost all the time in the sacred enclosure next to his *churinga*'.

Each individual thus owns two bodies: body of flesh and one of wood or stone, his *churinga*. We are told by Strehlow, missionary and anthropologist, that the *churinga* 'is regarded as the common body of a man and his personal totemic ancestors (...)': The man will only be given this materialization of his double at the last stage of his initiation when he receives his own *churinga*, his double. 'That double', says Strehlow, 'is called *iningukua* (the same). It is the man's secret protector, in other words his innermost self rooted in the life of his ancestors. In the world of doubles, invisible to our perception, its appearance is that of the living man when he puts on his festive garb'.

Life for the totem folk is based on beauty. Through his initiation, through his festive clothes, man becomes a creature of beauty, and that beautification rules his ethics and his rites. These ceremonies in their luxurious economy are grandiose events which are remarkably aesthetic. They glorify life by their striking colours, their harmonious movements, their quivering feathers bowing with the rhythm, the plethora of shining mother-of-pearl.

The rhythm helps man to be part of the cycles of time; the dancing helps him keep his place in space. His robes and his dancing keep his body one with the rhythm, with space and with nature. It has been mentioned repeatedly how in those countries the same life passes through mineral, vegetable, animal and human phases. Man is thus an integral part of the cycle of nature. His beautification serves that integration and thereby assures the eternity of humanity.

To be a 'real man' is to attain that beauty, source of all life. To achieve this requires harmony between each person and all that surrounds him. Hence, while a man sleeps and dreams, his double informs him of the right way to behave, the ceremonial ritual, its songs and its dances. Nothing in this should seem incongruous to us. It is the simple joy of being, the harmony between the imaginary and the mind.

For all these myths and rites and ceremonies are not aimed at hedonist happiness. They represent a search for unity, for harmony with the world. The totemized Australian, that 'aristocrat of nature', as he has been called, does not identify with nature but co-operates with it.

Is there any place in those societies for evolutionism and what Westerners call progress? Certainly not as we understand them. That is why they have been termed 'cold societies' in contrast to 'hot societies'. In *Le Temps retrouvé*, Claude Lévi-Strauss replaces the usual differentiation between 'people without history' and 'people with a history' by two other terms: 'cold societies' for those seeking through their institutions to eliminate almost automatically the effects of history on their equilibrium and eternity, and 'hot societies' for those keeping historic development to themselves so as to make it the driving spirit for their own development. If rural Europe was still a fairly 'cold society', then modern society in the West, where gross production per inhabitant increases fairly steadily, is a 'hot, not to say burning, society'. But in allying his philosophy to Adam Smith's ideas, Kant was preparing the ground for the changes awaiting our societies, although he may not have realized it: division of labour and discarding nature, the only productive factor being human labour.

Many people now believe that rational and technical civilization is incapable of resolving its own contradictions and seems to be leading the world to destruction. Neither liberalism nor pure reason can help in the understanding what 'real men' are. For them there is no question of disregarding nature. What characterizes totemic civilization is as far from notions of productivity as it is from notions of Christian charity, as indicated at the beginning of this chapter, stressing that syncretism between Christianity and totemism is impossible.

That other is founded on close co-operation with cosmic nature. Each element in the universe is integrated in the clan. The most exemplary result of these societies lies in that integration of the various elements of which it is composed: no poor, no outcasts, that great problem of the West where so many people and even groups live outside the pale of the society they serve.

With totemism, nothing on earth or in the heavens is left on one side. Man is an integral part of nature around him. It is not so much a question of classifying as of being part of the cosmos. The result is a balance which has permitted those societies to survive through various crises, leading their lives in the concrete reality of the moment, without splitting time up into arbitrary divisions nor dividing up their lives.

From there it is easy to understand the suffering expressed in poetry and in books by the bi-cultured, by those who are naïvely called 'civilized' because they have acquired culture in Western universities. They return home shod in shoes which deform their feet, and handicap their walking, clad in a suit, carrying a handbag and a transistor, and armed with a vast accumulation of knowledge yet not possessing their own true knowledge. Their glorious past, a past of a spiritual stone age founded on ethics, will enable them to dream, and then with clear and tranquill courage to invent new myths which will once more restore their ability to preserve the eternity of life.

For without their totems and the myths of the Time of Dreams true life would vanish and nothing would remain of man or nature.

# COLONIZATION

## THE REASONS FOR COLONIZATION

Colonizing is not a modern invention. We need only think back to the Phoenicians, the Greeks, the Romans — to cite but the most outstanding and best known among earlier colonizers. There have been many before them and many after them.

Before the appearance of the White Man, the Pacific Isles were the targets of many migratory movements, some peaceful, some violent like those from Polynesia and Japan, as we noted earlier. They all had similar characteristics, impulses and motivations:
- on the one hand were the natives to be colonized, averse to change, an aversion often complicated by political disarray, yet able to find common ground on a high level of civilization;
- on the other hand the aggressors with a spirit of adventure and a thirst for expansion, driven by demographic pressures, technically advanced, and with a certain lack of scruples more or less justified on grounds of philosophy, religion or ideology.

The nineteenth century was characterised by the dominance, not to say monopoly, held by Europe in the field of colonization. Europe raised the phenomenon of colonialism to a degree of perfection never before attained, for Europe's colonial expansion affected the whole world. In previous centuries it was mainly to the two Americas that European colonizers turned.

In the nineteenth century and at the beginning of the twentieth century they would turn towards Africa and Asia. Gradually Europe was to dominate the world, directly or indirectly.

This dominant position was achieved by gradual process, the various stages of which could not always be identified under the same label but which corresponded to the basic features of Europe's expansion: the great discoveries, the advance of missionaries, the major migration waves, colonial imperialism. In the ensuing chapters we shall have an opportunity to analyse those stages more thoroughly. Meanwhile we can already distinguish the fundamental and original features of this colonial expansion.

Previously colonial adventure had sprung from a lust for conquest, the lure of wealth, a need for alleviating excessive population. This was still true in the seventeenth and eighteenth centuries. What the Spaniards, Portuguese and Dutch were seeking beyond distant horizons was gold and spices. These primitive motives still held good. But the new colonizing powers of the nineteenth century had other aims in mind. Convinced of the superiority of their own culture, they sought to impose it on their future colonies. They wanted these to be instruments of their national might. There was no question of recognizing the potential values of the local civilization or of adapting them to enrich their own culture, as other colonizers had done before. The idea was to create new Europes all over the world.

The Pacific was the area furthest from the enterprising conquest-bent Europe. So colonial expansion had a more disorderly and less systematic effect on it than on any other part of the globe. But it did not escape. The essential features of European colonization were to be found there in various forms and for a much longer period of time: adventurous explorers, the missionary and military stages of conquest, colonial penetration, indifference towards indigenous civilizations, sometimes extermination of whole populations and creation of those new Europes which would later become Australia, New Zealand and New Caledonia.

The British protectorate of South-East New Guinea was proclaimed at Port Moresby on 6 November 1884 in the presence of a number of prominent figures from the British government. Germans and Dutch shared the rest of the island.

# AWAKENING INTEREST IN THE SOUTH SEAS

The tales of the great navigators aroused the interest of the crowned heads of Europe from the days of the very earliest voyages of discovery. They had returned from the ends of the world and navigated to its uttermost corners, and their descriptions of the beauties and delights of the Polynesian Islands seemed beyond belief. These were first found by mistake by Mendaña de Neyra in 1595 when he thought he was back at the Solomons which he had discovered twenty years earlier. However, he found the inhabitants looked completely different: they were indeed the tall brown-skinned Marquesans. He was dazzled by this nation of navigators and by the beauty of their womenfolk: 'Broad shoulders and narrow hips distinguish the Maori woman from all others' was how Gauguin described them later.

Although but a part of the immense Pacific, it was Polynesia that first aroused the admiration of the Europeans. And it was its most celebrated, if not its most beautiful island, Tahiti, that first awakened the interest of Western man in the south seas. Tahiti can be said to have been the real meeting place of the European and the Pacific. This densely populated island (240,000 inhabitants according to Cook) was ruled over by two chiefs, two Ariki, whose clothes revealed their importance at first glance: great robes of finest vegetable material garnished with plumes. Under them came the tribal chiefs in charge of their villages and the high priests watching over the *marae*. Tahiti was first discovered by Wallis, who spent several months there in 1767 and named it after George III. The following year Bougainville called there and gave it the beautiful name of New Cythera.

It was the island of the god Oro, founder of the Arioi Society, a kind of sect with a hierarchy of eight ranks, which had nothing in common with the other Pacific societies, especially not with the Melanesian societies. The Arioi wore no masks and were tattooed all over their bodies. They enjoyed absolute sexual freedom. Groups of wandering singers and dancers gave lavish shows called *upaupas*. These formed a part of every ceremony, especially weddings.

In his *Voyage autour du Monde* published in 1771, Bougainville described Tahiti as an idyllic country of love and pleasure where life went by with little need for work since 'a superb soil' yielded 'virtually all things without working it'. He was enchanted by his welcome to this New Cythera. In his description of their arrival, he writes about his men and himself: 'Our efforts were successful in containing the men, who were bewitched; not the least of our efforts had been in containing ourselves!' This so-called ease of life combined with the nudity of the natives and the unrestrained warmth of their welcome set imaginations aflame back in Europe, and almost a century later, in 1865, Chateaubriand was to refer to those same accounts in his *Génie du Christianisme*. It

Travellers returning from Tahiti told of the unfettered innocence of the people's habits. This engraving, entitled *Pleasures of the Otahitians and the English* could be used as frontispiece for Diderot's notorious pamphlet *Petit Supplément au Voyage de Bougainville* (1772).

In 1774 Captain Furneaux introduced Omai, a native of Huaheine, to the drawing-rooms of London. High society flocked around this 'noble savage', who was immortalised in his oriental costume by Sir Joshua Reynolds, the painter. Five years earlier Bougainville had introduced Aotourou of Tahiti to the court of Louis XV.

---

**Happiness and plenty in Tahiti**

If happiness lies in the abundance of every necessity of life, in inhabiting a superb land enjoying the most beautiful climate (the soil producing everything without the need for cultivation), in enjoying perfect health, in respiring always the purest and most salubrious airs, in leading a life of freedom, gentle, calm, divorced from all passions, even that of jealousy, surrounded by charming females; if those females may also partake of this happiness, I say that no people could ever be so blessed as the nation whose homeland is New Cythera.

LOUIS-ANTOINE DE BOUGAINVILLE, *Voyage autour du monde de la frégate* LA BOUDEUSE *et la flûte* L'ETOILE *en 1766-1769,* Neuchâtel 1772/1773, N. Ed. Paris 1958. p. 302

---

**Civilization and the 'Noble Savage'**

It were indeed sincerely to be wished, that intercourse which has lately subsisted between Europeans and the natives of the South Sea islands may be broken off in time, before the corruption of manners which unhappily characterizes civilized regions, may reach that innocent race of men, who live here fortunate in their ignorance and simplicity. (...)

If the knowledge of a few individuals can only be acquired at such a price as the happiness of nations, it were better for the discoverers and the discovered, that the South Sea had still remained unknown to Europe and its restless inhabitants.

GEORGE FORSTER, *A Voyage Round the World,* London 1777, pp. 303, 368

---

seemed that no-one realized that the 'nature' of these men was partly dictated by their social standing and that their so-called 'liberty' was fixed in a certain social structure.

It has been said that Bougainville found in Tahiti the very incarnation of Rousseau's ideas, although he described the natives as thieves, scroungers and crafty. But he was dazzled by their sexual freedom and painted the Tahitians as the noble savages of the Rousseau myth. To this conception of happiness Diderot, in one of the first anticolonialist publications, his *Supplément au Voyage de Bougainville,* added that of virtue, thus spreading abroad the vision of an Eden in the midst of the Ocean. But no-one tried to understand that Eden or the men who lived there. Society was only mildly interested when two Tahitians, Aotourou and Omai, were brought on a visit to Europe, the former to Paris by Bougainville and the latter to London by Cook.

Yet Cook gave a more objective notion of the problems; in his *A Voyage to the South Pole and round the World,* published in 1777, some passages gave warning of the dangers presented to those civilisations by the presence of the white man. But nobody seems to have heeded his words.

The lavish feasts staged by the Arioi seem to have contributed greatly to Bougainville's ecstasy. Yet life was not all licentiousness in the reign of the god Oro and his *ariki.* Cook, who had spent four months in Tahiti on his first journey, gives a very different description to Bougainville's. Weber's engraving supports Cook's reports and shows the greed for human lives displayed by Oro and his high priests. It depicts a ceremony which took place on 15 September 1777 at the Tauta *marae* in Tahiti. To the right are shown Cook, Weber and Anderson staring at a man tied up on the ground in the centre of the engraving.

To the left, musicians are shown singing and beating drums while cooks are removing the skin from a dog before cooking it and two men are digging a grave for the victim with staves. The human sacrifice was to ensure victory against the Mo'orea, against whom an attack was about to be launched. Added to the celebrations of Oro, Cook's arrival on the scene must have been a splendid omen to the attacking side!

But, Cook's descriptions apart, probably the two most popular works to spread knowledge about the south seas were *Hawkesworth's Voyages,* 1773, and the *Voyage Pittoresque autour du Monde* published in 1835 under Dumont d'Urville's supervision.

The first was well translated into French, German and Italian, and enjoyed great success. In it Dr Hawkesworth describes in particular Cook's and Bank's adventures on the ENDEAVOUR. He gives a romantic account of Bank's liaison with Queen Obarea and of her ladies' 'lascivious' morals. Cook was highly embarrassed by the book, which did not represent his thoughts. But when his own *Voyage towards the South Pole and round the World* came out four years later, many people felt that his descriptions of those lands, albeit so precise and exact, were simply not to be believed! A romantic and false idea of the Pacific had already taken solid hold of people's minds. It still persists.

*Voyage Pittoresque autour du Monde* tells of the discovery of the South Seas and the beauty of nature with its new varieties of plant and animal life. In it the 'native' cuts a poor figure next to the fabulous ecological and botanical findings reported by the explorers and the scientists who accompanied them. It contains such terms as 'this thing' when referring to the Australian aborigine, while talking of an animal of few yards away from 'this thing' as 'he'. All the rest is in this vein and can only lead to wrong impressions despite providing much new information of value.

Thus, to the puzzling discovery of a people living for pleasure came to be added exoticism and a degree of irrationalism, though based on concrete facts. *Moby Dick or the White Whale,* published in 1851 by an American, Herman Melville, tells of a 'cosmic battle' with the white whale which he is hunting. It is known that the story, full of very precise notes, is based on an experience which actually happened; the same is true of *Typee* and *Omoo,* which contain descriptions of great interest.

These three myths, one about the noble savage, another about a Paradise on earth and the third telling of the riches of Oceania, aroused immense interest. People who could afford it set out to see for themselves. A grandson of one the Vice-Presidents of the United States, Henry Adams, the memorialist, finished writing his *History of the United States,* and sailed off to recover from his disppointment with the West by visiting those distant shores. He found that the women of Tahiti with their skins of 'old gold' are the 'incarnation of archaic womanhood'. In 1893 he published the *Memoirs of Marau Taaroa, last Queen of Tahiti.*

Robert Louis Stevenson was at the time on almost those same islands. He settled there for good and died at Vailima in the Islands of Samoa in 1894. He succeeded in establishing contacts with the men of the Pacific. Author Stevenson's account of his relationship with Napaio, the braider of beards of the dead on the Marquesas Islands, is still a model for this type of literature. He learned Samoan, so that he was able to understand their many legends. Getting to know the civilization of those parts, he, like Bishop Dordillon of the same islands, reached the conclusion that 'The only lies are those told in travel books'. From then on his writings became strongly influenced by Oceanian culture.

Paul Gauguin, who died at Atuana in the Marquesas, was another artist who felt that same influence. But he became furious when he discovered 'the colonial world', the existence of which he 'did not suspect', and became a contraversial journalist in *Les Guêpes,* the Tahiti local paper, before founding his own paper, the *Sourire,* which he illustrated with wood-cuts based on Maori painting. He fought tooth and nail to defend his brothers' rights against the colonial administrators.

There are many other authors who should be mentioned. All of them display a certain disenchantment with their own civilisation. Pierre Loti was one writer who instanced this. But another officer, Victor Segalen, a naval medical officer, who assembled Gauguin's last works in Tahiti, avoided the colonial question, despite its being so prominent, in his novel *Les Immémoriaux* published in 1907. The basic reason for the interest aroused by those Southern Seas, which gave rise to so many dreams of escape, lay in the desire to find an universally good, unspoiled human and in the hope of finding an answer to the various stages of development of man as assumed by the Darwinian theory of evolution.

In these latitudes neolithic man still existed, and there was hope that studying their habits and work would help provide some knowledge about the lives of our own European ancestors. It was not too far-fetched to imagine that in some distant aera a single civilisation may have existed all over the globe.

An extraordinary fillip for science was provided by the outcome of the 1872 CHALLENGER expedition, which opened people's minds to the vast fields of study to be undertaken in all the varying forms of life. That curiosity about the Southern Seas was probably best put into words in the question about ourselves asked by Gauguin in his painting in 1897:

*Where do we come from?*
*What are we? Where are we going?*


# MISSIONARIES AND MARINERS

Was this awakening of interest in the South Seas to be a blessing or a curse? Would it result in an intermarriage of cultures to enrich the human heritage? What would Europe do with these newly found ocean spaces and islands? How would the peoples of the Pacific react to the arrival of hordes of new creatures: the whites?

As was seen in the chapter on customs, two totally contrary conceptions of the human being lie at the roots of the two civilizations: the Westerner, be he Christian or rationalist, is above all an 'autonomous' individual who differs not only from other human beings but from the rest of the world, from nature, from the dead and from his God who lives in unknown heavens, and increasingly induces a feeling of terror and guilt. Pacific man must on the contrary be in contact with the earth the moment he is born; from that moment his civilization becomes integrated with the animal, vegetable and mineral world surrounding him.

We shall see how the whites were received in a different manner by the Polynesians, already colonized by the Ariki, and by the Melanesians: whites settled more easily in Polynesia than in Melanesia. But wherever they went their arrival gave rise to murderous warfare thanks to their introduction of iron which altered the existing economic and political balance.

Distinction must be made between three successive waves: explorers, missionaries and mariners of all kinds, whalers, men in search of sandalwood or holothurians, adventurers and slave dealers. Finally the settlers, who will be the subject of the next chapter.

An imaginary speech made by a Tahitian chief to Bougainville

And thou, thou leader of a robber band, straightway remove thy ship from our shores: we are innocent, we are happy; and thou canst only destroy our happiness. We follow nature's pure instincts, and thou wouldst efface them from our souls. Here everything is for all; and thou hast attempted to preach I know not what distinction between *thine* and *mine*. Our daughters and our women belong to us all; thou hast participated in that privilege with us; and thou hast begun to kindle in them unknown passions...

We are free; and see, thou hast imported into our land the instrument of our future slavery. Thou art neither god nor devil: who then art thou, to make slaves of us? Orou! thou that knoweth the speech of these men; tell it to all, as thou hast told it to me, that which they have written on yonder fragment of metal: 'This land is ours.' This land is thine! and wherefore? because thou hast set thy foot upon it? Should one day a Tahitian disembark on thy shores, and carve upon one of thy stones, or upon the bark of one of thy trees: 'This land belongs to the inhabitants of Tahiti', what wouldst thou think? Thou art the strongest! What of it, then? When one of thy miserable playthings, which fill thy dwelling, wast taken from thee, thou hath cried it abroad, thou hath punished; and yet at the same moment, thou projecteth at the bottom of thy heart the theft of a whole country! Thou art no slave: thou wouldst suffer death rather than to become so, and yet thou designeth to enslave us!... We have respected our image in thine. Leave us our customs; they are more wise and more honest than thine; we desire not to exchange that which thou callest our ignorance against thy useless enlightenment. All that is necessary and good for us, we possess. Are we then worthy of blame, because we have not allowed ourselves superfluous needs? When we are hungry, we have food to eat; when we are cold, we have garments to wear... Seek where thou wouldst that which thou callest the commodities of life; but allow thou sensible people to stop, when they have nothing to gain by continuing their toil except imaginary benefits... Examine thou these men: thou see'st that they are unbowed, healthy and strong. Examine thou these women: thou see'st that they are unbowed, healthy, both sweet and beautiful. Take thou up that bow, it is mine; call to thy assistance one, two, three, four of thy companious, and seek to draw it. I bend it alone. I cultivate the soil; I climb the mountain; I traverse the forest; I travel over a league of the plain in less than an hour. Thy young companions follow me with difficulty, and I am over 70 years old. Unhappy is this Island, cursed are the Tahitians, and cursed will the future generation be, from the day that thou visited us! We knew but one disease; that which each man, each animal, and each plant is condemned to: old age; but thou hast brought us another: thou hast infected our blood... The notion of crime, and the fear of illness have come amongst us with you. Our pastimes, once so sweet, now bring with them naught but remorse and fear. That man in black, who is nigh thee, who heareth me, hath spoken to our sons; I know not what he hath said to our danghters; but our sons draw back; and our daughters blush. Shut thyself up, if thou so desirest, in depths of the forest, with thy perverse pleasures for thy companions, but leave thou the good and simple Tahitians to reproduce without shame, under the heavens and in the light of day.

DENIS DIDEROT, *Supplément au voyage de Bougainville,* 1772 (?), pp. 170-174

The paganism and licentious habits of the Oceanian civilizations were a source of concern for the missionaries, whose first duty was to convert the natives to Christian standards of morality. Catholic and Protestant missionaries vied constantly with one another to gain the goodwill of the people. Natives building the Catholic church at Mua in the Wallis Islands.

The appearance and strange habits of all these caused much astonishment, and all reports which it has been possible to assemble and translate confirm the amazement felt by the arrival of the whites.

'The canoe was bulky and hairy. The people of Matavai thought it was a floating island drifting in.

'(...) As the inhabitants paddled out from the shore towards the tall canoe to cast branches of peace on the waters there was a sudden burst of thunder: a man on the reef collapsed.

'No stone had struck him; no spear had entered his body. His companions held him up from behind: he bent over like a lifeless body.

'The strangers came ashore. They were pale, and some were seen taking off their hair'.

Such were the extraordinary tales being told around Tahiti. That 'bulky and hairy' canoe held the good *Uari* (Wallis) which arrived in 1767 just ahead of the *Tuti* (Cook). The natives had imagined it was a floating island arriving, just as had another long ago which their ancestors had seen and had skillfully tied on to their island. They soon understood that this was no island and that these were pale-faced beings with faces devoid of muscles, and the question arose: 'Were these men? Were they gods?' The question passed quickly from island to island across the vast Pacific. It was to the King of Hawaii that fell the honour of unmasking the white impostors, namely Captain Cook, whom he had first thought was the incarnation of the god Lono. The story is told in the song of Kupa, son of Kapupua, an oarsman for King Kalainuno, chief of Kealakekua:

Cook had 'discovered' Hawaii in 1778. Not knowing who he was, they received him with the honours due to a god. When he came back a year later, his identity still unknown, he was received with the same honours. But Kalamaino put his arms round him and hugged him, hugging so tight that Cook let out a cry of pain. '*He shouts, so he can't be a god*', cried the King, and slew the impostor. A massacre followed. In the words of Kupa's *Dirge. 'It was a strange thing, when we struck them they fell and bled like us.* We then understood that the whites were men like ourselves.'

Stories like that were collected by careful, disinterested observes such as Victor Segalen and Charles de Varigny who later published them, the former in *Les Immémoriaux* (Paris, 1907), and the latter in *Quatorze Ans aux Iles Sandwiches* (Paris, 1874).

Tahiti seems to have been the island most visited by explorers, most of whom cast anchor in Matavaï Bay, and later at Papeete. In the decades that followed, these strange and somewhat unclean creatures, who washed so little and who failed to pluck the hairs under their arms, kept arriving in ever greater numbers on all kinds of vessels ranging from broken down old whalers to three-masted warships carrying up to 60 guns, the fast and death-dealing frigates. Bligh, commanding the *Bounty,* also stayed there for five months in 1788. Soon after he sailed out of Tahiti a mutiny broke out and the mutineers took control of the ship and returned to Matavaï. Some of them settled down there for good, others went to Pitcairn, west of Gambier, taking a number of Tahitians of both sexes with them.

---

**The stranglehold of the Missions**

Mgr Bataillon appears to the Wallis islanders as a twelfth-century Bishop revived in our century. This grand old man... has made the island Catholic from one side to the other. He dominates it, captivating it by his devotion and by his charity, challenging it by his audacity, conquering dissidents by war and by exile. He has, in fact, the Queen Amélie supporting him. He brought her up, taught her, adopted her as his spiritual child, and continues to influence her. Through her, he is the master of the island. He has never let British missionaries establish themselves there. He inspires both his missionaries and the savages with awe and admiration. He made the people carry stones on their backs, to build him a cathedral. Heavy and massive with its two towers, it seems to reach to the heavens among the minute shanties so close to the ground, a bizarre monument to another age and another world. However, the Bishop's advancing age has made him anxious and morose. He has forced those innocents to bow beneath his yoke and his laws, so that they have neither the vices nor the virtues which belong to them. Alas, of the vices, there rests hypocrisy, and with their virtues, gaiety, naivety, and warmth have fled. As for the new virtues which are preached to them, they pay lip service to their names, they do not understand them, and if they practice them, it is in a desolate and beaten fashion. Is this then the reward of 40 years of exertion and of faith?

HENRI RIVIÈRE, *Souvenirs de la Nouvelle-Calédonie. L'insurrection canaque de 1878*, Calmann-Lévy, Paris 1880, pp. 63-64.

This succession of mariners, always well armed, could not fail to increase the power of the neighbouring chiefs. One of these, a small dark chief unlike the lighter skinned true *Ariki*, became well known under the name of Pomaré, meaning He-who-coughs-in-the-night, which he assumed in defiance of ancient custom.

Cook had already erected a fort to the North-West of Matavaï, and successive *Piratanes* used it as their residence. It was called the *fare Piritane*, the house of the British (from *Piratania* = Britain or England).

For Christians this European love of far-off expeditions, whether undertaken for trade, science or mere tourist curiosity, had become a matter of missionary zeal. The L. M. S. (London Missionary Society) was born from a combination of various faiths, episcopalian, presbyterian and independents. A ship was purchased, the DUFF, flying a flag bearing three doves with olive branches. On 6 March 1797 Captain Wilson brought her into the same Matavaï Bay with Christian crew, ship's surgeon, and twenty-six missionaries.

It may be recalled that the Polynesians, far more than the Melanesians, had aroused the admiration of the early navigators, so that it was no chance choice that brought the London Missionary Society to select Tahiti as their base. It had been from there that the intrepid Ariki had set out in their huge dug-outs to found their *marae* far and wide; like them, the L.M.S. would fan out from Tahiti to convert and civilize the pagan.

Tahiti is a suitable starting point to choose to bring comprehension of the impact of missions and of the problems which that impact would create for the indigenous populations. Later, those same problems will be found when the other Pacific islands are described.

For the time being the servants of Jehovah and the priests of Oro were face to face. What would happen, since in Tahiti everyone belonged to the powerful sect of the Arioi?

*'Arioi, I am Arioi, and may no longer on this earth be a father.*
*'Arioi, I am Arioi, my twelve wives shall be sterile; otherwise I shall strangle my first-born when he first draws breath'.*

So went the Arioi chant in the *marae* as offerings were brought to Oro, bunches of bananas, succulent fish, pigs with bound trotters and skinny dogs which had to walk on their hindlegs like humans. Then came the human victim carriers. The High Priest dug out their eyes with his nails, one eye for the gods and one for the King.

The coming of the missionaries surprised and perplexed them. Segalen again comments on this in *Les Immémoriaux*,:
'This was no longer a case of those rough and turbulent young men armed with shiny sticks which strike from afar with great noise. Not one of these warriors or chiefs had set foot on shore when they arrived. But a monotonous chanting of sharp words could be heard coming from the ship.

'Pale faced women could be seen. Until then there had been some doubt as to whether white women existed. These did not appear very different from Tahitian women, but they looked pale and thin (...) with cloven feet wrapped in animal skins; physically they lacked grace or proportion, and were dressed in hard tight-fitting materials (...). The coastal inhabitants of Atahuru told extravagant stories about them, saying that the new arrivals were too busy studying their white leaves marked with little hieroglyphics to go in for love-making in public.' These strangers had declined offerings saying it was the Lord's day, the Sabbath day. They angrily refused to give their muskets away and pushed away the women who had come to welcome them. The people gathered that the missionaries' bodies were taboo. Later, as a precaution when a boat arrived they themselves tabooed it with a strip of white *tapa,* designed to warn their women against going aboard.

Pomaré had the *faré* which the old-time navigators had built given over to the visitors. The newcomers had spent twelve days storing their provisions and shiny instruments.

Pomaré's son paid a call on the new visitors, 'carried there on the shoulders of powerful servants who took turns carrying their noble load and ran all the way (...). The crowd made way (...). He stared at the white man, who stared back at him (...). Not a word was spoken. Looks were exchanged as between warriors waiting to fire the first shot.'

'After Pomaré had visited their ship, the missionaries celebrated his arrival with generous offerings of the burning drink which makes people joyous. They themselves held back. Maybe they only use it at their solemn secret ceremonies. Haamanihi (the priest) was aware of the wonderful effects produced by that *ava,* which is stronger and more bitter than any Maori *ava* and beseeched them to let him have more:
— 'I need courage!' he announced. 'Much courage! I have two men to slaughter for tonight's sacrifice'.

The foreigners were startled and displayed stupid horror. But Pomaré had gayly taken hold of a long bottle of the precious beverage, saying:
— 'Give me your *ava piritané...* we are now *fetii*!'
— 'That drink is not good for chiefs. It makes people ill. It effects one's eye-sight and one's walking...' came the reply.
— 'Not good for chiefs? Not good for other people? Then I shall drink it all, like this'. And Pomaré took a deep drink. His eyes rolled and cried. He coughed a great deal, and suddenly began to strike the timbers of the ship with his head like a battering ram. Somewhat shaken, his companions set about trying to calm him. But he laughed and recovered his dignity and climbed the wooden gangway, built to lilliputian scale, to the top deck. There he felt like dancing and started to dance the *ori* to which is usually sung *Aué! a girl is...* There Haamanihi stopped him:
— 'Your legs won't carry you! You have drunk the foreigners' *ava.* Watch out! And look where you are going with your eyes all shining! Eha! The Rainbow!

'But by then Pomaré had already dropped down into a dug-out without caring and was demanding his farewell salute of musket shot. He promptly went to sleep while his wife started weeping at not having been able to get entangled with one of those new foreign priests. Meanwhile Haamanihi was considering the advantages of serving those foreigners so as to make use of their power to recover his own properties.'

'Which are your gods', demanded Noté*, with an expression of disgust on his face. He leant towards the King: 'Another heretic...'
'Tell me the name of the land where I eat.'
'Tahiti', muttered the judge in surprise.
'So, my gods are the gods of Tahiti. It's not surprising. Why should I have others. If I speak, is it not with my own mouth? Why steal from others their lips and their breath?...'
'This has nothing to do with your behaviour', interrupted Noté, 'nor with whom you are supposed to be...'
'Arioi! I am an Arioi...' The stunned immobility of the crowd enabled him to finish the incantation of the ancient high priests without interruption.
But as soon as the amazement died down, there came a torrent of laughter, of jeering whistles, of mocking shouts and gestures: 'Pagan! He's a real pagan. They still exist! Another one! The last of the dark ages! Ha! Ha! he worships wooden gods! he religiously eats the eyes of corpses, near the demolished *marae*!' Shouts of 'Eyeeater!' 'Savage!' 'Stupid oaf!' 'Shameless one!' 'Old wizard!' rang out. And the happy tumult rose, a permissible pleasure, pleasing both to missionaries and to Kérito**...
After a moment, Noté checked the laughter, and spoke without anger:
'My brother, I recognise you now. I know all about you, and I know that your eyes have not yet seen the Truth. I have told you, and you did not believe me, that there are no more *marae*, no more pagan gods. Come into the place where you will be taught to pray to our Lord, to read and repeat His Laws: in a short time, you will loose your ignorance, and you will be glad to leave it behind you.'
'A good speech', thought Iakoba. But the Arioi seemed determined in his impiety and obstinacy, replying:
'Read? Read the "Law" and all your other foreign words? Hie! I say to your faces: when the animals change their cries...'
A groan from the crowd smothered his words, but he repeated loudly:
'When a man changes his gods, it is because he is stupider than the buck, sillier than the tuna fish. I said, when I came back: "Aroha-nui for Tahiti." But where are its people? These? Are they Maoris?'
All this time, a tumult of hatred rose from the crowd, sometimes covering the pagan's burning reproaches, sometimes being overcome by them.
'They had their cherished gods, Maori gods, wearing the maro, or with naked breasts, stomachs and faces, tatooed with the noble marks... They had inviolable customs, the taboos that were never broken... That was the Law, that was the Law. No-one wanted to, no-one could mistake it. Now, the law is weak, the sickly new customs cannot stop what they themselves call crime, and they content themselves by giving a display of anger—afterwards. A man kills: strangle him, Stupidity! Can that revive the dead man? Two victims in place of one! Two men gone! Taboos once were a strong defence. Now they protect no longer.'

VICTOR SEGALEN, *Les Immémoriaux*, Paris, 1907

* The missionary Nott who baptised Pomaré. Paofai, the Arioi high-priest, was condemned by the missionary court.
** Christ.

The fact is that at the height of the god Oro's might the Society Islands had been a single unit with Raiatéa as its centre; but the tiny state had disintegrated in the course of epic battles between their gods and most of the individual islands had recovered their autonomy. Their nobles were still very powerful and the tiny nation of the *manahuné* had to pay them a kind of tribute and accompany them in their ceaseless battles. The arrival of the missionaries set off a state of silent hostility. The powerful Ariki and the resplendent scornful Arioi were jealous of their power and turned down the missionaries. But the smaller chiefs had been dispossessed of their lands and sought to make use of them with the backing of their own lower-ranking priests. So it was that the *Arioi* sect was divided within itself, and some of them, as will be seen passed over to the side of the missionaries and became their supporters. As they belonged to the nobility they had the power of the taboo. They tried to learn the new laws and to acquire a better understanding of these new strangers who behaved so differently from all those who had landed there previously. That was why Pomaré had paid his visit to the missionaries, accompanied by Haamanihi the Arioi. The latter would have liked to have been given a musket, but the missionaries had refused. They had also turned down the women who had stripped off their clothes and started to dance, singing 'The *tané* are deaf... the *tané* are deaf...!' much to the anger of the missionaries.

Haamanihi had then offered them a few human victims. They were to be carried to the *marae*, an altar would be built to welcome Jehovah, the missionaries' god, and the ceremony of the offered eye would be conducted: one eye for Jehovah and one for the missionaries.

The latter had again declined. They demonstrated incomprehensible signs of disgust and found the Tahitian habits 'indescribably obscene'; so they set about silently observing the missionaries' habits. On Sundays they preached, addressing their words indiscriminately to everone, meaning as much to the *manahuné* as to the *Ariki* and the *Arioi*, to slave and nobleman alike. And this constituted a grave danger.

A still greater danger arose when the missionaries announced that a feast would be celebrated the following Sunday. Undoubtedly that would attract many adepts. A crowd gathered. But on the table where Holy Communion was to be celebrated lay only a few breadfruits off the tree and a little of that intoxicating *ava* in a cup. The missionaries chanted and shared the 'bread' and the 'wine' amongst themselves as symbols of the 'body' and 'blood' of Christ, but with unpardonable bad manners failed to invite anyone to share their meagre repast.

Thereupon the top ranking Arioi, the Twelve with tattooed legs, approached them singing: *'Over land, over seas, we are the masters; masters of joy, masters of life'*, their powerful voices drowning out the prayers of the missionaries:

*'O Lord, let not Thy word be silenced by the tumult of the wicked...'*

— *'We are the masters, masters of joy, masters of life, masters of pleasure! Aué! E!'*, sang the Arioi.

157

— 'Lord, deliver us from evil', prayed the missionaries, and the Arioi sang back.

— 'In times of drought our provisions are safely stored away. In times of plenty our women become sleek!'

So the Arioi had concluded that the Christian god was of little use. But they were afraid of the wrath of the *Piritané* and set out in their dug-outs, one paddled by eighty braves and the other containing a long *faré* to shelter the Arioi from the burning sun. They headed for Raiatéa, the island of Great Knowledge, where they would await the reaction of the missionaries and calmly debate what steps they should take. But there was one man missing: Haamanihi. Ever since the missionaries arrived his behaviour had been strange, and he never left the side of little chief Pomaré, the man with dark skin and thick lips. Would one of the Arioi, admittedly a man of lower rank, really betray the sect? That would be serious and deserving of death. But the *Piritané* missionaries had the support of a powerful ship which sometimes spat out fire with the noise of thunder. Without waiting any longer for Haamanihi, the Master of the Arioi gave orders to depart.

The missionaries had come to convert a nation of savages who, they thought, were ready to embrace Jesus the Saviour. They had never dreamed that they would encounter so different a civilization, one so diametrically opposed to their own. They were shocked by the Tahitians' nakedness and by their habit of caressing each other and making love in public with no attempt at concealment. They were horrified by the human sacrifices and by the chief having to pull out the eye of the victim. They were profoundly shaken by the frequent infanticides, which were compulsory for the Arioi who made so many women pregnant yet were under no circumstances allowed to become fathers.

The aim of the London Missionary Society was to send out missionaries – preachers and craftsmen – and to allow the little community to set itself up as best it could. Captain Wilson went off to other islands. The eighteen missionaries who remained behind organized themselves, for Tahiti was not yet the tourist island it later became and they had to live off the country. The blacksmith and the carpenter of the group soon had many friends, but the evangelical service was less warmly welcomed. Eleven missionaries soon became discouraged and left. With unshakeable confidence, the remaining seven presented their forge and their provisions to Pomaré, returned their arms to the ship in which their friends were departing, and stayed on like that with only their faith and the strength of their arms to sustain them. In 1800 the L.M.S. sent them out a new missionary, Henry, who introduced tougher methods of evangelization: he went to the nobles and made them destroy their Tahitian sculptures and all their *tiki*. They were expecting to be reinforced by some thirty new missionaries when their ship, the DUFF, suffered the fate of European political strife and was captured by the French in 1799.

The Friendly Island mission had to be abandoned as three of the missionaries were slaughtered by the natives.

But in 1801 the ROYAL ADMIRAL brought another eight

Value of Missions to Commerce and Shipping

I am convinced that the first step towards the promotion of a nation's temporal and social elevation, is to plant amongst them the tree of life, when civilization and commerce will entwine their tendrils around its trunk, and derive support from its strength. Until the people are brought under the influence of religion, they have no desire for the arts and usages of civilized life; but that invariably creates it. The Missionaries were at Tahiti many years, during which they built and furnished a house in European style. The natives saw this, but not an individual imitated their example. As soon, however, as they were brought under the influence of Christianity, the chiefs, and even the common people, began to build neat plastered cottages, and to manufacture bedsteads, seats, and other articles of furniture. The females had long observed the dress of the Missionaries' wives, but while heathen they greatly preferred their own, and there was not a single attempt at imitation. No sooner, however, were they brought under the influence of religion, than all of them, even to the lowest, aspired to the possession of a gown, a bonnet, and a shawl, that they might appear like Christian women. (...) Thus wherever the Missionary goes, new channels are cut for the stream of commerce; and to me it is most surprising that any individual at all interested in the commercial prosperity of his country can be otherwise than a warm friend to the Missionary cause. We may simply glance at the commercial advantages which have resulted and are still resulting from these labours. In the South Sea Islands alone, many thousands of persons are at this moment wearing and using articles of European manufacture, by whom, a few years ago, no such article had been seen; indeed, in the more advanced stations, there is scarcely an individual who is not attired in English clothing, which has been obtained in exchange for native produce. Thus we are benefited both in what we give and in what we receive. (...)

Apart entirely from the value of Christianity, no enlightened *statesman* can regard labours which secure such results as those I have enumerated, with indifference: for new havens are found at the antipodes for our fleets; new channels are opened for our commerce; and the friends of our country are every where multiplied.

Rev. JOHN WILLIAMS, *Missionary Enterprises in the South Sea Islands*, London 1837, p. 580-588

The Sufferings of the Chamorros

The inhabitants prize their freedom so highly that they brook no diminution of it. The foreign yoke was too much for their pride... and led some of them to despair. Life became so hateful to them that they hung themselves. Some of the women sterilised themselves, or threw their new-born children into the sea, thinking it better for them to die than to live in such slavery.

PEDRO MURILLO VELAVERDE, *Historia de la Provincia de Filippinas de la Compañia de Jesus*, 1616-1716, Manila 1749, p. 292

Missionary work was not devoid of danger, and Melanesia at times gave them a bloody reception. When John Williams landed at Eromanga (New Hebrides) on 20 November 1839 he tried to pacify the natives with gifts; without a word of warning the cannibals leaped on him and killed and ate him. The anonymous author of these two pictures emphasized the ferocity of the Melanesians so as to justify the mission of this martyr.

missionaries to Tahiti. In 1803 Pomaré was succeeded by his son Otou. He supported the missionaries and tried to educate himself, but, over-fond of the bottle, he was beaten by the anti-Christian chiefs and fled to Aimeo (now Moorea) where he was followed by the missionary Nott. The other missionaries all dispersed.

Finally in 1811 Pomaré II summoned the missionaries back and asked to be baptized. He was given Holy Baptism by Nott, who used the same words as Jesus: 'I baptize thee in the name of the Father, the Son and the Holy Ghost'. Then another missionary proclaimed Pomaré 'King of the Tahiti and Windward Islands', conjuring him to show himself 'always worthy of his high profession and of his eminent position in the eyes of the angels, of men, and of the Lord himself'. He was then given the name of Pomaré II the Reformer. A church was constructed at Papetoai and soon there were fifty faithful. Another church was built at Raiatéa under the guidance of Wilson. For all that the war of religions was not ended and a number of native Christians were sacrificed. Pomaré had, however, gone back to Tahiti where he put an end to the strife by winning a battle on 12 November 1815, after which he became recognized by one and all as King Pomaré II.

There was a similar battle at Raiatéa with Tamatoa at the head of the Christians and Tahaa in command of the pagans. Tamatoa won and summoned everyone to a huge feast. The sculptures from the *marae* were destroyed and only a few priests stayed faithful to the god Oro. The same occured at Bora-Bora and in the other Society Islands. More missionaries came out from London in 1817, including the famous Ellis whose *Polynesian Research* is still regarded as authoritative where Tahitian customs are concerned. As homage to the King, he brought a printing press and a horse, no such animal having ever before been seen on the island where the reaction was: 'What a huge pig these men have brought!' In 1819 the Tahitian Mission Society was founded. It despatched a cargo of palm oil worth a large sum of money to the parent society in London. At about time the active missionary John Williams, the Apostle of Polynesia, arrived on the scene. With his missionary spirit he combined a strong sense of commerce with often met with the disapproval of the Director of Missions. He was fairly successful in Polynesia, especially at Raratonga, but when he wanted to civilize the New Hebrides, the Kanakas, who were no fools, decided to kill him (1839).

New problems soon cropped up on all sides in Tahiti. Methodist temples were springing up everywhere and indigenous missionaries were carrying the good word to other islands when Captain Kotzebue's Russian ship put in at the same Matavaï Bay, in 1824. His book *Neue Reise um die Welt* and what it says about missionaries are well known. The spirit of the Arioi began to stir, and men claiming divine inspiration started preaching what the missionaries discreetly described as 'the emancipation of the flesh'. It was a kind of synthesis between Christianity and Arioi customs. Hidden away in a distant valley the 'heretics' would gather by night to worship the spirit of a Spanish priest. He had

## White Cupidity

I am persuaded that the Polynesians, from Hawaii to Tahiti, are dying because of the suppression of the play-instinct, an instinct that had its expression in most of their customs and occupations. Their dancing, their tattooing, their chanting, their religious rites, and even their warfare, had very visible elements of humor and joyousness. They were essentially a happy people, full of dramatic feeling, emotional, and with a keen sense of the ridiculous. The rule of the trader crushed all these native feelings.

To this restraint was added the burden of the effort to live. With the entire Marquesan economic and social system disrupted, food was not so easily procurable, and they were driven to work by commands, taxes, fines, and the novel and killing incentives of rum and opium. The whites taught the men to sell their lives, and the women to sell their charms.

Happiness and health were destroyed because the white man came here only to gratify his cupidity. The priests could bring no inspiration sufficient to overcome the degradation caused by the traders. The Marquesan saw that Jesus had small influence over their rulers. Civilization lost its opportunity because it gave precept, but no example.

FREDERICK O'BRIEN, *White Shadows in the South Seas,* New York 1919, pp. 164-165

Besides bringing the 'Good News', missionaries helped to introduce European civilization and to promote trade. New and often harsh laws gradually replaced traditional rules; left, the title pages of two law books printed at Huaheine in 1823 and 1838. Indolent and gay by nature, Polynesians had henceforth to work and be decently clad. Games, dancing and singing are now banned under penalty of imprisonment. Under such austere and puritanical conditions the islanders lost their love of life (below); the birthrate fell alarmingly in the early part of the nineteenth century, to such an extent that people began to fear for the survival of the race.

arrived years earlier to preach for a short time the worship of Mary and had died shortly after. But his bones had been respected and his words had been faithfully kept in memory:

'I salute thee, Mary; the Master is with thee. Thou art chosen among all women. Blessed is Jesus, the fruit of thy womb!'

And in his own words the Master of the heretics would follow on with this prayer: 'Breath-of-God! Breath-of-God! come down in our midst! Help us chase out the impostors and those who have usurped thy name! O Kerito who is within me, Kerito whom we knew well long before they brought thee to us and whom we called upon long before they did, help us to make all Christians perish! May they die by thy name! by thy might! they who shamelessly use thee!'

They would then revert to their ancient customs and couples would embrace and give free rein to the pleasures of the flesh.

In the Pomaré dynasty, Pomaré III had succeeded Pomaré II the Reformer (1780-1821), and in turn, following a premature death, been succeeded by his sister Queen Pomaré. At first she sided with the anti-Christians, but missionary Pritchard soon brought her back to the fold.

Meanwhile Pope Gregory XVI charged the Picpus Jesuit Society, which had joined other societies to found the *Société lyonnaise de la propagation de la foi* with converting the Pacific islands. The Picpus priests first went to the Gambiers, where they baptized the population wholesale in 1835 in the presence of Bishop Rochouse, apostolic vicar of the Pacific islands. Said the Bishop: 'This island is the door which opens up Polynesia to us'.

In 1836 two priests, Father Laval and Father Caret, landed in Tahiti. They were put up by Moerenhout and almost immediately expelled from the island.

Father Caret came back in 1837. Expelled again, he went back to Paris to ask Louis-Philippe for help.

On 27 August 1838 the French frigate VENUS under Dupetit-Thouars sailed into the bay to demand satisfaction for the insult to the French.

In January 1839 another French frigate, the ARTÉMISE under the command of La Place, came and anchored off Papeete. La Place obtained freedom of action for the Catholics and the grant of some land to build a church. Moerenhout had meantime been named French consul. He made the four chiefs sign a pledge offering France dominion over Tahiti. But calm was not restored by this. The consul's flag had several times been insulted by the 'natives' and some foreign residents had had their property forcibly expropriated. In his book *Omoo* Melville gives full backing to the 'natives' who, he writes, 'were perfectly within their rights. The law governing the liquor trade was in force at the time, being sometimes suspended and sometimes applied. The Tahitians found a large quantity of alcohol in the possession of a certain Victor, a low-class adventurer from Marseilles acknowledging neither faith nor law, and declared it seized'. Further, at a huge gathering held on 15 January 1843, the Tahitians asked for England's support in full agreement

Lost smugglers, sailors on the run, convicts and adventurers of every kind infested the South Seas. Greedy and unscrupulous, they soon found ways of turning the latent primitive habits of the islanders to their profit. A particularly revolting trade grew up in New Zealand: buying tattooed and smoked heads from the Maoris and re-selling them to museums and collectors in Europe at a handsome profit.

Pedlars specialising in the macabre trade in human trophies selected their victims 'on the hoof' in exchange for guns, alcohol and trinkets. Below, a Maori chief offers good quality tattoos. The goods will be delivered the next time the trader calls.

Raiding, looting and other excesses committed by alien invaders explained the frequently murderous attitude of the natives. Below, survivors from the shipwreck of the *Saint Paul*, her crew mainly composed of Chinese, are massacred by the inhabitants of Russell Island in 1861. La Pérouse suffered a similar fate in 1788.

with the Protestant missionaries who loudly announced that ships and armies would come to their rescue. But England turned a deaf ear to their pleas despite the vehement protests of missionary-consul Pritchard who kept Queen Pomaré under his sway and probably tended to confound politics with religion, having already several bones to pick with the Catholic missionaries and the French authorities.

Instead of a British fleet it was Dupetit-Thouars who came sailing in with three ships. He had the flag bearing the royal crown taken down from the Pomaré residence, deposed the Queen, and took Pritchard prisoner and expelled him. War broke out again on the island, bringing death to both the French and the Tahitian sides.

Feelings ran high in Christian circles in Europe. From London, Paris, Berlin, Hamburg, Geneva came a stream of letters to Louis-Philippe from Protestants demanding 'freedom of worship' for the people of Tahiti. Even today the greatest care must be used when mentioning the Pritchard affair in Christian circles. As to the 'liberty of worship' so loudly called for, nobody seemed to realize that if it had really been granted, the Tahitians and their poor little queen would have probably put it to use to throw out both French and English, Catholic and Protestant.

Similar events occurred unfortunately almost everywhere in the Pacific. They were all part of that religious struggle which was known as 'the missionary war' which lasted from 1797 to 1870. During those years 'pastors counselled local dynasties to implore England for protection, priests to appeal to France' and 'naval officers considered it their patriotic duty to support claims by the missions in the name of their government'. It should be added that those officers felt that the missionaries, soldiers of Christ the Redeemer, were single-handedly carrying out a task of pacification which would have required large numbers of troops. So how could they not believe it was their duty to help them?

This was particularly true of the French navy, as emerges from the work on missions in Melanesia by Salinis, in which the author retraces 'the continuous common struggle! (the) battles engaged from coast to coast by the Catholic missionaries and the French sailors in the name of triumphant Christian civilization'.

From Tahiti the L.M.S. turned its attention to the Austral regions, to Tuamotu, Gambier, the Marquesas, Cook and Samoa islands, to Tonga, then to Melanesia and the Loyalty islands. New Zealand and Australia were evangelized by the Anglican Mission Society founded in 1800, the New Hebrides by the Presbyterians, and the Hawaiian archipelago and Micronesia by the American Board, related to the L.M.S.

The Catholic missions only came later. In 1835 two vicars were installed, one entrusted to the Picpus fathers, the other to the Marists. The former converted the Gambiers in 1834, amongst others, then Tahiti and the Marquesas in 1836-38. The Marists settled particularly on Wallis and Futuna from 1837 on, New Zealand in 1838, and Fiji and Samoa in 1844. Finally in 1843, ten years before France annexed it, they moved into New Caledonia, where the first Protestant missionary sent out by the Société des Missions Evangéliques from Paris only arrived in 1902.

As to the Gilbert Islands and New Guinea, they came under the Order of the Sacred Heart of Issoudun, founded in 1835, before the arrival of the Benedictines and the Salesians from Australia.

The activities of the Catholics differed from those of the Protestants, the opponent brothers having only in common the hatred they harboured for each other. As to the natives, they were divided between the two missionary sides for reasons which usually had nothing religious about them.

While the missionaries were converting the islands, traders of all kinds were busy exploiting them. Moerenhout has already been mentioned, who founded in Tahiti the leading trading establishment of the whole area. From Tahiti he ran several vessels of his own and kept up continuous trading from Pitcairn and the Gambias to Fiji, from New Zealand to Hawaii. On all those islands he recruited his 'workers'. He left two books of memoirs, which were entitled *Voyages aux Iles du Grand Océan*.

So while the missionaries kept on fighting and spreading the written law of the Bible to the unwritten civilization of these peoples, traders, smugglers, adventurers and sea folk from all parts were looting the area on their own account. They would make use of their arms for no other reason than the pleasure of shooting at a moving target and thus proving their skill and the superiority of their country which had reached such technical perfection. A great deal has been written to support this. It is only necessary read what the sailors and smugglers wrote, such as the letters of Herman Melville or Cheyne the sandalwood dealer.

Seals and whales were exterminated. The Pacific islands were thoroughly deforested by the efforts of the sandalwood merchants. Soon all this wealth was exhausted, and men had to turn to 'black-birding', the contemporary term for slave trading. They mostly took their negro slaves from Melanesia, and especially from the New Hebrides. But the prisoners fought back, and often managed to rid themselves of the crews, or to escape.

To reach an idea of what happened when any attempt was made to resist, the classic example of ninety 'enlisted workers' tightly packed into the holds of the brigantine CARL should be mentionned. They were slaughtered at point blank range by the panic-stricken blood-thirsty crew, who shot into the huddled mass and went on shooting. When they came to their senses the seamen slung the 'workers' overboard, washed the ship down and... started all over again. It never mattered what they did. Brute force was of course in order, with fire-arms to back it up, but so was the most extravagant cunning. Thus slave dealers would disguise themselves as missionaries to allay the suspicion of the natives and then entice them aboard only to sail out to sea with their human cargo as prisoners. The story goes that when the missionary Patterson happened to arrive just after a group of such treacherous slave traders, the infuriated inhabitants took him for one of them, a mistake which cost the good man his life.

To secure cheap labour, settlers resorted to slave-trading. Sometimes the slaves mutinied, like these natives from the Solomon Islands jammed into the holds of the *Carl* in 1871; order was brutally restored and seventy Melanesians were slaughtered. Dead and injured were cast overboard (above). Survivors were sold at £10 a head to Queensland planters in Australia.

Slave Trading

In March 1816, the RURIK's boats were attacked by the natives of Easter Island... all attempts to gain their friendship by offering them presents were in vain; Captain Kotzebue was only able to disembark under the protection of his musketry, and when he left, he again departed under a hail of stones. Arriving at Sandwich, the Russians asked an Englishman the reason for the hostile behaviour of the natives, who had given such a different welcome to Cook and Lapérouse. It appears that twelve of them, with ten women, were kidnapped from the island in 1809, by an American captain, who hoped to use them as slaves in the seal fisheries of San Fernandez. Three days after leaving the island, these unfortunates were freed from their irons, and promptly lept into the waves, never to be seen again. The women were with difficulty prevented in following their example.

HYACINTHE DE BOUGAINVILLE, *Journal de la navigation autour du globe de la frégatte* LA THÉTIS *et de la corvette* L'ESPÉRANCE (1824-1826), Ed. Arthus Bertrand, Paris 1837, pp. 549-550 (Nov. 1925)

These pictures show a gang of slave-traders operating off the coast of New Caledonia. Armed to the teeth, the traders had no hesitation in throwing their human cargo into the sea if coastguards appeared.

Naturally steps were taken to put a stop to that kind of activity. But with what results? It was still going on at the beginning of the twentieth century. To obtain a true picture of the terrible drop in the population of the islands of Oceania, on top of the ravages produced by the new diseases caught from the crews, it would be necessary to evaluate the parts played by the sandalwood dealers, the sea slug catchers, whalers and slave traders as well as the consequences of alcohol and even sometimes opium. The resultant colonization was achieved at a high price to the ecology of the area and in the lives of its inhabitants. But it is only right that the missionaries, whose selflessness must be emphasized, should be set apart from the series of uncontrolled invasions which fell upon the peoples of the Pacific. Nevertheless, as far as the original culture of those countries went, it is a fact that everyone concerned, missionaries and others, must inevitably share the blame for the wholesale ethnocide which took place.

# ECONOMIC AND POLITICAL FACTORS

'Yes, new markets are what our great industries need more and more now that the treaties of 1860 have turned them towards ever greater development... Are our governments going to leave the task of policing the mouth of the Red River to others? Are they going to leave it to others to dispute the territories of Equatorial Africa? ... If France wants to remain a great country she has to introduce her language, her customs, her flag, her arms and her genius wherever she can!'

No clearer definition of the real motives for colonization can be conceived. Jules Ferry, who addressed those words to the French Chamber of Deputies on 26 July 1885, had nothing of the extremist or the adventurer about him. He was a serious and moderate statesman, a republican, which means that for those days he stood politically somewhat to left of centre: he belonged to the *Gauche républicaine* (Republican left) party and was particularly noted for his courageous educational reforms. He instigated the introduction of free primary education in France.

He saw nothing contradictory in also being one of the fathers of France's second colonial empire. In that, as a matter of fact, he was merely imitating his European colleagues, especially the British, but also the German, Russian, Italian and, later, American. The nineteenth century was in effect the second era of European colonial expansion. The first had lasted for 300 years, from the beginning of the fifteenth century until 1830.

Although the British and French had participated in it, the leading protagonists had been the Spaniards and the Portuguese, and later the Dutch. Despite their lavish scale, the earlier colonial adventures had been relatively marginal in relation to their respective national politics. Discovery was carried out for the glory of it as well as for lucrative commercial purposes, but without the whole country being behind it. The initiative often came from dashing *conquistadores* who thereby reconciled their material ambitions with their hope for Life Eternal in their search for gold, glory and pagans to be converted. After 1830 things became different. Colonization began to be taken seriously, with the nations of Europe on the look-out for profit and prestige. In his speech of 28 July 1885 Jules Ferry was only putting into words the convictions held by most European statesmen of his day.

The aims of yesteryear would still continue to be presented as paramount, and indeed in some cases were those pursued by a few: exploring, discovering unknown lands and seas, converting the pagan, searching for rare items and precious metals, pioneering brave new settlements. But colonization had now become an affair of state, and integral part of the general politics of the great nations of Europe.

The same formula was certainly regarded as applicable to all the great states of late nineteenth century Europe as was applied by Paul Leroy-Beaulieu to France in his *De la colonisation chez les peuples modernes* published in 1874: 'For France colonization is a matter of life and death'. This novel conception could be attributed to a number of motives, economic, demographic and political.

Colonial imperialism appears as the inescapable consequence of the capitalist economy which was then booming throughout Western Europe.

This new form of economy was to cause real disruption: the progress of science and technology made it possible to set up huge industrial centres, ever more powerful, with constantly growing output and in need of parallel growth of financial resources and systematic bank support. Such expansion called for as plentiful and as cheap commodities as possible together with ever wider marketing outlets. These were at first sought on the spot, that is to say in Europe, at home and in neighbouring countries. But opportunities there were limited, thanks to the fact that many countries erected protective tariff barriers against competitors. In contrast, there appeared to exist almost unlimited opportunity in those new areas discovered by colonial expeditions which were now becoming closer to the colonising countries thanks to the progress in maritime transport. They offered raw materials, which at first glance seemed inexhaustible, at low prices while simultaneously providing profitable trouble-free markets for some of the manufactured products. European agriculture began to fall behind – another feature of capitalist economy – but that was now of less concern since the new countries could also provide enormous quantities of foodstuffs at prices beneficial to both the home country and the settler.

Europe thus became the factory of the world with England in the forefront, where two thirds of the world's consumption of coal was being extracted. But it was not all smooth running. There came in turn the 'great boom' from 1850 to 1875, the 'great depression' between 1875 and 1895, followed by the 'new boom' from 1895 to 1914. Such ups

The fascination of the South Seas attracted the first well-to-do tourists to whom the natives were able to sell their assagais, carvings and other souvenirs. Tourism had as destructive an effect as the missionaries, who meant well but were... narrow-minded.

In 1872 a group of 100 men off the French frigate *La Flore* destroyed a number of Easter Island statues (below). Of those, one is today in the Louvre and the others have been resold. A statue was worth the price of an officer's uniform. Such senseless vandalism recalls Admiral Dupetit-Thouars' action when he destroyed relics of Tahiti's past by cannon-fire in 1844.

167

Botany Bay

We learnt from a lieutenant that the English fleet was commanded by Commodore Philipp (sic), who had appeared the evening before on board the corvette SPEY [really the sloop SUPPLY], accompanied by four transport vessels, in search towards the north of a more convenient place to set up his establishment. The English lieutenant appeared to cloak Commodore Philipp's plans with mystery, and we refrained from questioning him on the subject. However, it seemed likely that the new site was not very near Botany Bay, for the longboats and gigs were under sail to reach it; on the other hand, the distance could not be very far, for it was not considered worthwhole to hoist in the small boats on board ship. Soon the boat's crew, less discreet than their officer, informed our crew that they were only going as far as Port Jackson, sixteen miles to the north of Point Banks. There Commodore Philipp himself had surveyed an excellent harbour which stretched for some ten miles towards the south-west. The ships could moor within a pistol-shot of the shore, in a sea as calm as in a harbour. We afterwards had all too many opportunities to learn more details of the colony, for deserters from it caused us much trouble and embarassment.

J.-P. DE GALAUP DE LA PÉROUSE, *Voyage autour du monde,* edited by L.-A. Millet-Mureau, Paris 1798, vol. III, pp. 313-316 (Jan. 1788)

In this romantic painting, British emigrants on their way to Australia are sadly gazing at a primrose, last souvenir of their homeland. Around 1820 there were not yet very many of them, Australia's coasts being mainly settled by convicts and political exiles.

and downs only served to intensify the interest of the industrial nations in their colonies. The latter continued to furnish the former with their raw materials and with the outlets they needed, but enabled them in times of crisis to keep their private markets more or les unaffected by the economic depressions. For example, the effects of the 'great depression' were far more severely felt in Germany which still possessed no colonies. Hitherto having shown little interest in colonial enterprise, Bismarck changed his mind as a consequence and from 1884 on resolved to follow in the footsteps of the colonial imperialists, footsteps which finally led him to New Guinea. That illustrates the growing importance being linked to overseas possessions. Industrialists, financiers, businessmen, not to mention politicians, all were coming to realize that colonial expansion was a necessary complement to, and one of the conditions required for, economic expansion in the light of the then capitalist system. The driving spirit of the French 'colonial party', Eugène Etienne, said so in so many words, crudely stating: 'The colonialist ideal is, and can only be, founded on self-interest... So it can be clearly seen that the only criteria to be applied is the extent of its usefulness, the sum total of the benefits and advantages which the home country can derive from it'.

At that time Europe was not merely the industrial and financial centre of the world. It was also one of its most densely populated regions beset by a notable population explosion, which had risen from 265 millions in 1850 to 400 millions in 1900 and to over 450 millions by 1914. France was in the lead with 38 millions but began to stagnate at that level, while the population of England grew from 27 to 31 millions in a quarter of a century. The same was happening in Germany and Italy. No doubt growing industry called for greater numbers of workers, but it was also responsible for a shift from the land besides being subject to periodical crises as from 1875 to 1895. In addition, there were areas like Ireland and southern Italy, which derived no benefit from the industrial boom. All these factors combined to give rise to a vast wave of emigration from Europe, first to America, then further and further afield towards the newly conquered colonies in the hands of western nations: in less than 70 years 30 million Europeans found homes in this way in the new countries.

The migrant wave rolled as far as the Pacific. In that far off area it took on a peculiar shape: penal emigration. First England then France made use of their largest Oceanian possessions to clear their prisons of the most undesirable elements among their convicts.

England led the way with Australia.

In spite of the glowing reports on the discovery of Australia sent back by Cook, England had shown no hurry to occupy the new territories. Her rulers had more important fish to fry. Among other problems they were taken up with the revolt of their North American colonies which soon grew into the War of Independence and led to the birth of the United States of America. And some of those colonies had for many years been used to free the prisons of England of some of their inmates. At that time England was ahead

in the industrial race and harbored record numbers of delinquents. Prison capacity was no longer sufficient. So the most dangerous and unwanted prisoners were being sent overseas, many being 'sold' to the American colonies to perform the roughest tasks. With independence this 'white slave traffic' came to an end. But that did not stop delinquency. What then could be done to relieve the pressure on these prisons? At first attempts were made to use hulks, pontoon lighters lying in the Port of London. But they soon proved inadequate. At that stage came the idea of turning to the territories discovered by Cook. Banks was called in for consultation; he warmly endorsed the project. So did James Matra, another former member of the crew of the ENDEAVOUR. He added that New South Wales (so named by Cook who had no idea that he had discovered the famous austral continent) could well become a prosperous British colony capable of taking the place of the lost American colonies.

So on orders from Sydney, the then Home Secretary, Captain Arthur Phillip was given the task of taking out a convoy of convicts and settling them near Botany Bay. After many hardships the little colony began to take shape. To enable it to stand on its own feet he initiated a system of land concessions open to both soldiers and convicts, subject to certain conditions. From 1800 onwards the first groups of free settlers began to arrive, workers from England in search of a better life. But for another twenty years Australia remained a land of convicts, be they felons or political prisoners. Of a total of 40,000 inhabitants in 1821 only 1,307 were free settlers. From that point on a tremendous effort was made to encourage migration.

The Australian colonies were beginning to take shape. As of 1840 the oldest of them, New South Wales, ceased altogether to be a penal colony. Its example was soon followed by the other colonies with the exception of West Australia where the barren empty spaces made it necessary to call on convict labour for a long time to come.

England's success in colonizing Australia, first as a penal settlement and gradually later as a free colony, probably inspired France to follow her example, albeit half a century later. In 1853 the French took possession of New Caledonia. Were they contemplating turning it into a penal colony? The idea was indeed mooted but the drive really came from the Marist fathers who were afraid that the island where they had worked so devotedly for ten years might fall into the hands of the Protestant British. At first it was a free and somewhat anarchistic colony. After five years of French rule the commander of the island wrote to his minister 'So far no serious settler has presented himself in New Caledonia; all there are today are a few stores and cabarets. The only exception is, I regret to say, an Englishman, Squire Paddon'.

Eight years after being taken over New Caledonia could only boast some 400 settlers. In 1861 Captain Guillain, later to become its governor, could see that the colony had scant hope of growing if left to its own devices and conceived the idea of adding to its population by turning it into a convict settlement, in which he visualized '... large numbers of settlers who would be forced to provide an agreed amount of working time...'. Planned along these lines '... the colonization of New Caledonia would be a prudent, generous and eminently moral task offering every advantage to Society'.

A law dated 30 May 1854 already provided for transportation, in other words transferring convicts out of the national territory with a view to 'making treatment more humane and moral by putting it to the benefit of French colonization'. This was first used for Guyana. Later, in 1863, New Caledonia was designated 'as a choice land for penal settlement'. So it came about that on 7 May 1864 the IPHIGÉNIE arrived with a first convoy of 250 convicts. Their numbers grew rapidly and they were joined in 1871 by some 4,000 political deportees from the Paris Commune. Convicts continued to be sent there up to 1896.

Acquiring colonies is not only dictated by economic and practical motives. It came more and more to be regarded as a factor of national prestige, a visible sign of power on the international scene. Gradually most of the world's available unoccupied areas were split up between the great nations of Europe.

The building of those immense colonial empires sometimes gave rise to violent conflict between the great colonizing powers, Great Britain and France, or alternatively between nations which had entered the race for colonies at a later stage, such as Germany and Italy. But such conflicts went no further than international political tensions which almost invariably ended in compromises, as at the time the colonial powers had a common interest: securing world domination.

Examples of this were to be seen even in the far off Pacific. An instance of this kind was the 1844 Pritchard incident in Tahiti, following the institution of French protectorate over the archipelago. As it involved an area recognized as coming under French influence, it was felt that it should not be allowed to affect the efforts being undertaken at the time by King Louis-Philippe and Prime Minister Gladstone to institute closer ties between England and France. Another such example was England's disavowal of the occupation of the eastern part of New Guinea by Queensland in 1883, because the intention was to reach an agreement with Germany on the subject. Like the rest of the world, the Pacific was carved up between England, France and later Germany and the United States.

Great Britain obtained the lion's share, including Australia, New Zealand, part of New Guinea and the Central Islands. Next came France with Tahiti, New Caledonia and joint ownership of the New Hebrides. Germany's share was more modest: the north-eastern part of New Guinea, the Carolines and the Marianas Islands and part of Samoa. The United States only entered the race after their victory over Spain in 1898; they secured Hawaii and the Philippines. Japan took Formosa and the Netherlands occupied the western part of New Guinea. There was no more land left to discover, no more islands to conquer. Almost all the Pacific was in the hands of Europeans.

The first convoy arrived in Botany Bay in 1788 with 700 convicts and 200 sailors, and dropped anchor off Port Jackson (Sydney). This 1791 caricature shows the prisoners taking leave of their families. Police are summoning them to board their ships for Australia. Their wives and children will be able to join them at the end of their sentences. But they have scant hope of ever seeing England again.

On arrival in Australia prisoners were mainly employed on road construction. Some worked on near-by plantations. At the end of their sentence they could acquire land and a wife. After 10 years of good conduct they might, if they could afford it, return to England. But many chose to settle in a country where class differences and social injustices were less.

Transporting convicts took a lot of organizing as the journey lasted several weeks. In 1843 the list of supplies for the *Lord Petre* included more than 1,000 lbs of lemon (against scurvy), 179 lbs of meat and soup rations, 43 pairs of handcuffs and 248 chains.

Rural postmen in the Australian outback were not without their problems!

# THE COLONIZED TERRITORIES

The second wave of colonial expansion in the nineteenth century was destined to envelop almost all the lands of the Pacific and bring destruction to everything that constituted their unity. Bound together by so many cultural and economic ties yet possessed of a civilization which Western minds of the day could scarcely comprehend, these territories would come to be split up and separated in proportion to the might of the colonizing powers involved. At that time little thought was given to the notion of respecting a different but indigenous civilization or of seeking knowledge of alternative cultures. With few exceptions, the old chiefs, who had fiercely resisted the invaders, would be replaced by new ones who were supported and often designated by the colonizing power. The traditional structure founded on 'respect for the chief' crumbled as the newly nominated chief bowed to the laws of the conqueror. From this point, the group would lose its cohesion and vitality, improverishing the social constitution of their society. The subjugated people could no longer depend on themselves nor on their long established interchange with neighbouring islands, and would have to turn to their new masters for help and support. Furthermore, the new intruders often caused serious damage to the ecology of those areas: indigenous flora and fauna suffered, often beyond recovery, as new species were introduced which gradually assumed dominance.

The existing natural balance thus destroyed, the colonized territories would become bound by new links such as a common language and especially Christianity. Following in the tracks of the great explorers, missionaries became the great colonizing scouts, bringing with them their nationalism and the great rivalry of Catholic and Protestant, although in fact the methods they used were not very different. To the colonized inhabitants, Western civilization appeared under the cloak of religion, and Christian morality was punctuated by cannon fire and gun shots from the armed forces. There were other unifying factors involved, particularly of economic, technological and political nature. Doubtless a distinction must be made between the various forms of administration, 'direct rule' and 'indirect rule'. But for the occupied people the over-all result was the same.

Thus the nineteenth century was destined to be a tragic period for the colonized territories, bringing as it did structural disintegration, often going as far as genocide and ethnocide. Over the ruins the colonizers would then try to superimpose new structures inspired by their own civilizations. By the end of the century the number of inhabitants throughout the colonized territories could be seen to have fallen catastrophically.

All in the day's work for a rural postman in North-East Australia in the 1880s. His mail round might stretch for 3,000 miles.

# AUSTRALIA

When England resolved to colonize Australia, she was in the process of an unprecedented economic and demographic expansion, and colonized with the primary aim of relieving the pressure on her overcrowded prisons.

Charged by the government with setting up a prison colony, Captain Arthur Phillip set out from Britain on 13 May 1787 in command of a squadron of two warships, the SIRIUS and the SUPPLY, and nine other vessels carrying 200 soldiers and sailors, 40 army wives and 750 convicts, of whom about a third were women. At the Cape of Good Hope they took on stocks of grain and cattle and after a journey of eight months – during which some 20 convicts died despite Captain Phillip's comparatively mild treatment – the 'First Fleet' dropped anchor off Botany Bay on 18 January 1788. They put ashore first the men and then the livestock consisting of 2 bulls, 5 cows, 3 foals, 29 sheep, 19 goats, 25 pigs with 49 young, 5 rabbits, 18 turkeys, 35 ducks, 29 geese, 122 hens and 85 pullets. But what they found had little in common with the descriptions provided by Banks and Matra. For Banks had been consulted. Matra, another old and from the ENDEAVOUR, had also supported the project for a penal settlement and added that New South Wales – so named by Captain Cook who had no idea that he had discovered the famous austral continent which had aroused the imagination of his predecessors, so no one yet referred to it as Australia – could become a prosperous British colony capable of taking the place of those which had just been lost in America.

Without further ado, Phillip set about finding a more suitable location for a colony. Three days later he discovered a bay enclosed by a narrow passage between tall cliffs.

He named this natural port, one of the the most beautiful in the world, Port Jackson, which was later to become the future Sydney Harbour. He decided to settle there. With that in mind he hastened back to Botany Bay where on 24 January he was astounded to find two large ships flying the French flag: the ASTROLABE and the BOUSSOLE which, under command of La Pérouse, had come to take a look at that Botany Bay so glowingly described by Cook and Banks. Relations between the two captains were courteous, but Phillip hastened to proclaim openly British sovereignty over the country. After staying six weeks the ASTROLABE and the BOUSSOLE departed and were never seen again, for they were wrecked at Vanikoro shortly after.

Captain Phillip reloaded all his party and landed them at Port Jackson, where the adventure of settling in began. It nearly ended disastrously. The convicts were not prepared for the job of pioneers expected of them. Nor had the military any intention of becoming builders and farmers, or of clearing the bush. There was pillaging and murder and a permanent court martial had to be set up. The animals disappeared into the bush. European grain and seeds planted in Australian soil produced the poorest of crops. Venereal

George Angas's water colours, painted when he visited Australia in 1840, show the country already in full development. Above, the little farming village of Angaston in South Australia.

Right, an animated street scene in Adelaide, future State capital of South Australia, founded in 1836 by Protestant settlers. The inhabitants worked hard and business flourished, thanks to the harbour 8 miles from town. Ten years after its foundation, Adelaide was already an important commercial centre.

Port Adelaide (below) was the gateway to the new continent. It exported silver, copper, barley and wool, and imported food, clothes and machinery from England or India. In the background is a huge warehouse from which goods were sent inland or shipped overseas.

175

Above, right: sheep-shearing in Queensland. Below, right: near Adelaide sheep-raising soon gave way to barley growing, more profitable in that area (watercolour by George Angas).

Australia's was essentially an agricultural economy. During the first decades settlers were faced by famine: the soil was arid, water scarce. Cultivatable land was limited to the 'fertile crescent' along the south-east coast. In 1797 Captain MacArthur introduced sheep. Others followed suit, and settlers came to be divided into three classes: small farmers, the free emigrants from England; freed convicts; and big sheep farmers (squatters). By 1840 there were 5,000 sheep farmers running a million head of sheep.

Left: cattle-raising at Inkerman station in the West.

Below: a typical landscape, painted in 1835 by John Glover.

177

disease and scurvy took their toll of the little colony of men and women. Meanwhile the mother country seemed to have lost all interest in Captain Phillip and his expedition. Appeals for help went unanswered. In 1789 they were on the verge of famine when a frigate put in from the Cape of Good Hope with a load of supplies. And on 3 June 1790 the 'Second Fleet' arrived, admittedly with more supplies but also with a new party of convicts, who were in a pitiful state.

But under Captain Phillip's leadership things began to take shape. To enable the colony to become self-supporting soldiers who agreed to stay on in Sydney were offered concessions. The same was done for the convicts, to whom a system of indulgences was applied. It produced results.

Obviously any land handed out in this way came from the properties of the natives, who felt cheated. They tried to put up a resistance against such encroachment. But faced with the means at the disposal of the whites their weapons were puny indeed. One of them gave up the unequal struggle and was welcomed to the Governor's table. The settlement was off to a good start. When Phillip went back to England in 1792, 3,470 acres of concession lands had been distributed.

There appears to have been some difficulty in finding a successor for Governor Phillip, with the result that authority passed into the hands of the military who took advantage to monopolise all the economic life of the country in their own hands. To be honest, the economic activity was limited – first and foremost to liquor trading, to agriculture, and to hunting seals and whales, which in many places were entirely wiped out, and in others seriously depleted. The convicts worked in the service of the military, who paid them in kind, mostly with liquor. The home country did manage to find governors, but not always very successfully.

By the time Governor-General Hunter came out to take charge of New South Wales, it was a colony of 5,000 people with more than 50 horses and mares, some 70 bulls and calves, about 100 cows and heifers, 54 bullcocks, 1500 sheep and as many goats and pigs.

The town of Sydney was taking shape, boasting numbered houses and separate districts. Prisons, schools, hospitals and churches were built and a special currency system created. Then settlers began moving inland where the first inhabitants of the country had taken refuge. This gave rise to unceasing skirmishes, but of what use could the most skillfully thrown assegai be against guns?

Captain Gidley King succeeded Hunter as Governor-General in 1800, at which time there also arrived a batch of English working families as the colony's first voluntary settlers. Victims of England's dawning era of industrialization, the penal colony appeared to them as a place of refuge. They had hopes of finding a better life in the promising land.

In 1806 Captain Bligh became Governor-General. He was not successful in putting a stop to the army's excesses. He had already distinguished himself during the mutiny of the BOUNTY. He was put under arrest by his own men, court martialled and finally deposed. There followed an interval without a government, until the arrival of the famous Colonel Lacklan Macquarie on 23 December 1809 accompanied

Australia needed women, and good conditions were offered to those willing to emigrate, provided they could show a good conduct certificate. This buxom matron is off in search of a husband. 'There are plenty of good husbands in Australia, they may be married without much dowry', she said. 'In England men will only marry money.'

EMIGRATION in SEARC
*of a*
HUSBAND.

In Queensland wooing was informal and not over romantic. It took only a few minutes to decide. Men wanted an economic, loyal and fertile wife. Women sought a protective, hard-working and even-tempered husband. The Australian pioneers had little use for psychological subtleties.

by his own regiment. He started by sending the New South Wales regiment back to England and restored order by putting an end to the commercial monopolies usurped by the military. He founded new towns: Windsor, Richmond, Wilberforce, Pitt and Castelreagh. But the most notable feature of his government, and probably the most positive, was to re-instate convicts to normal life at the end of their sentences, that is when they became emancipists.

Who were those convicts? Some were genuine criminals, but many were victims of the extremely severe penal code. There were also a number of political prisoners, mostly Irishmen in revolt against British rule. Macquarie introduced a system of distributing land concessions to any emancipists willing to become settlers. They were permitted to use the services of convicts still awaiting their freedom. Macquarie entrusted the emancipists with all kinds of duties: thus one of them was the architect of the future Sydney while others became doctors, bankers, magistrates and even senior police officers.

By such means the colony gradually moved towards becoming self-supporting. This was indeed necessary as Great Britain was fully absorbed and exhausted by its battles against Napoleon and had no intention of continuing subsidies to the colony.

Soon sheep farming was to provide the colony with its first export product. An army man who had arrived with the 'Second Fleet' had the idea of introducing the first merino sheep to the continent. He and his friends had obtained concessions of vast tracts of land and started to breed sheep. Their efforts were successful and in 1807 the first wool from Australia appeared on the London market. MacArthur was a picturesque character. A former army officer, he became the first of Australia's great sheep farmers. His actions were often scarcely within the limits of the law and he had many a brush with successive governors, yet adhered to a form of life as close as possible to that of the British gentry. His was a style of life which was kept up by many people in Australia even after it became politically independent of Britain.

In any event, when Macquarie left New South Wales in 1821 it could be said that the country had got off to a good start. There were almost 40,000 inhabitants. The capital, Sydney, was a subject of universal admiration for its good order, its location and its size. It had, however, not yet reached a stage of social cohesion. Macquarie's plan had been to amalgamate the different classes making up the population which consisted of the army, civil servants, convicts, emancipists and free settlers. But the latter were very much against the idea. Setting out to practise what he preached, Macquarie had invited emancipists to dinner at his residence, thereby earning the opprobrium of society, some of which went so far as to ignore his invitations.

Macquarie's troubles stemmed from the privileged classes, who levelled every kind of charge against him and managed to persuade London to send out a commission of enquiry in 1819. The commission could find nothing against him but his position had by then become so untenable that he resigned.

Kangaroo hunting was a favourite pastime. Kangaroos jump several yards at a time, and cross the bush at an average of 18 mph. Men on horseback with greyhounds chased them in herds till they were exhausted. The quarry then turned to face them, blows from its fore paws being capable of killing a dog. The hunter finished off the kangaroo with a club. Its meat can be eaten, its tail makes an excellent soup. The slower koala bear was hunted for its fur (left). The curious Australian fauna gradually retreated in the face of farming and cattle-breeding. Defenceless, they were decimated by new diseases, rats and imported dogs which reverted to the wild. Their total extermination was only prevented by their being able to retreat into the vast hinterland.

Up to that point only the area around Sydney was settled. England was exhausted by the loss of her American colonies and the Napoleonic wars and had no wish for further colonial adventure. But as time went on the memories of the lost colonies began to fade and the needs of British industry to become more urgent. Besides, there was still the fear of the old French rival. Might they not also start taking an interest in the far-off Australian continent? As early as 1802 the Baudin expedition with two ships, the GÉOGRAPHE and the NATURALISTE had carried out an extensive survey of the southern coast and had given it the name of the 'Napoleon Coast'. Was this an attempt to take it over?

The purpose of that expedition had in fact been strictly scientific, with scientists like Louis Freycinet and François Péron on board. But science can cloak a multitude of sins. In any event it was felt wiser not to stay confined to New South Wales but to occupy as many points of the Australian coast as possible.

A start was made with the Island of Tasmania which turned out to be much more fertile and rich in vegetation than New South Wales. Paradoxically, as a reaction against Macquarie's policies, Tasmania was first used as a branch of the penal colony. New South Wales was tired of its convicts and aspired to a respectable reputation. So they conceived the idea of sending the more dangerous convicts to Tasmania. There they were largely left in semi-freedom and indulged in every kind of excess, particularly at the expense of the indigenous population, until 1824, when Tasmania became an independent colony. An energetic governor, Colonel George Arthur, was sent to take control.

But that was not the only new development. Expansion was under way: soldiers and immigrants vied with each other to find places to settle all round the circumference of Australia. The government was busy occupying the strategic points which they were afraid might fall into alien hands, their first fear being of the French. The immigrants were in search of virgin land for farming and cattle breeding. This gave rise to the 'squatters' who were to play so important a part in the growth of Australia. The land belonged to whoever settled on it first. It was in this way that the future towns of Darwin, Perth, Albany, Adelaide, Melbourne, and Brisbane came to be founded. Around these centres autonomous colonies were formed: Western Australia, South Australia, Victoria, and Queensland. None of them felt any tie to the old proud New South Wales.

That was also the period when the fabulous whale oil trade started. Thomas Melville (see below), one of the captains from the London firm of Samuel Enderly & Sons, came out to Port Jackson with a cargo of convicts. On the way they had sighted a school of whales. With his whaler BRITANNIA, and accompanied by Captain Eber Bunker in the WILLIAM AND ANN, he ransacked the coast. Sometimes they would between them take in as much as seven whales in a couple of hours. Eber Bunker, a Nantucket man, was destined to play an important part in developing the whale oil industry of which industrial England stood in such need for lighting her factories and lubricating her new machines.

Tasmania had meanwhile been opened up to free settlers, although still remaining a penal colony. Around 1837 half of its population was made up of convicts, the other half of free settlers. The latter were of a variety of origins and religious faiths, which raised a certain number of problems. The convicts, who wore no uniforms or distinguishing marks, were used as servants and common laborers. If Alexandre Dumas' accounts are to be believed in his delightful *Journal de Madame Giovanni*, life there would seem to have been rather peaceful.

At the instigation of Sir John Franklin, Lieutenant-Governor of Tasmania from 1837 to 1843, a system of lay education was set up. This was an unique departure for the entire British Empire and is worthy of special mention. One hundred years ahead of the rest of Europe, Franklin looked on this as the solution of his problem of securing good relations between the various sectors of society. He obtained the support of Dr Arnold, headmaster of Rugby, the English public school, who had a good reputation in education circles of the day. Dr Arnold sent him out one of his principal assistants, Sir Phillip Gell, to help organize his new educational system. Gell arrived in 1840 and the school was founded. It was open to everyone, although everyone hardly included any 'natives' as they had been thrown into the sea in the 1832 manhunt. But the school made no distinction as to position, origin or — quite extraordinary at the time — religion. It raised a general outcry but Franklin held out.

## Discovery of a Continent:

On 26 and 27 March 1838 young Lieutenant George Grey was wandering around the Kimberley when he discovered rock paintings depicting Australian traditional mythology, including one of *Galaru* the Rainbow Serpent. He hastened to publish his findings in *Journals of two Expeditions of Discoveries* (London, 1841) where he described for the first time Australia's totem customs. It aroused some curiosity, but for Westerners it merely suggested some savage exotic art. Europe was too busy elsewhere to give thought to ancient myths from the other end of the world. Besides, Grey was himself unaware of their true significance. Yet those drawings of *Wondjinas*, chinless faces created in primeval times by the Rainbow Serpent, constitute a lasting bridge to the timeless past. They were the heros and the rulers. If respectful attention had been given to those men and women cavedwellers, the *Wondjinas*, if the message of the Rainbow Serpent could have been understood with its mythical expression of the meetings of contrasts, a mingling of past and present civilizations might have ensued, enriching both in mutual respect for each other and for life. Instead of becoming an outpost of a fundamentally racist Europe, Australia might perhaps have fulfilled an exemplary destiny: by 'merging the contrasting' like the rainbow, she would have become the source of life.

For the time being Australia was satisfied with a different

The daily life of the Bushmen was full of dangers. Sometimes they would be attacked by aborigines chased out of the few fertile areas. But it was an unequal struggle. Australia's original inhabitants had to retreat into the desert lands of the interior or be settled in reserves around the towns.

In the interior, trappers and Australian pioneers closely followed the explorers. Shepherds or farmers, they liked to settle near the few rivers and streams. Such adventurous living encouraged tough and resolute men, like these bushmen posing proudly in front of their shack (c.1880).

destiny: a 'colonization' which succeeded perfectly. A case of this kind is sufficiently uncommon to be worth noting.

Although the coasts were more or less known, nothing was yet known of the interior. There was a common belief in the existence of some inland sea, an 'Australian Mediterranean'. In the beginning people remained in the area around Sydney which was sufficient for their needs. The few efforts made to explore the chain of mountains which closed off the horizon to North and West had all met with failure. Climbers succeeded in crossing them for the first time in 1813. On the other side of the mountains they caught their first glimpse of vast, green and tranquil stretches of land.

The great exploration of the interior started in 1840. Several explorers lost their lives, among them Leichardt who, after a number of successful expeditions, tried to travel from Sydney to Perth in 1848, only to vanish with his six companions and seventy-seven animals. No trace of them was ever found.

Others were more fortunate, and perhaps more sensible. In 1841 John Eyre discovered the inland lake which bears his name. Failing to cross it, he turned back and made for the Nullarbar Plain which runs along the coast. After walking for months and losing some of his companions, he was on the verge of meeting the same fate as Leichardt when he sighted Capitaine Rossister's French whaler and was taken aboard. During the course of his long wanderings John Eyre made many interesting notes which appear in his Journal. He wondered at the aborigines being able to frequent so regularly those very areas where his companions had lost their lives. He said they were of 'indolent nature' and noted that walking 'without haste or worry they do not suffer from the effects of the heat or stress or the pangs of thirst which for Europeans are caused not only by physical exertion and the great efforts which they force upon themselves, but mainly by the feeling of lack of security and the resultant sensation of fear'. The aborigines whom John Eyre encountered set about finding food and water 'without haste or excessive concern, well before they really needed them'. In contrast, when whites noticed their provisions diminishing, even if they knew how to find food in the area, 'they always waited until the last moment before starting their search'. Exhausted, hot and thirsty, they 'were in a dreadful state, overcome by fear' and as a result, incapable of taking any constructive initiative.

That was how Elkin described the conditions in his *The Australian Aborigines* in which he tells of explorers often meeting in the desert with 'small groups of aborigines showing no sign of fatigue and even in excellent condition. In 1873 Colonel Warburton had such an encounter west of Waterloo Wells. He found these men 'handsome, well set up, most of them wearing beards, all in good physical condition', particularly when one considers their miserable and precarious existence'.

'The miserable and precarious existence was Colonel Warburton's opinion', writes Elkin, 'but the aborigines certainly did not think so. Their economic system was based on hunting and finding food which meant a daily search for nourishment (...)'. Wisely, they lived 'from day to day'.

Elkin likewise disputes John Eyre's epithet of 'indolent nature' applied to the aborigines, explaining that the aborigine is 'psychologically adapted' as is well expressed by their phrase 'This is my country. My country knows me'.

In 1844 another explorer, Charles Sturt, set out from Adelaide with a large party, in contrast to the habit of the aborigines of travelling in small groups and thereby reducing their needs. Stuart was attempting to succeed where his predecessor had given up three years earlier: he planned to get beyond the inland lakes discovered by Eyre. He failed.

Other attempts were made with similar lack of success. It fell to John Stuart, a member of the Charles Sturt expedition, to complete the journey from Adelaide to Darwin and back in two years and to raise the British flag in the very heart of the continent, near Alice Springs. When he got back to Adelaide he was given a triumphal reception, in December 1862. It proved to be a transient triumph, however, for he died shortly after from the effects of exhaustion. Another expedition had set out from Melbourne at about the same time and with the same goal in mind: crossing Australia from North to South. Led by a certain Robert Burke, who had been named and subsidised by the Royal Victoria Society, it ended in failure with the death of Burke himself and his companion Wills.

There were still many parts of that vast Australian continent to be discovered. But its 'mystery' had at last been uncovered with close-up glimpses of its deserts, its lack of water and its more fertile regions. It is none the less strange to realize that it took more than 150 years, from William Jensz to Cook, to trace the complete coastline – not to mention all the other explorers who sailed around and cruised along portions of the coast only to depart without knowing it; and almost another hundred years, as we have seen, before the interior became known. As to Australia's riches beneath the soil, these were only recently discovered.

## The gold rush

Meanwhile there occurred an event which was to shake the fragile burgeoning economy of Australia: the discovery of gold in 1851 in New South Wales and a few months later in Victoria. Until then the economy had been based essentially on wool exports. The squatters' main concern had been finding new pasture land. They paid little attention to Wakefield's theories recommending the maintenance of high prices for concession land to avoid 'dispersal'; instead they tried to obtain them at as low a price as possible and even for nothing. The lives of these rugged folk was strange indeed. If they were married they would generally leave their wives and children behind in the towns and go to live as bushmen, alone or with their mate, some companion with whom they shared their lives. But their prosperity depended on world wool prices which fluctuated wildly and often collapsed altogether. They might be former convicts

The differences between the lives and mentalities of the whites and aborigines raised an insurmountable barrier between them. Cattle-rustling or the killing of a white man met with appalling reprisals, and the arrival of settlers caused indescribable terror.

From 1828 on, the whites in Tasmania set about the total extermination of the aborigine. Hunting dogs were used to 'clear' the country systematically. This even became a sport. The last Tasmanian died in 1876. Genocide was complete.

Following double page: Australia proved to be rich in minerals. Countless ore veins honeycomb the subsoil. This watercolour by George Angas shows the Kapunda copper mines discovered in 1845 north of Adelaide, from which 1500 tons were extracted in two years, and exported to England in exchange for manufactured products.

or immigrants in more or less equal proportions. They were up against the settlers who had legal concessions for their land and behaved like territorial aristocrats.

The idea of searching for gold in Australia came from Edward Hargraves who had been in the California gold rush of 1848, although without much success. But his previous experience enabled him to locate gold-bearing sites quite quickly, and on 12 February 1851 he discovered the first nuggets not far from Bathurst at a spot to which he gave the biblical name of Ophir. The news spread in no time. His example was followed in Victoria where even richer deposits were found soon after. In July an aborigine working for a Bathurst farmer discovered the famous Hundredweight of Gold, a 106·1lb nugget. There followed a gold rush reminiscent of the earlier days in the United States. Within a few months Sydney, Melbourne and Adelaide were empty, with everybody away chasing the mirage of gold. Early in 1852 the ALBERGOYLE sailed into the Port of London to unload a ton of Australian gold. A far-sighted publisher immediately put out a guide to Australia. Within ten days it had sold 20,000 copies. By the end of the year hundreds of ships were setting out with thousands of passengers bound for Australia. There were Americans, Asians, Europeans, all hungry for gold. Soon the trip from England to Australia was cut down to 77 days thanks to Donald McKay of Boston who designed and built the 2,421 ton sailing ship SOVEREIGN OF THE SEAS. The technical advance that this constituted can be judged by the fact that the First Fleet had taken 249 days to complete the journey. To bring back the cargoes of gold and wool, ever faster ships were being turned out and soon the MARCO POLO, built in Canada for England's Black Ball Line, would be taking only 69 days between Liverpool and Melbourne.

Obviously the authorities were not slow to impose fees for the granting of the required licences. This, together with abuses arising from the methods of collecting the fees, gave rise to the only popular revolt known to have occurred in Australia. A resistance movement started in a place called Eureka. It was led by a young Irishman named Peter Labor who published a 'declaration of independence'. The army attacked the rebels when they were gathered in a camp, and they had to surrender. They lost thirty of their men and the army five. Peter Labor managed to escape. He later became President of the Legislative Assembly. But the Eureka affair was to have wide repercussions. It came to be regarded as symbolizing the birth of democracy in Australia.

The gold fever slowly died down. But it led as a result to the arrival of new immigrants from Europe. In 1850 there was a population of a little over 400,000. Ten years later this was doubled. And this time they were no longer convicts or their families as no more had been sent to New South Wales since 1840. There were still some in Tasmania and Brisbane and a very few in Victoria, but none at all in South Australia. Only West Australia kept asking for them because of the very hard conditions prevailing there. But Australia's days as a penal colony could be considered as over. It was the beginning of modern Australia.

Shut up in their reserves, the aborigines sought to adopt the clothing and habits of the invader. Some took to strong drink which helped them forget their tragic fate. Many others found work on the squatters' farms. They generally made very good shepherds.

After 1842, the Society for the Protection of Aborigines firmly opposed man hunts. But the presence of the aborigines vegetating miserably around the edges of the towns remained an apparently insoluble problem. Above, settlers hand out blankets to celebrate Queen Victoria's birthday in 1889.

The only good Aborigine... (Australia)

There are examples of young men from a station who used Sunday to hunt the nearby blacks, not just from 'necessity', but as 'sport'. There have even been colonists who have poisoned the blacks. A squatter from Logon Lagoon, in the interior of Queensland, became celebrated for distributing strychnine to the blacks, in order to kill of a large number at the same time. Even nowadays, ferocious acts of this description still take place. A farmer I met at Lower Herbert boasted of having burnt several blacks after shooting them with a rifle. He considered that as a sensible precaution, leaving no proof against him. The life of a black is worth very little, especially in the north of Australia, and many colonists have offered to kill them to give me their heads. On the outskirts of civilization a black is killed as easily as a dog.

In central Queensland, I have often heard phrases like: 'the only way to deal with the blacks is to shoot them'. A squatter from this district follows this advice faithfully, considering it an absolute necessity. All the aborigine men he discovers on his grazing, he shoots down, because to him, they are cattle-killers; all the women, because they are likely to breed cattle-killers; and all the children, because they will become cattle-killers. I have heard colonists say: 'they will not work, the only thing to do is to kill them!'

CARL LUMHOLTZ, 'Chez les cannibales', in *Le Tour du monde*, 1889, vol. I, p. 334

## Political structure

The colonies now all had their political structure. Although jealous and proud of their British origins, their dearest wish was to administer themselves in freedom.

Starting from 1823, New South Wales possessed its own legislative council responsible for assisting the governor and in 1842 it adopted the principle of representational government. In 1850 the British Parliament was wise enough to invite the colonies to work out their constitutions for submission to London for approval. Ten years later all the colonies, except West Australia where development had been slower, had their own parliamentary system inspired on the British system: a legislative Assembly elected by universal franchise, corresponding to the House of Commons, and a legislative Council corresponding to the House of Lords with members nominated by the governor or elected by indirect suffrage. The governor represented the Crown and appointed the Prime Minister and his cabinet chosen from the majority party, whose tenure of office could be terminated by the Assembly. Political thinking was often rather vague; opinion was particularly divided between supporters of free trade and protectionists, but the question of personalities was paramount.

## Progress and economic and social difficulties

Although gold soon began to run out, the new immigrants stayed on. This produced an abundance of labour which had hitherto been in very short supply. Industrial growth began to develop as feverishly and dynamically as before, bringing in an important influx of capital, as usual mostly from England.

The second half of the nineteenth century was a period of tremendous economic growth in every sector, often spaced with serious recessions as in the last decade of the century when Australia fell victim to 'the great economic depression, the great strike and the great drought'.

The great economic depression was brought on by the collapse of the prices of wool and agricultural commodities which led to bankruptcies, unemployment and lower wages. Ahead of the old world powerful unions were in existence and had already secured the eight-hour day, 'closed shops' and the requirement of union agreement before workers could be discharged. Faced with the threat of lower wages they set off a wave of strikes, especially among the sheep shearers, which had serious effects on the Australian economy. Finally came a terrible three-year drought to cap all their troubles.

Up to that point the colonies had been living in almost total isolation from each other, each proud of its own achievements and scornful of the others. In that respect, the rivalry of Sydney and Melbourne has always been notorious, but the same applied to relations between the other capitals,

189

After 1881 the discovery of gold deposits shook the Australian economy. The gold rush emptied the towns; merchants, sailors, even civil servants followed the call of gold. Each day saw hundreds of grub-stakers from all over the world landing in Australia. The population of Victoria doubled within a few months. It was often a job for the whole family, with husbands digging, sons panning and wives looking for nuggets while little girls loaded the sifted soil on barrows. There would be eager bargaining for the nuggets (right). Below, new arrivals queue up at Ballarat for gold diggers' licences.

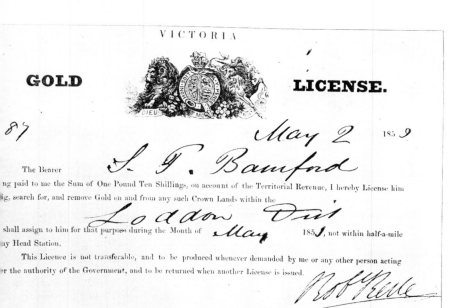

At Forest Creek in 1851 there were 12,000 gold diggers in an area of less than 10 square miles. Each one had paid 30 shillings for his licence, which had to be renewed each month. This kept the numbers down somewhat, by forcing out the unlucky ones. A real revolution broke out at Ballarat in 1854 when the police started checking licences. The military had to be called in, and 30 people were killed.

> **The discovery of gold in Australia**
>
> It was at Mount Alexander twenty-five miles from Melbourne, and hardly had three weeks elapsed before ten thousand individuals were working there. Many miners made a fortune in a few days; so all those who had lost their money, or never had any, left for the diggings. Two brothers, named Cavenagh, made in two weeks the sum of £3,600, which amounts to 87,500 francs. They found more than half of their fortune in half-an-hour, in the form of nuggets as big as pigeon's eggs. Three other individuals found £1,200 one morning before breakfast... At Melbourne, shops closed, the shopkeepers loaded their goods on wagons, and whip in hand, set off for the placers. Everywhere where manpower is needed, in mills, butchers, tanneries, work ceased for lack of workers. Gold-fever seized everybody...
>
> Nothing could be more surprising than the road to the goldfields just after the discoveries. All the travellers had an expression of joyous discovery, an unbounded confidence in making their fortunes. Money was thrown around freely, for nobody counted the cost when they dreamed of their future riches. A long caravan of carts drawn by oxen or horses, riders and travellers on foot, stretched from Melbourne to Mount Alexander.
>
> H. de CASELLA, Souvenir d'un squatter français en Australie, in *Le Tour du monde*, 1861, vol. I p. 83.

be it Adelaide, Brisbane, Hobart or Perth. Did the hardships which befell them all indiscriminately at the end of the century arouse any feelings of solidarity? In any case there was a strong move towards co-operation, and public opinion began to come out in favour of centralized government. Furthermore the Australian States were beginning to be aware of their growing importance and their potential influence in international life. Before, they had entertained few ambitions in that direction, leaving the task of their defence and of representing them abroad in the hands of the home country. They only kept two thoughts constantly in mind; to keep Australia white, which meant standing out against any immigration from Asia, and especially from China, and resisting any colonization attempts from any other source but England. France was always suspected of entertaining the worst designs in that respect, and her occupation of New Caledonia in 1853 aroused a storm of protest throughout Australia. The same happened in 1878 when London and Paris agreed to take joint possession of the New Hebrides.

A few years later a new threat appeared on the horizon, this time from Germany. Germany had become united too late to join France and Great Britain in the great colonial carve-up. She was now out to find such opportunities as were left anywhere in the world to raise the German imperial flag. There were possibilities in the Pacific, for instance in New Guinea where only the western half had been declared a Dutch possession. In an attempt to avoid the eastern part falling to Germany, Queensland did not hesitate to claim having annexed it. Unfortunately this brazen attempt was disavowed by London. But it did lead to an Anglo-German agreement in 1885 splitting the eastern half of New Guinea in two parts, one going to Germany and one to England. All this demonstrated that British and Australian interests were not always identical. In spite of their unswerving sentimental loyalty towards British forms and mentality, the colonies were beginning to find it increasingly difficult to bear their subjection to the home country. It was becoming clear that they could only hope to escape it by becoming closer knit, by uniting and assuming responsibility for their own defence. Certainly there was no question of their merging into a huge united and centralized state as each wanted to keep as much of its individuality and as wide an extent of independence as possible. But the need for ending their state of mutual isolation was becoming more and more imperative. The Prime Ministers met in Melbourne at the beginning of 1890. There they laid the foundations for what was, after many difficulties and some serious resistance, to end in the proclamation on 1 January 1901 of the Australian Federation: the Commonwealth of Australia.

The States retained their own institutions, but the Federation was accorded the basic powers of sovereignty: foreign affairs, national defence and finance. At its head stood a Governor-General representing the British Crown and charged with nominating a Prime Minister and the members of his cabinet who were to be responsible to Parliament. Parliament is made up of a Chamber of Representatives elected by universal suffrage (women obtained the vote at a very early stage) and a Senate with an equal number of States representatives.

At the beginning of the twentieth century the new Federation had a population of slightly under 3,800,000, very unevenly distributed. The greater part lived in the two States of New South Wales and Victoria, mainly in the cities. West Australia had less than 200,000 inhabitants. It is not known whether the aborigines were included in this figure: how many of these had survived by then the destructive campaigns waged intentionally or otherwise against them by the settlers? It is reckoned that there were only 250,000 left on the whole immense continent.

The first years of the young Federation were marked by political instability. Three parties fought for the popular vote: Conservative, Liberal and Labour. This followed British lines, even though the Australian pupil was sometimes ahead of his British teacher. The parties' differences were not doctrinal since no one thought of changing the free economy or the ties to Great Britain and everyone agreed with the policy of keeping Australia white and, if possible, British. The big farmers and land owners were the mainstay of the Conservative party and supported free trade. The Liberals, who were mostly drawn from the middle classes, sought to promote the burgeoning industry and were protectionists. Labour originated from the powerful unionist movement. Theirs was a purely pragmatic socialism. They were better organized than their competitors and from starting as a small minority were destined to become Australia's leading party.

Melbourne was selected as the temporary federal capital. The first federal cabinet would be headed by someone representing the oldest colony, New South Wales. After a fruitless attempt by its Prime Minister, William Lyne, who had always opposed federation and was forced to resign, Edmund Barton formed the first federal government in which were included the Prime Ministers of the colonies.

The first federal cabinets were generally short-lived, which gave the principal political leaders an opportunity to take turns at leading the country. Among them Deakin and Laborites Watson, Fisher and William Hughes are worth mentioning.

Despite so much political change there were a number of achievements. Most noteworthy were those concerning social legislation which was very advanced for the times: introducing the 8-hour day everywhere, creation of a system of arbitration with a Court of Arbitration headed by Henry Higgins who made a great name for himself there, and introduction of the concept of a 'fair and reasonable wage'. From the standpoint of economics the dark days of the closing century were being slowly forgotten and expansion started up again.

After several threatening attempts at secession, particularly in Queensland, the Federation grew stronger. A site was selected for the future federal capital and given an aboriginal name: Canberra. An army was raised, and later an independent navy. They took part in the Boer War alongside Great Britain, albeit without great enthusiasm.

The Kelly gang in Australia

The colonists of Victoria and New South Wales, on both sides of the River Murray, have repeatedly, in the past two years, been thrown into excitement by the unpunished outrages of a large party of robbers and murderers, headed by the brothers Edward and Daniel Kelly. They first began as horse-stealers, about three years ago, in the hill ranges at the head of King river, Delatite county, not much above one hundred miles north-east of Melbourne. Being aided and abetted by numerous family connections and other accomplices residing in the district, just like the Neapolitan, Sicilian, and Greek brigands of Europe, they evaded all police attempts to effect their capture. In October, 1878, they waylaid and killed three police constables near Mansfield. In December, they made a descent from the Strathbogie ranges upon the small town of Euroa, where they openly robbed the bank of £ 5000. The Victorian Government then sent a detachment of colonial militia, with artillery; but it could never meet the bushrangers, who next turned up, in February last year, at Jerilderie, in New South Wales. Here they made prisoners of the police, and locked them up, while the robbers put on the policemen's clothes, took up their lodgings at the best hotels, and seized all the money in the bank. The two Colonial Governments offered rewards amounting to £ 8000 for their capture, but in vain.

On June 26, at a place called Sebastopol, eight miles from Beechworth, in the Ovens Gold-Fields district, this band of outlaws surrounded the hut of a young man, Aaron Sheritt, who had formerly been their accomplice. He had since given information against them, and there was a party of four police with him in the hut that very night. They forced a German neighbour to call on Sherritt to come to the door, which he unsuspectingly did, as he knew the German's voice; and then a man named Joe Byrne shot him dead. The police within the hut did not venture to come forth, or even to fire a shot at the murderers, who sent a volley into the hut, and made an attempt to burn it down. But after staying out-side all night they rode away triumphant, and visited the town of Beechworth.

*The Illustrated London News,* 11 September, 1880

Ned Kelly (1854-1880) was an outlaw who was something of an Australian Robin Hood. Irish by descent, he revolted against the tyrannical rule of the squatters, the big Anglo-Australian landowners. From their lair in the forests of Queensland, the four men of the Kelly Gang carried out a number of cattle raids under the noses of the police and to the joy of the underprivileged. Their bullet-proof armour (right) made them invulnerable. In 1879 they occupied the village of Yerilderie in New South Wales. The following year Kelly was betrayed as he was preparing a daring ambush for a police convoy. The Glenrowan Hotel in Victoria, where the gang took refuge with forty-seven hostages, was surrounded. A massacre followed. Two of the bandits were killed, a third committed suicide. Kelly was shot in the leg and fell under the weight of his heavy bullet-proof armour. He was tried and hanged in Melbourne.

The First World War was to be Australia's first opportunity to project herself on the international stage and write a new page of her history. But Australia already enjoyed a legendary reputation because of her pioneers. The big economic growth of the nineteenth century had not lacked problems within its society which was still unstable and seething, composed as it was of bush clearers, fierce settlers, diggers and the notorious bushrangers, those Robin Hoods of the bush who were half brigands and half administrators of justice and had the well known Ned Kelly as their leader. Clad in his armour he too left his mark, in his own fashion, on the history of Australia.

But such legends paled beside the power of their British heritage, to which came to be added the traditions of the various peoples who came to make up the new nation. The time was approaching when Australian culture could no longer be satisfied to remain an echo of European culture, and would have to derive sources of national inspiration from within its own boundaries and historical background. It would also have to find a just solution to the problem of the aborigines living in their own country yet still a people who did not even possess names. The days of their physical extermination had become but a painful recollection. How many of them were there when the first Europeans arrived? Today a figure of 300,000 is generally given. The historian A. G. L. Shaw puts it at only 150,000 in his book *The Story of Australia* (Faber and Faber, London, 1955). But there may well have been many more; estimates at the time talked of one million indigenous inhabitants. But what is certain is that there are now but some 80,000, of whom scarcely 30,000 are of pure stock today. Twentieth-century Australia would have to face up to this problem. A. P. Elkin, the Australian professor, devoted himself to it with patience and

tenacity. He realized that a policy of assimilation could not save the survivors, who preferred to set up their tents outside houses which had been built for them and who wanted to retain their own customs. Professor Elkin felt they should be left to lead their own existence as they chose. This intelligent and generous man was thereby asking his country to face a whole ecological and economic problem. New hope began to emerge from the research made by universities and from many other efforts on the subject. Australia tried patiently to understand the history of the land where she had grown up, and young film producers are carrying out a remarkable and original task with government support. Ian Dunlop's beautiful film, *Desert People,* offers in this field an exemplary turning point in anthropology: the step from analysis to understanding.

In the nineteenth century Australia was still trying to find her position in relation to the outside world. By the twentieth century, in the course of the extraordinary struggles which shook the world, she would be trying to define her own specific character. Australia is part of the Pacific. This opens up a future which will have to be consolidated in the midst of ancient peoples of very different characteristics, rich in their native culture, who will soon be seeking to recover their independence after their long period of subjugation. The part to be played by Australia, a country still young yet already old, will not be an easy one. She already holds plenty of material trumps and will acquire more as the twentieth century unfolds, huge resources, vast geographical space, most of which is now more or less known. But will she be able to find within her own borders sufficient human wealth and creative imagination to become a link between Pacific and Western civilizations, far from the beaten track, in this world where hope is difficult?

Below: An engraving of an aborigine dance, made in 1861.

After 1830 free emigration took the place of the penal colony, many a tramp becoming an active citizen. New South Wales was the first to demand that deportation be stopped. This was granted in 1840. Still short of labour, only the western colony kept calling for convicts up to 1868. This cartoon from *Punch* shows an Australian pioneer telling John Bull to stop dumping his rubbish there.

By about 1850 the subdivision of the Australian continent was as good as completed. The boundaries were artificial, as the interior was still incompletely explored. Hardy travellers would venture into the great desert. Many lost their lives in the attempt. Above, the remains of an explorer found in the Lake Torrens desert (engraving by Gustave Doré).

Charles Sturt (1795-1869) methodically surveyed the river network of the South-East in 1829-1830, meeting many a dramatic situation. In their small craft Sturt and his men encountered hunger, bad currents, numerous sandbanks and often hostile tribes. Below, Sturt is pointing his gun at a threatening group of aborigines who withdrew.

Queensland Aborigines, showing tribal scars

The first attempt to cross the continent from south to north met with tragic failure. In 1860 Robert O'Hara Burke (left), an ambitious and rash individual, set out into the desert with fifteen men, twenty-three horses and twenty-seven dromedaries imported from India. The horses having died of exhaustion, the men ate the dromedaries. On 21 April 1861 Burke and two companions, William Wills and John King, went off in search of food. When they returned to Cooper's Creek they found their men had gone (below). Wills died. Burke, at the end of his strength, testified on a piece of paper (left) to King's valour. King was the only survivor, being saved by the aborigines. A year later John McDouall Stuart, the explorer, set out from Adelaide and managed to reach Van Diemen Gulf, west of Darwin.

This map shows the successive stages in exploring the interior of the continent, started in 1829 by Charles Sturt.

Sometimes in the desert, valleys formed in a wetter period are encountered, in which, after a storm, a torrent of mud will flow for some miles. But for many long months of each year the water channels are dry. Some 64 per cent of the surface is permanently cut off from the sea. The 763 lakes are mostly huge muddy wastes covered with a crust of salt. Below is a photograph of Red Centre (Northern Territory), dotted with the ubiquitous spinifex or porcupine grass.

Following double page: the monolithic mass of Ayers Rock in the heart of the desert.

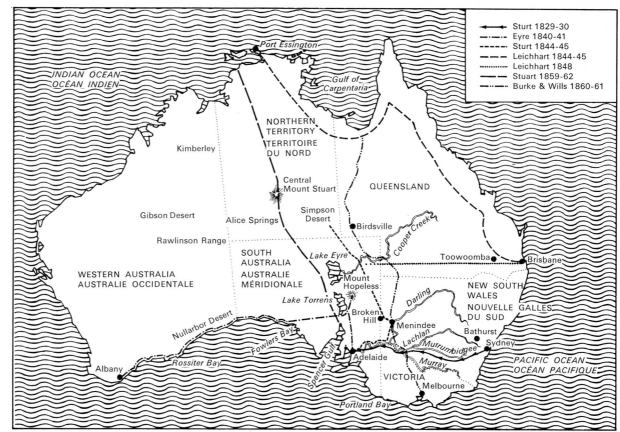

| | |
|---|---|
| ←—— | Sturt 1829-30 |
| —·—·— | Eyre 1840-41 |
| ——— | Sturt 1844-45 |
| — — — | Leichhart 1844-45 |
| ········· | Leichhart 1848 |
| — — — | Stuart 1859-62 |
| —··—··— | Burke & Wills 1860-61 |

# NEW ZEALAND

Te Ika a Maui, the fish of Maui – according to the Maori legend, that is the name given to New Zealand which the hero Maui fished up from the bottom of the seas, Maui, the myth continues, who was so helpful to man by not only giving him that wonderful country but by making the sun give it light and warmth, and who like Prometheus, seized fire from the god Mahouiké.

*Te Ika Maui* refers more precisely to the North Island, while the Maoris call the South Island *Te Wahi Punamu.* Later the South Island came to be known as *Aotearea,* Land of the Long White Cloud, when the Maoris were driven back to the island's extreme north and its central plateau in their attempt to escape annihilation; it became a promised land where the Maori nation could build itself up again.

On 6 February 1840, Maori chief Tamati Waka Neni signed the Treaty of Waitangi. On paper the Maoris recognized British sovereignty, while Great Britain guaranteed them 'full and absolute possession of their land'. Disregarding that clause, the New Zealand Company, assured of London's support, secured 400,000 acres of land and set up bases near Wellington and Taranaki. This ill-considered step by the authorities was to lead to the bloody Maori Wars.

## The Maoris

The Maoris were themselves immigrants. Had other inhabitants lived there before them, some more Melanesian race? This seems probable as references of such nature occur in a number of local legends but up till now no such earlier traces have been found.

Small groups of immigrants began to arrive between the tenth and thirteenth centuries, bringing their own culture of 'moa hunters'. This was followed by the big Maori immigration, the *héké,* around 1350. The Maoris are pure Polynesians. All their tribes claim to be descended from those who landed in one of the seven dug-outs which led the huge fleet: the first being *Te Arawa* (the shark) followed by *Tainui, Aotea, Takitimu, Tokomaru* and *Kurahaupo.* Were did these new settlers come from? They came from the same mysterious land to which legend ascribes the origin of all Polynesion migrations, be it Tahiti, Samoa, Fiji or Micronesia: *Hawaiiki,* land of the ancestors and simultaneously, according to some beliefs, the land where the brave and the good will meet again when they die. In the case of the Maoris it does indeed appear that their last habitat had been Tahiti whence they had migrated by way of the Cook Islands. Here again the courage of those Polynesian mariners has to be admired and the way in which, putting their trust in their nautical science and in the sturdiness of their boats, they unhesitatingly set out in groups on voyages covering thousands of miles across the Pacific Ocean to reach their destination in sufficient numbers to populate in a short space of time a country as vast as New Zealand.

---

**The theft of Maori lands**

A short distance from the Maori village there stands the small European hamlet of Havelock, which at present only consists of two houses. The natives consider that settlement as the extreme limit of the Pakehas' (Europeans) right to advance: 'Thus far and no further', they say. They stubbornly do their utmost to hold up the extension of the Great South Road, and during the Taranaki rising in 1861, William Thompson, chief of the Waikato tribes, declared that if troops crossed the Mangatawhiri, or if the roadbuilding was continued under army protection, it would be taken as an act of war which would provoke the outbreak of hostilities. The importance attached to the possession of the place is explained by the development that will take place there when the Waikato is opened to European commerce...

The natives consider that the Waikato belongs to them more than any other river in New Zealand. No European boat, I believe, has yet sailed upon this proud river; there are only native craft on its surface. Two mission stations, one near the mouth, the other at Taupiri, are the only European settlements along its course. The Maoris defend their national river with all the tenacity of a race that feels itself threatened in its rights and in its existence by the European immigration and colonization. They hang on with all their strength to their river banks, knowing full well that if they sell their land, they pour away their lifeblood, and if they let the river navigation pass into the hands of the Europeans, their pulse will stop.

FERDINAND VON HOCHSTETTER, 'Voyage à la Nouvelle-Zélande', in *Le Tour du monde,* 1865, vol. I, pp. 287-289

## The smoking island and the island of jade

This was a very different country from the ones they had left behind. The New Zealand climate may be subtropical in the north, but in the south it is more like Switzerland and further on like Scotland. The twin islands forming New Zealand stretch some 1,000 miles from north to south. Auckland is on approximately the same parallel as Melbourne, but Invercargill is the closest town to the South Pole. It is thus a land of contrasts. On one side are the New Zealand Alps, on the other Mount Egmont which could be called the 'New Zealand Fuji-Yama'. Vegetation ranges from the subtropical to the subantarctic. Fauna from Europe and flora from the west came to add to the diversity of its natural life.

The special feature of the North Island — the 'smoking island' as the whites were to name it — are its volcanoes. Some are big, and many of them are active. In 1886 Tarawera destroyed one village and Ruapehu started to erupt in 1945. Sometimes there are earthquakes. The subterranean instability of the central plain, with its lakes, its geysers, its warm water springs, causes all manner of phenomena brought on by shifts in the earth's crust.

The South Island, later known as the 'island of jade', is crossed by the New Zealand Alps with summits over 9,000 ft high, with glaciers and eternal snows.

*

*  *

As in Australia, native animal and plant life in New Zealand can show varieties found nowhere else. A deep-rooted fern constituted the first Maoris' principal foodstuff until they became accustomed to the sweet potato. They put phormium, a kind of flax with red flowers, to innumerable uses. The Kauri pine grows to 100 ft tall and the evergreen beech is found all over the south. Still further south vast flocks of sheep can be kept, thanks to the tussock grass. Except for two types of bats there were no mammals. But birds were plentiful, including the honey-eating tui and the bell-bird of which Joseph Banks wrote 'it emits the most melodious music I have ever heard'. There were also the kêa, a particularly friendly mountain parrot, and the kereku, one of the world's most beautiful pigeons. Of special interest are the totornis, a bird which forgot how to fly, the weka and the kiwi, which has hair and a long beak and lays enormous eggs, and has become the national emblem. There are also some original reptiles like the hatteria which dates back to time immemorial and can live for 300 years. It looks like a tiny dinosaur some 2 ft long.

To all these varieties of plant and animal life were added all kinds of western species, such as poplars, beech, pine, and fruit trees, together with cattle, sheep, horses, pigs, rabbits, stags, deer and others. Many of these constitute today some of the islands' richest resources.

## First contacts

Such was the land discovered in 1662 by the Dutch explorer Abel Tasman. He sailed along the west coast and mapped it, convinced that it was part of the antarctic continent. After him Captain Cook reached New Zealand on 7 October 1769. He took six months sailing around it, and discovered the straits between the two islands which bears his name, making a detailed map of the coasts. Unusually, most of his contacts with the inhabitants were hostile, and, according to a persisting Maori account, on 9 October 1769 *Te Mare* was shot dead by musket fire. Cook took possession of the country in the name of England, but London failed to ratify his initiative. In 1772 Captain Marion du Fresne and some of his crew were slaughtered and eaten for not respecting a taboo. His second-in-command proclaimed New Zealand a French possession and gave it the name of 'Austral France'. Finally in 1826 Dumont d'Urville finished outlining the country.

As a general rule the Maoris had proved hostile to outside contacts, and these expeditions often ended with bloody battles. Nevertheless a few Australian ships had the courage to come and trade. The first to succed in getting on good terms with a few Maori chiefs was Lieutenant King, Governor of Norfolk Island. British sailors at once began to be welcome. This was fortunate for British whalers, who had recently lost their Atlantic bases through the secession of the American colonies. They started by settling on the north-east coast in the Bay of Islands and were soon followed by French and Americans. Hundreds of adventurers of all kinds came and settled, establishing various lawless communities along the coast with much consequent abuse and extortions of all sorts. But it soon became obvious that the Maoris would not let their lands be taken away from them without a fight. Some of them had succeeded in obtaining guns and, excellent warriors that they were, showed no hesitation in taking to the battlefield if the need arose.

## Missionaries and land seizure

For their part the missionaries did not remain inactive. The Rev. Samuel Marsden, from the Anglican Missionary Society, was appointed to the Botany Bay penitentiary in Australia. He had on a number of occasions taken in Maoris who had been brought to Australia in British ships and left there. Thanks to that he was known to some of the Maori chiefs, amongst them Rouatara and Chongi. He managed to persuade them come to Sydney. Three months later he landed with them in the Bay of Islands and preached the first Christian sermon on New Zealand's soil on Christmas Day 1814. The early days of the mission there were full of troubles and disappointments. The Maori proved less than receptive and only the protection of Rouatara and Chongi kept the missionaries safe. By 1823 there were still only three missionary outposts.

Notwithstanding these difficulties, the Wesleyan Missionary Society sent out a group, and finally Monsignor Pompallier arrived with the rank of Apostolic Vicar. The Protestant and Catholic mission slowly began to extend their influence.

But anarchy continued to reign among the white settlers, and London turned a deaf ear to all appeals from Britons for someone to come and restore order and take measures to forestall any attempt by the French to take over the country. Ever since the arrival of Monsignor Pompallier the numbers of Frenchmen had in fact been increasing, and French warships were constantly putting in at Akaroa in the South Island, where there was a sizeable French colony. In fact, however, Paris was no keener than London to take the first step towards taking possession.

It was private initiative which finally forced both governments into action. Two expeditions set out from France and England at almost the same time, but the British arrived first. They immediately bought up huge tracts of land without any regard for the rights of the Maoris, which might well have had the effect of driving the Maoris to fight. Aware of the danger, the British government hastily ordered Captain Hobson to start negotiations with the Maori chiefs. This resulted in the treaty of Waitangi of 6 February 1840 by which the Maoris ceded New Zealand to England with the understanding that they retained 'full and complete possession of their land'. When the French reached Akatora the next day, they were faced with the accomplished fact.

## E.G. Wakefield or systematic colonization

The great instigator of the colonizing operation was Edward Gibbon Wakefield, who propounded the theory of systematic colonization and was one of those who contributed most to the rebirth of British colonial expansion of the nineteenth century, particularly in Australia and New Zealand. He had conceived and spread his ideas before ever having seen either country, basing himself merely on the stories and reports which had reached his ears. Studying certain resounding failures like the Swan River settlement in West Australia, he had reached the conclusion that three factors were essential for colonization to succeed: available land, capital, manpower.

In countries like Australia and New Zealand so-called available land was there in almost unlimited quantity; England at the time was overflowing with capital demanding investment opportunity; but there still remained the big problem of manpower. Experience had shown that 'natives' generally refused to lend themselves to working for the colonizers. Counting on convicts could only be an unsatisfactory and temporary expedient. Since the future lay with free settlement, manpower had to be imported from the home country. But when they arrived these workers preferred not to remain working for a wage, but to take their chance in buying land and themselves becoming free settlers. This

was facilitated by land being so very cheap or even in some cases available for nothing on a concession basis. As a result the 'capitalist' settler was soon unable to develop the immense land holdings he had acquired while the small free settlers were themselves without any labour and unable to cultivate the lesser holdings they had obtained. There were only losers on all sides and it was impossible for the colony to prosper. That is what happened at the Swan River Settlement. A Mr Peel had brought 300 people to his enormous estate; six months later he found he was alone and ruined.

The remedy was simple: stop giving out land on free concessions or at very low prices, and set the price of available land so high that imported labour from the home country could not afford to purchase it. Undoubtedly the labourers could save their money and become land owners in their turn, but that would necessarily take time, thus ensuring the stabilization of the free settlers and a reasonable return on capital invested.

This, in a few words, was Wakefield's theory of systematic colonization. Later he perfected it, particularly by encouraging the formation of two distinct classes in the new colonies; one, the capitalists, would be the land owners and become the colonial gentry; the other, the wage-earning workers, would be carefully chosen for their moral qualities and have their journeys subsidized. Under such conditions the colonies should be given a large degree of autonomy so as to be in a position to look after their own interests.

Wakefield's ideas found widespread followers among circles interested in the colonies. A Colonization Society was formed with him as its guiding spirit. The Colonial Office was interested but found it too late to apply his system in Australia. But New Zealand seemed to Wakefield and his friends to be the ideal country. So he founded the New Zealand Company and organized an expedition with his brother in charge, which ended by taking possession.

Once on the spot the Company had no intention to give up the land it had bought quite irregularly before the Treaty of Waitangi, nor had Captain Hobson any means to enforce this. He observed that of the 20 million acres which had been acquired by 300 buyers only 125,000 acres had been allocated in proper form. As was to be expected, the Maoris felt they had been betrayed and took up arms. It was the beginning of much hard fighting during the course of which the British forces did not always have the upper hand. Among the victims was Wakefield's own brother. These uprisings continued until after the arrival of Governor Grey.

## George Grey or comprehensive colonization

The other prominent figure of Britain's colonization of New Zealand was George Grey, who formed a contrast to Wakefield.

While still a young officer he volunteered to go out and explore West Australia. This gave him the opportunity of

The sale of native lands in New Zealand gave rise to many abuses, which led in turn to that series of revolts known as the Maori Wars. The famous King Tawhio, son of Potatau, fought Britain from 1860 to 1879. He finally surrendered in 1881, later to pay a visit to England in 1884. He died ten years later. Right: Chief Heke and his wife, 1865.

making direct contact with the 'natives' and of becoming friends with them. They in turn learned his language and shared much of their own knowledge with him. The Colonial Secretary was much interested by his account of the expedition and appointed him Governor of West Australia.

After a brief visit to England he was asked to take over South Australia, where the position of the colony was particularly critical. Here for the first time he came up against the system inspired by Wakefield. He let it be known that he was utterly opposed to excessive prices being set for the sale of land which thereby became available to only a privileged few. And he arranged for ownership of the newly discovered copper mines to be distributed as widely as possible.

This proved a success. Thanks to the additional revenue which this policy provided, the colony, which up to that time had been on the verge of bankruptcy, became prosperous once more.

The Colonial Office then asked him to try and restore order in New Zealand, where mutiny had broken out as a result of the extortions committed by Wakefield's New Zealand Company.

Using his knowledge of the 'natives' he approached the enemy on his own ground. He launched his attack on a Sunday, Sundays being *taboo* for baptized Maoris. He captured the centre of resistance without firing a shot. His boldness won him high prestige in the eyes of the Maoris, who came to regard him as blessed with *mana.* He helped small settlers to acquire homesteads, and embarked on policy of working with the Maoris, which at that time was regarded as very daring. He learned their language, and could thus talk personally with their chiefs. He came to know their civilization, which had been ignored, and his writings on the subject are still regarded today as authoritative.

In 1846 London sent him out a constitution. This was progress indeed, as it gave New Zealand semi-autonomy. But in Grey's eyes there were two things seriously lacking in it: only people who could read and speak English, which excluded the Maoris, could vote; also all vacant land or land occupied by Maoris became Crown property, in violation of the Treaty of Waitangi. Grey refused to apply the constitution and submitted his resignation. But the then Colonial Secretary in London was someone who respected a man of strong character. He refused to accept Grey's resignation and allowed him to alter the constitution as he saw fit.

In 1853 the constitution drawn up by Grey was promulgated. As Prime Minister Gladstone noted, this gave 'a wider measure of liberty than had ever been accorded to any colony'. Thereafter the Maoris were put, at least in theory, on an equal footing with Englishmen.

## The Maori wars

Within six years under Grey New Zealand had progressed from anarchy to a state of full development. But Grey had aroused the enmity of the big landowners and of Wakefield's supporters. So he was recalled to England. While he was away in South Africa on another mission the situation in New Zealand began to worsen again. The sale of natives' lands recommenced, and gave rise to all manner of abuses. The Maoris rose once more. This time the war lasted more than ten years, from 1860 to 1871, leaving numerous victims on both sides.

Grey was sent for again. His erstwhile friendship with the Maoris was no longer enough to quell the struggle. He had to engage in a fight which was all the more difficult because London failed to realize the difficulty of the situation and only extended him limited help. But he succeeded in containing the uprising and securing the submission of King Potatau after the fall of Orakau Pah. There were still a few centres of discontent left but he would undoubtedly have silenced them all had he been given time and means to do so. But he was again recalled in 1868, though fortunately not before he had had time to introduce improvements to his constitution and reach better understanding with the Maoris. It took, however, several more years before complete peace was restored under his successors.

The war was responsible for the birth of a new religion among the Maoris, known as 'Hau hau', which provided inspiration for resistance. During the fighting a British officer by the name of Lloyd had been killed and his blood drunk by the warriors, who declared that the Archangel

Maori resistance to British attacks

(...) It is understandable that with such a proud and energetic people, the British should have plenty of difficulty in conquering them. In fact, the history of their first years in New Zealand is a record of bloody checks, of guerilla wars in which the Maoris displayed as much ferocity as did the Spaniards towards Napoleon. I heard tell of a fort where eight savages sustained an assault by a battalion for six hours. And when the last survivor understood that all was lost, with his last gasp he dragged himself to the magazine, lit it, and blew up the fort and more than forty British.

Capitaine PRÉFONTAL, 'Chez les Maoris', account appearing in *Le Journal des Voyages,* No. 85, 17 July 1898, p. 99

Family portraits

Fish eat fish; the bird preys upon the bird; they only eat their prisoners!... Death in combat is preferable, in the islanders' eyes, to death of old age. They cut off the heads of their deceased fathers and mothers, embalm them, and keep them carefully at home, showing them as we would show our family portraits.

HYACINTHE DE BOUGAINVILLE, *Journal de la navigation autour du globe de la frégatte* LA THÉTIS *et de la corvette* L'ESPÉRANCE *(1824-1826)*, Paris 1837, p. 523 (August 1825)

The Maoris took up arms and fought with intelligence and indomitable courage. Left, Wiremu Tamihana, the rebel chief. He encouraged tattooing so as to preserve his people's cultural heritage. Below: British troops suffered severe losses in the course of an attack on a Maori *pah,* one of hundreds of fortified places scattered all over the island. After three successive compaigns, George Grey overcame the rebels, not so much by force of arms as by the confidence which his words inspired. He legalized the native farming customs (1865), set up Anglo-Maori land courts (1867) and had four Maori chiefs, elected by the tribes, admitted to the colonial Parliament (above).

205

Gabriel had appeared to them in a dream and revealed that Lloyd's skull would help the Maoris chase out the *Pakeha* (meaning the British) and retrieve their independance. Henceforward, the skull became an object of veneration. They dipped it in baptismal water, and it was supposed to call upon the protection of the Virgin Mary. The *Hau-hau* kept up the fight even after Potatau surrendered. They took to attacking the missions and Protestant missionaries, and a substantial number of Maoris gave up Christianity. It took the missions many years to recover their position.

## The growth of New Zealand

The war resulted in much of the natives' land being confiscated and handed over to the settlers. In addition, gold was discovered in 1860 in Otago and Westland Provinces, giving rise to an inrush of people in search of gold. Without attaining the size of the gold rush in Australia, it nevertheless greatly increased the number of immigrants. In 1865 there were 172,000 white inhabitants. But the principal activity was still cattle farming. Governor Grey's successors were wise enough to follow his policies and to keep land prices low enough to permit the formation of a large number of properties of modest dimensions. The main export products were wool and, after refrigeration had been perfected in 1882, meat and dairy products.

In 1840 New Zealand separated from New South Wales. We have already seen how she acquired a constitution in 1853 under Governor Grey. Then six provinces were created. In 1876 the provincial system was dropped, and the country was given a single government responsible to two Chambers, the Legislative Council and the Chamber of Representatives. New Zealand refused to join the Commonwealth of Australia, which was then in process of formation.

From 1891 on New Zealand had a Liberal government which embarked on a programme of social legislation which was extremely advanced for the times. Women were granted the right to vote in 1893; working conditions were controlled and regulated; procedures were laid down for arbitration and reconciliation between employers and workers. In 1907 New Zealand was given the status of a Dominion.

But there was still the problem of the Maoris. As soon as the war ended Grey began trying to enable them to participate in the life of the country. They were thus entitled to elect four members of the Chamber of Representatives, and a great effort was made to provide them with schools and improve their living conditions. But none of this could prevent a sharp drop in their numbers: by 1896 there were only 42,000 left. Was the Maori race to die out like the Tasmanians in 1877? We shall see that they had a happier fate and that New Zealand was in a position to enter the twentieth century under relatively better conditions than those prevailing in other areas of the Pacific.

The driving force of Gibbon Wakefield caused the New Zealand Company to bring in 15,000 settlers in 1844. Twenty years later there were 172,000 white inhabitants. A number of flourishing towns sprang up, the chief one being Wellington on the North Island. Due to its central location it replaced Auckland as capital. Above: laying the foundation stone of the Wellington Parliament in 1857.

The formation of New Zealand's steep mountains with their many lakes, dense forests, and alpine prairies, called for adequate means of transport. As in the Far West of America, a widespread network of stage coaches was available to travellers from one end of the island to another. Below: a staging post, circa 1890.

# THE OTHER PACIFIC ISLANDS

Australia, New Zealand and New Guinea are exceptional by their respective dimensions. The Pacific basically embraces myriads of islands scattered across its vast expanse. Their variety was a source of enchantment to the great explorers. Some, composed of coral, are flat and are little higher than sea level. Others are formed by volcanos and often reach to considerable height, while yet others are of combined volcanic and coral formation. They are seldom single units, being grouped together in archipelagos which become more numerous from east to west and from north to south.

In the north, the Aleutian chain is an extension of the Alaskan peninsula and forms a barrier shaped like a hollow lid composed of fifteen islands, the biggest of which is Unimak with two volcanos over 6,000 ft high. This group is itself surrounded by some hundred smaller islands. They were inhabited by about 30,000 Aleutians of somewhat mongoloid type, with coal-black eyes, who spoke an Eskimo language and subsisted by fishing. Later, trappers from Siberia settled there. In 1867 the Russians handed the islands over to the Americans. By 1885 there were scarcely 4,000 Aleutians left.

To the east of the Aleutian islands lie the thirty-two Kurile islands, forming a southerly extension of Kamchatka and bordering its eastern Pacific coast. This was the hunting territory of the ancient Aïnu folk, of whom some 20,000 still exist on Hokkaido, the northernmost island of the Japanese Archipelago.

Without going into detail, mention must be made of Japan, now regarded as Asian, Taiwan, the Philippines, which are separated from the Pacific by the Philippine Sea, and lastly Indonesia, a transitional region settled by the Dutch in the seventeenth century. The Philippines were a Spanish colony from 1571 until 1898 but became an American sphere of influence after the Spanish-American War. Taiwan was colonized by the Portuguese who named it Formosa, 'the beautiful', but was later occupied in turn by the Dutch in 1624, the Chinese in 1683, and the Japanese from 1895 to 1946. By then there remained only two per cent of the original inhabitants from the Pacific, who now live in seven isolated tribes.

## MICRONESIA

Before examining Polynesia, let us look at Micronesia, an area focused on the Equator, which is dotted from Indonesia to Polynesia by the thousands of islands, big and small, which make up the Marianas, the Carolines, the Marshalls, the Gilbert, Ellice and Phoenix groups, possessing some ten different languages, a complex assortment of cultures, and a remarkable variety of climates.

Micronesia was discovered very early on, being preserved for a long time as relics of Spain's colonial empire and used by deserters and travellers of all kinds. Whalers would winter in the Gilbert, Ellice, Marshall and Caroline islands and take their departures from them in pursuit of whales as far as the Bering Straits. In the Carolines pirates and adventurers held absolute sway over the entire population. Between 1840 and 1850 they came into conflict with a new adventurer, Captain Cheyne, whose journal is better known by the name of *A Description of Islands in the Waters of the Pacific Ocean North and South of the Equator* (London 1852). In it he gives a moralizing account of his sinister and cruel adventures, reporting in detail on his difficulties and on the opposition he encountered when he tried to set up a fishing base for sea slugs at Ponape. He had to arrest the uncontested leader of the local deserters, an Irish deserter named Boyd, and hand him over to justice. The affair was settled by compromise and Cheyne was able to establish a number of fishing stations in Micronesia, where he died. The years 1850 to 1875 were the days of the slave traders who carried off their 'workers' to the guano workings and coffee plantations of South America, and later to the Fiji, to Tahiti, Hawaii, and Queensland in Australia. There was fierce fighting, especially in the Gilberts where several ships were destroyed, whereas in the Ellice Islands the population defended itself less vigorously and was virtually decimated.

The southern part of the Marianas, inhabited by 100,000 Chamorros, put up long and stiff resistance to the Spanish explorers. They were discovered in 1521 by Magellan and converted between 1668 and 1672 by Father de Santivatoris, who died there. In the seventeenth century, seeing that they had no hope of winning, they abandoned their homes and put out to sea in their dug-outs with the Spaniards still in hot pursuit. Only one group managed to find refuge at Yap in the Carolines. Around 1857 the American Board of Missions took the place of the Spanish missionaries, and were followed by the Marist fathers, who settled down there at the end of the century.

After the Spanish-American War of 1898 Spain surrendered the Carolines, the Marshalls and the Marianas to Germany, with the exception of Guam, the most important of those islands at the extreme south of the Marianas, which was ceded to the U.S.A.

The Germans went to great pains to colonize and plant the coconut palm throughout the archipelagos that fell to them. The three other archipelagos gradually became British Crown possessions between 1898 and 1916. They were comparatively overpopulated and had nothing other to export than copra. Nauru and Ocean Island, two isolated islands west of the Gilberts, both put up a valiant defence against the whalers. Sir Albert Ellis discovered phosphates on them at the end of the nineteenth century. These were exploited from 1906 on by the Anglo-German Pacific Phosphate Company. Otherwise no-one paid much attention to them or to the eight little islands forming the Phoenix group on the way to Hawaii until the twentieth century.

# POLYNESIA

## The Hawaiian Archipelago

The islands of Hawaii form the northern tip of the Polynesian triangle. They too very soon fell prey to merchants, smugglers and pirates of all kinds.

The inhabitants of the area, where coral islands lie cheek by jowl to some of the tallest volcanos, a few them over 12,000 ft high, called themselves *Kanaka*. Kanaka corresponds to the *tangata* of South Polynesia. Kanaka, contrary to general belief, does not mean man. It comes from *Kana-ka,* meaning animal-man, from that Pacific form of civilization where the same life is breathed into animals, plants and humans.

Several *Kana-ka* chiefs shared the islands where the priesthood is hereditary. But at the end of the eighteenth century Kamehameha succeded in conquering, uniting and organizing almost the entire archipelago and became the first of a long dynasty of kings. What was more, he drove out the Spanish pirates, who had plagued all the Northern Pacific and used to sail up beyond the Aleutians to pillage.

In 1820 a branch of the L.M.S. set up in Boston sent out some American missionaries to convert the peoples of the archipelago, where they offered their skills and services to King Kamehameha I. In 1823 Kamehameha II took his favourite wife Kamamalou on a visit to the United States and London, where they were lavishly treated, but both succumbed to measles. Meanwhile back in Hawaii the missionaries were given high positions in the government, in administration and in the economy, and Christian conversion went ahead. The ancient gods Kané, Kou and Lono lost their powers and the sovereign's four wives became Christians. The story goes that their faith was so profound that in 1825 Queen Keopouclani climbed up to the crater of Kilauca, sanctuary of the goddess Pele who liked to dance and bathe there, threw in a bowl of water in which she had washed her hands, and sang a hymn to the glory of God. A few years later a mass conversion of 20,000 Hawaiians took place, and King Kamehameha III was persuaded by the Protestant clergy to issue a Declaration of Rights and grant a constitution. This new constitutional kingdom had an hereditary monarchy. The king appointed noblemen or naturalized foreigners as life members of the upper chamber, members of the lower chamber being elected by the people. Christainity was proclaimed the state religion. Hawaii thus became a kind of reserve for the Protestant churches. As a last step to wipe out any remaining traces of the ancient civilization, the *taboo* was forbidden.

In 1843 French troops blew up Fort Honolulu, claiming they were defending the rights of a merchant, and in 1858 a Franco-Kanaka treaty permitted the sale of distilled liquor.

Catholics had settled in Hawaii in 1827 but made slower headway. This resulted in a struggle between England and France. King Kamehameha IV (1855-1863) favoured England while his successor Kamehameha V (1863-1872) was rather more inclined towards France, whose representative at the time was Consul Charles de Varigny. The highest positions in church, school and state services were held by Christian Hawaiians. The Catholics had a seminary, a convent and fifty schools, and were beginning to make good progress. They erected a Cathedral at Honolulu. But it very soon became obvious that the Americans felt that the archipelago should be in their sphere of influence. They encouraged moves toward democracy. But King Kalauka (1874-1891) set about restoring the power of the monarchy, and the archipelago was still theoretically an independent constitutional monarchy in 1888 when Stevenson visited Hawaii and learned many ancient legends from the lips of the last king. This king was succeeded by his sister Liliuokalani, who was deposed in 1893 and a republic set up. In 1898 America annexed the islands. From then on their destiny was linked to the United States.

None of this was to benefit the populations of the islands in the way hoped for by the early missionaries. Cook had been full of admiration for the bravery, skill and charm of the Polynesians who so closely resembled the people he had found in Tahiti. At the time he estimated the population at 100,000. Since then it never ceased to diminish. More and more foreign labour of Japanese, Chinese and Philippine origin had to be used to maintain the plantations set up under the aegis of the missions. This was characteristic almost everywhere where the West extended its power. Western settlement would be followed by a decrease in the Pacific population and a corresponding increase of foreign races, mostly of Asiatic origin, imported for economic reasons. At the end of the century Blüchner, the traveller, complained that 'the beautiful Hawaiian race was fast dying out' in a Hawaii which was already heavily Westernised and where Chinese workers provided cheap manpower.

Happily we still have the splendid *Kumulipo* with its 2,000 verses, handed down orally from generation to generation, casting powerful light on a vanished civilization.

## Easter Island

Half way between Chile and Tahiti, at the far end of the submarine ridge of which Hawaii is one of the outcrops, lies wonderful, arid *Rapa nui,* Easter Island, discovered on Easter Sunday 1722 by Roggeven, the Dutch navigator. This volcanic island is inhabitant by a people of Polynesian origin who probaby migrated there fairly recently, having come, it is believed, from the Marquesas. This people was unable to explain the origin of the extraordinary monuments found on the island — vast paved terrasses with colossal stone statues, wooden statuettes and maces. The tools used to carve them were found intact, together with unfinished statues, on the edge of the crater of Rano Raraku where the unknown craftsmen abandoned them before leaving the island. More than a hundred years later Monsignor Tepani Jaussen thought he had found traces of an Oceanian script when he discovered some rosewood tablets with various hieroglyphics which he recognized as portraying a king with his plumed headgear and women wearing the dainty hats which Cook had so admired.

If these really were 'writings', they should be compared with those on Melanesian engraved bamboos and with the markings on Marquesa Island textiles or the tattoo marks on humans. These particular tablets helped to recall the text of a chant.

In 1862 a group of Peruvian slave-traders came and abducted the leading chiefs and decimated the population of the island which, in 1888, became a Chilean possession. The history of those immense statues set up to face the Ocean is still largely unknown.

## Pitcairn Island

Heading due west, we find Pitcairn, a tiny volcanic island chosen by the mutineers of the BOUNTY as their home. When they reached this desert island in 1789 and burned their boats, they found stone axes and *marae* with tall statues. Under the leadership of John Adams, one of the group, they constituted themselves a truly patriarcal society together with the Tahitians who arrived with them, although this was marred by a fatal dispute in which most of the men lost their lives. They were only discovered there in 1808, and in 1815 the island came under the protection of England. In 1832 England wanted to move the little colony of eight-seven persons of half-caste blood, speaking English as well as Tahitian, over to Tahiti, but they all preferred to go back to Pitcairn. There their uncontrolled deforestation caused the climate to deteriorate and the British government transported them again, this time to Norfolk Island, to the west of New Zealand. Although a few of them still preferred to return to Pitcairn, the Norfolk Island colony prospered and grew to 340 persons by 1871.

## The Gambier archipelago

Going still further west, the traveller finds at the extreme south of French Polynesia the Gambier Islands, the real name for which is Mangareva. Captain Wilson (see above 'Missionaries and Mariners') named them Gambier in 1797 after the President of the London Missionary Society, and called the highest point of the islands Duff, the name of the mission's ship. The islanders were originally from Raratonga and numbered some 4,000 persons. But by 1832 disease had brought their numbers down to scarcely 1,000, taking the average of estimates made between 1832 and 1834,

which ranged between 935 and 2,300. Although the Protestant missions failed to become established there, the Gambier Islands were the scene of an astonishing though not unique episode. The Picpus missionaries (see 'Missionaries and Mariners' page 154 above) had landed there in 1834. Father Laval was given charge of the main island, Mangareva. In less than a year he converted the entire population, despite their reputation of being fierce cannibals. Without displacing King Te Maputeoa, he exercised absolute power which, in the words of the officer commanding the *Etablissements français en Océanie*, reached a point of 'high tyranny sometimes attaining supreme ridicule'.

He had a cathedral for 1,000 worshippers built out of solid stone and decorated it with a mosaïc of mother-of-pearl. To do so, he instituted a system of forced labour, and it is said that many of his workers died on the job. The mission had taken for itself a monopoly on mother-of-pearl, which brought in substantial profits. Father Laval retained his hegemony in this way for 37 years. By the time the scandal was discovered and he was recalled to Tahiti after a complaint by Governor La Roncière, less than half of the population was left alive.

In 1844 Captain Penaud took over protection of the archipelago, but this was only ratified by the French government in 1871. France finally took possession in 1881.

## The Marquesa, Tuamotu and Society Archipelagos

Situated in the heart of French Polynesia, the Tuamotu islands are made up of a host of atolls and seventy-eight low-lying islands surrounded by coral reefs posing great danger to navigators. The western islands of the group were conquered by Pomaré I, who recruited his most powerful fighting men from them. One of those islands, Makatéa, barely rising above sea-level, contains rich phosphate deposits. France annexed the archipelago in 1880.

North of the Tuamotu, and close to the Equator, lies the Marquesa Archipelago composed of volcanic islands. The Marquesans belong to the extensive Maori family of Asian origin which is found from New Zealand to Hawaii and from Easter Island to the Carolines, and with whom they share common crafts and the same root-language. Colonization introduced them to alcohol and opium, and they were shamelessly decimated. *The Marquesa Journal* (edited in Canberra in 1974 by G. Denning) naïvely shows the different yet ever similar causes of the fatal impact of the whites. Its author, Robarts, was one of those alcohol distillers and a deserter from the whaler NEW EUPHRATES who settled in the Marquesas in 1804, that is to say *before* the collapse of the population. In *Typee* Melville provides much vivid historic detail. More than anywhere else the Marquesas suffered terribly at the hands of the whalers. Those from the United States were so powerful that in the first decades of the century they captured nearly fifteen British whalers and Captain Porter took possession of Nuku-Hiva on his own in

1813. At the time he reckoned the Marquesas population at 80,000. There were only 6,000 left when France took over in 1842. The whites with their alcohol and the Chinese with their opium had moved in. The Marquesans were dying and the magnificent *paepae* could only listen to their agony and to the complaints of the rare survivors, numbering only 400 in 1888, according to Stevenson!

## Tahiti

To the South of Tuamotu lies 'the enchanting image' of Tahiti, made famous by Wallis, Cook and Bougainville, whose accounts left their governments indifferent, unwilling as they were to become involved in such far-off lands, the economic advantages of which were hard to grasp. But the explorers were followed by missionaries. The L.M.S. sent preachers to Tahiti in 1797.

We have already seen the part which they played, encouraging the ambitions of one of the chiefs who became king and was converted in 1812 and subsequently asking for the protection of England. In 1824 the L.M.S. sent a young, intelligent, and ambitious missionary named George Pritchard. Combining the interests of his religion with commerce, he was appointed British Consul in 1837, thereby becoming the leading personality on the island. In 1836 two French Catholic missionaries had landed there and Pritchard contrived to have them expelled. The French government ordered Captain Dupetit-Thouars to demand that Queen Pomaré make amends for the 'insult to France' in the expulsion of the two missionaries. This initiated a struggle between Pritchard and Dupetit-Thouars, the latter greatly exceeding his instructions and the former vainly trying to secure Britain's protection. Dupetit-Thouars was promoted Rear-Admiral and occupied the Marquesas Islands. On 9 September 1842 he succeeded in making the queen ask for French protection. Guizot, the then French Prime Minister, took a long time to make up his mind to back up Dupetit-Thouars' initiative. The protectorate treaty was only ratified on 25 March 1843 after the British government had given its assent in return for a free hand in Hawaii.

Pritchard did not give up. He returned to Tahiti and promoted an uprising among the Tahitians. Dupetit-Thouars landed his troops, deposed Queen Pomaré who fled to a British ship, and took possession of the islands. Efforts were made in Paris and London to stop the struggle from escalating: the admiral was disavowed while Pritchard was transferred to Samoa. But on the spot the position continued to deteriorate. On 3 March 1844 Pritchard was arrested by Captain d'Aubigny and, after 5 days detention, put on a British vessel heading for England. This episode further incensed public opinion in England and France. It took all the skill of both prime ministers to avoid a serious conflict. The French government apologized and offered to pay an indemnity. The British government did not dispute French presence in Tahiti. After further months of troubles, Queen Pomaré came back from exile and in 1847 signed a

George Pritchard (1796-1883), a passionately sectarian missionary, was British consul in Tahiti. A sworn enemy of France, he used his political and spiritual position to drive the Catholics out of the island and affirm his country's hegemony.

The July monarchy ordered Rear-Admiral Dupetit-Thouars (left) to obtain amends for Tahiti's insult to France in expelling her missionaries. Under the threat of his guns, the Rear-Admiral made Pomaré sign a treaty of protection (9 September 1842). The following year Pritchard incited the islanders to revolt. The French put the British consul in prison (above) and Dupetit-Thouars' ships bombarded the island. The native mutiny went on until 1847, causing bloody strife in both Tahiti and the Marquesas.

new protectorate treaty. In 1880 King Pomaré V relinquished to France his powers over Tahiti and parts of the Society Islands, the Tubai Islands and the Tuamotu Archipelago. France obtained possession of the rest of the Society Islands in 1887.

## The Austral Islands (French Polynesia) and Cook Archipelago (British Polynesia)

South of the Society Archipelago, on the level of the Tropic of Capricorn, are the Tubai islands of Tubai, Rurutu, Rimatara, Raivavae and Rapa. They all belong to the same chain of now partially submerged mountains as the Cook Islands. Pomaré V surrendered Tubai and Raivavae to France in 1880. The two islands, where the missionary Ellis had arrived in 1817 to evangelize, followed by Tahitian preachers in 1822, had lost two-thirds of their population to an epidemic introduced by a visiting ship. The same ship was responsible for reducing the population of Rurutu from 6,000 to 314.

Rapa, which in 1791 Vancouver found to be defended by imposing fortresses and where he estimated there were 1,500 inhabitants, was also evangelized by Ellis (1817) and by the missionary Davies and two Tahitian preachers from 1825 on. In 1826 Davies estimated the population at 2,000. By 1831 he counted only 600, and the population continued to decline in fairly similar proportion to the other Pacific islands, which we have already estimated at about 80 per cent. The island also fell prey to sandalwood cutters, sea-slug fishers and others including the pearl industry. In 1864 a ship from Peru was responsible for another epidemic so that soon there were only 150 inhabitants left, according to Moerenhout, who noted that this was a 'strange and almost inexplicable phenomenon recurring without a single exception in all the islands where we introduced our religion and altered their habits'.

John Williams made no attempt to alter the traditional social structure with its *matai*, the powers of which are held by a Council, the *Fono*. The social structure is in fact very different from the Polynesian form and is closer to the Melanesian. Christianity thus came to be superimposed on the life of the people, and the Church of Samoa became one of the most prosperous in Polynesia. This helped the Samoans to remain for a long while safe from the covetous desires of the great powers. But when Germany decided that her turn had come to enter the colonial fray, she soon saw that the Samoa Islands were 'vacant'. This alarmed the New Zealanders, who pressed Britain into taking the initiative. Meanwhile the Americans were beginning to take a serious look at the Pacific. They all appointed consuls to Samoa, with the object of swaying the sympathies of the local authorities over to their side. The resulting tensions almost degenerated into war. On 16 March 1889 a German squadron found itself facing an American squadron in Apia Bay, the capital of Samoa. But a storm sprang up before combat

Tahiti's Queen Pomaré (1813-1877) with her husband Ariifaaité adopted European attire, but attempted to maintain a degree of autonomy in the face of the foreign powers. She shook off the yoke of English Protestant missionaries, and in 1836 drove out their French Catholic rivals. Competition between the colonial nations brought Europe to the brink of war.

could be engaged and destroyed both fleets, forcing them to negotiate. England withdrew, preferring to secure compensation in the Solomon and Tonga Islands. Germany was allotted the two large islands of western Samoa, including Tutuila with a natural harbour at Pago-Pago. The first German governor set up residence in the house which Stevenson had built himself at Vailima above Apia. In his *Footnote to History* Stevenson denounced the whites' spiritual and material vandalism towards the Samoans. When he died, after spending five years on the island, the people gave him a funeral as touching as it was grandiose.

In 1867 the Panama-New Zealand and Australian Mail Company began to display an interest in Rapa. France guessed their intentions and hastened to set up her own protectorate (27 April 1867). But when the French tried to take possession (1881) the Rapas categorically refused. However under the iron heel of ebullient Governor Lacascade they had to abandon their resistance and submit.

As to Cook Islands, which the great navigator named Harvey Islands when he visited some of them in 1773, their main island, Raratonga, was only discovered in 1820 by Captain Goodenough, and explored in 1823 by John Williams who established one of the L.M.S. bases there. In 1888 the island came under British protection, administered from New Zealand.

## The Samoan Archipelago

Here again it was the missionaries who brought Western civilization to the people. Rev. John Williams of the L.M.S. arrived there in 1830, coming from Raïatea via the Cook Islands which lie between the Society Islands and Samoa. He had with him a number of Samoans who had migrated to the Cooks and whom he had converted. He received a very warm welcome, the more so as the position of high priest was vacant as a result of wars and internal strife. He achieved rapid success, and within fifteen years the whole island was converted to Christianity.

## The Tonga Archipelago

The Tonga archipelago lies just south of Samoa and embraces several hundred volcanic and coral islands. Only a few are permanently inhabited, including the principal island of Tongatapu with the capital, Nukualofa. Like most of the islands in the area, the Tongas were affected by colonization. But instead of falling under alien domination they formed in independent kingdom, thanks to an astonishing sequence of events in which missions, or more precisely a missionary, played a preponderant rôle. The Tongan warriors had a reputation for great valour, of which they sometimes gave proof to the detriment of their Samoan, Fijian and Wallisian neighbours. At the end of the eighteenth century a number of claimants, more or less supported by the early white settlers and merchants, were struggling for

supremacy. One of them, Taufna'ahau, was heir to the most prominent title of *Tu'i Kanokopolou* and lived in Ha'apai Island north of Tongatapu. Two Wesleyan missionaries, John Thomas and John Hutchinson, settled there in 1826 and converted young Taufna'ahau to Christianity in 1828. This led him gradually to acquire authority over all the Tonga Islands and in 1847 to be proclaimed their king under the name of George Tupau. He swept away the few remaining vestiges of independence, which the Catholic missionaries more or less supported, and proclaimed Methodism as the state religion. But Tupou had other adversaries to face, who were far more dangerous than the Christians: the white merchants who were attempting to take over the economic life of his kingdom. It was at that point that, in 1860, a new Wesleyan missionary named Shirley Baker arrived. He was to become the king's loyal adviser and help him to assure the independence of the Tongas. Baker was a strange personality, unjustly criticized, ingenuous yet cunning, selfish yet generous, one of the earliest and most efficient defenders of an indigenous population.

After turning the Tonga mission into one of the most prosperous of all, he cut it off from the central mission in Sydney, and created the Free Wesleyan Church of Tonga with king Tupou as its head. This aroused the ire of his fellow missionaries, who set about having him recalled. In 1878 they succeeded. But Baker would not admit defeat. With the support of the king, he returned to Tonga and was appointed Prime Minister. Under his aegis the kingdom acquired a constitution and proclaimed its independence. In spite of all kinds of intrigue this was never challenged, and in 1899 Great Britain assured responsibility for guaranteeing it. Today the kingdom of Tonga is still independent, the Free Church is in communion with the Methodists but remains autonomous, and its head is still the Tonga sovereign, whose motto is 'God and Tonga, my heritage'.

# MELANESIA

## The Fiji archipelago

Fiji consist of some 300 islands spread across 7,083 sqare miles to the west of Tonga. The two largest are Viti Levu and Vanua Levu. They are a mixture of ancient volcanos and coral reefs. It is one of the wealthiest, most populated and most interesting regions of that part of the Pacific, forming a hinge between Polynesia and Melanesia. As the Capita-Watom proto-Polynesian potteries, found by archaeologists at Viti Levu, reveal, it was occupied by the Polynesians before the arrival of the Melanesians, which accounts for its cultural riches. Then came the Europeans. This brought conflict and struggles until the country came under British dominion in 1874. After that, large scale sugar cane plantation were started. But sugar cane requires plentiful labour, and the Fijians were loath to provide this themselves. They preferred to live on their own traditional plantations which provided them with a peaceful and well-balanced existence. So in 1879 the British administration sent for 60,000 Indian workers for the Colonial Sugar Refining Company plantations. They were given ten-year contracts, after which they were to return to India. But they had their womenfolk with them and liked Fiji, so they refused to go home. As their numbers increased unceasingly, the Fiji population diminished – from approximately 200,000 in 1860 to less than 100,000 by 1900.

Despair at seeing death awaiting their race gave rise to a phenomenon which is common throughout Melanesia: the certainty that the whites were *stealing* the food and possessions which their ancestors shared with the living became crystallized in the vernacular word *kago*. This word expressed the idea that the heavy bales of food and other items which were brought to the islands on board Western ships, and later by aircraft, and which the 'natives' had to unload, but which they were unable to use themselves, having no *share* in these imported riches. Hence various movements were set on foot to try and return to the idea of the past with its *gifts* and *return gifts,* so that possessions might once more be equitably shared and all might be able to live. The *Tuka* Movement started in 1885 and the Milne Bay Prophet Movement started in 1893 were examples of this.

Prompted by the French conquests in Polynesia, the British Admiralty sent out consuls to the Fiji and Tonga Islands (1848). Rather than proceeding by crude annexation, London preferred to negotiate with the native kings, appoint representatives and bring pressure indirectly. In this 1874 cartoon, Disraeli introduces the Fijians to Britannia: the acquisition was 'useful if not beautiful'.

## New Caledonia

The British-sounding name of Wallis was the name of the captain who found the islands in 1767 on his way from Tahiti. The archipelago is formed by the volcanic island of Uvea surrounded by small islands in the middle of a lagoon. As the Protestant missionaries took their time about following in Captain Wallis's footsteps, it was Monsignor Pompallier, the future Bishop of New Zealand, who sent in Father Bataillon. After a difficult beginning, he won the king's confidence, converted the people and had huge churches built. Consecrated Bishop and Apostolic Vicar of Central Oceania in 1843, he persuaded the king to request French protection. When the good Bishop died in 1877 he was the real ruler of the island.

Events developed otherwise in the Futuna Archipelago 150 miles south-west of Wallis, which is made up of the twin islands of Futuna and Alofi enclosed by a single barrier reef. Monsignor Pompallier had sent an exemplary priest there, Father Chanel, who refused to follow Father Bataillon's authoritarian methods. The islanders wanted no whites among them and killed him after three years. Father Bataillon thereupon took the situation in hand, and within a few years had converted the entire population. Under his aegis a real theocracy grew up; the kings and chiefs kept their positions, and France took the islands under her protection from 1886-1887 on, but the real power lay in the hands of the Church. The position remained unchanged until about the middle of the twentieth century.

West of Wallis is found the small Santa Cruz group, where the principal islands are Ndeni, also called Santa

In 1853 Napoleon III annexed New Caledonia, finding that it offered strategic advantages (proximity to Australia), economic advantages (nickel mines), facilitated trade with China and Japan and communications with Polynesia, and could be socially useful as a colony for deportees. To ensure the loyalty of the natives, the colonial authorities seized the sons of the Kanaka chiefs as hostages, and forcibly enlisted them in the army (above).

Cahier n° 41. — NOUVELLE-CALÉDONIE.
Village Canaque.

Cruz, Utupoa and Vanikoro. Their inhabitants put up a brave fight against all alien intruders. The missionary Patteson lost his life there in 1871, as did Commodore Goodenough in 1875. La Pérouse and his expedition were shipwrecked there. Whites only began to take an interest in the islands in the twentieth century. They came under British protection in the very last years of the nineteenth century.

Much the same happened in the case of the Solomon Islands with their seven main islands surrounded by smaller ones. A steep mountainous chain runs across the 'Big Land', Bougainville, and ends in the north with tiny Buka Island. This kind of formation is common to much of Melanesia, including, for instance, New Caledonia, which there too the largest island is called the 'Big Land' (Grande Terre) and ends at its southernmost point with a small island, Kunie.

The Solomon Archipelago was one of the first lands of the Pacific, like the New Hebrides, to be discovered by Westerners (Mendaña 1568) but for a long time Westerns prudently steered clear of it. The Marist fathers tried to settle there in 1845, but Monsignor Epalle lost his life there shortly after. Then in 1849 came Bishop Selwyn; his Anglican mission thrived and the islands slowly became a British protectorate. Trade did not develop until 1905 when the Levers Pacific Plantation Ltd started up, followed shortly after by Messrs Burns Philip and the Malaita Co. Densely populated, during the nineteenth century the archipelago was mainly used as a source of labour for other colonies, amongst them Queensland and Fiji.

This was also true of the New Hebrides (Quiros, 1606). There too were active volcanos, a varied landscape, and numerous inhabitants who became the prey of whalers, sandalwood cutters and other adventurers. The population was farther decreased by 'labour' being carried off to New Caledonia, Queensland and Fiji. Settlers, Caledonian and Australian merchants, all tried to move in there and persuade their respective governments to take over the archipelago. But neither London nor Paris saw fit to yield to their pressure. They only stirred when Germany began to manifest her colonial appetite. This led to a first Franco-British agreement in 1887 aimed at least in excluding other claimants from the New Hebrides, which later evolved into the curious system of condominium which still persists today.

Cook's journeys were undertaken essentially in Polynesia. Knowledge of that part of the Pacific and its population soon became quite extensive. As has been seen, this was not true of Melanesia, much of which was fiercely defended by the inhabitants and remained free of whites for many a decade. It is true that the Polynesians, like the Melanesians, took up their spears against the white invader, but the Melanesians also kept up an aggressive and continuing cultural resistance, exemplified by the *kago* movements. Mariners and missionaries have told of the Polynesians' 'superstitions', but when referring to the Melanesians they spoke of a 'devilish religion'. As the nineteenth century still had a lingering belief in the devil, this may be an involuntary tribute paid to the reality and strength of Melanesian culture. Many were the travellers and missionaries who sadly took note of the Melanesians' scorn for the white man with his pale face and flabby muscles. Still more numerous were the whites who fled in terror before the Melanesians' expressive 'wide nostrils', swarthy skin and 'cannibal teeth'. The diversity of languages presented another obstacle. In Melanesia alone there were 263 languages spoken as against 37 in all of vast Polynesia. All of which explains why the whites were so slow to penetrate that part of the Pacific.

## New Guinea and the Bismarck Archipelago

With New Guinea we leave the 'South Seas' and reach the borders of the West Pacific. The huge island is more like a continent, since its area is half as much again as that of France. It is formed around a central chain with a number of summits over 14,000 ft high and a northern chain where some of the peaks exceed 12,000 ft, and which extends into the Bismarck Archipelago, including the islands of New Britain and New Ireland. These chains contain several active volcanos and enfold some fertile valleys. There was an extensive population, speaking a number of different languages, who greatly impressed the early European navigators. Most of the great explorers landed there, but Western nations gave scant attention to those unexplored, malaria-ridden regions before the nineteenth century.

The first white man to attempt to discover New Guinea without ulterior motive was the Russian explorer Miklaukho-Maklaï. As such he deserves to be likened to Stevenson, Gauguin and Melville. He put ashore at Bonga in Astrolabe Bay in September 1871 with two companions, and immediately set about establishing friendly relations with the local people. This proved no easy task, and he had to face many critical situations. But his cool courage and generosity slowly won them over. He sought to protect them from the abuses of Europeans who would succeed him. So when he departed in 1877 he told them that he would give a 'sign' to anyone whom they could safely welcome as his own brothers or friends. Thus when in 1878 gold prospectors from the DOVE tried to land without having his sign, they were obliged to depart post haste.

Quite the reverse happened to the German Frisch in 1881. When he unjustifiably claimed friendship with Maklaï, he was confidently welcomed and was able to extend German influence over that part of New Guinea.

Missionary work started there in 1871, when the L.M.S. sent out the Rev. Murray and the Rev. MacFarlane with eight others from Lifu (in the Loyalty Islands at the other end of Melanesia) to the Torres Straits coast, which was already being raided by adventurers diving for pearl shell and sea-slugs. The mission settled in discreetly, but two of the party were killed by their new converts during prayers. The next step was to explore around Port Moresby (discovered on 20 February 1873 by Captain Moresby), where a first mission post was installed in 1874. Finally the Rev. McFarlane, together with the Italian naturalist Albertis, explored some distance up the course of the Fly River.

Other preachers followed and founded new missions. Life cannot have been easy for any of them, but a particularly noteworthy incident involved the missionary Brown, who had four of his mission killed and eaten. A punitive expedition was thereupon organized and some sixty natives were executed.

Slowly other missions took root on the island, the Order of the Sacred Heart in 1885 and an Anglican mission in 1891. Finally it should be noted that a *kago* movement, the Mansren Myth, took root in West Irian and reached its zenith during the Second World War.

When in 1828 the Dutch took the western part of New Guinea (Irian Barat) as an extension of the Dutch Indies, they captured several natives and sent them back to Holland; but they never managed to colonize or develop the area. The huge territory was thus still 'available' when Germany began to take a serious interest in colonial expansion. In the person of 'Queen' Emma they found a picturesque ally. Mrs Emma Forsyth was a half-caste of Samoan descent, widow of an Englishman. She had managed to build up a little colonial empire centred on Duke of York Island, between New Britain and New Ireland. She got on so well with the managers of the German Company of New Guinea that she let them transfer their headquarters to her land at Kokopo in New Britain when malaria drove them out of New Guinea, and, on marrying one of their managers, Captain Kolbe, sold them all her plantations.

Concerned at the advance of the German Company of New Guinea, Queensland proclaimed sovereignty over the south-east part of the island. London disavowed this initiative but agreed to open negotiations with Germany. These resulted in a treaty in 1885 which gave the north-east to Germany (Kaiser Wilhelmsland) and the south-east (Papua) to England, which in turn transferred the responsibility to the newly formed Australian Commonwealth.

## New Caledonia and the Loyalty Islands

At the far end of Melanesia, at the southernmost point of that arc between the Coral Sea and the Pacific formed by New Guinea, the Solomons and the Hebrides, New Caledonia stretches for 300 miles before disappearing into the ocean to re-emerge some distance to the south and form the Island of Kunié. Along a chain running parallel with the east coast of the Grande Terre rise the Loyalty Islands: Maré (properly called Nengone), Lifu, and Uvea. The latter is smaller but more fertile, and bears the same name as Uvea Island in the Wallis Archipelago, being likewise mostly inhabited by Polynesians.

*The discoverers* – In 1774 Cook landed at Balade, in the extreme north-east of Grande Terre, and was filled with admiration of the climate, the beauty of the *maciri* well planted across the landscape, the architecture of the houses with their tall pointed roofs, the rich plantations, the kindliness of the people and the chastity of their womenfolk.

Continuing southwards, he sighted Kunié which he named the Isle of Pines. He was probably followed by La Pérouse, and finally by d'Entrecasteaux who was sent out in 1792 in search of the lost discoverer.

*The adventurers* – The L.M.S. brig CAMDEN put into Kunié in 1840 and 1841, each time leaving behind two Samoan novices. From then on, adventurers, ever on the look-out, were able to obtain information about the place. After being repulsed from Grande Terre when he tried to land there, Cheyne hastened over to Kunié, which he largely depleted of its sandalwood. He then headed for Nengone, where he was met by armed resistance, and only saved at the last moment by the timely action of two other sandalwood vessels. Although enemies and competitors in business, white did help white when 'savage cannibals' put up resistance against invaders seeking to ravage their lands.

Cheyne then procceeded to Lifu where he collected 40 tons of sandalwood, and went on to Ovea where the JUNO under Bank, also a sandalwood cutter, had already called. Ever eager to further his profitable trade, Cheyne determined to make another attempt on Grande Terre, and put ashore at Balade on 15 October 1842 to fish for sea-slugs. Two days later he was attacked and a bloody battle ensued, which went against him. He took flight and was back in Kunié on 19 October. There he found that, in the face of the hostility of the Kunié people, his two Samoan novices had embarked on another sandalwood ship, the STAR, commanded by Captain Ebrill. Discouraged by his menacing reception at Kunié, Cheyne set sail for Norfolk Island. He left the well-known Charles Bridget in the Loyalties, a former East India Company sailor, who decided to remain with the Kanakas at Lifu. Cheyne made a rather significant note about this: 'It is difficult to believe that a man born in a Christian country (...) should banish himself from the society of his own countrymen, and voluntarily exchange the habits and customs of a civilized life for those of the most degraded savages'.

Meanwhile Captain Ebrill, still with his novices on board, came back to Kunié to take on a last load of sandalwood. His skull was split open, and the same fate befell the novices and all the crew. As to Cheyne, he returned to Uvea on 4 November 1842 where the cannibal meal served him so repulsed him that he left Melanesia to try his fortune in Micronesia as has already been recounted. That same year LA MARTHA's sandalwood longboat was attacked at Nengone and her crew slaughtered. The New Caledonian group managed to put up a stiff resistance to the Western invader.

*The beginnings of French missions* – A small group of Marist missionaries landed at Balade on 21 December 1843 under the leadership of Monsignor Douarre who had recently been promoted by the Holy See to the position of Apostolic Vicar of West Polynesia. The very same people who had fought the bloody battle of 17 October 1842 against Cheyne the sandalwood cutter now offered a warm welcome to the new missionaries. Completely cut off from the Western world, the mission lived humbly side by side with the Kanakas. But from 15 November 1845, when they were visited by Monsignor Epalle aboard the MARIAN-WITSON, more and more ships began to call. Each time they brought with them both moral support and material supplies. But instead of sharing those supplies with their Kanaka hosts as these had shared their yams and taros with them, the thrifty missionaries took to preserving their food under lock and key, thus outraging the convention of reciprocity (gift, return gift) which was held paramount in those parts. Quite logically, according to the convention, Father Blaise, who kept the key to the stores, had either to hand over his key to the Kanaka chief or take the consequences for having flouted the custom. In 1847 he was killed and the stores looted. A series of raids and reprisals followed, the navy coming to the missionaries' aid in much the same way as in Polynesia. The missionaries had no choice but to leave, taking with them a number of neophytes whom they kept safely in 'enclosures' in the Wallis and Futuna Islands. They themselves tried several times to go back but only succeeded in 1851. The crews of a number of longboats anchored off the coasts were likewise systematically attacked, and the tribes of the north made pacts amongst themselves not to allow a single white to set foot on their shores. At the same time a *kago* movement grew up, possibly precipitated by the thoughtless action of the missionaries, but few details of this are known.

*The beginnings of British missions* – The British were at that time taking care of the Loyalties. In accordance with the original L.M.S. precepts teachers and island novices had been sent as scouts to every island of the archipelago.

Although in Kunié the teachers had been slaughtered, the Loyalty Islands missions were successful, and in 1853 Rev. Graegh and Rev. Johns, both British, succeeded in settling in Nengone. There, like their Tonga colleagues, they refrained from changing the traditional social structures.

*The Missionary Wars* – On 24 September 1853 Rear-Admiral Febvrier-Despointes landed at Balade in New Caledonia to take possession of the island in the name of France, just 79 years after Cook had 'hoisted the British flag' on the same spot and 'taken possession of the country in the name of His Majesty King George III'. As was the case in other islands, where the titles to possession were signed by Protestant or Catholic missionaries, so here the act bore the names of not only the Rear-Admiral and his officers but of Marist missionaries Rougeyron, Vigoureux and Forestier, Monsignor Douarre having died six months earlier without living to see the result of his efforts. Febvrier-Despointes then set out for the Isle of Pines (Kunié) where Father Goujon, a Marist missionary who left an indelible mark on the island, had been installed since 1848. On 29 September 1853 a 'convention' was signed between France and Vendegu, the island's Catholic Chief.

By 1857 English Protestant missionaries had explored the whole of Nengone Island, where they estimated there were 8,000 inhabitants. Of these, 3,000 had already been

217

converted, a situation which led to fratricidal violence between Christians and pagans from 1860 to 1861. In 1859 two missionaries, Rev. MacFarlane and Rev. Sleigh, went to Lifu and founded a school of novices, while Rev. Ella took up his post at Uvea.

Then on 2 May 1864 the Governor of New Caledonia, Commandant Guillain, ordered the French flag to be hoisted and the novices' school to be closed. The people revolted. On 21 June the Governor himself reproached the missionaries for having moved into a French island without leave. He was followed by a detachment of 150 soldiers who took possession of the island. Fighting broke out, the mission was surrounded and the village burned down, the coconut groves were destroyed and the novices made prisoner. Commandant Guillain's parting shot was to call upon the people of Lifu thereafter to learn French. A similar scenario was unfolding meanwhile at Maré (Nengone). Catholic priests then set about moving into the islands and the situation remained in a state of flux for a number of years.

After the recall of Governor Guillain in 1870 things began to calm down. Kunié took in a thousand Catholic refugees from Nengone, and the Catholic religion began to take solid roots there. But Nengone's Naisseline chiefs had always supported the Protestants, and Protestantism continued to thrive there even after the archipelago became French (1866).

Meanwhile in New Caledonia Marist missionary work had for fifty years continued unopposed. It developed successfully, founding schools and supporting the natives against the settlers and their abuses. To the honour of the missionaries it must be said that their letters show that they always felt themselves safe among the Kanakas, even at the height of the revolutionary wars which tore the islands asunder. Unlike the Loyalty Islands, Grande Terre escaped the missionary war which spread throughout Oceania in the nineteenth century. The first Protestant missionary, albeit a Frenchman, Maurice Leenhardt, only appeared in 1902. He installed his mission, Do Néva, close to that of Father Hilly. Although belonging to different 'parties', the two men had the good sense to keep on as polite terms as possible. Thereafter the Grande Terre contained both Catholics and Protestants, but the real solid alliance continued to be those formed by the ancestral bonds of the *vibe* which link the Grande Terre Kanakas to those on the islands, and which still persist to this day.

*Colonization* – The start was slow and shaky. In 1858 there were scarcely a hundred settlers, bar and store operators, with but a single serious settler, an Englishman, Mr Paddon, who founded the township of Païta with a group of emigrants and was one of the first to promote an industrial, commercial and agricultural start for New Caledonia.

*Transportation* – Governor Guillain came to New Caledonia in 1862 and had the idea of forming a penal colony there with the object of 'providing the infrastructure essential for the island's development'. A number of military outposts were set up and the first convicts (then called 'transportees') arrived on 7 March 1864. By 1872 there were nearly 6,000, with 1,000 convicts liberated but subject to forced residence in New Caledonia. The benefit they brought to the island was minimal.

*Deportation* – To the figures mentioned above must be added those of the deportees from the Paris Commune, who arrived in 1872. Some, like Henry Bauer, Henri de Rochefort and Louise Michel, were deported to the fortified enclosure on the Ducos peninsula near Nouméa. Others were sent to the Isle of Pines. Among these were Jourde who had held the post of Finance Delegate for the Commune; Dr Rastout, who had been the Commune's Chief of Health Services, had tried to escape but been shipwrecked with nineteen other companions; Achille Ballière, who was later to found the New Caledonian newspaper 'La Bataille'; and Mourot, a journalist who had been de Rochefort's secretary. In the space of a few months there thus arrived in that Isle of Pines which Father Goujon had in less than a quarter of a century turned into a peaceful theocracy, almost 3,000 'blasphemers and libertines', the deported 'assassins' of the Archbishop of Paris. To save the pious inhabitants of Kunié from being contaminated by them, the deportees were spread out along a strip of coast from which the inhabitants had been evacuated. To those deportees from the Commune were added some 100 Kabyles and Arabs from the 1871 Algerian revolt; this group was assimilated to the former, but unlike them they were not freed when the amnesty of 11 July 1880 was proclaimed after being supported by Victor Hugo and Clémenceau. They settled down in the island, many of them bringing up large families.

*Free colonization* – During the time it took to form the penal settlement, free colonization was being slowly organized by means of grants of large land concessions. In 1876 the total number of such settlers had reached 2,753. On the east coast there were a number of small farmers and cattle-breeders, while on the west coast the big land holdings were monopolized by only 40 settlers. That was where Mr Higginson, of British descent, founded the Société du Mont d'Or, forerunner of the Société le Nickel. For lack of capital the other settlers were unable to develop their thousands of acres, so they decided to introduce cattle. As in Australia, they started intensive cattle-farming on an island where, before the coming of the whites, no four-footed animal existed save only a small water rat. Soon there were 80,000 head of cattle destroying the Kanakas' taros and plantations and reducing them to starvation. But who cared about the Kanakas? All the settlers thought about was taking their lands; there was always the navy to put down the revolts, which occurred all over the island. The Kanakas were facing extermination. So one of them, Ataï, patiently attempted to lay the problem before the governor. It was of no avail. Ataï then tried to make new allies, and sought to marry the widow of a settler whose lands marched with his own. The woman turned him down. Driven out by the new settlers

A decree of 2 September 1863 turned New Caledonia into a centre for deportees and remained in force until 1896. Some 40,000 convicts were sent to the island. But this pseudo colonization was a failure which set the island's development back fifty years. Left: the penal settlement on Nou Island, off Nouméa, circa 1880. Prisoners are cleaning, watched by a gendarme. Right: a cell holding rebellious convicts in the boiling heat.

Among political deportees were a number of Kabyles from the 1871 Algerian revolt and 3,900 Communards. Henri Rochefort, one of the Commune leaders, is shown below seated in front of his hut on the Isle of Pines. Nearly all survivors returned to France after the amnesty.

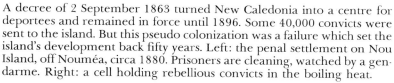

The penal colonies of New Caledonia

On the Island of Pines, the free deportees follow a way of life that is less rigidly ordered, more active, and less silent. The island is surrounded by sandy beaches, and is covered with pine trees and banyans. Nigger-heads of coral, their bases eroded by the constant movement of the waves, stand out of the water like baskets of flowers. A fine road, some 15 km long, first follows the beaches, then strikes off into the centre of the island. The penal settlements are sited along this road at 2 km intervals.

The last of these, furthest from the sea, is reserved for the Arabs who took part in the Algerian rising of 1871. They can be seen, passing hither and thither, resigned or stoic beneath their long white burnouses, bound to their heads by camel-hair ropes. Their eyes contain a gentle flame, half extinginshed; they bow, with typical dignified humility, whenever a white chief passes. Every evening, at sunset, they bow down, kissing the enemy's ground, which none the less for them still belongs to God. As for the other settlements, there is the French village, a collection of low huts, built of straw or palm fronds most often. The rain, or the moonlight, traverses their low roofs. No-one settles in these far-away countries. This is not true of the deportee alone, but of all the French colonists everywhere. Voluntary exiles or not, they all dream of returning to France.

HENRI RIVIÈRE, *Souvenirs de la Nouvelle-Calédonie,* Paris 1880, pp. 77-78

from the village of Komalé where he was born, he had to go as far as La Fonwhari before finding somewhere for himself at a spot known as Banian Ataï, which the whites prophetically called Ataï's Barrier. Ataï's Barrier was to become the rallying point for the Kanaka people.

*The 1878 Revolt* — Ataï took ten years to prepare, forming alliances from *maciri* to *maciri*. The Kanakas plotted amongst themselves, observed the white man's techniques, learned the uses of their methods of communication such as the telegraph, all the while hoarding cartridges one by one until they had 2,000, and preparing camps and farms in hidden areas to be able to hold out as long as possible. Even their women, who in traditional wars were kept far from the scene of combat, were trained to play their part in the struggle for freedom, being made responsible for logistics such as food and ammunition supplies. They participated so whole-heartedly in the fight that many of them hung themselves, preferring death to slavery, when the governor proposed handing his women prisoners over to the conquerors.

Spearpoint of the 1878 revolt were the tribes on the west coast who came from the same *maciri* and spoke *ciri*. Ataï was the leader of the mutiny which eye-witnesses described as having broken out like a thunderclap out of a clear blue sky. There had been no more uprisings during the 10 years of plotting and preparing, and the whites believed that their blacks were subjugated. All of a sudden on 25 June 1878 La Foa was attacked and its police slaughtered, followed by the prison at La Fonhwari and the Teremba and Bouloupari outposts. Lt-Col. Galli-Passebosc made a survey on the spot. The massacre had taken a heavy toll. On the two days of 25 and 26 June some twenty settlers and as many officials had been killed along with substantial numbers of convicts, transportees and freed men. A significant fact was that the slaughter had also included Kanakas from Grand Terre and the New Hebrides who were closely associated with the life of the settlers.

There was great anxiety at Nouméa. The *Nouvelle-Calédonie* newspaper stated 'This was an army come to attack the settlement at its most important centre'. Governor Olry decreed a state of siege.

The uprising kept spreading for the next three months, spilling blood over two thirds of the area. Colonel Galli-Passebosc was killed in the Red Mountains on 3 July. His place was taken by Major Rivière. On 1 September Ataï and Chief Baptiste were killed. They were succeeded respectively by Naïna and Kaupa. The revolt escalated to a general insurrection in October, with 200 posts pillaged and burned down. The troubles subsided at the end of April 1879, all the leading chiefs being by then dead or deported.

The French had had to call on 4,665 soldiers and sailors, who were supported by settlers, convicts and freed men, and a few tribes who took fright and surrendered. These acted as guides for the French, leading them to the Kanaka hiding places and thereby contributing to the defeat of their fellows. Further support was provided by a fighting unit supplied by republicans and patriots from the Commune.

New Caledonia was dotted with military outposts to protect the 1,300 settlers. In 1878 a general rebellion broke out, in reply to the continual invasion of Kanaka farms by the European's cattle, the brutal expropriations, women stealing, and the general blunders of the missionaries. Above: One of the military posts, probably Canala.

Chief Ataï made skilful use of the Kanakas' discontent. A brilliant strategist, he led a real guerilla war against the French forces. More than 100 Europeans were massacred, often eaten. Below: the Bouloupari outpost being pillaged and burned down on 26 June 1878. This was the starting point of the revolt.

The rising was put down with implacable cruelty. For the 100 European
dead, the French killed 1500 Kanakas. To overcome the revolt, 4,665 soldiers were used, among them some of the exiles from the Commune,
who formed a special unit (above).

Among all of them, only one deportee felt any sympathy
and understanding for the Kanaka cause, Louise Michel. On
page 359 of the 1886 edition of her *Mémoires* she writes: 'I
particularly regret my black friends (...). Well, yes, I loved
them and, to tell the truth, people who during the revolt
accused me of hoping they would recover their freedom
were right (...). There should be an end to supremacy if all
it has to show is destruction'.

# THE MYTH OF PARADISE LOST

Three-fold disappointment was to succeed the three-fold
myth which had grown up around stories of the Southern
Seas, the myth of the noble savage, the myth of a paradise
on earth and the myth of fabulous riches awaiting those
who might discover them.

The first of those myths, about the noble savage, arose
from idealist visions and was bound to die in the face of reality. But it should be remarked that the enchantment did survive among those who knew how to appreciate their human
heritage and share it, permitting it to be enriched by intermarriage between the two cultures and the two civilizations
on an equal footing. Of such was Stevenson, whose admiration and affection for the men of the Pacific never faltered.
The white invasion filled him with sadness and a feeling of
impotence. He himself had 'gone native' and was regarded
by other white men as a despicable renegade. When Henry
Adams and his friend La Farge, the painter, came upon him
they were horrified by his primitive living conditions and
the scantiness of his attire. They were mutually unable to
make contact, and that evening Stevenson merely wrote
'Two Americans visited me (...), one being an artist called La
Farge (...) I do not recall the name of the other man.'

Such a 'meeting' as that between Stevenson and the men
of the Pacific was to remain exceptional. But mention
should also be made of Gauguin and others less famous
than Stevenson and Gauguin, who were equally open-
minded. But visitors to the South Seas who came to find
their *alter ego,* happy and confidant, neither disappointed
nor disillusioned, nevertheless held to their Western values,
and came back disenchanted to vent their spleen across
both hemispheres. Many of them, including Julien Viaud, a
naval officer better known as the author Pierre Loti, used
the exotic as a glittering mask to conceal their private
thoughts. Such exotic literature, making a travesty of what
they were supposed to be describing, truly expressed the
colonial mentality. Hence came the plethora of films and
novels known as 'colonial' which were often insipid and
failed completely to give a true picture of the Pacific despite
being set in its colourful scenery. Loti's portrait of
Vahékéhu, a woman of the Marquesa Islands, on page 224,
provides a good example of the ethno-centricity of such
illustrations. Much more honest was another naval officer,
Segalen, who made a discreet note in the margin of the

## The Kanaka Revolt in New Caledonia

Grave news arrived at the end of dinner. The district surrounding Bouloupari was in full revolt. The Ouameni tribes, the Owi and the Koa were running through the bush, plundering and burning the houses, and slaughtering the colonists. About midday, a band of natives spontaneously attacked a position, killing the gendarmes there, hacking up a surveyor, and slaughtering the telegraph clerk, M. Riou, at his post at the very moment when he was warning Nouméa of the Kanaka rising...

We had hardly arrived at Bouloupari when we were alerted. A horseman dashed out of the bush. This messenger brought news that only three kilometres from the position, in the bush that bordered it, Captain of Marines de Joux was surrounded by the Kanakas. The Captain had left in the moning on reconnaisance, taking with him some twenty men and a few Moriceau horsemen. He was returning towards the end of the day when 2-300 natives surged all around him. He beat them off with a volley; but the savages, ducking and weaving with astonishing speed, or taking cover behind trees, were not hit. They had a few guns and revolvers, and succeeded, by killing his horse, in dismounting a rider. This success inflamed their courage; they maddened themselves, as is their custom, with shouts and stamping. Brandishing their weapons, they drew their ring closer around the little company. This was the crucial moment, for they were about to make a concerted rush that would not be stopped. De Joux, hard pressed, put a bold face on matters. However, over the gloomy woods, night was falling... This was the story the horseman told me.

HENRI RIVIÈRE, *Souvenirs de la Nouvelle-Calédonie,* Paris 1880, pp. 130 and 173-174

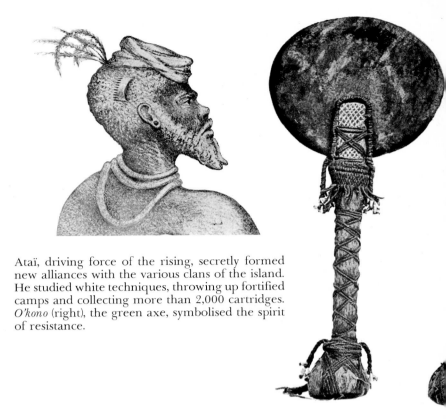

Ataï, driving force of the rising, secretly formed new alliances with the various clans of the island. He studied white techniques, throwing up fortified camps and collecting more than 2,000 cartridges. *O'kono* (right), the green axe, symbolised the spirit of resistance.

A view of Port-de-France, New Caledonia, engraved in 1861.

222

UMA;
OR
THE BEACH OF FALESÁ.
(BEING THE NARRATIVE OF A SOUTH-SEA TRADER.)
BY
ROBERT LOUIS STEVENSON

Like America's Herman Melville, Robert Louis Stevenson from England visited the Marquesa, Tuamotu and Gilbert Islands in a vain search for the earthly paradise. Stevenson not only recounted fascinating exotic tales (frontispiece, above) but also passionately defended the natives against the white administrators.

Stevenson (right) and his wife (second from left) settled in the Samoa Islands where they adopted native habits and customs. When he died in 1894, sixty Samoans in tears took turns to bear the author's body up to the top of a high peak overlooking the Pacific.

poems, which he chose not to publish: 'Too much lived to be written about'.

The three best writers about the Pacific, Stevenson, Segalen and Melville, were good observers and judges. Segalen provides us with an account of Tahiti of remarkable historic and ethnological precision. He describes the *Arioi* sect and its effect on the population. As to the friendly Melville, he sets about seeking a solution to the problem of blacks and whites. His works reveal the ambivalent attitude of seamen towards the blacks. The feature common to these three authors was exceptional in that they recognized the existence of the Pacific man in its entirety.

The second myth, regarding a paradise on earth, vanished within a few decades of the white man's invasion, incomplete as this still was. The qualities of that Oceanic Eden were not so much due to the climatic conditions of the region, which is anyway liable to fearsome cyclones, as to its peculiar ecology arising from an elaborate balance between man and nature. The 'black' Melanesian 'headhunters' were looked upon by the terrified Europeans as the most savage among men, yet were in fact merely *As-mats,* meaning Tree Folk, whose birdmen were on the look-out for fruit-skulls to give life to their children. The first whites were sandalwood traders, whalers and adventurers in the South Seas. They upset the balance of nature by their excessive deforestation and by exterminating some of the fauna and flora. What they first did to the animal and vegetable life of the region they did later to human life with their slave trading or 'black-birding'. Eden was being impoverished. As to the settlers, 'pioneers' as they were then known, propaganda in Europe aimed at populating the colonies had from the outset filled them with illusions about the vast areas of virgin land just waiting to be grabbed. The opposition they encountered on arrival filled them with bitterness.

If those Europeans had but found a smiling and docile source of manpower among the natives, the worst problem of the colonies would have been solved and the whites' bitterness and disappointment might not have been so great. But this was not to be: the 'natives' remained allergic to any form of co-operation.

The third myth concerned the fabulous riches to be uncovered and proved likewise somewhat disappointing. The search for gold had not been very rewarding in New Caledonia or in Australia. The apparent signs of the existence of various metals took a long time to be exploited in both countries, except for the copper mines in Australia. It was not until 1873 that an Englishman, Mr Higginson, founded near Nouméa the Société du Mont d'Or, the predecessor of S.L.N. (Société Le Nickel) which soon brought fame to New Caledonia. The phosphate deposits on Nauru, Ocean Island and Makatea were not discovered until the close of the century.

Probably the only persons who were not disappointed were the geographers and scientists. The Pacific offered them rich fields for research. But the philosophers, hoping to find a picture of universal man, failed to appreciate the true worth of the men of the Pacific. They did their utmost

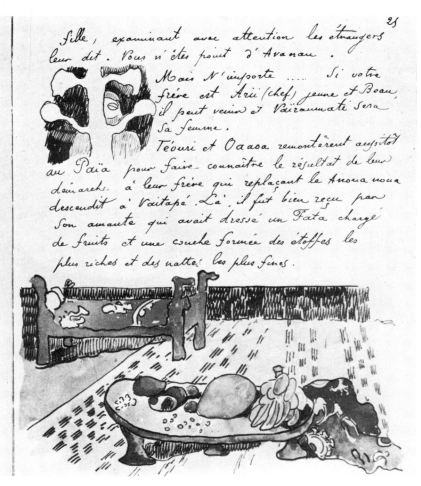

## 24

*Soeurs d'aller la voir pendant qu'il remonterait à leur demeure, au sommet du Paia. En approchant, les Deesses la saluèrent, louèrent sa beauté, et lui dirent qu'elles venaient d'Avanau district*

*de Bora Bora et qu'elles avaient un frère qui désirait s'unir à elle Vairaumati (c'était le nom de la jeune*

*fille, examinant avec attention les étrangers leur dit. Vous n'êtes point d'Avanau.*

*Mais N'importe ..... Si votre frère est Arii (chef), jeune et Beau, il peut venir et Vairaumati sera sa femme.*

*Téouri et Oaaoa remontèrent aussitôt au Paia pour faire connaître le résultat de leur démarche à leur frère qui replaçant le Anoua noua descendit à Vaitapé. Là, il fut bien reçu par son amante qui avait dressé un Fata chargé de fruits et une couche formée des étoffes les plus riches et des nattes les plus fines.*

Tahiti inspired Paul Gauguin to paint his best pictures and his pamphlets (right: *Tahitian Women with Flowers*, 1899). Recognized protector of the Marquesans, he engaged in futile struggles with the local authorities. At his death in 1903 the people were heard lamenting over his tomb 'Gauguin is dead, we are lost!' Above: Pages from Gauguin's *Ancien Culte Mahorie*, showing life on the islands.

Pierre Loti's soft and nostalgic evocations brought dreams to a generation of Europeans pining for the exotic. Above: a drawing by Loti which appeared in 1873 in a tourist guide to Nuka-Hiva. The island queen can be seen talking to her children.

---

**Gauguin on Tahiti**

I had to return to France; imperative family business called me back. Farewell, kindly soil. I leave you two more years – younger by 20 years, more earthy and yet more cultivated.

When I left the quay to board the ship, Tehamana, who had cried for many nights, melancholy and drooping, was seated on a rock. Her legs hung loosely, her two large solid feet brushed the salt water. The flower she wore above her ear had fallen to her knees – withered.

All around others watched stupified the heavy smoke of the ship that was carrying us all away, lovers for a day. From the gangway, it was possible to use a spyglass to see their lips moving to the old Maori refrain:

*You, light breezes of the south and the east, you who meet to play and to caress one another above my head! hasten together to the other island. There you will see he who abandoned me, seated in the shade of his favourite tree. – Tell him you saw me in tears.*

PAUL GAUGUIN, *Noa Noa* (first ms), 1st edition, Paris 1966, p. 45

The fascinating story of the *Muting on the Bounty* has stirred people's imagination for two centuries. Three films were made of it (Above: Lewis Milestone's version of 1961).

Films helped to spread the myth of the Pacific. In 1931 F. W. Murnau and Robert Flaherty made *Taboo,* a tragic love-story filmed in the Marquesas with Polynesians in the cast (above).

The first fiction film made in Polynesia was *White Shadows* (1928). Producer W. S. Van Dyke (centre, with helmet) tells of the shameful treatment of pearl fishers by white traders.

to reconstruct an image most closely conforming to their theories. Far from discovering universal man, they often buried themselves in sterile evolutionism with consequent ill effects which persist to this day.

So faded the three myths which we have just described. They were soon followed by yet another myth of possibly more harmful nature, that of the heavy burden to be born by the whites ('the white man's burden', as Kipling put it). Feeling their prestige threatened, the whites educated the savage with the aid of ethnologists and missionaries.

But the savages had formed their own picture of the characteristics of the whites, a shrewd and true picture. By now they were aware that the latter were neither gods nor people representing their ancestors returned to visit their descendants and share their riches with them.

&#10047;  &#10047;  &#10047;

From this point, they began to be afraid of the whites as poor landless folk who had come to steal other men's lands. This gave rise to many bloody uprisings throughout the nineteenth century. Furthmore, the 'savages' were given only the most meagre education and were unable to understand the wide technological gap between the two civilizations. They tried to remedy this by adopting the laws of the gods of the Christians. They zealously had themselves baptized and recited Protestant and Catholic prayers and litanies, and diligently observed the various Christian *taboos*. But all to no avail. Ships kept unloading rich supplies for the whites only, who refused to share with them. So they came to believe that the missionaries had only imparted a portion of their knowledge and kept the real name of their god to

themselves; a god whom the Oceanians took to fearing as a civilizing hero of white technology. From this belief there grew up all over Melanesia a host of different movements, messianic, dualistic, generally known under the term 'cargo-cult', or more precisely *kago*. These cargoist movements were essentially mythical expressions of their political aims. They too were harshly repressed. Disenchantment and mutual misunderstanding grew worse on both sides.

Referring back to that first myth of a terristial paradise dominating the awakening curiosity about the South Seas, it may well be wondered why the whites, instead of taking advantage of the remarkable ecological balance achieved in those regions, found nothing better to do than do destroy it? We have already considered this problem from the standpoint of its economic importance by listing Europe's needs at that time. But that is an old story which comes up again with each new generation and has lasted for thousands of years. It dates from before the earliest recorded history, going back to the Exodus of Biblical times when manna from Heaven fed the people of Israel after the crossing of the Red Sea, who needed only to pick it up each morning and be filled. But if anyone tried to store it away thriftily instead of living 'from day to day', instead of being filled they would only find food that was 'filled with worms' and 'infected'. (Exodus, chapter XVI).

Herein lay the difference between the two civilizations. The white man, over systematic and rational, had need of the culture of the Pacific. Perhaps he would soon lay down his heavy burden and renounce his lasting illusion of being entrusted with a mission of civilizing, and would at length become aware of the other culture and admit its values. Despite the disenchantment felt by both factions, it is reasonable to suppose that such a 'meeting' may soon take place. But it will require much soul-searching.

# THE PACIFIC IN THE TWENTIETH CENTURY

## CONFLICT OF THE GREAT POWERS

Rivalry among the great industrial powers gave rise to two World Wars in the first half of the twentieth century, involving most nations and their populations, and profoundly upsetting established patterns. Yet their effects on the Pacific area were very uneven: the First World War brought but few direct changes to its archipelagos which, however, were to become one of the principal centres of operations in the Second World War.

In the early part of the century the three leading powers were Great Britain, France and Germany. More and more capital was being invested in the colonies, giving birth to huge plantations, and powerful trading, mining and shipping operations throughout the Pacific. Except by missionaries, little attention was given to educating the inhabitants. The sole aim was to make use of their manpower and especially of the raw materials on their land and beneath its soil. Home governments counted their wealth in proportion to the extent of the colonies they possessed. The balance of power, however, was altered by the First World War. On 3 August 1914 Germany declared war on France; on 13 August the British, allied with France, landed in Boulogne; at the same time Japan entered the war against Germany and, while declining to join the conflict in Europe, set about gradually taking over Germany's possessions in China and the Pacific. When Germany was beaten in 1918 her place in the concert of colonizing nations was taken by Japan.

The United States entered the war on the side of the allies on 4 April 1917 and took advantage of the victory over Germany by building up powerful military bases in the Pacific, as did Japan. On the other hand, victorious France and England were seriously impoverished by the war which cost them millions of lives. Furthermore, doubts were beginning to be cast on certain 'intangible' feelings and moral values. Louis Gilloux's novel *Sang Noir* (1935) can be singled out as expressing one of the many new trends of thought characterizing the period between the wars. Its description of society in 1917 constitutes an unassailable condemnation, still true today, of society at the time.

But unlike developments in Europe, the first four decades of the twentieth century were relatively peaceful in the Pacific. Admittedly uprisings did break out occasionally, but the local population had been decimated by the white man's expansion in the nineteenth century, their decline seeming to have been hastened by the effects of colonization, by political subjugation and by cultural ethnocide. Finally, thanks to the attention which ethnology focussed on those civilizations which were thought to be vanishing, the authorities were able to dominate the islanders without resorting to the bloodbaths witnessed in the previous century. But somehow or other the native population began to increase to an extent never foreseen by the settlers at the beginning of the century.

Sydney is the oldest city in Australia, and has the most inhabitants. Today there are no reminders of the convict settlement of 1786. Port Jackson bay proved particularly suited to being developed as an international port.

The British Empire's colonial policy was moving towards the looser formation of the Commonwealth. The older colonies of Australia and New Zealand were taking their first steps towards autonomy, rather timidly where foreign policy was concerned, but much more firmly in the field of economics. Soon Australian and New Zealand capital would be supporting and even supplanting British interests in some of the islands of Oceania. This was to help Australia and New Zealand to develop markedly by comparison with the other Pacific colonies which the Westerners shared out, at first among themselves and later with the Japanese.

# DEVELOPMENT FROM 1900 TO 1940

## *The divided Pacific:*

'Colonial policy is the child of industrial policy', remarked Jules Ferry. And it was indeed the five greatest industrial powers of the time which carved up the lands of the Pacific during the first half of the twentieth century.

North of the Equator lay the realm of the United States: the Aleutians, Hawaii, Midway and Wake Islands, then Guam, the essential stepping-stone to their larger possessions in the Philippines. In 1916 the latter were granted a status of partial autonomy which was gradually to lead to independence. But thanks to disturbances they remained in fact under the tight control of America, which set up powerful naval and military bases between the wars, both in the Philippines and on Guam. As to the people of Hawaii, by 1937 scarcely 21,389 of them were pure Hawaiian out of a total population of 400,000, which at the time included some 158,000 Japanese.

Up till 1914 Germany was represented on both sides of the Equator, in the Marianas (excluding Guam), the Carolines, the Marshall Islands and the North-East of New Guinea with the important Bismarck archipelago (New Britain, New Ireland, New Hanover, – Lavongaii – and the Admiralty Islands). Samoa was divided between Germany, which held Western Samoa, and the United States which held the Eastern Islands of Samoa. After the First World War the German possessions were divided up between Australia, which took north-eastern New Guinea and the Bismarck Archipelago, New Zealand, which was given Western Samoa, and Japan, which was alotted by the League of Nations responsibility for the Marianas, the Marshall and Caroline Islands including Yap Island, a relay point for trans-oceanic cables.

Japan was at the time in full expansion. In the face of its continuously increasing demographic pressure (45,000,000 inhabitants in 1900, 55,000,000 in 1920 and 65,000,000 in 1930), its hope was to settle some of them in the 'over extended' territories conquered by the whites in the Pacific. Its balance of trade, in deficit up till 1914, was now showing a surplus. Its navy was the world's third largest and required bases. The nationalist conception of a 'Great Oriental Asia' under the aegis of Japan was beginning to take shape.

Further south, England held sway over archipelagos made up of the Gilberts, the Ellice, Fiji and Cook Islands as well as south-eastern New Guinea and the Solomons. She entrusted some of them to the care of her two dominions, namely Cook Islands and Papuasia to New Zealand and Australia, which by the Second World War thus became themselves colonial powers.

On either side of Britain's possessions France held the Marquesas, Tuamotu, Society and Gambier Islands to the east, and, to the west, New Caledonia, the Loyalties, Wallis

By the QUEEN.
# A PROCLAMATION.

Alarmed by rumors of war in Egypt and South Africa, the Prime Minister of New South Wales, Sir Henry Parkes, issued a clarion call for the Australian continent to unite. On 1 January 1901 the Australian colonies and Tasmania, after much hesitation, formed the Commonwealth of Australia. Queen Victoria declared the new federation in being, and her proclamation was published in the newspapers. The election poster below recalls the Commonwealth motto: 'One people – one flag – one destiny'.

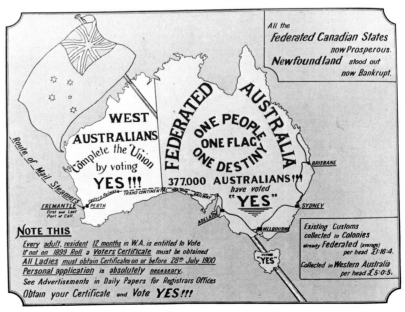

Right, a cartoon of the British lion congratulating and encouraging the Australian team on its 'first appearance': 'Well done, chaps' he cries to his cubs, 'Pull together!' Below, a constitutional conference was held in Sydney as early as 1891. On 1 January 1901 Australia celebrated its independence and Sydney crowds gathered in Martin Place to the sound of brass bands.

and Futuna. Finally there were the New Hebrides which have been held since 1906 under joint rule of a Franco-British condominion.

## Development:

Until the end of the First World War Europe held sway over the Pacific. Her hegemony was disputed by neither Japan nor the United States. Both were still in Europe's debt, and the world's biggest banks were still British, French or German. It was they which provided the capital required for colonial enterprise and they that took most of the profits.

The Americans first took an interest in phosphates. Companies were set up to extract them in the Phoenix and Line Islands. They were followed by Australian and New Zealand firms, particularly on Malden Island. Among others, the Australian firm of Arundel & Co is worth mentioning; when guano became exhausted they turned to plantations. But the largest phosphate deposits lay on three islands: Makatea in the Tuamotu Archipelago, which belonged to France, Ocean Island in the Gilberts, which was British, and Nauru in the Marshalls which became British after having belonged to Germany. There were thus three companies, which worked in harmony: the Compagnie Française des Phosphates de l'Océanie, the Pacific Phosphate Company, and the Anglo-German Pacific Phosphate Company. The last two later merged with the help of Australian and New Zealand capital to become the British Phosphate Company, which proved of valuable assistance to farmers in the two British dominions. But in the economics of colonization, at that time the phosphate industry was in an unique position by comparison with the two main colonial activities of planting and trading. The rôle played by the planters, their actions, their successes and failures could all provide material for many an adventure novel, some dramatic, some grim, but all truly colourful.

Those who made good often combined both activities as planters and as merchants, sometimes forming their own fleets and shipping lines as well. Some names came to the fore which are still worth recording as examples of these.

It is hardly surprising to note that in French Polynesia the first names were British, since the islands started by coming under the influence the London Missionary Society. A number of them had founded homes with members of Tahiti's aristocratic families. In Tahiti, Brander started with pearl trading before creating huge plantations on the Leeward islands. Stewart set up the Tahiti Cotton & Coffee Plantation Co. Ltd. which owned, among others, the 18,000-acre Antimaono estate. The Coppenrath trading network, with the Bambridges, covered all French Polynesia and beyond.

Married to a Brander daughter, Gustav Godeffroy from Hamburg formed the Compagnie du Commerce et de Navigation Océanienne; based at Apia, capital of the Western Samoans, it operated throughout the Southern Pacific. His successor, Weber, 'discovered' copra, or dried coconut, which was practical and economic to use and became one

From the earliest days of the colony, the majority of Australians settled around the south-east edges of the country, in the 'fertile triangle'. Melbourne, capital of the State of Victoria, was founded in 1835 by settlers from Tasmania. It grew very rapidly thanks to the birth of the cattle industry, Melbourne being one of the biggest wool markets, and to the gold rush of the 1850's. By the dawn of the twentieth century Melbourne already possessed all the attributes of a modern city, teeming and dynamic. Below, an 1889 engraving of Collins Street. Above: Bourke Street around 1930.

The 1914 war went almost unnoticed in Oceania itself. But New Zealand sent over 100,000 men to the Western Front (above). Germany did not have enough troops to defend her distant possessions. On 21 September 1914 an ANZAC (Australian-New Zealand Army Corps) corps, formed in Melbourne, landed in New Guinea and New Britain, forcing the German colony to surrender unconditionally.

The 1884 conference of Australian colonies brought pressure to bear on the Colonial Office to set up a British protectorate over the south-east coast of New Guinea ahead of the Germans. This acquisition opened the way for ethnologists and explorers. They hoped to study the lives and habits of the local inhabitants. Below, an expedition led by Henry O'Forbes of Scotland photographs the village of Hunuabada.

The hilly plateaux of Australia's east coast are covered by forests which stretch down to Tasmania. The main feature of these often dense forests are eucalyptus trees, some more than 330 ft tall. Gradually the forest had to give way to civilization. The photographs below and right show clearing operations in the State of Victoria towards the beginning of the century. The nineteenth century political division left each State to construct its own railways without consulting their neighbours. So the various States adopted different gauges. A resolution to coordinate the system was only passed in 1971. Left, a train crossing an isolated part of Queensland in the 1890's.

234

of the great sources of wealth for the area. The Godeffroy enterprise became the spear-point of German colonization in the Pacific, even after its difficulties in Hamburg which led to its being replaced by the 'D.H. & P.G.' (Deutsche Handels und Plantagen Gesellschaft.)

Australia joined the fray with John T. Arundel, already mentioned above, and especially with Burns Philip & Co. Ltd which established offices and shipping lines all over the South Pacific. One of the aims of its founder, Sir James Burns, who died in 1923, was to maintain a British and Protestant presence in that part of the world to contain the French and German expansion.

Many other names should be recorded, such as the Lever Brothers, Morris Hedstroem, Philip Carpenter, not to mention the powerful Colonial Sugar Refining Co, backed mainly by Australian capital, which gained a particularly powerful hold on the Fiji Islands. Sugar cane planting became the main activity in the Fijis and led to the immigration of Indian workers: between 1879 and 1916 60,965 Indians were brought to the Fiji in 87 convoys. Their refusal to go home at the end of their contracts led to problems which have not been solved to this day.

Manpower shortages in fact were to cause serious difficulties everywhere. Where it had been available, as in Australia and New Caledonia, convict labour had by now become a thing of the past. The 'slave trade' had at last been banned after reaching such proportions in the second half of the nineteenth century, particularly from the Solomons and New Hebrides, that the numbers of 'indentured workers' deported to Fiji, Australia, New Zealand and New Caledonia are estimated at 150,000. Only a very few of them ever saw their homelands again. The native population itself generally refused, for understandable reasons, to work for the colonial enterprises. Hence the need to look further afield for labour: Java, Indo-China, China and, as we have noted, Fiji and India.

The 1929-1933 world economic crisis also affected the colonial companies which found themselves facing collapsing prices for raw materials, a fall in world trade and increasing difficulties in obtaining finance. Many of them disappeared while others were only saved by support from their respective home countries. But it turned out that those distant islands were less seriously affected than the three big Pacific countries of Australia, New Zealand and New Caledonia, which were already to becoming industrialized.

## New Caledonia, New Zealand and Australia

In New Caledonia a great effort had been made under Governor Feillet (1894-1902) to replace the penal colony by a free settlement of immigrants from France. At the same time large-scale mining prospecting was being carried out with promising results when gold nuggets, chromium, cobalt and especially nickel began to be discovered. This was followed by a stream of prospectors and the formation of

companies which devoted themselves to the triple tasks of cattle-breeding, planting and trading, such as Ballande, Lafleur, Barrau, Johnston, Pentecost and, the biggest of them all, John Higginson. Among its many enterprises, it was Higginson who, in conjunction with the geologist Garnier, created the Société le Nickel and later the Cie Calédonienne des Nouvelles-Hébrides to compete with James Burns of Australia.

Quite soon Société le Nickel came under the control of the Rothschild Bank. In 1909 the Ballande firm founded the Hauts-Fourneaux de Nouméa which after the First World War became the Société Calédonia and was financed by the Banque d'Indochine and the Société Générale de Belgique. The 1929 crisis brought much of this merging to a standstill and put a number of companies into serious difficulty. But recovery was rapid. Finally the Société le Nickel took over the Société Calédonia, and in 1939 it had a capital of 224,400,000 francs.

As elsewhere, the labour problem was becoming acute. It was not helped by the preference of the descendants of Chief Ataï 'to have no children rather than see them exploited by the whites', as Maurice Leenhardt noted in 1902. So they looked to the New Hebrides for labour, and then to Asia. In 1929 there were 6,230 Tonkinese, 7,690 Javanese, and 1,500 Japanese out of a total population of 57,000 which included 17,000 whites.

Since 1901 and 1907 Australia and New Zealand had respectively been developing their powers, based on their new autonomy as British dominions. At the beginning they showed no eagerness to cut loose from the mother country. They left their foreign relations in the hands of Britain's embassies abroad and their defence to the care of the British Royal Navy. They were content with taking part in the Imperial Conferences which met in London from time to time. This gave their representatives the opportunity of seeing that the world situation was moving towards a major conflict and that some precautions ought perhaps to be taken. So it was decided in 1907 to create a small Australian fleet and in 1909 to institute compulsory military service. Further, possible recruits were not allowed to leave the country. Political life in Australia was extremely unsettled: between 1901 and 1914 there were nine different governments. Of the three original parties (Conservative Free-Traders, Liberal Protectionists and Labour, supported by the unions) only the last two still existed. Labour took office in 1910 and held it until 1913, to return again on 17 September 1914 just after the beginning of the First World War.

The economic situation was not brilliant in the early days of the Federation, but it was improving. Cattle and wool sales were growing, and industry was beginning to be really important. The Broken Hill Proprietary Company had already become a big mining and metal undertaking. Lastly, the population had grown considerably thanks to immigration, which was of course white and preferably British. By 1914 Australia had almost reached the 5,000,000 mark.

New Zealand was moving ahead along parallel lines. There, too, the political parties were Conservative, Liberal

Civilization moves in: In 1910 Carterton, New Zealand, was still but a township of gaudily painted houses, its architecture and the picturesque characters in its streets recalling some frontier town of the American Far West. Yet a clock tower, telegraph posts and a car tell of increasing prosperity and progress.

Air travel is almost the only way to cross the huge stretches of Australia's grass lands. The first trains went through the Alps by 1868, but vast areas were still hard to reach. After the 1920's air transport assured more regular communications between the farming regions of the interior and the cities on the coast.

At left immigrants are shown landing on the quayside at Nouméa in about 1900. In 1891 there was almost no immigration to Australia. It was only resumed on a large scale after the Second World War. The alarming competition of the Asian races was controlled by enormous immigration taxes. Travel and settling-in subsidies for Europeans were no longer paid by the colonies. Free settlement made great advances in New Caledonia after the suppression of the convict settlements, particularly between 1896 and 1902, but was suddenly stopped in 1903.

Below: A view of the Auckland landing stage in full activity (around 1890). The New Zealand islands saw tremendous economic growth after the end of the Maori wars in 1869. Cattle farming flourished, the discovery of gold and development of Kauri fossil gum brought fortunes to the new settlers. Later, at the beginning of the century, material interests gave way to search for political and social reform. A Dominion of the British Commonwealth after 28 September 1907, New Zealand became a model socialist state.

Sydney's agricultural show was one of its great attractions (the photograph was taken about 1900). From 1933 until the start of the Second World War, Australia's farm produce made up 75 per cent of her exports; Australia already possessed the world's biggest flock of sheep! In 1891 it numbered 106 million head. By 1902 it had fallen to 54 million owing to the great droughts. But the numbers subsequently rose again.

A cargo of frozen meat from Sydney being landed at Millwall Docks, London. For New Zealand a new era of prosperity dawned in 1882 with the despatch of the first shipload of frozen meat for England. After wool, meat and dairy products were to play an increasingly important part in the export trade of New Zealand and Australia.

and Labour. But political life there was not so unsettled. The Conservative party took over from the Liberals in 1912 and remained in power until 1930. But the economy was slower in going ahead. The gold rush, which had taken place in about 1860, had the consequences of at last providing the State with some resources and bringing in additional numbers of immigrants. Mainly based on cattle, the economy stayed on a modest level but did gain relative prosperity from wool exports as well as frozen meat and dairy products. In 1914 there were 1,000,000 inhabitants.

A feature common to both dominions was their social legislation which was extremely progressive for those days, and well ahead of Western nations. New Zealand gave women the vote in 1893.

When the First World War broke out Australia and New Zealand joined on England's side. They formed the famous ANZAC corps (Australian and New Zealand Army Corps) which distinguished itself in 1915 in the Dardanelles, at Gallipoli, in Palestine where the Australian cavalry drove in the Turkish lines with its famous charge of 31 October 1917, and lastly in France, in the Somme area, where they were led by Australia's General Monash and broke the German attack of 4 April 1918 and took part in the final assault on the Hindenburg Line, which they pierced at the end of September. They suffered considerable losses: almost 60,000 Australians and 17,000 New Zealanders, Australia's Prime Minister William Hughes had been beaten on the question of conscription and broke with the Labour party. With the Liberals, he formed the 'National' party which won the 1917 elections. He took an active part at the Peace Conference which led to the Treaty of Versailles on 21 June 1919. It was his hope that the sacrifices of his country would be rewarded by allowing it to share the former German possessions in the Pacific with New Zealand.

However Japan came on to the international stage, so New Zealand only received the Western Samoans while Australia was awarded tutelage over the south-east of New Guinea by the League of Nations. In fact Australia administered New Guinea as one, making no distinction between the mandated portion and Papua.

During the twenty years between the two World Wars two events of importance came to mark the history of Australia and New Zealand: the 1929-1933 economic crisis, and the coming of independence within the framework of the British Commonwealth.

After a short period of apparent prosperity, the youthful economies of the two dominions had to face the full brunt of world recession. Economically both were closely tied to Great Britain and the United States and depended largely on them for external loans. They had no means at their disposal to withstand the Wall Street crash, the City's inability to provide new loans, or the fall of the prices of wool, wheat, meat and minerals. Once again, common history was made in Australia and New Zealand: when things were at their worst, both countries turned to Labour.

Cattle farmers and planters in Australia saw a threat in the rise of industry and had formed a new agrarian party which supported the National party in the Bruce government up to 1929. But as soon as the effects of the crisis began to be felt Labour returned to office. It was the worst possible time, and they had to resort to such brutal measures as deflation, lower salaries and devaluation. This put an end to full employment in Australia for the first time in many years. A third of the working population was reduced to unemployment. To succeed with his plan for recovery the Labour Prime Minister, Lyons, did not balk at following the example of his predecessor Hughes and leaving his party to join forces with the National party. He was to remain in power until 1939.

In New Zealand, also, the depression brought on unemployment, lower standards of living and the fall of the Conservative government. The Labour party took over and set about implementing a determined social policy: national health service, free medical care, pensions and health insurance, 40-hour week, and a large-scale low cost housing programme.

Recovery started to be felt from 1933 on and the Australian and New Zealand economies began to expand again.

First the war and then the great depression afforded the two dominions an opportunity to evaluate their weak and their strong points – weakness stemming from their lack of external autonomy, and strength from their position in the Pacific, their expanding economy and the part they had played in the First World War. They united with the other dominions to demand that Great Britain review their status.

That was the objective of the Balfour Declaration of 1926 which recognized the dominions as possessing full autonomy, external as well as internal. The outcome was the 1931 Statute of Westminster, whereby the former dominions became truly independent countries, freely associated within the British Commonwealth.

The other dominions hastened to ratify the Statute of Westminster and apply its provisions, but Australia was in no hurry to follow their example. Of course 1927 had witnessed the solemn inauguration of her new federal capital. But Australia still did not see her future otherwise than as an appendage of England and protected by her. It was not until 1935 that she set up a ministry of foreign affairs separate from the Prime Minister's office and 1942 when she began to realize her isolation and her own international responsibilities and ratified the Statute of Westminster on the outbreak of war in the Pacific.

New Zealand appeared even less eager to take on full sovereignty and did not ratify the Statute of Westminster until 1947.

Sheep farming is still New Zealand's primary resource. It takes up 89 per cent of the agricultural land surface. The prevalence of sheep farming is due to the exceptionally mild climate. Grass grows all the year round. The land is hilly, therefore ill suited to cropping, and labour is scarce. The shepherds shown in this photograph, taken in 1910, could easily imagine they were in their native Scotland. Below: A view of Melbourne, engraved in 1861, when the artist felt goats fitted in the landscape better.

# THE PACIFIC WAR

On Sunday morning 7 December 1941 the Japanese air force attacked
the American fleet riding at anchor at Pearl Harbour, Oahu Island, in a
surprise attack. Within two hours the Americans lost a battleship and
45 aircraft; 8 destroyers, 3 cruisers and 7 battleships were badly damaged.
The onslaught brought the United States into the war.

The First World War did not seriously affect the Pacific, even though some countries like Australia and New Zealand did take part in it under the leadership of Great Britain, while Tahiti and and New Caledonia fought with France as part of her 1st Pacific Batallion, and Germany's ephemeral possessions were transferred to other imperialist hands after her defeat. But the Second World War, which broke out in Europe in September 1939, was very different. The conflict spread directly to a large part of the Pacific, and, more important still, it brought profound changes there as in the rest of the world, with particularly as far as the economic and political supremacy of Europe was concerved.

It all began at dawn on 7 December 1941. That morning 300 Japanese aircraft attacked Pearl Harbour without any warning. Pearl Harbour was America's greatest air and naval base in the Pacific, situated close to Honolulu on the west coast of Oahu Island in the Hawaiians. With no time to fight back, the Americans lost 10 battleships, 240 planes and 3,300 men in the space of a few hours. It was the greatest disaster in America's military history, and marked the opening of the war of the Pacific.

That surprise attack precipitated the American nation into the war. Up till then the United States had watched the lightning victories achieved by Hitler's armies without feeling themselves directly threatened by the dictators, including Germany's Japanese and Italian allies. Pearl Harbour put an end to such illusions.

Japan had long been waiting for the right opportunity. The aim of her leaders was to secure dominion over South-East Asia and the Pacific. They had become involved in Manchuria and Formosa. They had invaded China in 1939 and Indo-China in 1940. France and the Netherlands were practically eliminated while Great Britain was besieged on her island. That left only Russia and the United States. In June 1941 Hitler launched his massive attack on Russia. Thus Japan had no-one to face but the United States which, as a matter of fact, showed no signs of wanting to become involved. The Americans were to be taken by surprise and faced with the accomplished facts: a Japanese delegation headed by Admiral Kurusu was in Washington discussing ways and means of maintaining peace in the Pacific on the very day when the Pearl Harbour attack was launched. Indeed, through a clerical error the Japanese declaration of war was delivered half-an-hour after the attack had started.

That first action was to characterize the entire Pacific war, which became essentially a war in the air and on the seas. By destroying most of the American fleet, the Japanese gained an important advantage. But they had under-rated America's industrial might which was turned over to war production and soon showed itself ever more powerful than that of Japan, and above all, the attack had not succeeded in destroying the American aircraft carriers which were absent from Pearl Harbour when the raid was launched. This was to be of vital importance in the new type of amphibious warfare that developed in the Pacific.

The Pacific war lasted three years and nine months, and can be divided into three separate phases: the first was Japan's lightening offensive which propelled them irresistibly to the Solomon Islands and New Guinea; then began the phase of indecisive fighting which mostly took place in the jungles and which, without seriously affecting Japan's military potential, nevertheless prevented them from attaining their apparent targets of New Caledonia, New Zealand and Australia; the final phase saw the Americans regaining their supremacy in the air and at sea and playing their extraordinary game of island 'leap-frog' which was to lead to the fall of Tokyo within a few months.

## The Japanese offensive:

The Japanese crossed the frontier between China and Hong Kong on the same day as they attacked Pearl Harbour. Then began a serious of astonishing achievements. On 10 December the PRINCE OF WALES and the REPULSE were sunk and Guam was captured. Before the end of 1941 the Philippines were being attacked, Wake Island and Hong Kong had fallen, Thailand had joined in on the side of Japan, which occupied the Gilberts and North Borneo with its rich oil wells. The early monts of 1942 witnessed more Japanese successes on every front: the Dutch East Indies were besieged on all sides and 'impregnable' Singapore surrendered on 15 February. It was a disaster: 125,000 allied soldiers were captured, including a whole division of 17,000 men, which meant one quarter of that country's forces. This was followed by the fall of Batavia and Rangoon. Admittedly there were still points where resistance was still going on, such as the Philippines where General MacArthur was beginning to make a name for himself. But 30,000 American and Philippine soldiers had to surrender in April and the Corregidor fortress, their centre of resistance, was abandoned on 6 May. The Japanese occupied New Ireland and New Britain almost without firing a shot and started to set up a powerful air and naval base at Rabaul. It seemed that nothing could stop them as they drew near to the shores of Australia, New Zealand and New Caledonia. If those were taken it would become extremely difficult, if not impossible, for America to mount a counter-offensive, since it could only be based on Hawaii, which was separated from Japan by vast stretches of ocean.

And all three countries possessed only extremely weak means of defence which appeared in no way capable of resisting a massive Japanese attack.

## Out of breath:

The Americans and their British, Australian and New Zealand allies made every effort to halt the Japanese tidal wave, often attempting spectacular feats. Thus on 19 April 1942 they launched an air attack on Tokyo from aircraft-carriers. There was no hope of the planes ever returning to base. If possible, they would have to land in China or elsewhere. Some got through... Before that they had

A squadron of battleships lying at anchor off Hawaii in prewar days. Below: Landing craft head for the shore at the Okinawa landing.

bombed the Marus, Marshall and Gilbert Islands. But the Americans were pulling themselves together and firmly took charge of operations. Admiral Chester Nimitz became Commander-in-Chief of the Pacific Fleet, while General MacArthur was appointed Commander-in-Chief of the Allied forces in the Pacific. He arrived in Australia on 17 March 1942 after proclaiming, as he was leaving the Philippines, 'I will return'. It would seem that relations between the two men were not always very harmonious, but their association was more fruitful than harmful and both of them proved to be courageous war leaders.

So far the means at their disposal were inferior to those of the enemy. Although America's industrial and technological power was fully mobilized, the losses at Pearl Harbour and in the early fighting were not yet made up. It was vital to gain time at any cost.

Fortunately they seemed to be helped in this by the Japanese who reached Rabaul on 23 January and appeared to be hesitating. Obviously they were aiming for Australia and New Zealand. But for several weeks it was impossible to tell which of the two they were aiming for first. On 19 February their air force bombarded Port Darwin. Did that mean that Australia was to be their next target? If they had followed up their first push they would probably have had little difficulty in taking New Caledonia and then New Zealand, thereby putting America and her allies in peril.

It was true that the Japanese forces were engaged on many other fronts, in Burma, and in the Dutch East Indies. But Japan had had all the time it needed to get ready materially and strategically for these numerous actions. When they made up their minds, it was too late: surprise was no longer on their side. In any case, their plan was ambiguous, for in the beginning of March their troops landed almost simultaneously at Lae, Salamaua and Finschhafen on the south-east coast of New Guinea and on Bougainville Island north of the Solomons. New Guinea would open the door to Australia, while the Solomon Islands were on the route to New Zealand. And on 10 March an American division took up position in New Caledonia while General MacArthur concentrated all available Australian and American forces on holding Port Moresby. On 7 May Vice-Admiral Ghormley moved into Auckland, while the American forces in New Caledonia were further reinforced.

It can be assumed that the Japanese felt it necessary to set up a solid intermediary base before pushing further south. That base would be formed to the north at Truk, the 'secret' island which they had turned into an 'unsinkable aircraft-carrier', and to the south at Rabaul, where they hastily built powerful installations and where they soon had a garrison of 200,000 men.

In any case, they allowed the Americans valuable weeks of respite, and both routes which they had selected proved to be studded with obstacles. They literally became bogged down, and it was very soon seen that they had reached the limits of their push to the south.

This first became apparant in New Guinea. The island is covered with dense jungle, deep marshes, and posseses myriads of insects and uncrossable mountain ranges. The Australians were more familiar with the territory and its difficulties than the Japanese and made friends with the Papuans, even though some of the latter saw the coming of the Japanese as a means to rid themselves of white domination. The Australian coast watchers, who knew the area perfectly and stayed on the spot behind the Japanese lines, played a decisive part as observers and informers.

The Japanese extended the area they occupied along the south-east coast of New Guinea, but not without difficulty. They suffered heavy losses in the Battle of the Coral Sea which was fought in the air from 4 May to 11 May; this prevented them from sending in the reinforcements they needed. Of course they counter-attacked. On 1 June four or five midget submarines forced their way into Sydney Harbour, and a few days later they launched a powerful naval attack as a diversion against Midway Island in the very heart of the Pacific. But by then the Americans had broken the Japanese secret code and had advance knowledge of the project. The Americans suffered severe losses but the attack failed. But the Japanese did not lose heart. On 25 August they landed at Milne Bay at the southern point of New Guinea in order to provide support on the west coast for their offensive against Port Moresby. Once again the Americans and Australians were forewarned and the Japanese were thrown back into the sea within a week of their landing. They then attempted the impossible; a direct attack on Port Moresby by crossing the fearsome Owen Stanley Mountains. They launched their offensive on 14 September from Buna and Gona. They carried Kokoda, in itself no mean exploit, and reached the top of the Owen Stanley Mountains. But they made no further progress. The Australians counter-attacked with American air support. Actually it took the Allies several months of savage combat to reach the south-east coast, but the basic aim of the Japanese, the capture of Port Moresby, was now beyond their grasp.

Kokoda was only retaken by the Australians on 4 November, and Gona and Buna were reoccupied by the joint American and Australian forces on 10 and 14 December. That did not mean that New Guinea was cleared of the enemy, far from it. Driven out of the southern extremity, the Japanese continued their resistance for a long time further north. On 27 January 1943 they made another attempt at Port Moresby, launched from the Lae-Salamana area which they still held solidly. But the Battle of Mau turned against them. MacArthur only managed to conquer Salamana and Lae in September 1943 after a daring airborne operation.

Meanwhile tougher battles still were being fought on land, on sea and in the air to conquer the Solomons. The Japanese had taken over two-thirds of the archipelago, Bougainville, Choiseul, Vella Lavella, New Georgia, Florida, and at the beginning of July 1942 they landed at Guadalcanal. Complete possession of the archipelago would form an excellent take-off point towards the New Hebrides, then New Caledonia and finally New Zealand, even though the position of the Allies there was better by mid-1942, as has been shown, than it was at the beginning of the year.

The Americans selected Guadalcanal to block any further advance by the Japanese. A month later, it was their turn to land there, after taking the Isle of Tulagi and Gavutu and Tanambogo between Florida and Guadalcanal. There then ensued what became tragically known as the 'Verdun of the Pacific', such was the ferocity of the fighting, so implacable its nature, so murderous the hand-to-hand combats. On the American side, it was the first taste of battle for General Vandegrift's Marines; on the Japanese side it revealed their indifference to death and the stubbornness of the soldiers of the Rising Sun.

Tremendous sea and air battles were being fought at the same time for Guadalcanal, at ever greater cost of life and limb. They showed what was to be expected in the two years ahead. First came the Battle of Savo on 8 and 9 August 1942, where the Japanese took the Americans by surprise and took severe toll of their fleet, obliging it to withdraw and leave the Marines behind at Guadalcanal. Then, on 24 August, came the Battle of the Solomon Islands, which was less decisive. Finally the Battle of Cape Esperance avenged Savo, for the Japanese were taken by surprise and their fleet severely defeated.

While the navies and air forces of the two sides were waging their battles, more exhausting and murderous fighting was taking place on land as each side kept sending in more reinforcements. On 12 October and again on 12 November two convoys of 6,000 American marines each were put ashore. On the Japanese side, the 'Tokyo Express' was bringing in men, material, supplies and munitions, and shelling the American positions. The struggle was implacable but valueless: each day the advances gained the day before at such cost of human lives would be wiped out.

The naval engagement known as the Battle of Guadalcanal, 'the most savage fleet action in modern times', took place on 12-13 November. The Japanese wanted to bring decisive support to their defenders at Guadalcanal. The American fleet was in a very definitely inferior position, but once again had advance knowledge of the enemy's plans and immediately sailed into the invaders, forestalling their attack. The mêlée was worthy of olden days. Two American admirals lost their lives on their ships, nearly all their vessels were sunk or damaged, but they mauled the enemy so badly that he had to turn back, leaving their troop transports to continue alone towards Guadalcanal, possibly in the belief that the Americans were no longer in a position to intercept them. But the American air force was receiving continuous reinforcements and plunged in for what turned out to be a massacre: 20,000 Japanese soldiers were drowned.

On 30 November the Japanese tried again, but in vain: the American fleet had in the meanwhile been able to reform.

The balance immediately changed in favour of the Americans. Each night they attacked the 'Tokyo Express' and supplies and reinforcements for the Japanese troops on Guadalcanal became more and more scarce while the Americans kept improving theirs. The Japanese made a few counterattacks but fortune was now decidedly on the American

In the Philippines, Corregidor Island bars the entrance to the bay of Manilla. Its fortifications served MacArthur as a base for his troops, who held off the Japanese advance for several months. On 7 May 1942 the Americans surrendered. Above they are seen marching out of the fort under the white flag. But the American general staff was already preparing a major counter-attack. Troops were being trained for jungle fighting and the strategic positions of the Pacific islands were being carefully studied with an eye to the forthcoming invasion (below).

From 1944 the fortunes of war began turning in favour of the Americans. The assault on Japanese bases was carried out with amphibious tanks under cover of heavy fire. On 14 July 1944 the Americans landed at Saipan (top to right) on 14 September on the Palau Islands (right), and finally at Okinawa (below) on 31 March 1945. This was the greatest amphibious operation of the war in the Pacific, and enabled the Americans to set up air bases within range to bomb the cities of Japan and destroy Hiroshima.

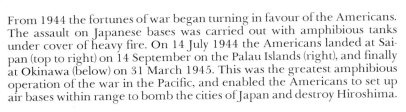

side, and on 9 February 1943 Tokyo announced the evacuation of Guanalcanal. It took many months before all resistance ceased. But, as in New Guinea, the Japanese had to give up their goal. The route to the south by way of the Solomons was denied them for ever.

In the following months there were still a number of serious actions both in New Guinea and in the Solomons, but the positions had turned in favour of the Allies. American naval and air power was now superior to that of the Japanese and that superiority would continue to grow.

The Japanese had lost the impetus of their attack. Undoubtedly they still reacted fiercely. They did not hesitate to bomb long-distance targets such as Port Darwin in May and June 1943, or to undertake naval battles as they did off New Georgia at the beginning of July. They seemed, however, surprisingly loth to follow up their local successes. This was noticeable on a number of occasions as, for instance, after their naval victory at Savo, or again at Midway, or later when the Americans landed at Leyte. They seem to have less well informed about their enemy's intentions than were the Americans. In short, they were now on the defensive almost everywhere.

## The reflux:

At this point the Americans started their counter-offensive which was to propel them in two years from New Guinea and Guadalcanal to Tokyo.

The advance was carried out along twin south-north parallel lines: to the west by the army under General MacArthur from New Guinea to the Philippines and Okinawa, and to the east by the navy under Admiral Nimitz by way of the Solomons, Gilberts, Marshalls, Marianas and Iwo Jima. At Okinawa on the two forces joined hands.

The twin forces were actually very similar in composition: both comprised ships, planes, aircraft-carriers, tanks, guns and infantry. The difference lay rather in the temperament and military background of their respective leaders. Despite personal rivalries they managed to work together on important occasions, both using the same 'leap-frogging' tactics, by-passing enemy strong points and leaving them to wither on the vine.

Between Guadalcanal and Tokyo lay some 10,000 islands, all wholly or partially occupied by the Japanese. Had they to be taken at the rate of one month for each island — and we shall see that it often took much longer than that — a systematic recovery of all the islands would have required 800 years! Doubtless that was the idea of the Japanese: to make the project seem too lengthy for America to undedrtake.

It was to counter this that MacArthur and Nimitz developed their island-hopping tactics: to concentrate on taking the few islands considered to be indispensible for cutting the Japanese communications and ignore the rest, which would have to surrender after the fall of Tokyo.

This could only be done thanks to great material superi-

In one of the bloodiest battles of the Pacific at Iwo Jima (19 February 1945) the Americans only took a few prisoners (above). The Japanese garrison numbered 20,000 men, most of whom were killed or took their own lives. The occupying forces did their best to help the distressed native population by distributing medicines and food. Below G.I.'s are seen handing out sweets to the children of Papua and water to an old woman at Okinawa.

ority. Here lay the great common feature shared by the two men: they only launched their double counter-attack when they were certain of having material means at their disposal which were much superior to those of their enemy. For they had observed in the fighting at New Guinea and Guadalcanal that the Japanese never surrendered and was prepared to fight on until he died. 'The individual tenacity of the Japanese soldier is astounding... During the attack on the Solomons only three Japanese surrendered.' This observation by General Vandegrift, who was in command of the American Marines, is confirmed by figures quoted below. 'Hitting them where they ain't' was third among the tactics used by MacArthur and Nimitz. But, as will be seen, it sometimes led to painful surprises when they found the Japanese where they were not supposed to be.

The first major operation in the east was fought in the Gilberts. On 20 November 1943 after a heavy bombardment the American marines landed on Betio Isle, part of Tarawa atoll, which is 2 $^1/_2$ miles long by 770 yds wide. It took 72 hours of furious combat to overcome Japanese resistance as against the 42 hours originally expected. Some 100 ships took part in the operation and 3,000 tons of bombs were dropped on the little island. Almost 1,000 Americans lost their lives and 2,311 were wounded, while the Japanese lost 4,690 men killed out of a garrison of 4,836.

Next came the capture of Kwajalein Atoll on 31 January 1944 and Eniwetok on 18 February in the Marshall archipelago, followed by Saïpan Island on 15 June, Guam in the Marianas on 21 July and finally Palau Island. The first truly Japanese soil was taken on 19 February 1945 at Iwo Jima in the Volcano Islands archipelago.

All these operations followed more or less the same pattern, although the Americans learnt from their costly landing on Tarawa: first, bombardment to knock out defensive installations and their garrisons, then the landing, and lastly, immediately afterwards or some time later, to better surprise the invaders, a fierce counter-attack by the defenders who still survived despite the bombing, and who fought on until they died. But American equipment was overwhelming, as a few figures will illustrate:

– 15,000 tons of bombs were dropped on the tiny atoll of Kwajalein with its area of only 1 $^1/_2$ sq. miles. It might be thought that not a living creature could have survived. Yet it took four days to subdue the defenders. The cost: 8,500 Japanese and 356 Americans killed.

– It took one month to capture Saïpan. The fierce fighting cost the lives of 3,246 Americans with 13,000 wounded.

– Iwo Jima is a little larger, 5 miles by 2 $^1/_2$. The Americans dropped 40,000 tons of bombs on it. 'Everything above ground was totally destroyed, but the inferno beneath was extraordinary'. The Japanese had constructed thousands of underground pill boxes, most of which withstood the bombing. The first day 40,000 Americans went ashore. At first they were allowed to move forward until suddenly murderous fire was turned on them from all sides. Plans called for the island to be over-run within 5 days; instead, it took 26 days. Then followed the desperate *kamikase* attempts and

the suicide of the conquered. Rather than surrender, the Japanese preferred to commit suicide. This was true of the military when their ammunition gave out, but also of civilians, men and women, who even took their children's lives too, while *kamikaze* pilots deliberately crashed their suicide planes with their bomb loads on the decks of American ships. That was how the BISMARCK SEA was sunk with her complement of 350 men.

The eastern route offensive started before the one along the western side, as MacArthur had been fully occupied improving his position in New Guinea. But as soon as he felt certain that the Japanese were beaten, that is after he had taken Lae, he decided that his next objective must be the Philippines, skipping all the Japanese-occupied areas in between. This was a very different undertaking as it involved a huge area with islands stretching for over 1100 miles, populated by over 13,000 people. They were all occupied by the Japanese who had built over 70 aerodromes in the area. The operation was planned down to the minutest detail with the main landing on Leyte Island scheduled for 20 December. But once again MacArthur's fiery temperament came to the fore. He felt that the Japanese should be taken by surprise, unable to believe that the Americans could advance so rapidly. He landed at Leyte two months ahead of schedule, on 20 October, at the head of 124,000 men and with the support of three American fleets.

On land things went fairly well. His troops met with little opposition. They were also helped by an internal resistance movement which proved invaluable to the Americans.

But at sea the operation nearly ended in disaster. The supporting American fleets were set on by three Japanese fleets, resulting in one of the greatest battles of the war in the Pacific, which was fought from 20 to 24 October 1944. In the opening stages the Americans' co-ordination was bad and at one point the Japanese fleet was in a position to destroy the ships effecting the landings, which were left unprotected. Once again the Japanese hesitated at the very moment when everything seemed lost for the Americans, turned tail and failed to follow up their advantage. Thereupon the Americans pulled themselves together and inflicted heavy losses on them, virtually putting paid to the Japanese fleet. On 12 November the Japanese managed to send in reinforcements to Leyte, but it was again too late to stop the American advance. On 26 December Leyte was entirely in the hands of the Americans who, at the beginning of January 1945, landed in force at Luso, entering Manilla on 3 February. Two weeks later they landed on Iwo Jima.

By then the Americans and their Allies were at the gates of Japan. True, numerous islands and entire countries were still in Japanese hands, left to wither on the vine, but almost everywhere the Japanese had suffered enormous losses in men, ships and planes, while the American navy and air force were becoming more powerful every day.

Then came the air raids on Tokyo and the big cities of Japan, followed soon after by American ships bombarding the coasts.

After bombing for a month without cease, the Americans landed on Japanese soil on 1 April 1945 at Okinawa under the guns of an armada of 1,400 ships. For the first four days of their attack they encounterd almost no resistance at all. But on 5 April their advance was halted by a system of underground strong points even more formidable than those that had awaited them at Iwo Jima. On the morning of the 6th of April the Japanese air force attacked the American fleet. The *kamikazes* came in in groups, flying old machines surrounded by new ones. Each one chose his target, the ship on which they would crash with their bomb loads. In the evening what was left of the Japanese fleet came in to attack. In was to be the last naval battle of the war in the Pacific. The Japanese plan, to let the American troops land and then trap them by destroying the ships that had landed them, failed utterly. Damage to the American fleet was minimal. The results achieved by the suicide-planes were more psychological than material. They did in fact succed in sinking 35 ships and damaging a further 300, but their own losses were tremendous. The number of Japanese planes shot down in the one day of 6 April has been estimated at 500. Such a desperate way of fighting so shocked the Americans psychologically that their morale would have been badly shaken had it lasted any longer, the more so as it was followed up by the manned flying bombs. These were bombs dropped from planes, and flown by one man who could use his controls more or less accurately to steer the bomb and crash his craft on to his chosen target.

One such caught the destroyer ABELE which was cut in two and sank immediately.

The conflict was too unequal, and the Japanese lost their last big battleship, the YAMATO, and had to give up. It was the end of the Japanese fleet. They launched one more offensive on land but, battered by naval bombardments and air attacks, they could not hope to do more than delay the American advance. They kept up their resistance until 21 June, losing 117,000 dead against 7,000 on the American side.

All Japan's major cities were then subjected to massive air raids. Four unforgettable dates put an end to the whole tragic conflict:

– July 27: the Allies delivered an ultimatum calling for unconditional surrender, but received no reply.

– August 6: the first atomic bomb wiped out Hiroshima, causing 100,000 deaths.

– August 9: the second atomic bomb was dropped on Nagasaki with the loss of 80,000 lives.

– That same day the USSR declared war on Japan and invaded Manchuria.

– August 15: the representatives of the Allied powers accepted Japan's offer of unconditional surrender in Tokyo.

The war in the Pacific was over.
The atomic age had dawned.

# THE PACIFIC TODAY

## INTRODUCTION

Not only was the Second World War the greatest armed conflict of all time; thirty years later it is still today impossible to gauge the extent of its effects in many fields.

Its most obvious and almost immediate effect was the redistribution of world power. The nations of Europe lost their former supremacy. Their mantle was first inherited by the USA, whose industrial and financial might seemed capable of dominating the world. But her position soon came to be challenged by another power, Soviet Russia, whose economic power was assisted by an aggressive communist ideology having previously had, or still retaining, a hold on the population. The Second World War was soon succeeded by the cold war, until the two super-powers came more or less tacitly to agree to divide up the world when they both became convinced that a new conflict might destroy them both and most of the rest of humanity in atomic warfare.

But there emerged a new element, also a consequence of the World War, to upset the understanding between the two super-powers: the appearance on the scene of China, also communist but fast setting itself up against Russian leadership and proving to be the great power in Asia.

This was to mean the American withdrawal from South-East Asia, the loss of Indo-China, and American presence on the major archipelagos of the Pacific, the outer circle constituted by the Philippines, Taïwan, Okinawa and Japan and the inner arc by Guam, the Marianas and Hawaii. Powerful American bases were set up at all those support points, but was the Pacific to become an American lake?

Worldwide decolonization was the next great consequence of the Second World War. At least the European kind of colonization was coming to an end. For a new and subtler type of colonization was taking over: the rule of the dollar, the universally recognized currency, stronger than gold, had started. It was to last until the free economy crisis of the 1970s.

These disturbing developments were accompanied by a third consequence of War, with results which may over the years prove even more shaking: a worldwide denial of the accepted values of Western civilization. People's minds and consciences were profoundly troubled by the events immediately preceding and following that war. Christian churches were themselves involved in the soul-searching that was taking place everywhere. Meanwhile the gap was widening between rich nations, which were seeking to equal the American living standards, and poor nations living in penury and ever worsening under-nourishment. The former embraced the formula of consumer nations, generally leading to wastage, while the latter suffered the miseries of the many, contrasting with the luxuries of the fortunate few. Indifferent to such shocking inequalities, technolgical progress spread its tentacles everywhere. In particular the vast distances which formerly separated the islands from the mainland seemed to melt away with the progress in flying and telecommunications.

But a start is being made to giving consideration to the dangers which these developments may hold in store for the future of humanity and the equilibrium of nature. At a time when a serious economic energy and monetary crisis seems to be shaking our contemporary industrial economy, there are beginning to be doubts about the advantages of unlimited growth, and the protection of the environment is becoming daily a more general concern.

It is in this world context that the nations of the Pacific are now situated. They are not affected by the dilemmas of rich and poor nations. But after living through such profound changes over the past century and a half, their future is still fraught with uncertainty.

The famous Sydney Harbour Bridge, with its huge arched span, is almost a symbol of Australia.

# THE RE-EMERGENCE
# OF THE PEOPLES
# OF THE PACIFIC

The main resource of the Hawaiian islands is sugar. But the cane fields are mostly in the irrigated flatlands on the coast, while pineapple is grown (above) on the higher slopes of Oahu Island, where they cover 75,000 acres. In many places they are planted along the contour lines to avoid erosion.

In what terms is it possible to write about as shifting an epoch as the 'atomic era'? The very foundations of the former world balance of power are at stake, and it is hard to foresee in these present times which of the many currents struggling for the upper hand will emerge pre-eminent. But it certainly seems an established fact that, among other short term effects, the last World War has tolled the knell for the imperialist rule of Western Europe and paved the way for a new balance.

The general evolution of all the 'third world' countries formerly subjected to white domination has already begun to be felt in countries overseas along particular lines which are worth examining. Undoubtedly the position of the two former British dominions continues to differ from that of the other Pacific lands, but it will be seen that certain features are shared by all those countries, thereby undermining the clear distinction which could formerly be drawn between those two parts of the Pacific. They are still only pointers which it may be rash to link together, but the two most significant of them are the re-emergence of the peoples of the Pacific and the beginnings of notions of solidarity between them, both of these factors being encountered when the most recent developments in the area are studied.

Facts disproved the belief, so widely held throughout the nineteenth century and even in the early part of the twentieth century, that the peoples of the Pacific and their civilization were disappearing progressively but rapidly, due to extermination or assimilation, or by simple desuetude.

Colonization did in fact almost achieve this result. But after the First World War and more so after the Second — when Pacific troops always came in on the side of the Allies to help defend their own lands — there was a reversal to the trend, the position improved and the peoples recovered their dignity.

The demographic recovery became clearly evident with the 1930s, as a few examples below will illustrate:
In 1922 there were 32,600 native Samoans on the island. By 1947 there were 65,000 and more than 100,000 in 1961. In the Tongas the figures were 27,000 in 1931 and over 64,000 thirty years later, in the Solomons 91,500 and 130,000 respectively for the same years, and in New Caledonia's Grande Terre 17,000 to over 30,000. The indigenous population of the Marquesas climbed from 2,255 in 1926 to 4,000 in 1956. Admittedly their numbers are all well below the figures of past centuries, but they are still growing. The new Zealand Maoris have the highest birthrate in the world at 39 per 1,000; there were 200,000 of them in 1966, 60 per cent of these being under 21 years old. The position of the Australian aborigine was worse: in 1966 there were only 50,000.

To what factors was this recovery due? Undoubtedly to a combination of circumstances. After the attrition of the nineteenth century the inhabitants were no longer in any condition to react collectively or with violence, and colonization had achieved its objects and settled down. The natives were now left in the reserves where they had been moved. At the same time, from the medical point of view, a real effort was made to take care of their diseases, especially

In 1959 Hawaii became the 50th State of the Union. Left, an Hawaiian newsvendor triumphantly waves the special edition of the *Honolulu Star Bulletin* announcing the news. The archipelago's rapid growth and economic prosperity transformed the lagoons of former days into a seething jungle of sky-scrapers, luxury hotels and apartment buildings for millionaires. Honolulu's concrete streets and Waikiki's tourist beaches are a worthy match for California (below). Memories of the past are kept alive by a few native relics like this statue (right) of the great King Kamehameha I (1782-1810) festooned with flowers. It was he who gave the archipelago its political union before the Presbyterian missionaries came.

those which the whites had introduced and which had brought about such serious and lethal epidemics among the natives. The last epidemic in the twentieth century was the Spanish influenza after the First World War which struck at the colonizer and the colonized without distinction. Finally, the missions taught their converts to read and write in their schools and helped to save them from the evils of drink which the white man had brought with him, thereby giving the inhabitants some chance of standing up against the extortions to which settlers and traders subjected them.

But the demographic recovery may also be partly due to new grounds for hope. The ubiquitious presence of the white settlers may have become more felt than ever, but the initial trauma of colonization had been gradually overcome. Such developments as the fighting between whites witnessed in the First War, and the flood of Japanese giving way to the American tidal wave in the Second War, had given the people grounds for reflexion: were the whites really as monolithic and powerful as they had first seemed? Since they were so busy robbing and fighting each other, might it not be possible to lay hands on the material wealth which made them so strong and turn it against them?

These vague hopes, which certainly contributed to restoring hope and enthusiasm to some of the population, such as the Melanesians, could be detected in a variety of ways, including the revival and occasional stiffening of the *kago* cult, the beginnings of which had started to appear in the nineteenth century (see previous section).

## Kago: cargo cults: cargo-loaders movements

Under the heading of 'cargo cult' come a number of very varied phenomena which nevertheless possess certain common features, which are all the more surprising for occurring in places far apart. Some contemporary ethnologistes like Burridge, Jean Guiart, Peter Lawrence, have made detailed studies of some of them. Cargo (*kago*) refers to all goods procured and used by colonizers which come in either by ship or, after 1945, by air. The Melanesians felt that they would be able to make use of them just as much as the whites, but the whites kept them for their own exclusive use. What was needed therefore was to propitiate those responsible for the *kago* and thus find the requisite means to be able to share it.

The whole of New Guinea became an example for the *kago* cult manifestations, which took many forms in Irian, Madang and Gona to pave the way for a new turning point in the history of those peoples. Among the many different outbreaks of the phenomenem, some require particular notice:

— In today's Irian the *Mansren Myth*, started in 1867, reappeared in 1942: an army was formed with its own officers and imitation weapons, which was subsequently massacred by the Japanese.

— In Madang, where Peter Lawrence studied five different forms of *kago* cults covering a little over a hundred years, the origins of the movement go back to the arrival of the first whites, in this case the Russian Nikolaï Miklouho-Maclaï (see above). Because of the colour of their skin, these whites there as elsewhere taken for some sort of gods, the ancestors revisiting the living. The islanders brought gifts, which was normal and right, showing proper respect for the ancestors But as the the whites increased in numbers they ceased to bring gifts. Furthermore they suffered from diseases, which proved that they were human. Then came the missionaries. According to the rules of reciprocity (gift and counter-gift) observed by the people it was obvious that adopting the Christians' god would mean sharing the missionaries' riches. This did not mean abandoning their own beliefs, but merely adopting new knowledge which was considered more efficacious. In order to qualify for this new *kago*, considered as gifts from the ancestors, they became converted. The missonaries taught Bible reading, but they refused to reveal the 'real name' of God, which would in its turn reveal the secret of *kago*. After 1944 and the end of the turn the ideals of decolonization drove the Australians to encourage the country's economic and cultural progress. People began to understand that there were two kinds of goods: those provided by their ancestors but also, those manufactured by their own industries, and this last was a significant discovery. It led to changes in the different forms of *kago* which, from being cargo cults became cargo movements, developing a much more political nature. The principal leader, Yali, was mainly concerned with the old form of 'cargo cult'. He was held in prison for a number of years before being elected to office in the elections organized in Papua-New Guinea in preparation for the coming of independence.

In the south, the Papuans had been pacified since the coming of the Anglican mission in 1891. In 1942 they were amazed to see the people who preached a peaceful religion becoming soldiers. But the explanation of this metamorphosis was so well put across that it convinced some Papuans to join the Australian army. With the Japanese advance a number of whites were evacuated, but the missionaries decided to stick to their posts. Had it occured to them that they were thereby endangering their Papuan converts if the Japanese should win, which then seemed extremely likely? Did Christians require that Papuans should die for Australia?

In short, when the Japanese occupied Papua, feelings began to rise among the people, feelings which foreshadowed the fight for independence.The patriotic missionaries were unable to grasp those feelings. To give but one typical example, Father Holland found this out to his cost when, still unable to believe that his faithful followers would betray the cause, he was informed by one of them that 'now' the days of Papuans being willing to live with Europeans were 'over'. The spirits of the dead were now appearing, dressed as soldiers of the Rising Sun, and would soon be briging great quantities of wealth and provisions, quantities

Every kind of race rubs shoulders in Honolulu. There are many types of half-castes to be seen, with the Asian element predominant. Hawaii's wealth is exclusively in the hands of the white and Asian races, the latter being the better workers. The indolent Polynesian has only adopted the easier sides of the American way of life: they particularly like to spend their afternoons in Pool halls.

Hawaiian pineapples are canned in a number of factories around Honolulu. This seasonal work is generally performed by women of Polynesian or Japanese descent. Three quarters of the world's pineapple fruit and juice canning is in the hands of five Hawaiian companies, linked together by trade and family ties.

of *kago*, on their ships and aircraft. Astounded at being addressed in this manner, Father Holland replied that they should not believe in such 'nonsense'. Incensed at not being taken seriously, his informant knocked him down. Father Holland was later killed by the Japanese. At the same time an old man at Oïtanandi was declaring publicly that all Europeans should be killed, if only to escape Japanese reprisals.

Taking different shapes according to the time and to the various stages of advancement reached, there grew up a current of thought throughout New Guinea which would finally give birth to the independence movement.

On other islands *kago* cults took different forms. To understand them it is necessary to appreciate the important part played by the huge quantities of material brought in by the Americans in the days of the allied victory. That wealth, the friendliness of the gum-chewing GI handing out tinned foods, cigarettes and all kinds of equipment, the democratic appearance of their army and the riches they showered on all who worked for them – all that started the natives thinking when the war ended and the Americans departed, leaving everything behind.

It was then that a movement known as the *Marching rule* started in the Solomons, on Malaïta Island, some 60 miles from the Guadalcanal base. The Americans' withdrawal left a tremendous trauma. The men of Malaïta went on imitating them, but this time they were keeping up the war on their own account and moving with the times.

The island had 50,000 inhabitants. They made wooden guns looking like American guns, pointed assegais, built up fortifications, conscripted armies and even proclaimed a Malaïta Declaration of Independence. There was hardly any violence, but a lot of marching and singing; and the inhabitants just refused to pay taxes or recognize authority. In the words of a Protestant missionary 'The island had become pratically independent and beyond any kind of control. Even the missionaries did not dare go there any more'. But despite the 'impressive call-up of thousands of men' there were few 'acts of violence' but rather 'passive resistance'.

Another community movement like the *Marching rule* also took place in the Solomons in 1959 on Buka Island. The natives deserted their churches and set up a system of sharing all their resources under the leadership of two former Catholic novices, women and children being taken care of by the community.

At Tanna in the New Hebrides, where some of the inhabitant had worked at the American bases in the war like the people of Malaïta, there grew up what was know as 'the John Frum cult'. Overnight the island, almost entirely converted to Christianity by Presbyterian missionaries, saw its churches deserted. John Frum, it was held, was the black brother of President Roosevelt whose power he shared. He therefore lived in the United States, but was soon to bring to Tanna all the supplies which he was busy collecting on great white ships escorted by squadrons of planes. He was in communication with his Melanesian brothers by wireless as well as through the intermediary of the great volcano Yahué. When he arrived all rivalry would vanish, the island

be united, and its inhabitants become masters of the riches and techniques of the white man, living peacefully and comfortably for ever after.

As in Malaïta, new arms were made: American guns and ancient weapons like the assegai, linking ancestral tradition to the present day. In Tanna, as in Malaïta, the new faith was founded jointly on the volcano *and* on wireless, and showed proof of the people's vitality and capacity for thought as they tried to bring themselves up to date without denying their past in their attempts to deal with their problems. Many of its aspects were thus very positive. But as at Malaïta, the colonial authorities failed to understand anything about it and their reactions could only turn the movement more against them. The John Frum supporters acquired themselves a flag and an army, the T.A.-USA (Tanna Arma United States of America). On 17 July 1957 they went on parade with wooden guns and red bamboo bayonets.

Many other such movements sprang up in the New Hebrides. To mention only one, there was the 'Naked cult' which was short-lived and was mostly taken up by the pagan peoples. The leader Tsek's object was to try and restore the balance between man and nature. To achieve this he called for elimination of property ownership, destruction of manufactured goods, in-breeding and nakedness.

In New Caledonia, there probably did exist customs comparable to the cargo cults, such as when the Kanakas started going down to the beaches to meet in-coming ships dressed in missionaries' hats, cassocks and stoles, and carrying a breviary. But the little information the auther has been able to gather about the movement is too sketchy to give a valid picture of it. It was soon absorbed into the 1878 uprising which was so firmly put down that the island remained 'pacified' for a long time. Of that occasion Doumenge writes that the Melanesians 'were brushed aside by the inroads of big cattle ranchers, smallholders and penal colonies, so violently that their consequent trauma was so profound that their only reaction was despair'. But at the time of the the First World War war there were some stirrings near Mount Panié in the north of the island, and again an attempt from 1920 to 1938 to revive ancient traditions at the time of what was known as the case of the 'divine Pwagae', a healer who was consulted by Europeans as well as by Kanakas. As Jean Guiart wrote in his article entitled 'Birth and abortion of a messiah', Kanaka society was for ever trying, despite its difficulties, 'to escape from the vicious circle which led them relentlessly from the head-tax to providing services and being conscripted, with no hope in sight of ever being anything better than cheap labour, regarded, by reason of their goodwill, as the 'auxiliary of colonization', the official term.

The few instances cited above show how much there is to be learned from those various movements. They all share a common feature: a desire to break with the whites and the colonial authorities, and a return of their own ways. The Melanesians (*kago* was essentially a Melanesian phenomenon) had two different ways of demonstrating their pride and indepence according to time and circumstance: open rebellion or *kago* cults. We have already seen how all this

259

caused them to reflect more deeply on the values of Western civilisation.

Formerly their desire to adopt the white man's culture had often sprung from their having lost faith in their own traditional culture, which they now felt was out of date since it had been vanquished. So they had started by welcoming Christian religions as the pillars of the white man's powers. But successive mutterings from the *kago* cult adepts, and the contributions of the Second World War had made them understand that such might and wealth must be backed by more intellectual and technical knowledge.

It was now time to stop 'acquiring/dropping cultures'. They wanted to be equal with the whites and grasp the fruits of their technique without renouncing their own individuality. A big step forward had been taken, leading to rapid development of their minds.

## Assimilation

Obviously the colonial authorities at first made no effort to encourage this desire for intellectual knowledge. They were quite willing to teach the natives the rudiments needed for the services expected of them. Indeed the missionary schools took care of that quite adequately. But there was no question of admitting them to secondary education or higher education. Up till the Second World War only a minute number of young people had matriculated, still less had a university degree. A prerequisite for this was the necessity of moving to the nearest capital town, which was very costly. But this trend found little support later on when assimilation began to be advocated. Faced with the spectacular demographic growth of the native population, a few of the whites began to realise that the people would not be prepared to stay for ever in the inferior position to which colonization relegated them. So they had to be helped to climb up to the level of the whites and to become part of Western civilization. By shaking off their customs and primitive mentality or pre-logic, some of the natives would thus later be able to help their fellows take advantage of modern technical and intellectual progress.

Those who believed in such assimilation soon found that it had its limitations – some still sincerely believe in it – because it could only be tolerated in so far as the maintenance of European supremacy remained unquestioned. It often led to people not belonging anywhere. Some deeply cultured Tahitians, for instance, were overcome by periodical waves of despair brought on by a confused feeling of having given up their own culture and lost their own roots. Finally, as Maurice Leenhardt commented in *Do Kamo* 'In his enthusiasm it does happen that the [assimilated native] grasps misleading realities, when the white man preaches to him about the myth of assimilation. Police and senior administration officers have been each stupider than the other in the way they have destroyed the Kanaka ethics in favour of the supremacy of the art of the barracks. The

indigenous farmer in his zeal sought to get away from traditional farming and to produce corn with the aid of paid labour. He convinced his family to become coolies. He soon found himself up against the problems of capital in the face of a vigorous but ruined proletariat. His was the bitterness of the deluded.' As an illustration of Leenhardt's observations there was Chief Henri Naisseline, of Nengone, who complained at the beginning of the twentieth century 'When I speak my language I call my people 'brothers'; when I speak French I am told to call them 'subjects'. Can Christian and Western civilization really not do better than transform 'brothers' into 'subjects' and lands of 'peaceful living' into 'States'?'

White intrusion into the Pacific, with all its consequences, is now an accomplished historic fact which cannot be escaped. But who can say today whether the peoples of the Pacific are going to allow their culture to disintegrate under the effect of this shock, or whether they will manage to integrate this event into their own development?

That, however, does not depend on them alone. The West bears its own share of responsibility, and has no right to keep on for ever withholding the best of its cultures from those whom it has itself colonized. Autonomous schools and universities have only been quite recently founded there, thanks to the coming of independence to a large part of the Pacific. Hitherto people who were unable to travel to London, Paris or the USA for their education had to seek it in Australia or New Zealand. Today the South Pacific University at Suva, capital of the Fijis, takes in English-speaking students from most of that part of the Pacific. But that autonomous seat of learning is subject to the same doubts and problems as those suffered by the governments of the new independent states in the Pacific.

## Steps towards independence

One of the prime consequences of the Second World War was the granting of independence to most of the former Pacific colonies. But once granted, that political independence has not been able to wipe out all the human, social and economic aftermaths of colonization.

The fate of the former American colonies has varied. Hawaii was not only assimilated, but was integrated with the USA, becoming the 50th State in 1959. There the population, now approaching 800,000, is of mixed background – Japanese, Philippine, Chinese, Porto Rican and, of course, American. Since becoming American citizens those of pure Hawaiian stock are no longer counted separately. There is only a small minority of them, and theirs is one of the few cases of diminishing numbers today (21,389 in 1937, 12,206 in 1950). The Archipelago is daily becoming more American and will soon cease to count as Polynesian territory any longer. Today Hawaii's principle resources are sugar cane, pineapples, tourism and military bases. At the other end, the Philippines became an independent republic on 4 July 1966.

New Caledonia is a prosperous island. This is due to its low population, for lack of manpower leads to higher salaries. The presence of American forces for a number of years brought wealth to the island. Nouméa, with 40 per cent of the population, looks like some little market town of Southern France. The Town Hall (above) faces a huge shady square. Production from New Caledonian mines has grown rapidly since the last war thanks to the world demand for nickel and chromium. Below is an aerial view of factories A and B of the Société Le Nickel at Doniambo.

But they stayed under America's economic and political sway in spite of the *Huk* movement, which had been the centre of anti-Japanese resistance during the war, and other more recent resistance movements like the communists and the NPA (new people's army). As to the other American possessions, Midway, Wake, Caroline, Marshall, Marianas and Eastern Samoa, all remained under direct US administration. In some, such as Guam, the Americans built powerful military bases. Their administration is often severely criticized, even by many Americans. Recently newspaperman Jacques Decornoy reported the opinion of an American official in the Eastern Samoan islands: 'Ours is a seventeenth century colonialist policy'.

The British are the people who have developed independence furthest: Tonga, Fiji, Nauru and the Western Samoans are today all independent countries. Only the Gilbert and Ellice islands are still British colonies, while the South Solomons are British protectorates. Independence for Papua and New Guinea was scheduled for September 1975. This presented serious problems for Mr Somare, Prime Minister of Papua-New-Guinea since 1972 when his *Pangu Pati* coalition party won the elections. He had hard taskahead. In January 1975 Simon Kaumi formed a provisional republican government and announced the formation of an army of 'liberty fighters' in Papua. On 16 March 1975 Miss Abajah, head of the *Papua Besena* nationalist movement, unilaterally proclaimed the independence of Papuasia at Port Moresby, while New Britain and Bougainville announced their own intention of becoming independent.

The case of Bougainville is interesting. That island forms the 'Grande Terre' of the Solomon archipelago. It was only attached to Papua-New Guinea for economic reasons, being 640 miles distant. Unlike the lighter-skinned New Guineans, its 90,000 inhabitants are jet black. It contains major copper mines, and there are reasons to believe that even more extensive deposits may be found there. These mines are being worked by an Australian company, a subsidiary of Rio Tinto Zinc of London, in which the Papua-New Guinea government holds 20 per cent of the shares. Following very violent strikes and the breakdown of discussions between the Minister for Foreign Affairs, Commerce and Defence, Sir Maori Kiki, and the separatists, M. Sarei and Father John Momis, Grande Terre, backed by the Roman Catholic church in the person of Bishop Gregory Sinkai, proclaimed that it would secede from the New Guinea Confederation and declared its independence unilaterally on 1 September 1975, just 15 days before Australia granted full independence to the Confederation.

It remains to be seen whether all the separatist leanings will be able to see the light of day or not. But this is an example of the intricacy of the problems facing those new independent countries in which foreign firms are so keenly interested. At the birth of their independence, when their thoughts should be turned to solving their own problems within the Melanesian picture, the new leaders of these lands of the Pacific find themselves faced with difficulties inherited from colonialism which vitiate their position.

261

This is where lies the responsibility of the former colonial powers, which sometimes appear to be seeking to take back with one hand what they give with the other in granting independence more in form than in reality. We should recall the case of Tonga which had retained its independence as a kingdom, merely placed under British protection after 1890, where England's influence had been predominant mainly because of the influence of the missions.

Queen Salote reigned from 1918 to 1967 and was head of the Church. She firmly held to the unchanging system of the great feudal leaders holding all the land and all political power, while capital remained in the hands of foreign companies. So young people began to emigrate and take jobs in Auckland. If they returned to Tonga they had but slim hope of finding work answering to their aptitudes or aspirations.

The same has happened in Western Samoa which became independent on 1 January 1962. Following the principale of indirect rule, the British kept to the traditional *mataï* system of heads of family communities. The system was not only retained but in fact reinforced. Only the mataï can vote, and they use their powers much more to their own ends than to help the people whom they are supposed to represent. It is a kind of feudal democracy which admirably suits the purposes of the foreign companies running the country's entire economic life.

Fiji has been independent since 10 October 1970. In fact it is the well-known CSR of Australia (the Colonial Sugar Refining Company) which has been effectively running the country since 1972 when the new State bought up its sugar industry. Now Fiji is faced with the problem of Indians who outnumber the Fijians. The Indians have the sugar economy in hand, as well as most of the industrial and commercial life of the islands. Admittedly the Fijians are still the sole proprietors of the land as the former British authorities had ruled, and the Prime Minister, Ratu Sir Kamisese Mara is a Fijian. But no-one can foretell how this Fijian-Indian confrontation is going to develop and how it will be settled. Meanwhile tourism is growing but mainly to the benefit of foreign enterprises which run it, and the Burns Philip Carpenter companies control the rest of the economic activity ever since the C.S.R. gave up. But the influence of Fiji on the other islands is considerable, and many of the young folk there turn to Fiji in their search for an escape from the consequences of colonial domination.

Many other examples of the results of colonialism could be cited. It is enough to mention what has happened to Ocean Island, one of the three main phosphate islands, which provides a glaring example. Most of its population, the Banabans, had been deported by the Japanese during the Second World War to the Carolines, Nauru and the Gilbert Islands. After the war the British Phosphate Company took advantage of this to try and exploit the whole of Ocean Island. They managed to prevent the Banabans from being repatriated and to have them all transported to Rabi Island in the eastern part of Fiji. There they are in fact paid some form of royalty, but the Banabans consider themselves as exiled and are anxious to return to their own island. But will they be able to when all the phosphates have been removed? A similar move was planned for Nauru, but the inhabitants there opposed it fiercely, and Nauru is now an independent republic since 31 January 1968.

France did not follow the British example. None of her possessions in the Pacific have been given independence. But in 1956 an outline law was passed which has been modified several times since and which gave her territories a specific new régime mid-way between assimilation and internal autonomy. This was the law of the 'overseas territories' which freed the tribes from the ancient colonial servitudes and made the 'natives' into 'full' French citizens.

French Polynesia is comprised of five archipelagos (the Marquesa, Tuamotou, Gambier, Society and Tubu islands with Clipperton and Rapa islands). The population totals some 120,000 inhabitants, one quarter of whom live in Papeete, the capital. They live under the statutes of T.O.M. (Overseas Territories) and have an elected Territorial Assembly and a partially elected Government Council. But the executive power lies with the Governor, who is nominated by Paris and has direct authority over the administration. A system of communes has been installed along French lines, collaboration between the communes and the Territorial Assembly being not altogether smooth. This status is continuously evolving, in principle towards an ever greater degree of autonomy.

French Polynesia was one of the first French colonies to join General de Gaulle at the beginning of the Second World War. This was voted by a semi-official referendum organized in Papeete by a 'Committee for Free France' which obtained a large majority (5,564 for de Gaulle against 18 for Pétain) and deposed the Governor, Chastenet de Géry, who refused to recognize its authority. He set up a provisional government which came out on General de Gaulle's side on 2 September 1940.

Before that the Tahiti Maoris and most of the other islands had organized public demonstrations in favour of the common cause. Eric de Curton, the Medical Officer, left a discreet and humorous book about the events of the time, *Tahiti 40,* and was later named Governor of Tahiti. On 14 July 1940 he summoned a grand palaver at Raiatea attended by many of the chiefs who rallied to his support. One of them, Teriiero, chief of Papenco, declared 'The *Prutia* (meaning the Germans) have not yet vanquished the territories of France which are so vast that the sun never sets on them. They are not in Tahiti, nor the Windward Islands or the Tuamotou. They have not conquered the Maoris! Today all Tahiti is astir. The spirits of the valley and the spirits of the sea are on our side in the fight, and the fierce gods which haunt the heights of Aoraï and Orochena have descended among us to support us in the great battle...

Right: the population of Tahiti is over 36,000, almost half the total number of people found in French Polynesia. The scenery is breathtaking, particularly at sunrise and sunset.

The wind is getting up, the great war wind of the Maoris... We shall think of nothing but the war until victory is achieved!'

One of the provisional government's first actions was to raise a corps of volunteers, which was sent to New Caledonia to form the 2nd Pacific Battalion.

After the war life returned to normal: subsistence-level economy, fishing, pig and poultry breeding, exporting copra, vanilla and mother of pearl. But a new element came to disturb the peace of the colony: in 1964 came the C.E.P. (*Centre d'expérimentation du Pacifique* – Pacific Experimental Centre). France had selected that far-away area to pursue the development of her nuclear arms. It brought in great numbers of service personnel and technicians and especially money, which brought a false prosperity and seriously unbalanced the economy and the outlook of the Tahitians. The prosperity was indeed artificial and temporary. The dual pressure of the recession and of the protests from States on the coasts of the Pacific forced France to give up its nuclear experiments in the atmosphere and drastically cut down her personnel and expenditures on the C.E.P... This resulted in immediate repercussions on the local economy. For the time being, however, even the opposition, Mr Sanford's *Te E'a Api* party and Mr Pouvanaa Oopa's *Pupu Here Ai'a* are only asking for autonomy. But it is by no means certain that the rising generations will not seek to go much further.

New Caledonia in French Melanesia has since 1946 also enjoyed the progressive status of French overseas territory, with a Territorial Assembly, a Government Council, a High Commissioner holding the real executive powers, and a system of communes which is still being set up. Its population is approaching 100,000, 47 per cent of whom are Melanesians and 39 per cent Europeans, the rest being made up of Asians, Indonesians, New Hebrideans, Wallisians and, since the end of the war, West Indians. Most of the Vietnamese, previously quite numerous, were sent home after the war.

Contrary to other French territories in Oceania, New Caledonia's wealth is mainly derived from its mineral resources and their allied industries. Quite apart from its chromium, cobalt, iron, copper and other metals, New Caledonia sits on a solid block of nickel which is extracted in a number of places, particularly at Thio. The large metal works at Doniambo gets its power from large dam at Yaté.

New Caledonia followed Tahiti's example early in the Second World War, joining the Free French on 19 September 1940, following a referendum organized on 25 June 1940 which produced almost unanimous support for the cause. But Governor Pélissier only pretended to accept it, and kept on temporizing. He was recalled by Vichy and replaced by Lt-Col. Denis as military commander. Meanwhile in the New Hebrides Mr Henri Sautot, the French Commissioner, did not hesitate to make a stand, and rallied to the cause of General de Gaulle. On 13 September he was appointed Governor of New Caledonia and landed there on the 19 September from the Australian cruiser ADE-LAIDE. He received an enthusiastic welcome from the

In Australia horse racing is the favourite sport of miners, metal workers and dockyard hands. Every Saturday afternoon thousands of spectators gather in the stands to watch horse and greyhound races. Above and below: the tote counters and bookies' stands at the Newcastle races in New South Wales doing a thriving business.

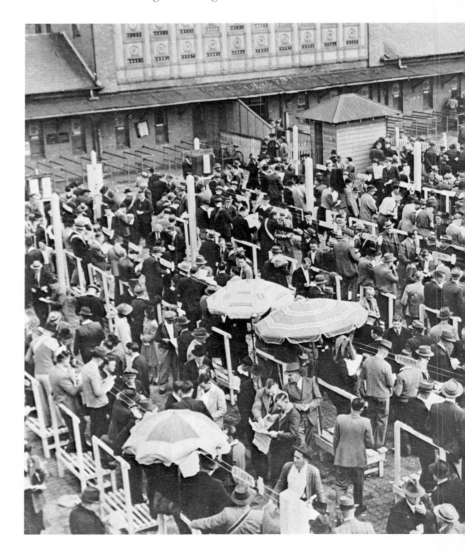

In the twentieth century gold diggers cross the Australian bush in trucks. These vehicles are esential for carrying tools, food and 40 gallon drums of water (upper left). Men sleep under blankets on the ground and only resort to tents when it rains. Should they stay on the same spot for any length of time, they run up a small shanty (right).

In some parts of New South Wales the countryside has hardly changed since the end of the nineteenth century, and truly rural scenes may be glimpsed (below). Distribution of cattle is largely a matter of abundance of rain. The big sheep and cattle holdings are generally to be found in south-east Australia where there is adequate rainfall.

Some 70·80 per cent of aborigines live in shanty towns, unable to cope with the problems of modern life. Life in contact with whites has led to their becoming detribalized and often losing their moral standards. Any who have any earnings – about one third of the coloured population – do not share the white man's needs. These uprooted folk spend their wages on liquor and tobacco. The Australian government has today admitted the failure of its assimilation policy and is trying more and more to give the aborigine a relative independence with rights to the lands of their ancestors.

Life in the interior is tough. Often the only way to reach the huge isolated ranches is along tracks with terrible ruts. In cases of emergency, wireless and planes are the only means of communication. A Flying Doctor medical centre at Alice Springs is shown at the foot of the page. The notice above urges motorists to check their provisions of food, water and petrol as the next service station is 168 miles away. Aborigines who have not been driven out into these starved areas live in government-run camps where missionaries play an active part, as at Hermannsburg, below.

people in the face of Lt-Col Denis' opposition. On 5 May 1941 the first contingent to the 2nd Pacific Battalion landed at Nouméa under command of Major Broche. It was made up of New Caledonians and Tahitians, and was to serve with great distinction at Bir Hakim and in the Italian campaign. From then on New Caledonia became a base for the American and New Zealand forces.

After the war New Caledonia resumed its economic activities, with interruptions occasionally caused by fluctuations in the price of nickel. It was distinguished from the other countries, whose present position has been discussed above, by having been a colony for immigration, so that its largely European population almost equalled in numbers the size of the Melanesian population. The Europeans, mostly French, for the main part lived in the capital and retained most of the economic and political power in their hands. The position is now changing, as for some years more and more Kanakas from Grande Terre and the Loyalties have come to settle at Nouméa. It is still too early to tell how the latent racial segregation more or less prevalent on the island will develop. The French outline law of 1956 has given the Kanakas a measure of self-expression by having their elected representatives sent to the Territorial Assembly and to the Government Council. So far these have mostly come out in favour of as wide a degree of autonomy as possible. But the first signs can be detected of the younger Kanakas beginning to think about their future. They are very conscious of their own individuality. This has given rise to a number of demonstrations and arrests. In 1969 a young chief, Nidoish Naisseline was arrested when he came home from ten years of studies in Paris and expected to resume his life among his brethren at Nengone. The shock and scandal of this arrest resulted in the formation of a number of movements, foremost among which are the *Foulards rouges* (Red Scarves) with their newspaper the *Réveil Canaque* (Kanaka Awake) and the *Union Multiraciale de la Nouvelle Calédonie* (Multiracial Union of New Caledonia), led by Yann Celene Uregeï. The latter became president of the Territorial Assembly and requested the French government to set up a referendum on independence. If this is conceded, what will be the outcome of such a referendum?

It should be recalled that Nouméa was chosen as the seat of the I.F.O. (French Institute of Oceania) which was formed in 1946 and carries out scientific research over all the French territories of Oceania, and of the *Commission Internationale du Pacifique Sud* (International Commission for the South Pacific), set up in 1947 to undertake an extensive economic, social and health programme. On the other hand the project for a Kanaka university at Nouméa has not yet seen the light of day. It is easy to guess how heavy must be the sacrifices which families have to make to send their children for advanced studies which have today become so indispensible. Whereas the Papuans have long had their Papua-New Guinea University at Port Moresby, and numerous English-language universities exist in Oceania, French-speaking students have to go to the antipodes if they want to go on to higher studies.

267

Wallis and Futuma islands come under the administration of New Caledonia. Their resources are so slender that almost half the population has had to emigrate. Many go to New Caledonia to work as labourers, mainly in the mines. This situation explains the discontent and the recent demonstrations to which the kings of Wallis and Futuma lent support.

In the New Hebrides progress has been held up by the hybrid Franco-British condominium. England would rather favour giving them independence, but not so France, especially since the *Cie. Française des Phosphates de l'Océanie* (French Oceanian Phosphate Company) started to exploit the rich manganese mines at Forari on Vaté Island. Paris and London have, however, recently begun to show signs of reaching agreement to move ahead from their hide-bound position and to grant the islands a more liberal régime.

## New Zealand and Australia

Contemporary evolution in the Pacific is obviously dominated by, and to some extent geared to, that of the two biggest countries, New Zealand and Australia.

In the Second World War New Zealand played an important part in the allied effort. This helped strengthen her sentimental and economic ties to Europe and particularly to England. The New Zealand government even kept rationing going for some years after the war ended in order to help Great Britain overcome her continuing food shortages. Cattle, wool, dairy products, exporting beef, mutton and lamb were still the base of New Zealand's economy, 80 per cent of her foreign trade coming from agriculture.

Successive National and Labour party governments struggled to develop industry and diversify foreign markets with the aim of becoming self-sufficient. Up to 1958 56 per cent of New Zealand exports went to England; by 1973 this proportion had fallen to 27 per cent. But the constitution of the E.E.C. (the European Economic Community) presented a serious problem: might not the preference to agriculture given by the community keep New Zealand produce right out of the English market? Nevertheless Mr Rowling, Prime Minister of New Zealand, was in favour of England joining the Common Market. There were two reasons for this. Firstly, New Zealand's export trade could recover from the market as a whole what she would lose on the British market alone: indeed 36 per cent of New Zealand's foreign trade already goes to E.E.C. countries, and negotiations are in hand to consolidate and improve this share. Secondly, New Zealand was beginning to feel the need of taking stock of her own immediate surroundings, without in any way denying her links with Europe. Mr Rowling declared: '(We must) strengthen our position as a country belonging to the South Pacific area'. Internally one of their main problems was relations with the Maoris. New Zealand is a multi-racial nation with universities open to all comers. Of her 3,000,000 inhabitants 7 per cent are Maoris, and the proportion is increasing. The Maori wars belong to the past. The Maoris have for a long time enjoyed the same rights as the rest of the nation. They can aspire to the highest offices in the land, including becoming ministers. But serious doubts are beginning to be felt about the legitimacy of the policy of assimilation as practised so far in a situation of 'perfect equality'. Does it really meet with the Maori people's aspirations?

In Australia the Labour party, whose contributions to the war in the Pacific are referred to on earlier pages, remained in office for another four years. On 10 December 1949 a coalition of the new Liberal party and the remnants of the Agrarian party won the elections. With Mr Menzies at the head, the coalition stayed in power for twenty-three years, and Labour only returned to office in 1972, with Mr Whitlam as Prime Minister.

Such stability of government is a new feature of Australia's political history. It made it possible for Australia to face up to the major problems of the postwar era.

Great Britain had handed over some of her former Pacific colonies to Australia, which now found itself having to carry out decolonization operations, particularly in Papua-New Guinea, as has been mentioned above.

Three other factors played an important part in the history of Australia over the past three decades: immigration, mineral discoveries, and Australian foreign policy becoming much more independent than in earlier days.

The dangers to which the last war had exposed Australia highlighted the insufficiency of her population, which in 1939 was under 8,000,000, spread over all that vast continent. There had never been any serious attempt to increase the rate of immigration which, it was always felt, should be limited as much as possible to anglo-saxons. Compared with her overcrowded Asian neighbours Australia was still an empty continent. For how much longer could she hope to hold off yellow immigration which she had always sought to avoid?

'Our first immediate need is to increase our population' announced the government as soon as the war ended, and a ministry of immigration was set up.

They first sought volunteers from Europe's refugee camps with their hundreds of thousands of displaced persons, victims of the war and political upheavals. Later, agreements were signed with some twenty countries, mostly in Europe. This led to the creation of an Australian Immigration Department, the aim of which was to find candidates and fit them into the economic life of Australia. This brought in over 2,000,000 New Australian settlers, less than 40 per cent of whom were British. The remainder were Germans, Belgians, Dutch, Italians, Greeks, Turks and Jugoslavs.

This rapid growth of the foreign population may have raised some real problems, but at least it helped Australia to cope with the second major factor, the discovery of minerals. In Queensland silver, lead, copper and uranium were found at Mount Ysa and the world's largest bauxite deposit at Weipa; in West Australia Hammersley became one of the biggest iron ore producers. Australia was found to conceal

New Zealand is often referred to as the Switzerland of the Pacific owing to the mountainous nature of the country. The rugged landscape in the photograph below shows the town of Queenstown on the shores of Lake Wakatipu; in the background are the Remarkable and Double Cone (7800 ft) mountain chains. Urban development in New Zealand since the beginning of the century has been less violent than in Australia. There are no sprawling cities; only a series of medium-sized towns, trading centres for 15,000-35,000 inhabitants. Life is centred on a street bordered with little shops with awnings. Four cities act as regional capitals: Auckland, Wellington, Christchurch and Dunedin. The Maoris live in villages like Ohinemotu (right); their houses have porches and old-fashioned carved gables, and rub shoulders with modern buildings.

The peculiarity of Australia is that it is essentially an urban country. While 75 per cent of its exports are farm products, 80 per cent of the inhabitants live in towns. Alice Springs is a township of 2,000 people in the heart of the desert, at the centre of the continent (above far left). But most people live on the coast and one Australian in five lives in Sydney. The State capital of New South Wales has over 2,000,000 inhabitants. The historic centre has today been taken over by the business quarter with parallel streets bordered by huge buildings (below left). An immense bridge crosses Port Jackson, leading to the north shore of the bay (above left).

Sydney's residential areas and suburbs stretch out for miles, as Australians share the British taste for small houses with gardens. An impressive network of highways lead off to the various parts of the bay. The industrial areas are mainly in the south (Botany Bay) and west (Paramatta).

The Maori minority has a very high birthrate and is mostly to be found on the North Island, New Zealand, where it is beginning to play an ever more important part in the life of the country. They live from mixed farming, mostly cattle. Despite certain protest movements, their handicrafts and traditional national dress are tending to die out. There is little effort to keep them alive (right and below). The new generation of Oceanians is slowly yielding to the temptations of the modern world like this Papuan in blue jeans (left-hand page).

a wealth of resources beneath her soil in almost every area, the extent of which is still far from being known. Even petroleum and natural gas have now been found. In her present state of development Australia has not only become self-sufficient but able to supply energy and mineral raw materials on a big scale to a part of the world where all these were thought to be in short supply and where in some countries like Japan shortages were becoming serious.

Following upon her participation in the Second World War and her action throughout the Pacific, this situation was bound to have a decisive influence on Australia's foreign policy. This constituted the third factor which so greatly marked the life of Australia over the past three decades: an attitude of ever greater autonomy towards England. Australia remained a loyal member of the Commonwealth, and never relinquished her sentimental bonds towards British forms of life and thinking. But she felt that she had her own interests to defend, which on occasion differed from London's, and that she should conduct her foreign policy independently. This evolved along three main lines: very definite new links with the United States growing out of the 1963 agreements and participation in the ANZUS and SEATO pacts; growing interest in South Pacific affairs, and lastly a more open attitude towards Asia, first towards Japan and more recently towards China.

Like his New Zealand opposite number, the Prime Minister Whitlam was in favour of Great Britain joining the E.E.C. This identical attitude adopted by the two most loyal members of the British Commonwealth was significant. Both had become aware that their future was no longer solely tied to the old mother country but was now dependent on many other factors, foremost among them being the future of the Pacific.

This photograph illustrates the countless difficulties encountered by the peoples of Melanesia as they face up to decolonization and the interference of the great powers. Will Papua-New Guinea's 700 tribes be capable of making the leap from the stone age to the jet age without troubles? For them, the aircraft is the symbol of *Kago*.

274

# CHANGES IN THE PACIFIC

## Pollution and Parasities:

Cook had already noticed the changes and the dangerous effects to be expected from the mere presence of whites in those countries. Three centuries later François Doumenge the geographer wrote in his *L'Homme dans le Pacifique Sud*\*(Man in the South Pacific) that after the Second World War 'the American forces left behind an impressive quantity of weeds and animal parasites (...), every archipelago and almost every island being at a more or less advanced stage of change, and this is general throughout the Pacific.' What Doumenge says is true everywhere in the Pacific, which is affected today by the white intrusion: the Western form of economy and the wars which it causes have polluted its lands and even its ocean, where the coral is dying.

## Ecology:

The ecology is today very different from the one so admired by men like Forster and La Billardière. Sheep, cattle, coffee, and food crops have taken a solid hold. At the same time other vegetable and animal species have been destroyed, and some which were formerly to be found everywhere subsist only marginally. In New Caledonia the wood warbler, with its exquisite flesh, has become a prey for hunters, often being pursued into secluded thickets and left to die from its wounds. The silvery niaouli bush, which produces soothing oil and provides so many cures with its bark, disappear into paper factories, while the nickel works spew their red dust into the air to darken the once crystal clear waters of the rivers. Bit by bit the healthy climes of those 'peaceful days' are vanishing.

Who cares? Rich herds of cattle are now feeding off the fields where once broad avenues led up to the homes of chiefs Ataï and Naïna. Meanwhile modern medicine is there to cure diseases which were formerly contained by a better adaptation to natural life, and remains obstinately oblivious to the ways of the ancient Kanakas whose farming methods were so effective.

Admittedly there is now a tendency to be concerned over the situation. To cite but a single yet significant example, the *Jonah* project has come to the rescue of the hunted whale by warning off the mammals when hunters are approaching. Studies are being made to find ways and means to safeguard the original fauna and flora of the Pacific. But the greed of neo-colonial economy scarcely complies with the dictates of the ecologist, and everything that has been written in warning about the Pacific has so far produced no visible results of any real value.

\* See Bibliography.

## The men of the Pacific:

An author from the northernmost parts of that immense ocean, Iouri Rytkeou, a Soviet Chukchi, recently stressed in *Zvedia*, No 3, 1975 the 'characteristic common to the cultures of the Pacific from the tropics to the poles'. He writes of the Pacific that it has 'always been a *centre of life* from which a cultural community was born'. Rytkeou himself belongs to that community. In his *Contes de la Tchoukotka*\* he tells of the Chukchi folk who, until the Russian revolution, lived off the produce of the sea, using tusks to fashion marvellous *pilikens*. For the peoples of the North, whale hunting took the place of bonito fishing for their brethren of the South, so that at such different latitudes the men of the Pacific, that 'centre of life', derived from its waters both their very existence and the wherewithal of their art. In his preface to that work, which in its poetry constitutes true pages of history and ethno-sociology, Rytkeou concludes 'I owe my existence as a man and as a writer to being part of these arctic folk who survived and managed to preserve the noble title of man for centuries under the harshest and most extreme conditions of nature'.

Western anthropology and ethnology brought to light the morphology and social formations of the men of the Pacific, but only knew how to classify them according to the ideas of their own civilization. Rytkeou was astonished that our ethnologists did not feel themselves more directly concerned by the subjects of their studies.

Worse still, ethnology was not always unconnected with the process of colonization. It is only in quite recent times that to some extent the superiority of the Western civilization has been put in doubt and recognition given to a plurality of cultures. Professor Berndt, who shares with Professor Elkin the distinction of possessing the closest knowledge of the Australian aborigine, wrote in 1967 'It is not many decades since anyone interested in the problem was regarded as eccentric and mad...' Is the position any different elsewhere...? Or worse still?

Yet the problem existed everywhere. The Kanakas in the bush put it clearly into words as Kumalau Tawali shows in *Modern Poetry from Papua – New Guinea* (Papua Pocket Poets, Port Moresby, 1972):

> Every white man the *gorment* sends to us
> forces his veins out shouting
> nearly forces the excreta out of his bottom
> shouting: you *bush Kanaka*.
>
> He says: you al les man!
> Yet he sits on a soft chair and does nothing
> just shouts, eats, drinks, eats, drinks,
> like a woman with a child in her belly.
> These white men have no bones.
> If they tried to fight us without their *musiket*
> they'd surely cover their faces like women.
>
> Kumalau Tawali

\* See Bibliography.

Obviously colonization has brought about much that cannot now be expected to be undone. The whites have arrived, and it is hard to see how they could ever relinquish countries like Australia or New Zealand. Whole populations have been moved, like the Indians settled in Fiji. Crossbreeding has taken place, considered by many, as in Tahiti for instance, to be a long-term means of gradually solving the present racial conflicts. The half-castes indeed often form an important portion of the population, at least in some countries – for instance in Australia where there are 50,000 half-castes in addition to the 50,000 aborigines mentioned earlier. But the position of the former is not always as enviable as might be thought. As pointed out by Mrs Elphick, member of the Council of Aboriginal Women for South Australia, it is still an unhappy solution, as the half-castes live between two worlds, two sets of laws, and have lost their identity. In her book *A Question of Choice** Mrs Elphick poses the question 'My people are generally referred to as "an Aboroginal problem"! But have we paused to think seriously about this? May it not be a white problem?' (...) 'white people want to tell us what to do and to take over from us. Our greatest problem is with the European – not with our own people (...)'.

Finally we have the demographic recovery; there is every reason to believe that it will continue. In a few decades it may substantially alter the present position.

Culturally this demographic recovery is still far from producing any significant impact. When they landed, the whites were so convinced of the superiority of their civilization that still today 'relations between settlers and non-whites, who have accepted to deny their own background, amount to hypnotism. It is enough for a missionary to appear for the native to lose all will-power.'** 'To become civilized' or 'advanced' for many people still means to adopt Western habits, which, in the essential, means losing their own identity.

It is true that at certain times and places it has been possible to see how natives were led to share that belief in the superiority of Western civilization, which was clearly demonstrated by the power and material wealth it gave to those who possessed it. This accounted for the temptation to exchange cultures which was still so common at the beginning of the century, and which today's youth is now disputing. It is easily understandable that it was a great temptation for many of those who paid long visits to industrialized countries and came to know the extraordinary facilities of the modern world. Hence N. Naisseline's severe condemnation of the 'non-whites denying their own background'. Could that denial be lasting? Has it not led to those psychological tragedies which we are now witnessing? How profoundly can people be affected by a culture which does not give expression to the deepest faculties and values of their own society? It can only end by 'uprooting' people and making them belong to nowhere, 'I was born without a soul and I have no indentity' said Fijian Novick. Herman Talingapua

* See Bibliography.
** See Bibliography, Naisseline.

was giving expression to the same kind of feeling when, returning home after acquiring western knowledge abroad, he wrote 'Hidden Power' published in *Modern Poetry*:

# HIDDEN POWER
Herman Talingapua

\*

Slowly the moon climbs
along its silvery path
over Kumbu mountain.
Palm trees cast the shadows
of their rough bodies
across my path,
their wombs
heavy with sago.
Avoiding the wind,
coconut trees bend low.
*Leleki* baskets
hang from the roof of the men's house
pregnant with secrets
and power.
But I,
the 'modern man',
complete with suit,
despatch case and transistor set,
shall never know
what hidden happiness or strength
is tied up in these baskets.
My age and 'learning' notwithstanding,
I am excluded.
Uninitiated,
condemned to sleep with women,
unfit to carry shield and spear.

It was a fact that the more the men of the Pacific mastered Western culture the more they felt ill at ease with it, finding it closed in on itself and oppressive. Counting their riches, calculating their profits, Europeans, Asians, Americans took over everything, lands and brains, and the men of the Pacific felt lost. They felt they had to call a halt to take stock of themselves and wipe out the changes brought on by colonization. Many of them, after acquiring Western culture, underwent a reaction and returned to their original culture, sought out its deeper significance and the opportunities for independent progress. 'With no apprenticeship in reaching our present situation, we have a feeling of insecurity', explained Nidoish Naisseline. 'We are horrified to discover that one can go through life missing out on it'.

This discovery of a 'bi-culture' is echoed by the great majority of bush Kanakas who now want to be heard, and by those who have exchanged cultures and are affected by the sight of the younger generations raising their heads. They are all united in seeking to retrieve the essential roots of their own civilization and to cast off the changes brought in by colonization.

In the light of this perspective, does the future, at least in a transitional phase, belong to the bi-cultured, to those who can take on both cultures – their own and that of their former colonizer? Young people returning from French- and English-speaking universities in Europe, Australia, New Zealand, Port Moresby and Suva (Tahiti and New Caledonia still have no university) do not seem to have acquired the knowledge they will need to cope with the problems in their countries after two centuries of Western imperialism.

Communications developing between archipelagos present a new element to be considered. Air travel has been taken up with remarkable facility, and knowledge of French and especially English promotes ease of communication. Lastly there are the various organizations and societies which have been formed and where writers and artists from the Pacific lands can meet.

Population increase is everywhere accompanied by a cultural awakening as yet in its earliest stages, to a background of unrest among the recently independent, of all too many mistakes by the former colonizers, and of indifference and ignorance displayed in Europe. But as their view of Western civilization became clearer, the people of the Pacific obtained a better grasp of its consequences: the last World War with its millions of dead, followed by nuclear experiments, opened the eyes of some of them to its tragic but logical consequences. The so-called 'war of dissuasion' was the answer to a faultless logic. As Leenhardt wrote in the concluding passages of his *Do kamo*: In helping Melanesians 'to grasp human realities by means of myth, *mythical knowledge* enabled them to find in those realities the values which are essential for organizing society (...)' and to 'enjoy that plenitude where the Kanaka feels himself *do kamo,* a real person...'

'(...) By antithesis the view of the Melanesian helps us to imagine that if primitive man had been content to adhere to knowledge supplied by reasoning, then he would have followed an order of perfect technique, which would take him beyond the insect, limited by its instinct, to the logical pursuit of his logic to exhaustion, revulsion and death. So what could be more logical than organizing a total war?'

Almost twenty years later, on a different continent, another professor, Douglas Oliver, ended his work on *The Pacific Islands* (New York 1961) with the following disillusioned comment: '(...) it does not make sense to expect... the islanders to arise as one man to defend a civilization which has deprived them of so much and given them so little...'

Thus the cultural awakening referred to earlier also has its political aspects. Many people are asking themselves whether the forms and policies adopted by the new independent young States are not following in the footsteps of colonization rather than representing the aspirations and real needs of their people. Albert Wendt of Samoa wonders whether the University of the Pacific at Suva is not, like American universities, 'a factory among many others mass-producing technicians'. Another Samoan, the workman poet Eti Sa'aga asks 'When does my time come?'. And Apisai Enos cries out about his own country, New Guinea:

(..., Awake, awake, awake,
wake up, New Guinea
(...................................................)
(...) Be quiet New Guineaa
ancient cocoon
be still!
Don't you know that I am your husband
betrothed to you in childhood
promised to you in the womb?
I have come to celebrate our wedding
I have come to elope with you
into better times.

Most of the former Pacific colonies may now be politically independent, but it must be observed, alongside the majority of authors such as those quoted here, that that independence is not yet absolute. There is still a heavy inheritance of administrative habits and forms. Above all these is still economic dependence. As Maori writer Marjorie Tuainekore Crocombe says: 'Their economy is still in foreign hands'. And this may be true not only of the islands and archipelagos of the 'separated' Pacific but maybe also of New Zealand and Australia. In support of Mrs Marjorie Tuainekore Crocombe we might quote Australia's Labour Prime Minister, Mr Whitlam, who declared on resuming office 'It is time to put an end to foreign domination, it is time for Australians to start reconquering Australia'.

## Economic and industrial neo-colonialism:

In this field the change introduced by the Second World War was the predominance of American capital. Political conquest in the Pacific gave place to economic conquest, better concealed but no less efficient than the former. The great beneficiary was America, which swamped all the Pacific with the 'American way of life', westerns, multinational trusts and huge scale American tourism. Therein lies the great challenge today to the people of the Pacific. With their weak resources, will they succeed in overthrowing the aftermaths of the first type of colonization to which they fell victim without being overcome by the second?

The most insidiously destructive form taken by this new colonization is the huge blanket of tourism covering independent countries, French overseas territories, former American colonies and others. A few small islands, like Uvea, have managed to escape by refusing to permit 'holiday clubs' on their territory, but the whites brandish powerful arguments in favour of tourism.

Peter Kros goes into this in an article 'Tourism: does it help to preserve our culture?' In it Kros explains how humiliating it is for a new country to sell its hospitality and be looked upon as a zoo by teeming crowds of crude creatures with pink faces and knees, and states his belief that in its present form tourism is far from promoting international goodwill but rather adds to racial prejudice. Can it be said, nevertheless, that it brings any economic or social advantages in its wake? No. Jobs offered are only of the 'lowest order' such as prostitutes, guides, chauffeurs, maids, waiters. Does it help promote local arts? No. If tourists do pay to see dances or to buy sculptures and handicrafts, their lack of taste and ignorance encourage artists to produce works in the worst taste. And Peter Kros goes on to say that the tourist's peculiar taste and demands soon influence the work of local artists. Thus in Arnhem Land in the Northern Territory of Australia, artefact dealers have encouraged Aboriginal bark painters to paint outsize penises on the *mimi* images because this is apparently what sells.

Peter Kros clearly points out the contradictory aspects of exotic tourism. People come from industrial countries to escape from the oppression of their own immense cities and find rest and a certain way of life in those countries which this is still comparatively well preserved. But in so doing they spoil and defile everything they approach. And he ends by asking: 'Can a country promote tourism purely on its own terms?'

The Pacific also is filled with potential resources which go far beyond the mere economic. The myth of the Southern Seas is no more, but among those waters, those countries and their people are hidden treasures of inestimable value for the rest of the world.

Those treasures do not consist in opportunities to develop large-scale tourism along American lines, as some may believe through misguidedness or personal interest. As journalist Jacques Decornoy writes 'The growth of tourism [turned out to be] a plague which only leads to humiliation and cultural prostitution'. The author had the opportunity to observe on revisiting some places after an interval of several years how, wherever tourism was introduced, it merely succeeded in disfiguring the countryside and in ruining the ethics, cultural life and health of the local population. It is enough to look at what has happened to Waikiki beach in Hawaii. Tourism is entirely in the hands of foreign companies, mostly American and Australian, and brings no benefit to the economy of the country where it has taken hold. Except for the limited quantity of local manpower employed, most of the profits return to the pockets of those who finance and create the projects.

Quite a different form of tourism could be devised which would aim to build a bridge between the civilization of the Pacific at its most authentic and the world's other civilizations, while yet bringing an important part of those resources to the countries in question which need them at present to maintain their positions in the concert of nations. But such original type of tourism must belong to the people of the Pacific, who must be allowed to control and devise it themselves. Their profits should come from a form of tourism which they would organize themselves according to their own tastes. An opportunity lies there which should not be ignored.

# CONCLUSION

A culture's authenticity cannot be gauged by its static qualities, but by its ability to enrich the course of history with its most essential values. One of the constant features of Pacific culture was surely its capacity of absorption. The crisis today is a formula generally admitted as designating the profound upheaval which has overcome the industrial nations following the last war. A time when Western society is starting to be concerned at the serious imbalance brought on by the inroads of industrial economy against the environment is surely the time for giving attention to the aid which the peoples of the Pacific could offer, knowing still so well, as they do, how to find a balance between man and his natural surroundings. As the systems which were the strength of the industrial nations seem to be weakening today, might it not be the moment to study, with a view to finding new solutions for Western colonial commercialism, the origins of the economic systems prevailing in the Pacific before it was invaded, and to which researchers display a remarkable indifference – and to do so regarding them not as something prehistoric but as a source of ideas? In these days when Western society seems to be suffering from State hypertrophy, with states becoming ever further removed from the citizens they govern and therefore resented by them as being oppressive, does it not seem equally surprising to find that the societies of the Pacific were highly structured yet remained societies with no State? Were evolutionists right to believe that the existence of a State was a sign of civilized progress? And are the societies of the Pacific condemned to equip themselves with States to prove that they are 'civilized'?

No matter how great the material power of industrial nations may still be, they force blame and controversy from many sides, no longer in a position to give advice to other peoples on what they must and must not do. If, without cutting off aid, tourism, for instance, is allowed to be developed locally and on its own, without looking to Western prototypes, than yes, that kind of tourism would be a positive element for the economy of those countries and for an interchange of cultures.

A similar case can be made for many other economic and intellectual activities. In the small world of today no one nation can make itself free alone. And, strange to realize, Western liberation also depends on the way in which the Pacific peoples will be freed, and on the ability to accept their complete 'decolonization' without obstructing it.

The history of decolonization may be the great question mark of the twentieth century. It will also be a tribunal: a civilization cannot pass judgement on itself alone but can only do so in terms of the links it has been able to establish with other civilizations.

# INDEX
## OF GEOGRAPHICAL NAMES
## AND
## APPENDICES

Acapulco 17, 20
Adelaide 174, 175, 178, 181, 184, 191, 196, 208
Admiralty (Islands) 69, 92, 230
Africa 12, 13, 15, 21, 23, 70, 79, 104, 151, 166, 181
Africa, South 204, 230
Aimeo 160
Akatoa 202
Akatora 202
Alaska 32, 55, 69, 207
Albany (Australia) 181
Albany (USA) 23
Aleutians 32, 70, 74, 207, 208, 230
Alexander (Mount) 191
Algeria 219
Alice Springs 184, 267, 270
Alofi (Island) 214
Alps, Australian 237
Alps, New Zealand 201
Amazon 14, 20
Ambon (Island) 22
Amédée (Lake) 139
America 15, 17, 18, 20, 21, 23, 26, 28, 32, 33, 34, 69, 70, 74, 105, 106, 151, 170, 171, 277
America, British 35, 37, 181
America, Central 14, 69
America, North 26, 55, 132, 155, 170, 178
America, South 11, 20, 106, 207
Andes (the) 20
Angaston 174
Angola 23
Anourourou 119
Antartic (Continent) 53, 60, 63, 69, 201
Antilia 13
Antilles (West Indies) 14, 17, 18, 31, 41, 42
Antimaono 232
Aotearoa (New Zealand) 74, 200
Apia 80, 232
Arctic (Ocean) 69, 70
Arguin 23
Arnhem (Land) 69, 75, 85, 279
Ascension (Island) 31
Asia 13, 17, 21, 32, 69, 70, 151, 253, 273, 277
Asia, South East 75, 244
Astrolabe (Bay) 216
Asuncion 20
Atahuru 156
Atlantic (Ocean) 13, 17, 20, 23, 31, 32, 54
Auckland 201, 206, 238, 246, 262, 269
Austral (Continent), Austral (Lands) 22, 26, 28, 31, 32, 33, 36, 42, 55
Australia of the Holy Ghost 22
Australia 11, 23, 25, 26, 28, 31, 55, 56, 60, 61, 62, 63, 64, 65, 66, 69, 74, 75, 76, 77, 79, 85, 86, 91, 92, 93, 95, 104, 105, 106, 108, 109, 119, 120, 130, 131, 133, 135, 136, 139, 140, 142, 143, 144, 151, 153, 163, 164, 165, 170, 171, 174 et seq, 201, 202, 203, 206, 207, 215, 216, 218, 223, 229,

230, 231, 232, 233, 234, 236, 237, 239, 240, 244, 245, 246, 256, 258, 260, 261, 262, 264, 265, 266, 267, 268, 271, 273, 276, 277, 278, 279
Australia, North 106
Australia, Central 143
Austral France 201
Ayers Rock 197
Azores 17
Aztec (Empire) 18, 20

Bahamas (Islands) 13
Balade 217
Baliem (River) 273
Ballarat 190, 191
Banian Ataï or Ataï's Barrier 220
Bantam 28
Bass (Straits) 60
Batavia 22, 28, 32, 54, 62, 245
Bathurst 188
Benguala (Current) 17
Bering (Sea) 70
Bering (Straits) 32, 69, 70, 207
Betio (Isle) 250
Bio-Bio (River) 20
Bir Hakim 267
Bismarck (Archipelago) 67, 69, 71, 92, 131, 216, 230
Bojador (Cape) 13
Bonga 216
Bora Bora (Island) 45, 48, 55, 58, 103, 111, 144, 160
Borneo 245
Boston 208
Botany Bay 42, 170, 171, 174, 201, 271
Bougainville (Island) 215, 246, 261
Bouloupari 220, 222
Brazil 14, 17, 20, 21, 23, 31
Brisbane 181, 188, 191
British Empire 182, 229, 239
Broken Hill 236
Buenos Aires 20
Buka (Island) 215, 259
Buna 246
Burma 75, 246

Cajamarca 20
Calicut 15
California 21, 31, 32, 55, 188, 256
Callao 20, 26
Cambodia 75
Canada 188
Canala 220
Canaries (Isles) 13, 14, 41
Canberra 192, 209, 240
Canton 55
Capocate 15
Cape Verde (Isles) 15, 17, 21
Capricorn (Tropic of) 15, 22, 26, 28, 212
Carolines (Islands) 54, 60, 69, 92, 171, 207, 209, 230, 261, 262

Carterton 237
Castlereagh 179
Cebu (Island) 15
Central Sepik 80, 85, 117
Ceram (Island) 15
Ceylon 22
Chile 12, 20, 21, 26, 32, 69, 208
China 11, 12, 13, 14, 21, 42, 61, 126, 129, 215, 244, 245, 253, 273
China (Sea) 26, 31
Choiseul (Island) 246
Christchurh 269
Cipango 14
Clipperton (Island) 262
Commonwealth, British 229, 239, 273
Commonwealth of Australia, see Australia
Conception 20
Congo (River) 13
Cook (Island) 69
Cook (Isles) 67, 119, 163, 200, 212, 213, 230
Coopers's Creek 196
Coral (Sea) 22, 26, 69, 106, 216, 246
Corregidor 245, 247
Cuba 14, 17, 20
Curaçao 23
Cuzco 20

Dardanelles 239
Darien (Isthmus) 14
Darwin 181, 184, 196, 208
Decres (Island) 56
Desirade (Island) 14
Dominica (Island) 14
Don (Cossacks) 11
Doniambo 261, 264
Dorei 92
Double Cone 269
Ducos (Peninsula) 218
Duff (Mount) 209
Duke of York (Island) 216
Dunedin 269

Easter (Island) 32, 69, 74, 86, 87, 92, 93, 106, 167, 208, 209
Egmont (Mount) 201
Egypt 230
Eldorado 20
Elmina 23
Ellice (Islands) 69, 75, 86, 207, 230, 261
Eniwetok (Atoll) 250
Eromanga 159
Etablissements français en Océanie 209
Eureka 188
Euroa 192
Eyre (Lake) 183

Falkland (Islands) 31
Far East 42
Far West 206, 237
Fiji (Islands) 28, 54, 60, 69, 83, 85, 163, 200, 207, 213, 214, 215, 230, 236, 260, 261, 277

Finschhafen 246
Florida (Island) 247
Fly (River) 216
Fonwhari (la) 220
Forari 268
Forest Creek (Island) 191
Formosa 75, 171, 207, 244
Fort Orange 23
France (Island) 68, see also Mauritius
French Colonial Empire 166, 229
Friendly (Islands), 45, 121, 158 (see also Tonga)
'Fuji-Yama' (New Zealand) 201
Futuna (Islands) see Wallis and Futuna

Gallipoli 239
Gambier (Islands) 155, 162, 163, 209, 212, 230, 262
Gavutu 247
Geelwink (Bay) 92
Gilbert (Islands) 60, 69, 99, 164, 207, 223, 230, 232, 245, 249, 250, 261, 262
Gilolo 16
Goa 21
Gona 246, 257
Good Hope (Cape of) 11, 13, 16, 22, 32, 174, 178
Grande-Terre (Bougainville) 215, 261
Grande-Terre (New Caledonia) 83, 126, 130, 134, 143, 216, 218, 220, 256, 267
Great South Road 200
Greenland 12
Guadalcanal (Island) 20, 246, 247, 259
Guadeloupe (Island) 14
Guam (Island) 20, 207, 230, 250, 261
Guanahani (Island) 14
Guyana 13, 171

Ha'apai, Hapai (Island) 68, 121, 213
Haïti (Island) 14
Hamersley 268
Harvey Islands 213
Havelock 200
Hawaii (Islands) 11, 12, 52, 54, 67, 69, 70, 78, 80, 86, 95, 97, 107, 119, 125, 132, 137, 140, 155, 160, 164, 171, 207, 208, 209, 230, 244, 245, 253, 255, 256, 258, 260, 279
Hawaiiki 67, 74, 138, 200
Hermannsburg 267
Hermit (Islands) 98
Hiroshima 248, 251
Hispaniola 14
Hobart 191
Hokkaido (Island) 74, 85, 207
Hong Kong 245
Honolulu 208, 244, 245, 256, 258
Horn (Cape) 28, 31, 32
Huahine (Island) 97, 152, 161
Hudson (Valley) 23
Hunuabada 233

Iceland 41
Inca (Empire) 20
India, 11, 21, 68, 196, 214
India (road to) 13
Indian (Ocean) 15, 16, 21, 23, 28, 31, 32, 42
Indies, Dutch or East 15, 22, 63, 216, 245
Indochina 75, 244, 253, see also Vietnam
Indonesia 15, 22, 66, 69, 75, 80, 139, 207
Inkerman Station 176
Invercargill 201
Irian 216, 257
Irian Barat 216
Isabella City 14
Islands (Bay of) 201
Isle of Pines (the) 217
Iwo Jima 249, 250

Jakarta, see Batavia
Japan 13, 14, 21, 23, 36, 74, 171, 207, 215, 229, 230, 232, 239, 244, 245 et seq, 253, 273
Java 16, 22, 28, 62
Jerilderie 192
Juan Fernandez (Islands) 28, 31

Kaiser Wilhelmsland 216
Kalabu (Island) 91
Kamchatka (Peninsula) 11, 32, 55, 70, 207
Kapunda 184
Kayakakowa 107
Kermadec (Island) 70
Kilauca (Volcano) 208
Kimberley 182
King George III 152
King (River) 192
Koghi 136
Kokoda 72, 246
Kokopo 216
Komalé 220
Koné 80
Kumbu (Mountain) 277
Kunie (Island) 215, 217, 218
Kurile (Islands) 70, 74, 207
Kwjalein (Atoll) 250

Labrador 21
Ladrones (Islands) 15
Lae 246, 250
La Foa 220
Lapita 95
Lavongai (Island) 230
Lebuka 85
Leeward (Islands) 232
Lemaire (Straits) 28, 32
Leyte 249, 250
Lifu (Island) 217, 218
Line (Islands) 232
Logon Lagoon 189
Louisade (Archipelago) 69, 124
Lower Herbert 189

Loyalty (Islands) 60, 69, 97, 163, 216 et seq, 230, 267
Luanda 21, 23
Lucayas (Islands) 14
Luf 98

Macao 32
Mactan (Island) 15, 16
Madagascar 75, 80, 95
Madang 257, 258
Madeira (Island) 13
Magellan (Straits) 15, 16, 21, 28
Mahaïtea 67
Makatea 32, 209, 223, 232
Malacca 15, 21, 22
Malaita (Island) 259
Malaysia 26, 63, 69, 75, 91
Malden (Island) 232
Malikula 130
Mallicolo 117, 144
Mana (Island) 78
Manchuria 244, 251
Mangareva (Islands) 209
Mangatawhiri 200
Manilla 20, 26, 32, 55, 250
Mansfield 192
Maprik 80, 91, 123
Marus (Island) 246
Mare (Island) 216, 218
Marianas (Islands) 15, 61, 62, 69, 171, 207, 230, 249, 250, 253, 261
Marquesas (Islands) 11, 20, 55, 67, 74, 86, 91, 93, 97, 133, 152, 153, 163, 209 et seq, 221, 224, 227, 230, 254, 262
Marshall (Islands) 54, 69, 100, 207, 230, 232, 246, 249, 250, 261
Massim 104, 129
Matavaï (Bay) 155, 156, 160
Mathias (Islands) 69
Mauritius (Island) 28, 61
McDonnell Ranges 108
Melanesia 67, 69, 74, 75, 83, 92, 95, 98, 99, 112, 124, 125, 126, 129, 130, 131, 135, 154, 159, 163, 164, 212, 213 et seq, 223, 227, 257, 259, 278
Melanesia, French 264
Melbourne 178, 181, 184, 188, 191, 192, 193, 201, 232, 233
Mendoza 20
Mewstone 56
Mexico 11, 17, 18, 20
Micronesia 62, 67, 69, 74, 75, 91, 92, 97, 99, 100, 137, 163, 200, 207, 217
Midway (Islands) 230, 246, 249, 261
Milne Bay 214, 246
Moapa 85
Moluccas (Islands) 15, 16, 21, 22, 23, 28
Mombasa 15, 21
Mongo (Lake) 75
Montserrat (Island) 14
Moorea (Island) 28, 50, 58, 144, 160

Motu Tapu (Island) 50
Mount Ysa 268
Mowée (Island) 87
Mozambique 16
Mua 155
Mulboutu 139

Nagasaki 55, 251
Nantucket 181
Napoleon (Coast) 181
Nauru (Island) 207, 223, 232, 261, 262
Navidad (Fort) 14, 17
Navigators (Islands) 91
Ndeni (Island) 214
Negapatam 22
Nengone (Island) 216, 217, 218, 260
New Amsterdam 23
New Britain 31, 32, 40, 69, 216, 230, 233
New Caledonia 31, 55, 69, 83, 85, 86, 93, 95, 97, 103, 104, 106, 112, 119, 120, 125, 126, 129, 130, 137, 138, 155, 163, 165, 170, 171, 191, 214 et seq, 222, 223, 230, 236, 238, 244, 245, 246, 254, 256, 259, 261, 264, 267, 268, 276, 278
Newcastle 264
New Cythera (Island) 55, 152
Newfoundland 31
New Georgia 246
New Guinea 23, 26, 27, 28, 31, 32, 53, 54, 55, 60, 66, 68, 69, 72, 74, 75, 79, 80, 83, 85, 88, 91, 92, 93, 104, 105, 112, 113, 117, 120, 123, 127, 128, 129, 130, 134, 135, 136, 140, 151, 164, 170, 171, 191, 207, 216, 230, 233, 239, 245, 246, 249, 250, 257, 258, 259, 261, 267, 276, 278
New Hanover (Island) 69, 230
New Hebrides 22, 26, 55, 69, 80, 88, 93, 106, 117, 120, 130, 135, 159, 160, 163, 171, 191, 215, 216, 220, 232, 246, 259, 264, 268
New Holland 31, 60
New Ireland 28, 67, 69, 72, 92, 131, 216, 230, 245
New South Wales 131, 142, 170, 174, 178, 179, 181, 184, 188, 189, 192, 193, 206, 230, 264, 265, 271
New York 23, 178
New Zealand 25, 28, 54, 55, 56, 69, 74, 78, 80, 86, 92, 93, 97, 117, 120, 127, 129, 140, 142, 162, 163, 164, 171, 200 et seq, 207, 209, 213, 214, 229, 230, 232, 233, 236 et seq, 244, 245, 246, 256, 260, 268 et seq, 277, 278, 289
Niutao 86
Nomuka 121
Norfolk (Island) 201, 209, 217
North Island (New Zealand) 200, 201, 206, 273
North West Passage 21
Nou 219
Noumea 214, 220, 223, 236, 238, 261, 267

Northern Territory 197, 279, 289
Nuku-Hiva (Island) 133, 210, 244
Nullarbor (Plain) 183

Oahu (Island) 244, 245, 255
Ocean (Island) 207, 223, 232, 262
Oceania 67, 69, 74, 75, 79, 85, 86, 87, 91, 92, 97, 104, 106, 110, 112, 119, 130, 153, 155, 166, 170, 209, 214, 218, 223, 227, 232, 233, 264, 267, 268
Ohinemutu 269
Oitanandi 259
Okinawa 248, 249, 251, 253
Oopoa 131
Ophir 188
Opoa 67
Opulu 124
Orakau 204
Orinoco (River) 14
Otago (Province) 206
Otutu 74
Oualan (Island) 92
Ouameni, Ouamenie 214, 222
Owen Stanley Mountains 246
Oyapoc (River) 14

Pago Pago 213
Païta 32, 218
Palau 69, 137, 248, 250
Palestine 239
Panama (Isthmus) 14
Panama (Town) 20, 26
Panié (Mount) 259
Papeete 155, 162
Papetoai 160
Papua (Gulf) 128
Papua (Region) 75
Papua (Territory) 216, 230, 239, 246, 258, 261
Papua — New Guinea 69, 72, 75, 83, 85, 88, 104, 106, 112, 114, 117, 123, 129, 135, 258, 261, 267, 268, 276
Paraguay (River) 20
Paramatta 271
Parana (River) 20
Patagonia 15, 60
Pearl Harbour 244, 245, 246
Persia 23
Perth 181, 183, 191
Peru 11, 20, 21, 26, 32, 69
Petropavlovsk 32
Philippines (Islands) 15, 17, 20, 21, 26, 31, 42, 63, 75, 171, 207, 230, 245, 247, 249, 250, 253, 260
Phoenix (Islands) 207, 208, 232
Pines (Islands) 217, 218, 219
Pitcairn (Island) 155, 164, 209
Pitt 179
Plate (River) 15, 20
Polynesia 11, 54, 62, 67, 68, 69, 74, 75, 85, 93, 95, 97, 103, 110, 112, 119, 121, 125, 129, 130, 133, 138, 152, 154, 156, 160, 161,

162, 200, 207, 208 et seq, 213, 214, 215, 227, 258
Ponape 207
Port Adelaide 174
Port Darwin 246, 249
Port Jackson 68, 77, 171, 172, 174, 229, 271
Port Moresby 93, 151, 216, 246, 261, 267, 276, 278
Porto Rico 14
Pyramid 56

Queensland 164, 171, 176, 179, 181, 189, 191, 193, 207, 215, 216, 234, 268
Queenstown 269

Rabaul 245, 246
Rabi (Island) 262
Raïatea (Island) 67, 74, 157, 158, 160, 213, 262
Raivavae 212
Ralik (Islands) 100
Rangoon 245
Rano Mafana 75
Rapa (Island) 212, 213, 262
Rapa-nui 208
Raratonga 160, 209, 213
Red (Mountains) 220
Red (River) 166
Red (Sea) 227
Remarkables (Mountains) 269
Richmond 179
Rimatara (Island) 212
Rio de Janeiro 15
Rota (Island) 61
Rotouma 83
Royal Bay 54
Ruapehu 201
Rurutu (Island) 212
Russell (Island) 163
Russia 32, 207, 244 see also USSR

Sabana (River) 15
Sadera Makera 85
Sagittaria (Island) 26
Saint Julian (Bay) 15
Saint Pierre et Miquelon 41
Saint Thomas (Island) 14
Saipan (Island) 248, 250
Sakhalin (Island) 74, 85
Salamaua 246
Samoa (Islands) 28, 60, 62, 80, 95, 121, 124, 153, 163, 171, 200, 210, 212, 213, 223, 230, 254, 261, 262, 278
San Cristobal (Island) 20
San Domingo, Dominica 14, 17, 18
Sandwich (Islands) 55, 80, 87, 119, 164 see also Hawaii
San Salvador (Island) 14
Santa Cruz (Islands) 20, 26, 69, 99, 214, 215
Santa Isabel (Island) 20
Santiago 20

Santo (Island) 26
Savo (Island) 247
Sebastopol (Australia) 192
Senegal 13
Sentani (Island) 117
Sepik 91, 123
Siberia 26
Simpson (Desert) 138
Singapore 245
Society (Islands) 28, 55, 69, 78, 97, 119, 144,
   157, 160, 212, 213, 230, 262
Solomon (Islands) 20, 26, 28, 40, 55, 60, 69,
   101, 135, 152, 164, 213, 215, 216, 230,
   236, 245, 246, 247, 249, 259, 261
South (Island, New Zealand) 200 et seq
South (Pole) 22, 153, 201
Spanish America 20, 32
Spanish Empire 20, 21, 32, 207
Spiritus Sancto 93
Springsure 181
States Territory 28
Suva 260, 278
Swan River Settlement 202
Switzerland of the Pacific 269
Sydney 77, 171, 174, 178, 179, 181, 183, 188,
   189, 201, 213, 229, 231, 239, 246, 271

Tahiti (Island) 11, 12, 26, 50, 54, 55, 62, 67, 70,
   75, 79, 85, 93, 95, 97, 105, 107, 110, 111,
   120, 129, 131, 138, 152, 153, 154, 155,
   156, 157, 158, 160, 162, 163, 164, 171,
   200, 207, 208, 209, 210 et seq, 224, 232,
   244, 260, 262, 264, 267, 277, 278
Taïwan 207, 253
Tanambogo (Island) 247
Tanna 259
Taomarama (Island) 70
Taputapu-Atea 67
Taranaki 200
Tarawa (Atoll) 250
Tarawera 201
Tasman (Island) 56
Tasmania 28, 56, 60, 75, 181, 182, 184, 188,
   230, 232, 234

Taupiri 200
Tauta 153
Te Ika a Maui 200
Tenochtitlan 18
Teremba 220
Ternate 22
Terra australis de Spiritu Santo 26
Te Wahi Panamu 200
Thailand 75, 245
Tierra del Fuego 31
Tidore 16, 22
Timor 16, 31, 62, 69
Tinian (Island) 32
Tokyo 245, 249, 250, 251, 262
Tolaga 127
Tonga (Islands) 27, 28, 68, 95, 121, 163, 213,
   214, 217, 254, 261, 262
Tongatapu (Island) 213
Torrens (Lake) 195
Torres (Strait) 23, 26, 92, 112, 129, 216
Trinidad (Island) 14
Trobriand (Island) 83, 85, 88, 105
Truk (Island) 246
Tuamotu (Island) 26, 28, 163, 209, 210, 212,
   223, 230, 262
Tubai (Islands) 67, 212, 262
Tucapel 20
Tulagi (Island) 247
Turtle (Island) 31

Unfortunate (Islands) 16
Unimak 207
USA 37, 153, 170, 171, 188, 207, 208, 212,
   229, 230, 232, 239, 244, 245, 246, 253,
   256, 259, 260, 273, 278
USSR 244, 251, 253
Utupoa (Island) 215
Uvea (Loyalty Islands) 214, 216, 278
Uvea (Wallis Islands) 216

Vailima 153
Van Diemen (Gulf) 196
Van Diemen's Land 28, 56
Vanikoro (Island) 61, 174, 215

Vanua Levu (Island) 213
Vaté (Island) 268
Vella Lavella (Island) 246
Venezuela 14
Vera Cruz 18
Verde, Cape 17 see also Cape Verde (Islands)
Victoria 181, 184, 188, 190, 192, 193, 232,
   234, 265
Vietnam 75
Vinland 12
Virginia 21
Virgins (Cape) 15
Viti Levu (Island) 213
Volcano (Islands) 250

Waigeo (Island) 68
Waikato (River) 200
Waikiki Beach 256, 279
Waitangi 200, 202
Wakatipu (Lake) 269
Wake (Island) 230, 245, 261
Wallace (Frontier) 69
Wallis and Futuna (Islands) 69, 83, 155, 163,
   214, 217, 230, 231, 268
Washington 244
Waterloo Wells 183
Watling (Island) 14
Weipa 268
Wellington 200, 206, 269
Westland (Province) 206
Wilberforce 179
Wilson (Promontory) 56
Windsor 179
Windward (Isles) 160
Winton 179
Witt (Islands) 56

Yahué (Volcano) 259
Yap 207, 230
Yaté 264
York (Peninsula) 69
Yucatan (Peninsula) 18

Zanzibar (Island) 11

# BIBLIOGRAPHY

BAKER, J.N., *Histoire des découvertes géographiques et des explorations,* Paris, 1959.

BARRAU, Jacques, *Plants and migrations of the Pacific peoples,* Honolulu, Bishop Museum Press, 1963.

BATCHELOR, J., *The Ainu and their folk-lore,* London, 1901.

BATESON, Gregory, *NAVEN:* Cambridge, 1936.

M. BAUDOT, H. BERNARD, H. BRUGMANS, M.R.D. FOOT, H.-A. JACOBSEN, sous la direction de, *Encyclopédie de la guerre 1939-1945,* Casterman, 1977.

BEAGLEHOLE, J.C., *The Exploration of the Pacific,* London, 1947.

BEAUJOUN, J., *Supplément d'Histoire et Géographie,* Paris, 1882.

BERNDT, C.H. and BERNDT, R.M., *The barbarians: an anthropological view,* London, 1971.

BERNDT, R.M., *Australian Aboriginal religion,* Leiden, 1974.

BLOND, G., *La grande aventure des océans. Le Pacifique,* Paris, 1973.

BROCHE, François, *Les bataillons des guitaristes, l'épopée inconnue des F.F.L. de Tahiti à Bir-Hakeim,* 1940-1942, Préf. du Gén. Koenig, Paris, 1970.

H.C. BROOKFIELD and Doreen HART, *Melanesia, a geographical interpretation of an island world,* London, Butler and Tanner Ltd., 1971.

BROSSARD, Amiral de, *Lapérouse. Des constats à la découverte,* Paris, 1978.

BROSSES, Charles de, *Histoire des navigations aux terres australes,* Paris, 1756.

CHALMERS, James, *Works and adventure in New Guinea,* 1877 to 1885. By James Chalmers ... and N. Wyatt Gill, London, The Religious Tract Society.

CHAUNU, P., *Conquête et exploitation des nouveaux mondes,* Paris, 1969. *L'Expansion Européenne,* Paris, 1959.

Captain CHEYNE, *A description of islands in the western Pacific Ocean north and south of the equator: with sailing directions, together with their productions, manners and customs of the natives and vocabularies of their various languages,* London, 1852-1969.

CODRINGTON, R.N., *The Melanesians studied in their anthropology and folklore,* New Haven, H.R.A.F. Press, 1957.

CODRINGTON, R.G., *The Melanesian languages,* Oxford, 1885.

COOK, James, *The Journals of Captain James Cook ...* ed Beaglehole, London, 1955-67.

CROCOMBE, Marjorie Tuainekore, *THE WORKS OF TA'UNGA, Records of a Polynesian traveller in the South Seas, 1833-1896,* Canberra, 1968.

de CURTON, Eric, *Tahiti 40, Récit du ralliement à la France Libre des établissements français d'Océanie,* Paris, Musée de l'Homme, 1873.

DAHLGREN, E., *L'expédition de Martinet,* Paris, 1913.

DENNING, G. (Ed.), *The Marquesa Journal,* Canberra, 1974.

de VARIGNY, Charles, *Quatorze ans aux Iles Sandwiches,* Paris, 1874.

DODD, Edouard, *Polynesian seafaring,* New York, Dodd, Mead and Co, 1972.

DOUGLAS, Oliver, *The Pacific Islands,* (rev. edn.) New York, 1961.

DOUMENGE, François, *L'homme dans le Pacifique Sud,* Paris, Musée de l'Homme, 1966.

DOURNES, Jacques, *Potaö, une théorie du pouvoir chez les Indochinois jörai,* Paris, Flammarion, 1977.

DOUSSET-LEENHARDT, Roselène, *TERRE NATALE, TERRE D'EXIL,* Paris, Maisonneuve et Larose, 1976.

DOUSSET-LEENHARDT, Roselène, *COLONIALISME ET CONTRADICTIONS, Nouvelle-Calédonie 1878-1978,* Paris, L'Harmattan, 1978.

DOUSSET-LEENHARDT, Roselène, 'En Nouvelle-Calédonie: A propos de kamo cynomorphes', in Archives de Sociologie des religions, N° 24, Paris, 1967.

DOUSSET-LEENHARDT, Roselène, 'A propos du totémisme autour de la mer de Corail', in: Archives de Sciences sociales des religions, N° 40, Paris, 1975.

DUMAS, Alexandre, *Journal de Madame Giovanni.*

DUMONT d'Urville, J., *Voyage autour du monde,* Paris, 1848.

DUNMORE, John, *French Explorers of the Pacific*, Oxford, 1965-67.

A.P. ELKIN, *The Australian Aborigines*, Sydney: Angus and Robertson, 1938.

Ellis, W., *A la recherche de la Polynésie d'autrefois*, Paris, 1972.

ENOS, Apisai, *TABAPOT*, in: Papua Pocket Poets, Port Moresby, 1971.

FAIVRE, J.-P., *L'expansion Française dans le Pacifique*, Paris, 1953.

FIRTH (R.), *Rank and Religion in Tikopia: a study in Polynesian paganism and conversion to Christianity*, Boston, 1970.

FREYCINET, L.C., *Voyage autour du monde*, Paris, 1824-44.

GAUGUIN, Paul, *Oviri, Ecrits d'un sauvage*, choisis et présentés par O. Guérin, Paris, Gallimard, 1974.

GAUGUIN, Paul, *Le Sourire*, Collection complète en Fac-simile, Introduction et notes par L.J. Bouge, ancien gouverneur des Etablissements français d'Océanie, Paris, Maisonneuve et Cie, 1952.

GERBRAND, *Adrian, Wow-Ipits, Eight Asmat Woodcarvers of New Guinea.* Leyden, 1972.

GREY George, *Journals of Two Expeditions in West and Western Australia*, London, 1841.

JOURDAIN, Pierre, Commandant, *Pirogues anciennes de Tahiti*, Société d'étude polynésienne, 1969.

LARACY, H., '*Marching Rule and the Missions*', from: Journal of Pacific History, N° 6, 1971.

LAWRENCE, Peter, *Road belong cargo*, Manchester University Press, 1964.

LAWRENCE, Peter and R.M. BERNOT, *Politics in New Guinea*, University of Western Australia Press, 1971.

LEENHARDT, Maurice, *Gens de la Grande Terre*, Nouvelle-Calédonie, Paris, Gallimard, 1937.

LEENHARDT, Maurice, *Arts of the Oceanic peoples.* Photographs by Emmanuel Sougez. Translated from the French by Michael Heron, London, Thames and Hudson, 1950.

LEENHARDT, Maurice, *Vocabulaire et grammaire de la langue houaïlou*, Paris, Institut d'ethnologie, 1935.

LEENHARDT, Maurice, *Do kamo. La personne et le mythe dans le monde mélanésien.* Paris, Gallimard, 1947.

LEENHARDT, Maurice, *La structure de la personne en Mélanésie.* Recueil de textes présentés par Claudio Rugafiori, S.T.O.A. Edizioni, Milano, 1970.

LEROY-BEAULIEU, Paul, *De la colonisation chez les peuples modernes*, Paris, Guillaumin et Cie, 1874.

LEVI-STRAUSS (C.), *Le totémisme aujourd'hui*, Paris, 1962.

LEWIS, David, *We, the navigators,* Canberra, Australian National University Press, 1972.

LONG, J., *Voyages and Travels of an Indian Interpreter*, London, 1791.

LOTI, Pierre, *Le mariage de Loti*, Paris, 1892.

MALINOWSKI, Bronislaw, *Argonauts of the Western Pacific*, London, George Routledge and Sons, 1932.

MARTIN-ALLANIC, J., *Bougainville navigateur et les découvertes de son temps*, Paris, 1966.

MELVILLE, Herman, *Moby Dick, or the White Whale*, New York, Harper, 1950.

MELVILLE, Herman, *Omoo: a Narrative of Adventures in the South Seas*, London, 1850.

MELVILLE, Herman, *Typee: a peep at polynesian life during a residence in a valley of the Marquesas*, London, 1850.

METRAUX, Alfred, *Ethnology of Easter Island*, Bishop Museum Press, (reprint) 1971.

MICHEL, Louise, *Mémoires de Louise Michel écrites par elle-même*, Paris, F. Roy, 1866.

MICHEL, Louise, *Légendes et chants de gestes canaques*, Paris, Kéva et Cie, 1885.

MIKLOUCHO-MACLAY, Nicolai Nicolaevich, *New Guinea Diaries 1871-1883*, Kristen Press, Madang, P.N.G., 1975.

MOERENHOUT, J.-A., *Voyages aux îles du Grand Océan*, Paris, A. Bertrand, 1837.

O'REILLY, P., *Bibliographie de Tahiti et de la Polynésie française*, Paris, 1967.

PUKUI, Mary K. and Korn, *The Echo of our Songs, Chants and Poems of the Hawaiians* − Honolulu, The University Press of Hawai, 1973.

RUTHERFORD, Noël, *Shirley Baker and the King of Tonga*, Melbourne, Oxford University Press, 1971.

RYTKEOU, Iouri, *Contes de la Tchoukotka*, Paris, Publications orientalistes de France, 1974.

SEGALEN, Victor, *Les Immémoriaux*, Paris, 1907.

SHAW, A.G.L., *The Story of Australia*, London, 1955.

SIMON, J., *La Polynésie dans l'art et la littérature de l'Occident*, Paris, 1939.

SPENCER, B., and GILLEN, F.-J., *The Natives Tribes in Central Australia*, 1899.

SPENCER, B. and GILLEN, F.-J., *The Northern Tribes of Central Australia*, 1904.

STANLEY W. HOSIE, s.m. *Anonymous Apostle, The life of Jean-Claude Colin, Marist.* New York, William Morrow and C°, 1967.

STEVENSON, R.L., *Dans les mers du Sud,* 1896.

STREHLOW, T.H.G., *Aranda traditions*, Melbourne University Press, 1947.

TAILLEMITE, E., *Bougainville et ses compagnons autour du monde*, Paris, 1978.

TURNBULL, Clive, *Black War; the extermination of the Tasmanian Aborigines*, Melbourne, F.W. Cheshire Pty, 1948.

WILLIAMSON, J.A., *Cook and the Opening of the Pacific*, London, 1966.

WORSLEY, P., *The trumpet shall sound*, London, Paladin, 1968.

ZEMP, Hugo, '*Field report from the Salomon Islands*', Society for ethnomusicology, Middletown, V.5., N° 3, 1971.

# PHOTOGRAPHIC ACKNOWLEDGEMENTS

a·above; m·middle; b·bottom; l·left; r·right

Afrique-Asie-Photos/Boutin: 111a, 266al, 266ar, 266bl, 266br – W. Andersen: 70bl – Archivo General de Simancas: 23 – Atlas-Photo: 77a, 264b, 267a, 271bl – Lénars: 58a, 106b, 136ml, 145, 148, 197b, 198-9, 267m + b, 269a, 270, 272, 273 – Popper: 264a, 265 – Potentier: 223b – Bibliothèque cantonale et universitaire, Lausanne: 12, 40a, 44al, 48-9, 53b, 54b, 56a + b, 60-61, 61a, 62, 63, 66, 64ar, 64-5, 65, 68-9, 70a, 72, 77b, 78ar, 78b, 81, 85a, 92a, 96a, 97a, 107a, 110, 119b, 121a, 124b, 125b, 127, 131, 132a, 133, 135, 150, 161a, 167, 180al, 188br, 189, 193al + b, 203l, 205ar, 206a, 211ar, 223a, 224b, 232b, 239b – Bibliothèque du Muséum d'Histoire naturelle, Paris: 44ar – Bibliothèque Nationale, Paris: 15, 24-5, 27, 152al, 215b – British Library, London: 19al, ar + ml, 22, 54a + m, 60a, 120-121, 171m – Commonwealth National Library, Canberra: 176b – Foreign and Commonwealth Office Library, London: 84, 85b, 233b – Library of the Hispanic Society of America, New York: 19b – Missionsbibliothek, Basle: 210 – Mitchell Library, Sydney: 191, 196a – National Library of Australia: 164, 168-9, 171a, 178, 182-3, 183a, 188mr, 205b – Royal Commonwealth Society Library, London: 171b, 190, 234a – State Library of Victoria, Melbourne: 195ar, 196m + bl – A. Turnbull Library, Wellington: 205al, 237a, 241 – Universitätsbibliothek, Basle: 31 – The Castle Howard Collection, York: K. Gibson: 152al – Cinémathèque Suisse/H. Dumont: 226, 227ar – Congregazione dei S.S. Cuori, Rome: 106a – Documentation française/Délégation de la Nouvelle-Zélande: 269b – Morin: 261a – Le Nickel: 261b – Dole Photo: 255 – R. Dousset: 22al – Australian News and Information Service: 73, 105, 108a – Linden Museum, Stuttgart: 4 – National Library of Australia: 82-3 – F. Drihon-Buchanan: 165, 215a, 219, 220a, 238a – Edita, Lausanne: 155, 161b, 162b, 163, 176a, 177a, 179, 180ar, 184b, 185, 188bl, 194, 195al, 197a, 203r, 206b, 211ar, 212, 214, 230, 238b – Editions Laffont, Paris: 53al + am – Explorer/Boizot: 136al + am – Du Boutin: 102b, 113, 114l – Walker: 122 – Fotoarchiv des Rautenstrauch-Joest Museums f. Völkerkunde, Cologne: 128r – Giraudon, Paris: 10 – Goldner, Paris: 59b, 70br, 71, 74ar, 76a, 101, 108b, 109, 232, 237b – R. Holkar: 29, 89, 103, 111b, 263 – Institut Géographique national, Paris: 45a – Jacana, Paris/Bassot: 142m – Fritz: 142am – Vincent: 136ar – J. Jobé, Lausanne: 142 – H. Kiwas, Cologne: 274-5 – Collection J. Kobal, London: 227al – H. N. Loose, Klefhaus: 128l – British Museum, Natural History, London: 64al, 104 – City Museum and Art Gallery, Plymouth (GB)/Chapman: 18b – National Gallery of Victoria, Melbourne: 196br – National Maritime Museum, Greenwich: 18a, 38, 39b, 41, 43al + b, 44b, 45b, 46-7, 52, 53ar, 57, 96-7, 107b – The Metropolitan Museum, New York: 225 – Musée des Arts africains et océaniens, Paris/Giraudon: 37 – Musée d'Art et d'Histoire, Berne: 125a – Musée de l'Homme, Paris: 74al, 112, 119a, 162a, 221, 222ar – Coll. Alix de Rothschild: 124a – Musée de la Marine, Paris: 211al, 211b, 220b, 233a – National Ethnographic Museum, Stockholm: 94b – Peabody Museum, Salem (USA): 59a – Pitt Rivers Museum/Coll: Forster, Oxford: 91 – Royal Scottish Museum, Edinburgh: 94ml – Science Museum, London: 40b, 41ar – University Museum of Archaeology and Ethnology, Cambridge: 94mr – Victoria & Albert Museum, London: 159 – New Zealand House, London: 200 – Photo Researchers/Cooke: 144 – Fields: 30, 102, 116, 141ar + br – Gahan: 142b – Holton: 88, 114-5, 142al – Hunt   : 137b – Lindgren: 140r – McCoy: 137am – McHugh: 140l, 141al – Ord: 141ml – Roberts: 136b – Russ Kinne: 137ar, 137mr, 141bl – Wayman: 137al – Weckler: 51 – A. Poignant: 76b – G. Koch, Berlin: 86, 90 – Museum f. Völkerkunde, Berlin: 66, 94a, 95, 98, 99, 100, 117a – Public Record Office, London: 160 – Radio Times Hulton Picture Library, London: 193ar, 231a – Rapho, Paris/Gerster: 256ar, 256-7b – Gritscher: 228, 271a + br – Haar: 258a – Koch: 258b – Zuber: 146-7 – Ringier Bilderdienst, Zurich: 247a – Royal Geographic Society, London: 70b, 78al, 92m, 117b, 118, 132b, 174-5, 177b, 180b, 184a, 186-7, 231b, 234b, 235, 239a – Service Hydrographique de la Marine, Brest: 58b – Stadtbildstelle, Cologne/Zimmermann: 92b – G. Thiemann, Baierbrunn: 123 – USIS, Paris: 242-3, 247b, 248, 249, 256al, 257a.

This book published under the direction
of
AMI GUICHARD

Editorial responsibility and supervision
by TIM CHILVERS

Produced under the direction of CHARLES RIESEN

Designed by MAX THOMMEN

Printed by GEA, Milan
and bound by Maurice Busenhart, Lausanne